REGULATING LAW

Regulating Law

Edited by

CHRISTINE PARKER
COLIN SCOTT
NICOLA LACEY
JOHN BRAITHWAITE

OXFORD
UNIVERSITY PRESS

OXFORD
UNIVERSITY PRESS

Great Clarendon Street, Oxford OX2 6DP

Oxford University Press is a department of the University of Oxford.
It furthers the University's objective of excellence in research, scholarship,
and education by publishing worldwide in

Oxford New York

Auckland Bangkok Buenos Aires Cape Town Chennai
Dar es Salaam Delhi Hong Kong Istanbul Karachi Kolkata
Kuala Lumpur Madrid Melbourne Mexico City Mumbai Nairobi
São Paulo Shanghai Taipei Tokyo Toronto

Oxford is a registered trade mark of Oxford University Press
in the UK and in certain other countries

Published in the United States
by Oxford University Press Inc., New York

British Library Cataloguing in Publication Data

Data available

Library of Congress Cataloging in Publication Data

Data available

ISBN 0-19-926407-4

1 3 5 7 9 10 8 6 4 2

Typeset by Newgen Imaging Systems (P) Ltd., Chennai, India
Printed in Great Britain
on acid-free paper by
Biddles Ltd., King's Lynn

Acknowledgements

This collection, like all edited collections, is a collaborative venture between the editors and the contributors. Having conceived the regulating law idea, the editors assembled a group of the best legal scholars whom we could persuade to join us in our enterprise and who we believed had enlightening ideas about law as regulation and the regulation of law. We wrote a short briefing document and invited each contributor to write a paper that demonstrated how a regulatory lens might apply in their own area of legal scholarship. The papers were presented at a lively workshop at the Regulatory Institutions Network (RegNet), Australian National University in Canberra.

We would like to thank and acknowledge here our debt to all our contributors not only for the work they put into preparing, presenting, and then revising their own papers after the workshop, but also for their contributions to each other's papers and to the whole project. We especially need to single out Hugh Collins for thanks, not only for contributing a new paper on regulating contract law to this collection and a mini-keynote address to the workshop, but also for being such a good sport in suffering with good humour the criticism of all the other authors who were asked to emulate and improve upon his pioneering juxtaposition of regulatory theory and legal doctrine in *Regulating Contracts* (Oxford University Press, 1997) in their own domains. Clifford Shearing, David Soskice, and Terence Daintith were each co-opted into pre-reading and presenting commentaries on the papers at the workshop. We are most grateful for their comments and for those of Suzanne Corcoran, Paul Finn, and the other observers at the workshop.

Both the workshop and also editorial assistance in the preparation of the manuscript for publication were made possible by funding from Australian Research Council Discovery Grant DP0344638, 'Meta-regulation and the Regulation of Law', granted to the four co-editors for 2003–5. Bron Stuart cheerfully implemented all the organizational arrangements for the workshop, and for the Regulating Law web site, which allowed contributors to read each other's papers in advance. Natalie Stepanenko assisted Bron, and also efficiently and painstakingly completed much of the final editing and preparation of the manuscript. Leah Dunn, the administrator of RegNet, capably supported all our activities, as usual. Oxford University Press also kindly supplied copies of Hugh Collins's *Regulating Contracts* to all our contributors before the workshop, no doubt contributing to his own discomfort but enhancing the level of intellectual engagement between contributors and their contributions.

Finally, John Braithwaite and Christine Parker would like to acknowledge that although Nicola Lacey and Colin Scott have humbly declined to be named as co-authors of the concluding chapter to this collection, our four-way conversations before, during, and after the workshop in real, virtual, and regulatory space greatly contributed to the ideas set out there both in substance and in clarity of expression.

Contents

List of Contributors

Julia Black is a Reader in the Law Department and research member, ESRC Centre for the Analysis of Risk and Regulation, London School of Economics and Political Science.

Stephen Bottomley is Professor of Commercial Law and Director of the Centre for Commercial Law in the Faculty of Law at the Australian National University.

John Braithwaite is an Australian Research Council Federation Fellow, a Professor in the Law Program, Research School of Social Sciences, and Chair of the Regulatory Institutions Network, Australian National University.

Peter Cane has been Professor of Law in the Research School of Social Sciences at the Australian National University since 1997. For twenty years before that he taught law at Corpus Christi College, Oxford.

Hilary Charlesworth is Professor and Director of the Centre for International and Public Law, Faculty of Law, Australian National University.

Christine Chinkin is Professor of International Law, London School of Economics and Political Science, and Overseas Affiliated Faculty, University of Michigan.

Hugh Collins is Professor of English Law, Law Department, London School of Economics and Political Science.

Angus Corbett is Senior Lecturer in the Faculty of Law, University of New South Wales.

John Dewar is Pro-Vice Chancellor (Business and Law) at Griffith University in Queensland, Australia. He is Chair of the Family Law Council and Vice-President of the International Society of Family Law.

Peter Drahos is a Professor and Director of the Centre for Competition and Consumer Policy, Research School of Social Sciences, Regulatory Institutions Network, Australian National University.

Richard Johnstone is a Professor and Director of the National Research Centre for Occupational Health and Safety Regulation, in the Regulatory Institutions Network, in the Research School of Social Sciences at the Australian National University, and Co-Director of the Socio-Legal Research Centre in the Faculty of Law at Griffith University.

Nicola Lacey is Professor of Criminal Law at the London School of Economics and Political Science and Adjunct Professor of Social and Political Theory at the Research School of Social Sciences, Australian National University.

Imelda Maher is Senior Lecturer in Law at the London School of Economics and Political Science. The research for her contribution to this book was undertaken while she was Director of the Centre for Competition and Consumer Policy, Regulatory Institutions Network, Australian National University.

Richard Mitchell is Professor and Director of the Centre for Employment and Labour Relations Law in the Law School at the University of Melbourne.

Christine Parker is a Senior Lecturer in Law at the University of Melbourne and Senior Research Fellow at the Centre for Competition and Consumer Policy, Regulatory Institutions Network, Australian National University.

Colin Scott is a Reader in the Law Department and research member, ESRC Centre for the Analysis of Risk and Regulation, London School of Economics and Political Science. The research for his contributions to this book was undertaken while he was Senior Fellow in Public Law in the Research School of Social Sciences, Australian National University.

Jane Stapleton is a Professor in the Law Program of the Research School of Social Sciences, Australian National University, and Ernest E. Smith Professor of Law at the University of Texas School of Law.

Table of Cases

Table of Legislation

Statutory Instruments

United States of America

New York

Table of Treaties and Conventions

List of Abbreviations

BBA	British Bankers' Association
BCBS	Basel Committee on Banking Supervision
CAFC	(US) Court of Appeals for the Federal Circuit
ECHR	European Convention on Human Rights
FSA	Financial Services Authority
FSMA	Financial Services and Markets Act
GAU	Gender Affairs Unit
GFA	General Framework Agreement for Peace in Bosnia and Hercegovina
IAIS	International Association of Insurance Supervisors
IFOR	Implementation Force (in Bosnia-Hercegovina; subsequently SFOR)
IMF	International Monetary Fund
INGO	intergovernmental organization
INTERFET	International Force East Timor
IOSCO	International Organization of Securities Commissions
IPTF	International Police Task Force (in Bosnia-Hercegovina)
ISDA	International Swaps and Derivatives Association
NCSC	National Companies and Securities Commission
NGO	non-governmental organization
NHS	National Health Service
OECD	Organization for European Cooperation and Development
OHCHR	Office of the UN High Commissioner for Human Rights
OHR	Office of the High Representative
OHS	occupational health and safety
OSCE	Organization for Security and Cooperation in Europe
PIC	Peace Implementation Council
RegNet	Regulatory Institutions Network
SFOR	Stabilization Force (in Bosnia-Hercegovina; previously IFOR)
UNMIK	UN Interim Administration Mission in Kosovo
UNTAET	UN Transitional Administration in East Timor

Introduction

CHRISTINE PARKER, COLIN SCOTT, NICOLA LACEY, and
JOHN BRAITHWAITE

Just as we think it is useful to look at regulation through a legal lens, we
hypothesize at the outset of this project that it might prove useful to look at law
through a regulatory lens. We consider what it means to see law as a form of
regulation and as something that is itself regulated by other forms of regulation.
The chapters of this book, therefore, use the tools of regulatory theory to ask
questions about a variety of areas of legal doctrine. They were chosen by reference
to the main subject areas in the legal curriculums of the common law countries.[1]
The concluding chapter will come to see law as one (significant) strand in a regulatory web that is growing in its complexity and plurality. This final chapter will
deploy the inductive methodology frequently used in regulatory scholarship
to ground new explanatory and normative theory and shed light on existing
scholarship.[2]

When we speak of applying a regulatory lens to law, what do we mean by
regulation? Definitions of 'regulation' abound, and for different intellectual
purposes there is merit in defining regulation in different ways—excluding or
including regulation by non-government actors, excluding or including governance without rules, including only intentional attempts to influence behaviour,
or including all actions that have regulatory effects.[3] For scholars of regulation,
the core area of study is 'regulation' in the sense of 'the intentional activity of
attempting to control, order or influence the behaviour of others'.[4] This definition is broad in the sense that 'regulation' is not limited to targeted rules that
are enforced and monitored, nor is it limited to state intervention in the economy
and/or civil society. It incorporates three basic requirements for a regulatory
regime: the setting of standards; processes for monitoring compliance with the
standards; and mechanisms for enforcing the standards.

For the purposes of assessing the regulatory significance of law, however, this
definition of regulation may be in certain respects too narrow. For example,
if we were analysing how the invisible hand of the market sets the price of

---

[1] Some areas, such as environmental law, where a regulatory perspective is already pervasive, have
been left out.

[2] See e.g. J. Braithwaite, 'Beyond Positivism: Learning from Contextual Integrated Strategies',
Journal of Research in Crime and Delinquency, 30 (1993), 383; C. Parker, *Just Lawyers* (Oxford:
Oxford University Press, 1999), 4–6.

[3] See J. Black, 'Decentring Regulation: Understanding the Role of Regulation and Self-regulation
in a Post-regulating World', *Current Legal Problems*, 54 (2001), 103. See also the introduction in
R. Baldwin, C. Scott, and C. Hood (eds.), *A Reader on Regulation* (Oxford: Oxford University Press,
1998), 1, 2–4; C. Parker and J. Braithwaite, 'Regulation', in P. Cane and M. Tushnet (eds.), *Oxford
Handbook of Legal Studies* (Oxford: Oxford University Press, 2003), 119.

[4] J. Black, 'Critical Reflections on Regulation', *Australian Journal of Legal Philosophy*, 27 (2002), 1.

a particular product, we would say this was economics, not regulatory studies. If, however, we were studying decision-making about how and when to design institutions so as to increase exposure of prices to the non-purposive control of the market, we would say this was an example of regulatory studies. If we were undertaking Foucauldian research on how the mute bars and barriers of Disney World make certain kinds of hazardous conduct impossible, we would not be doing regulatory research.[5] But if we incorporate such research within a study of the agency of the designers of the architecture of Disney World, or the internet, with their intent to shape the way we play and compute, then this is regulatory research.[6] The most influential theories of regulation involve some conception of private or public intent to shape the flow of events. Yet it makes no sense to study the effects of our intended agency without simultaneously examining the unintended effects of that agency. We cannot study competition law as a regulatory activity without also examining structural effects of markets; we cannot study how Bill Gates regulates cyberspace without analysis of how the architecture of the internet shapes our information choices; we cannot assess the regulatory significance of criminal law or the law of torts without understanding the indirect, legitimizing effects of doctrines which, though not designed for specifically regulatory purposes, may be a condition for such regulatory efficacy as these areas of law have. Our methodological bias is that we see best when our regulatory lens is multifocal, sometimes narrowly focused on intentional rule-making by public actors, sometimes widening its horizon to private, non-rulelike, or non-intentional, modalities of control over the flow of events.

In applying a regulatory lens to legal doctrine we are assuming that all law can fruitfully be seen as 'regulation'. Few would argue that law is not intended to regulate, even if just by maintaining order or regulating the resolution of disputes through the courts. Yet, as the contributions to this book show, finding clear regulatory purposes in some areas of doctrine is difficult. This does not mean it is not fruitful to see those areas of law as 'regulation' (although they might be less tightly coupled to the insights of regulatory theory). It does mean that much of the work in applying a regulatory perspective may lie in identifying implicit, indirect, or partial regulatory purposes and effects. It also means that much of the value in a regulatory perspective on law is likely to be the insight it gives us about how different areas of law with different levels of regulatory intent interact, and interfere, with one another.

There are at least three different, but overlapping, ways in which the contributors to this collection apply a regulatory lens to law.[7] In each, the meanings and levels of analysis of 'law' and 'regulation' differ. But the three connect

---

[5] C. Shearing and P. Stenning, 'Say "Cheese!": The Disney Order that is not so Mickey Mouse', in Shearing and Stenning (eds.), *Private Policing* (Newbury Park, Calif.: Sage, 1987), 309.

[6] L. Lessig, *Code—and Other Laws of Cyberspace* (New York: Basic Books, 1999).

[7] The following three sections follow Hugh Collins's informal keynote to the Regulating Law Workshop, in which he set out three themes that he thought the project was intended to have.

and interrelate in ways that give us a fuller perspective on regulating law. The *first* involves a dialogue between lawyers and regulationists[8] about the questions and methodologies in their respective areas of scholarship and how they can and do intersect. The *second* involves the consideration of the varying regulatory purposes or orientations of different areas of law, and how they interconnect and compete with each other. The *third* focuses on how law (seen overall as just one form of regulation in society) interacts with other forms of regulation or normative ordering.

Dialogue between Legal and Regulatory Scholarship

At one level this book is about bringing together what lawyers and regulationists do as scholars, the different methods, questions, and foci that each style of scholarship brings to the study of law, and asking how they can enlighten one another. Typically regulationists concern themselves with analysing various types of regulatory norms, techniques, and organizations (legal and non-legal) and how effective each is in different circumstances. In relation to law,[9] a regulatory perspective asks empirical questions about the proactive effects of law on society as a whole (or at least the target segment of society)—for example, the extent to which enforcement prevents and remedies wrongful conduct—and normative questions about how law and regulatory technique can be designed to be most effective at accomplishing social goals. The methods of regulation research are often empirical, and theory is generally aimed at elucidating the impact of law on social practices and institutions external to law and vice versa. Legal scholars, by contrast, typically take an internal approach to law that focuses on the content of legal doctrine and its coherence.[10] In common law systems their methodology is influenced both by the case-based reasoning of the common law (a form of inductive reasoning) and by the principles-based approach which is common to both civilian and common law traditions.

In most systems, legal scholarship is to a significant degree oriented to eliciting and examining distinctive legal doctrines characterized by a certain degree of normative complexity and autonomy. Of course many legal scholars already find it helpful to use sociological and political science regulatory research in their own scholarship. Nevertheless, regulatory scholarship has mainly been applied, by both lawyers and regulationists, to certain areas of law, in particular, specific legislative programmes and/or regulatory agencies for the social and

[8] The term is ugly but is a useful shorthand for scholars of empirical and theoretical research on regulation.
[9] Regulation researchers also concern themselves with a variety of non-legal regulatory practices.
[10] See E. Rubin, 'Legal Scholarship', in D. Patterson (ed.), *A Companion to Philosophy of Law and Legal Theory* (Oxford: Blackwell, 1996), 562. For an extreme version of the internal perspective to law in legal scholarship, see E. Weinrib, 'Legal Formalism', in Patterson (ed.), *A Companion to Philosophy of Law and Legal Theory*, 332.

economic regulation of business (either on an industry basis such as financial services, nuclear energy, and telecommunications, or on a topic basis such as environment, health and safety, and competition). More recently, public law, broadly defined, has also been conceived as the regulation of government and governance.[11] This book widens the range of regulatory legal scholarship by asking what light can be shed on the various branches of mainstream law using the tools, concepts, and methods of regulatory theory, regardless of whether these areas have traditionally been seen as 'regulatory' or not. This broadens regulatory scholarship by looking for the regulatory intent and effect in the content of legal doctrines that regulationists rarely consider, even if that intent and/or effect is implicit, episodic, or indirect.

The Different Ways that Law Regulates

Because the regulatory perspective in this book takes legal doctrine seriously on its own terms, the contributions are able to identify some of the ways different areas of law operate and 'think' about themselves as regulation, and how those different modes of regulation within law interact with one another. Much legal scholarship that relates to regulation draws a crude distinction between two modes of reasoning within law—instrumental, forward-looking, or policy-oriented ways of thinking and backward-looking, principled, or rule-based doctrinal reasoning.[12] The latter way of thinking about law emphasizes the autonomy of legal reasoning from society, while the former sees law as the tool of society. To draw a distinction here between legislation as embodying a modern, instrumental, and purposive approach, in contrast with the doctrinal approach of the common law, is too simple and liable to be misleading. Within some common law systems, notably that of the United States, it is widely suggested that courts have long favoured an instrumental approach to legal reasoning, even in the absence of instrumental legislation.[13] By the same token, legislation may be deployed to reinforce or develop the universalistic principles more commonly associated with the common law.

Accordingly these two distinctive 'mentalities' of law—contrasting understandings of 'how the law thinks'—are analytically elusive. We are not simply

---

[11] See Baldwin *et al.* (eds.), *A Reader on Regulation*, for a summary of the regulation literature. For examples of the regulation of government literature, see C. Hood, C. Scott, O. James, G. Jones, and T. Travers, *Regulation inside Government: Waste-Watchers, Quality Police, and Sleazebusters* (Oxford: Oxford University Press, 1999), and at the broadest level—the regulation of governance via international law, see J. Braithwaite and P. Drahos, *Global Business Regulation* (Cambridge: Cambridge University Press, 2000).

[12] e.g. R. Cotterrell, *Law's Community: Legal Theory in Sociological Perspective* (Oxford: Oxford University Press, 1995), 164–8, on 'voluntas' and 'ratio'; H. Collins, *Regulating Contracts* (Oxford: Oxford University Press, 1999).

[13] M. J. Horwitz, *The Transformation of American Law 1780–1860* (Cambridge, Mass.: Harvard University Press, 1979).

dealing with contrasts between statute and case-law, or public regulation and private law.[14] The instrumental mentality associated with regulation is about influencing the behaviour of people to accomplish particular social objectives.[15] The regulatory intention is frequently explicit and forward-looking, although it may be politically contested. For the doctrinal, universalistic mentality, associated with classical common law reasoning, regulatory intention is not central, although the law may have various regulatory intentions and effects in specific contexts. As some of our contributors show, there are not just two ways of thinking and regulating within law—rather law is 'multidimensional'.[16] Thus a regulatory perspective on law may be able to illuminate multiple innovations in, or recasting of, legal doctrines that have occurred as a result of the blurring of distinctions between public and private law, statute and case-law, regulation and common law.[17]

A regulatory perspective on law looks for ways in which the various regulatory goals in law connect or collide with each other, and with the more implicit regulation of the common law. It also looks for ways in which the converse is true, that common law interacts and influences the operation of law that is intended as instrumental regulation. It asks, What is the impact of the instrumental and common law mentalities upon each other, both within and beyond legal doctrine? For example, can we, as Hugh Collins does in *Regulating Contracts* (discussed below), generalize about a 'productive disintegration' of doctrinal reasoning under instrumental regulatory pressure, and under what conditions could such a productive disintegration occur?

As one would expect, chapters organized specifically around areas of doctrine— such as contract, property, and tort—that apply to a wide range of social practices and contexts tell a more complex, variable, and tentative story of law's regulatory import than do chapters organized around areas of social practice— work, competition, the family—in which law has been invoked with more specifically regulatory intent. If the objective of the collection were only to describe and understand regulation more fully, it would certainly have made more sense to assign chapters on the basis of different areas of social life.[18] This is the way that much regulation research is organized. Our decision was to allocate chapters according to doctrinal categories aimed to provoke a new dialogue between regulatory theory and research, and legal doctrinal scholarship. Whether we look at contract law or the social practices of contracting through a regulatory lens, it is possible to ask questions about the ways that law can be usefully seen as subjects and objects of regulation. How do the laws that apply in that space regulate and how are they regulated?

---

[14] Julia Black makes these possibilities particularly clear in Ch. 2 in this volume.
[15] Peter Cane's 'Administrative Law as Regulation' (Ch. 10 in this volume) helps to clarify this.
[16] Angus Corbett and Stephen Bottomley, Ch. 3 in this volume.
[17] Collins, *Regulating Contracts*, 53–5. Collins talks about the 'productive disintegration of private law' as its discourses of reasoning are transformed and reconfigured through clashes with the discourses of economic and social regulation.   [18] See Nicola Lacey, Ch. 7 in this volume.

META-REGULATION: THE INTERACTION BETWEEN LAW AS
REGULATION AND OTHER FORMS OF REGULATION

The insights in the second aspect of the regulatory perspective (above) relate to how different modalities or regulatory programmes *within* law interact. But regulation research is also interested in blurring the boundaries of law itself by inquiring into how law interacts with other forms of normative ordering. Thus it is useful to think about the relationship of law and society or law and economy in terms of various layers of regulation each doing their own regulating. At the same time, each layer regulates the regulation of each other in various combinations of horizontal and vertical influence.[19] The label 'meta-regulation' has been applied to this concept.[20] In Hugh Collins's book *Regulating Contracts* private law regulates the self-regulation of the parties in contract while regulatory law regulates private law, and now in the UK the Human Rights Act re-regulates the private law. Some regulatory researchers have argued that such interactions between public regulation and private law are just one manifestation of the more reflexive, meta-regulatory relationships between regulatory institutions of all types (legal and non-legal) in a 'new regulatory state'.[21]

One of the characteristic concerns in the study of regulation is how various regulatory tools impact on (or fail to impact on) daily life in their attempt to order it in accord with some set of norms;[22] and the extent to which the values represented in regulation and the techniques used to monitor and enforce compliance with regulatory standards fit with pre-existing norms and social ordering in the target population.[23] Much of the evidence shows that apparently

---

[19] See C. Shearing and J. Wood, 'Nodal Governance, Democracy and the New "Denizens": Challenging the Westphalian Ideal', *Journal of Law and Society*, 30 (2003), 400; C. Scott, 'Accountability in the Regulatory State', *Journal of Law and Society*, 27 (2000), 38.

[20] C. Parker, *The Open Corporation* (Cambridge: Cambridge University Press, 2002), Ch. 9; Parker and Braithwaite, 'Regulation'; C. Scott, 'Speaking Softly without Big Sticks: Meta-regulation and the Public Audit', *Law and Policy*, 25 (2003), 203. See also P. Grabosky, 'Using Non-governmental Resources to Foster Regulatory Compliance', *Governance: An International Journal of Policy and Administration*, 8 (1995), 527; B. Morgan, 'Regulating the Regulators: Meta-regulation as a Strategy for Reinventing Government in Australia', *Public Management: An International Journal of Research and Theory*, 1 (1999), 49, and R. Rhodes, *Understanding Governance: Policy Networks, Governance, Reflexivity and Accountability* (Buckingham: Open University Press, 1997).

[21] See J. Braithwaite, 'The New Regulatory State and the Transformation of Criminology', *British Journal of Criminology*, 40 (2000), 222; C. Hood and C. Scott, 'Bureaucratic Regulation and New Public Management in the United Kingdom: Mirror-Image Developments?', *Journal of Law and Society*, 23 (1996), 321; Parker, *The Open Corporation*, 12–15; G. Majone, 'The Rise of the Regulatory State in Europe', *West European Politics*, 17 (1994), 77; M. Moran, 'Understanding the Regulatory State', *British Journal of Political Science*, 32 (2002), 391.

[22] The choice of norms is often a separate question, though norm-form and tool-form are sometimes subjects of simultaneous construction of normative and explanatory theory (see John Dewar, Ch. 4 in this volume).

[23] e.g. I. Ayres and J. Braithwaite, *Responsive Regulation* (New York: Oxford University Press, 1992); R. Baldwin, *Rules and Government* (Oxford: Clarendon Press, 1995); E. Bardach and R. Kagan, *Going by the Book: The Problem of Regulatory Unreasonableness* (Philadelphia: Temple University Press, 1982); J. Black, *Rules and Regulators* (Oxford: Clarendon Press, 1997); N. Gunningham and P. Grabosky, *Smart Regulation: Designing Environmental Policy* (Oxford: Clarendon Press, 1998);

effective legal regulation that is not responsive to non-legal normative orderings ultimately fails to accomplish its goals.[24] It can be fruitful to think of regulation occurring in a 'regulatory space' in which the operation and competition of various regulatory regimes influences regulatory impact.[25] At this level of analysis, regulatory research also examines how the intended effects of regulation are modified and mediated by social customs and structural realities (non-legal ordering). Hence it makes sense to ask how law itself is regulated by other forms of ordering, that is, how it is modified and mediated by social relations and customs so that the actual effects of the law might be quite different from those intended.

This third question about the interaction of legal and other forms of regulation raises broad historical and comparative questions about the conditions under which legal and non-legal regulation can be effectively coordinated—'structurally coupled', as Gunther Teubner has put it.[26] Some regulatory scholars have diagnosed a structural change in the regulatory approach of late modern Western states towards a style oriented to 'steering' rather than 'rowing' or 'government-at-a-distance'—a hypothesis which would suggest important changes in the interaction between legal and non-legal regulation, and in the specific (increasingly 'meta-regulatory') style of legal regulation. By contrast, several of the authors in this collection point to the long history of law's regulatory role, and question whether contemporary changes in the style and scope of state power are as radical as theorists of the 'new regulatory state' have suggested.

HUGH COLLINS'S *REGULATING CONTRACTS*

Hugh Collins's *Regulating Contracts* was the inspiration for this book in the sense that it demonstrates that it is possible to apply a regulatory perspective to law in a way that is salient to both regulationists and legal scholars.[27] This does

N. Gunningham and R. Johnstone, *Regulating Workplace Safety: Systems and Sanctions* (Oxford: Oxford University Press, 1999).

[24] See P. Selznick, *The Moral Commonwealth* (Berkeley: University of California Press, 1992), 463. Cotterrell, *Law's Community* (304–5), describes at least five dimensions of the 'moral distance' between the normative expectations of 'law-government' and those of the field of social interaction it attempts to regulate—that regulation is too generalized, absolutist, inflexible, impressionistic, and democratically weak.

[25] C. Scott, 'Analysing Regulatory Space: Fragmented Resources and Institutional Design', *Public Law* (Summer 2001), 329; C. Shearing, 'A Constitutive Conception of Regulation', in P. Grabosky and J. Braithwaite (eds.), *Business Regulation and Australia's Future* (Canberra: Australian Institute of Criminology, 1993), 67.

[26] J. Paterson and G. Teubner, 'Changing Maps: Empirical Legal Autopoiesis', *Social and Legal Studies*, 7 (1998), 451, 457.

[27] As one reviewer has said, 'Collins' book displays an attitude towards the law of contract which is exemplary. He deepens fine contractual scholarship by combining it with empirical studies and social theory in just the way that exclusively formal legal scholarship does not'; D. Campbell, 'Reflexivity and Welfarism in the Modern Law of Contract', *Oxford Journal of Legal Studies*, 20 (2000), 477, 485.

not mean that the particular theories, concepts, and historical assumptions about the development of law and the regulatory state in *Regulating Contracts* need be taken as defining hypotheses of a regulatory perspective on law more generally. Rather, *Regulating Contracts* is a model of the type of scholarship that combines regulatory and doctrinal research. It is certainly the most systematic treatment we have of any field of law as an institution that regulates and is regulated. Firstly, Collins's book uses the conceptual and empirical tools of regulatory theory to examine the law of contract and ask how effective and efficient it is in regulating markets and contracts via standard-setting, monitoring, and enforcement.[28] As Collins points out, this approach assumes that the law of contract can be seen as 'a regulatory technique, equivalent to other techniques of social and economic regulation of business, though it differs in its forms, attributes and capacities' and that 'private law pursues instrumental purposes like other types of legal regulation of markets' (at least as one strand of discourse).[29] Collins identifies a number of structural weaknesses in regulation by the private law of contract, but also argues that the 'private law' of contract has the capacity to overcome many of these limitations, especially as it interacts with public regulation.

This leads to the second theme of *Regulating Contracts*. Collins suggests that 'we have reached an interesting historical moment' in which the nineteenth-century systems of private law have been demonstrated to be 'defective instruments of regulation'. At the same time the 'welfare or public regulation' adopted in the twentieth century to resolve these problems in command and control mode has also been shown to suffer from weaknesses in efficiency and efficacy.[30] However, the interaction, interference, and dialogue between public and private law regulation of contract, according to Collins, has created a fresh productive capacity for regulation. In particular the self-referential, closed nature of private law is 'productively disintegrating' and being transformed so that instrumental or policy concerns become more dominant.[31] Nevertheless, Collins argues that in this process private law retains, and even enhances, its main advantages as a regulatory tool, that is normative complexity that gives it the 'capacity to provide a more sophisticated, contextualised, and efficient system of regulation in many instances [than public regulatory systems]'.[32] So the 'collision' that Collins describes between the private law system of contract and the public law regulation of contractual practices (e.g. consumer protection, fair rents, minimum wages) is ultimately seen as productive. The goals and policies of welfare regulation have been included in contract law's normative domain through doctrines such as abuse of rights, unconscionability, and good faith. Once incorporated into private law doctrine, these norms (originating in public law regulation) have been

---

[28] See esp. ch. 4, and also ch. 2. Each of ch. 5 to 16 apply a combined regulatory and doctrinal analysis to each of various issues raised by the use of contract to regulate the construction of markets and the distributive outcomes of markets.   [29] Collins, *Regulating Contracts*, 56.
[30] Summarized from *Regulating Contracts*, 361.   [31] See esp. ibid., ch. 3.
[32] Ibid. 358.

applied by private law to many more varied situations than ever contemplated by the original legislation.[33] The private law of contract informs the public law of consumer rights and is in turn regulated by and transformed by that public law. Conversely, the trend to privatization and corporatization in government has meant that concepts from the private law of contract now have an increasing significance in the public sector and its regulation.[34] So, for Collins, the regulatory lens reveals to us a productive hybridity between public and private law doctrine as these two legal traditions regulate each other.

The interpenetration of private and public law is not only descriptively accurate, it can also be normatively desirable. Public regulation can transform private conflicts into public issues. An example is individual problems of people signing loan documents they do not understand being addressed by regulatory legislation requiring disclosure in simple English. Under certain conditions, justice can also be enhanced when private law is used to enforce public standards. Here an example is Collins's discussion of contracts between businesses mandating compliance with process of production standards for assuring quality, safety, or environmental responsiveness.[35] Where private contractors have greater practical capacity to monitor compliance with the standards within the routines of their contracting than do public inspectors, then direct public regulation less adequately serves the purposes of public regulation than do public law standards that percolate into private contracting.

The chief advantage of the private law of contract, according to Collins, is its capacity to be 'reflexive' or 'responsive'[36] to other forms of non-legal regulation:

[Private law regulation of contracts] devolves an extensive discretionary power of self-regulation to the parties. Subject to the requirement of a negotiated consensus, the rules produced will then be routinely enforced by the legal system through the agency of the ordinary courts. By conferring autonomy upon the parties to devise their own regulation, private law achieves considerable flexibility, which in turn achieves the advantage that the regulation permits experimentation with novel types of business transaction that might enhance productive efficiency.[37]

As the private law of contract is transformed by public regulation, it also develops the capacity to incorporate 'references to externalities, public goods, and the articulation of policy objectives for regulation' into its reasoning and makes 'procedural adjustments, such as permitting amicus curiae, granting standing to collective groups, the admission of statistical evidence, and using the burden of proof for the purpose of detection of violation of regulatory standards'.[38] It is 'reflexive' in that it allows itself to be regulated by other forms of instrumental regulation while also facilitating the self-regulation of those that it seeks to regulate:

The underlying advantage of private law regulation is the way it commences with a respect for the self-enforced, self-regulation of the parties to the contract, so that every

---

[33] Ibid. 46–52.   [34] Ibid. 303–20.   [35] Ibid. 297.
[36] See ibid. 65–9 for an explanation of these terms.   [37] Ibid. 67.   [38] Ibid. 93.

[regulatory] intervention has to be justified as either one which better achieves their objectives or one which pursues important distributive objectives. This style of reflexive regulation ensures that interventions confront the context of transactions and provide regulation tailored to the particular circumstances of the transaction.[39]

Transformed private or common law, in Collins's conception, can occupy a significant coordinating function among the interactions of various types of regulation. According to Teubner any regulatory intervention that attempts to change social institutions will face a 'regulatory trilemma'—either the legal rules may fail to have an impact on social practice, or they may subvert desirable social practices by making impracticable demands, or the law may lose the coherence of its own analytical framework by seeking to incorporate socio-logical and economic arguments in its reasoning to respond to instrumental concerns.[40] Collins argues that the transformed private law of contract avoids the problem of the 'regulatory trilemma' through the 'subtle' assessment of competing discourses around contracts.[41] But can Collins's hypothesis about the responsive potential of contract doctrine be generalized to other fields of law such as crime or torts, in which there may be distinct limits on the extent to which doctrinal responsiveness to social norms is desirable?

CONCLUSION

As we have seen, Teubner argues that any regulatory intervention that attempts to change social institutions will face the possibility that it is either (1) 'irrelevant'; that is, it is *ineffective* because people fail to comply; or (2) 'produces disinteg-rating effects on the social area or social life'; that is, it is *non-responsive* to exist-ing norms, values, and social orderings; or (3) produces 'disintegrating effects on regulatory law itself'; that is, it is *incoherent*.[42] In the original briefing document sent to contributors to this project, the editors suggested that much contemporary regulatory research could be characterized as being concerned with effectiveness, responsiveness, and/or coherence.[43] One need not adopt systems theory, as Teubner does,[44] to see these as a useful heuristic for the types of question that lawyers and regulationists might ask about regulating law. These are indeed the questions that characterize the contributions to this book.

[39] Collins, *Regulating Contracts*, 358. Selznick, *The Moral Commonwealth*, 463, also sees com-mon law reasoning as inherently 'responsive'.

[40] G. Teubner, 'Juridification: Concepts, Aspects, Limits, Solutions', in Teubner (ed.), *Juridification of Social Spheres* (Berlin: Walter de Gruyter, 1987), 408.

[41] See Collins, *Regulating Contracts*, 358.

[42] This is Collins's paraphrase in *Regulating Contracts*, 68–9.

[43] See also Parker and Braithwaite, 'Regulation', 127–9, for an attempt to summarize the themes in the regulation literature in this way.

[44] Teubner's analysis of the regulatory trilemma is based partially on his systems theory analysis of the problem of inadequate structural coupling of politics, law, and social life. The problem arises because in contemporary society these areas are both increasingly autonomous and increasingly interdependent: Teubner, 'Juridification', 407.

Firstly, we ask questions about the *effectiveness*[45] of law as regulation. How do different areas of law operate as a form of regulation in the social world— what is its regulatory impact on daily life? Much regulation research is concerned with identifying the extent to which target populations comply with regulation, why people comply, or fail to comply, and how the meaning of compliance is adapted, interpreted, negotiated, and influenced by both regulators and regulatees.[46] It investigates the impact of different styles of rules, legal instruments, monitoring, and enforcement techniques on compliance and attainment of regulatory objectives.[47] This book asks these same questions about a wider range of laws than regulationists have traditionally examined.

Secondly, we ask questions about the *responsiveness* of law, how it fits with other forms of regulation. To what extent does each area of law include doctrines and practices that allow responsiveness to social facts and norms or that perpetuate dominations and injustice at large in society as a whole? Descriptive regulatory research often charts the extent to which the values represented in regulation and the techniques used to monitor and enforce compliance with regulatory standards compete and interact with pre-existing norms and social ordering in the target population.[48] A central concern in the normative literature on regulation has been 'to consider how regulation can acquire the qualities of being simultaneously rationally planned and purposeful, and also deeply rooted in social and cultural life'.[49] This book applies those questions to law so as to illuminate law's place in the overall scheme of social regulation.

Finally, we ask questions about the *coherence* of law when it is seen through a regulatory lens. To what extent do plural norms and forms of regulation interact to form a whole? Or does multifaceted regulation fragment any semblance of integrity in law? For example, does the consequentialism inherent in effectiveness and responsiveness inevitably corrupt law's non-instrumental commitment to doctrines and principles associated with values such as distributive or procedural justice? Coherence is a typically legal concern compared with the other two sets of questions above. Lawyers have sometimes been concerned that the doctrinal coherence or values inherent in law's analytic framework can be threatened by the primacy of instrumental policy concerns in legislative regulation.[50] Legal scholars of regulation have been particularly concerned with the extent to which

---

[45] Here 'effectiveness' should be read widely to refer to the impact of law in real life, and perhaps its efficiency. Since in many areas of law there may not be one clear regulatory purpose, it cannot mean just effectiveness at achieving its purposes.

[46] e.g. H. Genn, 'Business Responses to the Regulation of Health and Safety in England' *Law and Policy*, 15 (1993), 219; B. Hutter, *Compliance: Regulation and Environment* (Oxford: Clarendon Press, 1997), and *Regulation and Risk: Occupational Health and Safety on the Railways* (Oxford: Oxford University Press, 2001); K. Hawkins, *Environment and Enforcement: Regulation and the Social Definition of Pollution* (Oxford: Clarendon Press, 1984); F. Pearce and S. Tombs, *Toxic Capitalism: Corporate Crime and the Chemical Industry* (Aldershot: Ashgate, 1998).

[47] See Baldwin *et al.*, introduction to *A Reader on Regulation*, 14–21.

[48] See references at n. 23 above.   [49] Cotterrell, *Law's Community*, 308.

[50] Ibid. 283–4.

constitutional guarantees, human rights, and fundamental legal principles[51] are observed in the practice of instrumental, policy-oriented legal regulation, and also in the diverse sites, methods, and agents of other quasi-legal and non-legal regulation (e.g. self-regulation).[52] The regulatory perspective on law in this book, however, also produces fresh insights into how different areas of legal doctrine (with varying levels of explicit regulatory purpose) can interact with one another and with other forms of regulation to produce complex, multidimensional fields of regulation. In this interaction there may be greater capacity to be responsive and effective than any one field of law or form of regulation has on its own.

[51] For example, openness, accountability, consistency, proportionality, and procedural fairness (list of principles taken from K. Yeung, *The Public Enforcement of Australian Competition Law* (Canberra: Australian Competition and Consumer Commission, 2001), 1). They are also concerned with the potential failure of effective and responsive regulation to secure certainty, consistency, and predictability in legal principles and values.

[52] For examples of this type of scholarship, see D. Galligan, *Discretionary Powers: A Legal Study of Official Discretion* (Oxford: Oxford University Press, 1986); C. Graham, 'Is there a Crisis in Regulatory Accountability?' (1997), repr. in Baldwin *et al.* (eds.), *A Reader on Regulation*, 482; Yeung, *The Public Enforcement of Australian Competition Law*. See also Cotterrell, *Law's Community*, 283, where the author observes that 'It is often remarked that policy-oriented regulatory practices are potentially incompatible with the ideal of the Rule of Law—regarded as a set of specifically legal values of predictability and consistency in rules, and coherence, equality and fairness in adjudication.'

1

Regulating Contract Law

HUGH COLLINS

To perceive contract law as a regulatory mechanism requires most lawyers to buy a new pair of spectacles. Instead of the conventional view that the law of contract facilitates market transactions, the application of a regulatory lens demands that we evaluate the general law of contract as a governance mechanism for steering and controlling markets or private ordering. To speak of 'regulating contract law' requires a further refocusing of the inquiry: the rules of contract law, now regarded as a regulatory mechanism, themselves become viewed as the subject of further regulatory mechanisms. That perspective invites us to investigate what kinds of regulation in fact steer and control the law of contract. We may discover such instances of meta-regulation in other branches of law such as constitutional law, in transnational legal orders, or in non-state institutional arrangements for private ordering that exclude or confine ordinary contract law.

This unfamiliar line of inquiry about the law of contract seems promising for a number of reasons. Firstly, a regulatory perspective on any aspect of governance asks whether the mechanisms function efficiently and effectively. The law of contract provides the basic rules governing most market transactions and, therefore, one of the principal sources of wealth. Every society needs to ensure that these rules function efficiently and effectively, so that they do not place unnecessary costs on market transactions, or obstruct potentially profitable deals, or permit rogue traders to subvert confidence in the market as a mechanism for generating wealth. Secondly, a regulatory perspective asks whether the effectiveness of the mechanisms of governance could be improved. In the context of globalization and regulatory competition between nation states, national governments need to be concerned that their laws governing commercial transactions do not put their economies at a competitive disadvantage, with the potential deleterious consequence of driving capital investment and business towards other jurisdictions. Similarly, to the extent that governments increasingly rely upon private companies to deliver public services and use competitive markets to ensure that those services are produced efficiently and effectively, the rules of contract law need to be assessed for their adequacy in contributing to the pursuit of that objective. Thirdly, in so far as the regulation of markets contributes to what a society regards as a fair scheme of distributive justice, we need to ask whether the rules of contract law contribute effectively and accurately to the production of an acceptable scheme of social welfare. Finally, we can assess the levers of meta-regulation from similar regulatory perspectives: do the mechanisms such as transnational legal orders that control contract law satisfy the criteria of efficiency, effectiveness, and steering towards an acceptable scheme of social justice? All four considerations point to the need to inspect the law of contract with the benefit of a regulatory lens.

In approaching these broad themes within a brief compass, I enjoy the advantage of having traversed much of this route before.[1] As a consequence, I address cursorily some central issues of the regulatory perspective on contract law, and concentrate on novel lines of inquiry. I commence by explicating more fully than before some methodological difficulties. Next, I rehearse in a more systematic way the reasons for believing that the general law of contract should be regarded as a governance mechanism and a part of the state's regulatory structure. Instead of then providing an evaluation of contract law as a regulatory mechanism, a task to which my earlier work was largely devoted, my discussion jumps to an examination of the issue of regulating the regulatory mechanism of general contract law. That inquiry requires reflection on the adequacy of this legal mechanism of general contract law in the performance of its tasks of governance and how its defects may be rectified by mechanisms of meta-regulation.

CONTRACT LAW AS A MECHANISM OF GOVERNANCE

A regulatory perspective poses such questions as whether the rules of the law of contract achieve their goals cheaply, secure high levels of compliance from participants in the market, achieve their goals effectively, and whether the rule-setting mechanism is democratically accountable to the extent that the rules affect the public interest.[2] To tackle those questions, we need to identify what may be regarded as the rules of contract law. Lawyers may immediately point to the material discussed in the legal treatises on contract law. Those books concentrate their attention on private law, and in particular the rules of the law of obligations regarding the creation and enforcement of voluntary legally binding obligations owed between citizens.

Studies of regulation heighten our awareness that many kinds of governance mechanism may contribute to the steering of social practices. In securing the goals of contract law, the law employs other steering mechanisms in addition to private law, such as particular legislative interventions, constitutional provisions, and international treaties. Beyond these materials, all of which might uncontentiously be called law, a regulatory perspective requires that we should examine the role played by other non-legal steering mechanisms on the social practice of making contracts. These other forms of regulation may provide an

[1] H. Collins, *Regulating Contracts* (Oxford: Oxford University Press, 1999).
[2] For a richer and fairer account of regulatory studies: R. Baldwin, C. Scott, and C. Hood (eds.), *A Reader on Regulation* (Oxford: Oxford University Press, 1998).

effective steering mechanism on their own, or they may be inserted into and revise the legal regulation. To evaluate contract law from a regulatory perspective, therefore, we need to place the general private law of contract in the context of overlapping and interacting regulatory mechanisms.

Once the focus of investigation becomes not merely contract law as traditionally conceived by lawyers, but rather all the governance mechanisms that serve to regulate contractual behaviour, the scope of the inquiry has to be determined not by a legal category but by reference to a social practice. The relevant topic is regulating contractual practices, or, more pithily, *regulating contracts*. By framing the investigation in a particular social context, we can examine how the different types of law, soft law, and other institutional mechanisms, interact and contribute to the steering of social behaviour. Having taken that methodological step, however, we encounter two further problems for determining the object of the inquiry.

In the first place, we need to form a view of which kinds of social practices should be regarded as contractual practices. The legal classification of a practice as contractual may provide an unreliable or dysfunctional guide for a regulatory approach. A regulatory perspective needs to adopt its own conception of contractual practices and not be constricted by the legal answer. For example, a void contract such as a gambling contract may not count as a contract in law, but a regulatory perspective needs to examine this social practice, because it will want to ask such questions as whether making the contract void is an effective way of achieving the social policy behind this prohibition. If the policy aim is to deter gambling, for instance, it is evident from the proliferation of high-street betting shops and internet gambling sites that the legal determination that placing a bet is not a contractual practice has no deterrent effect whatsoever and is wholly ineffective. In any event, the legal determination of whether or not a social practice should count as a contract often proves uncertain and controversial itself. The one case that every student of the common law of contract knows, namely *Carlill v Carbolic Smoke Ball Co*,[3] is devoted entirely to this issue of what should count as contractual behaviour: was the action by a manufacturer of placing an advertisement in a newspaper, which had the effect of inducing a consumer to purchase the product from a retailer, sufficient to create a contract between the manufacturer and the consumer? Although the legal determination of what counts as a contractual practice may provide valuable insights, a regulatory approach cannot avoid the task of providing a sociological conception of contractual practice.

To provide such a conception, we can commence by seeking some central instances of contractual practices, such as a written agreement between two people to purchase some specified goods. Beyond those agreed central cases, however, we need to use a hermeneutic method to examine whether the actors regard their conduct as involving contractual practices. For example, is the

---

[3] [1893] 1 QB 256, CA.

casual action of boarding a bus a contractual practice? Similarly, if I rescue a neighbour's cat from a tree, and she promises to give me a plant for my garden in thanks for my service, is this promise a contractual practice for these purposes? The answer to these questions depends, I suggest, on the meaning of these events to the participants. In order to determine whether this meaning should count as contractual, we require an independent criterion or theory for determining what kinds of meaning attributed to events by the participants should be regarded as amounting to a contractual meaning. Hence, in my earlier work the first task I addressed was to develop a theory of the meaning of contractual practice, in order to define the scope of the investigation.[4] Applying a regulatory perspective to contract law, therefore, requires not only that we should determine the scope of inquiry by reference to social practice rather than law, but also, in our conception of what counts as the relevant social practice, which is a contractual practice, we need to develop a view of the meaning of contract which is independent of the legal conception of a contract.

The second methodological problem presented by the regulatory perspective's insistence that we examine all the relevant governance mechanisms for contractual practices concerns the teasing ambiguity in the phrase *regulating contracts*. Agreements between people, especially if they are recorded in documents, are evidently being used as a mechanism for steering and controlling a relationship between two people for the future. Many contracts are, therefore, analogous to regulation themselves, for they purport to establish binding standards for future conduct and specify the sanctions that will be imposed in the event of breach of standards. The private law of contract, with its respect for freedom to set the terms or for private autonomy, delegates to the parties a substantial power to fix the rules that will govern the economic relations or contractual practices between participants in the market. In this sense, many contracts represent an instance of self-regulation at a micro level. The topic of *regulating contracts* requires us to view contracts both as the subject of regulation, and, at the same time, as a type of regulation governing contractual practices.

Furthermore, we need to appreciate that this regulatory capacity conferred on private actors enables them in many instances to determine through their agreement what legal regulation, if any, will apply to their transaction. As in the examples of 'letters of comfort' and 'letters of intent', the parties to an agreement can declare that their arrangement will not be legally enforceable, thereby excluding it from the province of legal regulation and control.[5] To the extent that legal regulation is comprised of default or supplementary rules such as implied terms, again the legal regime permits the parties through express terms to prefer their own standards over those supplied by legal regulation. Even when legal regulation imposes mandatory rules that cannot be excluded by agreement, it is often possible for the parties to structure their relationship in ways that avoid

---

[4] Collins, *Regulating Contracts*, ch. 2.
[5] *Kleinwort Benson Ltd v Malaysia Mining Corpn* [1989] 1 WLR 379, CA; *Rose & Frank Co v JR Crompton & Bros Ltd* [1925] AC 445, HL.

the application of regulation. For example, the terms of an employment relationship may be reformulated as a contract for services, with the effect that the mandatory rules of employment law do not apply to the relationship.[6] As a regulatory mechanism, therefore, contracts have the potential to regulate contract law itself in the sense of controlling and modifying its application.

To sum up these preliminary observations briefly: an examination of the subject of regulating contract law requires both an inclusive view of law that encompasses all kinds of soft law, not least the self-regulation by the parties to a contractual agreement, and at the same time the development of a social rather than a legal perception of what should be regarded as a contractual practice for this purpose. Only once these methodological steps have been taken does it become possible to ask the kinds of question posed by a regulatory perspective, such as whether or not a system of regulation operates effectively and efficiently.

The Effectiveness of Contract Law

Even after taking those preliminary steps, does it make sense to ask whether contract law is effective? The question presupposes that the law can be analysed as regulation, motivated by an identifiable goal, which it pursues by the promulgation of standards backed up by enforcement mechanisms. Although such an analysis might fit easily over some measures of consumer protection or employment law, lawyers experience considerable difficulty in accepting that the same analysis should be applied to the general law of contract. Lawyers conventionally regard the private law of contract as performing an essentially facilitative role, one which permits citizens to do something, namely, to make legally enforceable contracts, rather than one which purports to control business behaviour by reference to enforceable standards in the pursuit of a particular goal. On this conventional view, if any goal can be attributed to the law of contract, it amounts to no more than a way of respecting the basic right of citizens to freedom of association, which is not so much a goal but a pre-political settlement concerning the framework of rights that every citizen should enjoy. At least four strands of argument challenge this conventional view. Acceptance of any one, or any combination, compels an acceptance of the view that it is appropriate and meaningful to ask the regulatory question whether the private law of contract is effective. These arguments will be briefly rehearsed here.

Distributive Justice

A market system supported by a broadly facilitative law of contract does not impose on society a detailed pattern of distributive justice. Indeed, the system

---

[6] e.g. *O'Kelly v Trusthouse Forte plc* [1984] QB 90, CA; *Express & Echo Publications Ltd v Tanton* [1999] ICR 693, CA.

rejects any claims to inherent rights to superior wealth or minimum levels of welfare. The justice of this system is defended either on the ground that each individual chooses his or her own lot according to their efforts in making beneficial transactions, or on the ground that no justification is called for, because the state does not seek to impose any pattern of distribution at all.[7] On this view, contract law merely enables individuals to pursue their own goals, an aim which can be achieved by respecting freedom of contract. The absence of any patterned distributive aim seems to render it impossible to ask whether the regulation is effective in achieving its goals, for there are no ostensible distributive goals being pursued.

In response to that libertarian denial that one can ask whether the law of contract is effective in achieving its goals, we should first observe that the outcomes of a free market are foreseeable and predictable. Those citizens and legal entities with superior resources and natural advantages are likely to acquire greater wealth and power than those with few resources and disabilities. Because this outcome is foreseeable and at least to some extent avoidable, it calls for a justification.[8] Furthermore, the regulation of contract practices cannot avoid taking a stand on which resources and natural advantages can be employed to obtain wealth through market transactions. For example, the law must determine whether lying will be permitted, what kinds of pressure can be exerted to induce another party to consent to a transaction, and whether a person can use information known only to him or herself to obtain favourable transactions. Regulation of this kind of behaviour cannot be based solely on some pre-political view of the rights of individuals, but must be determined ultimately by reference to the consequences of the rules on the distributive outcomes of markets.[9] These consequences might be set by reference to some criterion of distributive fairness or wealth maximization, but whatever the standard, the regulation of contracts necessarily embraces a distributive goal. Therefore, it becomes meaningful and intelligible to ask whether the regulation is effective in achieving this goal.

Logic of Social Types

A second argument for resisting the view that regulation of contracts involves the pursuit of social aims relies on a claim about the distinctive form of legal reasoning. In its most articulate formulation, Dworkin's theory of 'law as integrity' expresses the idea that legal reasoning can proceed according to a process for the reconciliation of individual rights without the need to employ consequential or policy arguments in order to reach determinate results.[10] In the

---

[7] F. von Hayek, *Law, Legislation and Liberty*, ii (London: Routledge & Kegan Paul, 1976), 65; R. Nozick, *Anarchy, State, and Utopia* (Oxford: Blackwell, 1974), 159.

[8] H. Collins, 'Distributive Justice through Contracts', *Current Legal Problems*, 45/2 (1992), 49; R. Plant, *Modern Political Thought* (Oxford: Blackwell, 1991).

[9] A. Kronman, 'Contract Law and Distributive Justice', *Yale Law Journal* (1980), 472; I. Ramsay, 'Consumer Credit Law, Distributive Justice and the Welfare State', *Oxford Journal of Legal Studies*, 15 (1995), 177.   [10] R. Dworkin, *Law's Empire* (London: Fontana, 1986).

private law of contract, for instance, it is argued that judicial decisions involve the weighing-up of competing rights according to a scheme of principles, and that courts do not need to refer to social policy goals in order to determine the outcome of a case. This seductive theory enables lawyers to insist upon the autonomy of legal reasoning, by which is meant the idea that legal reasoning is distinctive from any kind of political or policy reasoning because it employs this unique process of evaluating individual rights.

Although Dworkin's work has been criticized from various quarters on many different grounds, the fundamental problem with this type of claim for the autonomy of legal reasoning lies in its reliance upon what Unger calls the 'logic of social types'.[11] In order to believe that legal reasoning can operate on the basis of a calculus of competing rights, it is necessary to assume that the social and political order contains within it a coherent, interrelated, and, in its essentials, a fixed scheme of individual rights. Once such a scheme is assumed, it becomes possible to imagine that legal reasoning is devoted to the discovery of the logic of this scheme of rights, so that each right is awarded its appropriate level of protection in order to preserve the scheme. On this view, for instance, the question of whether a person can rely upon secret information in order to obtain a favourable deal can be answered by an investigation of the pre-existing scheme of rights with respect to information, which are themselves linked to a scheme of property rights and rights to privacy and liberty.

The most fundamental objection to this idea of the autonomy of legal reasoning is simply that no such pre-existing scheme of rights exists. Legal systems can take different views on what rights to award individuals, and there is no constraint on the allocation of rights owing to some inherent logic of a liberal, democratic market order. One legal system may require disclosure of secret information, and another may permit an individual to use it to his advantage in the market. The choice does not depend on an examination of some supposed logic of the market system underpinned by individual rights, but rather on the preferred distributive outcomes. When courts decide such disputes, or when a general rule is enacted in a code of private law, the selection of the rule is based on a view about the desirability of the foreseeable distributive consequences. A rule favouring disclosure of information is designed to combat asymmetries of information in order to protect the weaker party from entering into highly unfavourable transactions. A rule permitting the stronger party to keep the information secret provides an incentive to acquire information by enabling those with superior information to profit by it. Either rule, or some combination of them, may be a defensible scheme of distributive justice, but no particular rule can be derived as a necessary ingredient in some inherent scheme of rights to be discovered in the law or the foundations of the market order.

---

[11] R. M. Unger, 'The Critical Legal Studies Movement', *Harvard Law Review*, 96 (1983), 561; and in more depth, R. M. Unger, *False Necessity: Anti-Necessitarian Social Theory in the Service of Radical Democracy* (Cambridge: Cambridge University Press, 1987).

Once it is accepted that there is no underlying logic of social types, no coherent scheme of individual rights embedded in the social and political institutions of a society, it becomes possible to examine the legal rules with a view to assessing their objectives and whether or not those objectives are achieved. In the case of a non-disclosure rule, for instance, we may ask whether the rule gives sufficient incentive to discover information or whether some other rule might provide a better incentive for individuals to acquire information from which they can make advantageous transactions. In the case of a rule that requires disclosure, we can ask whether weaker parties are adequately protected by the rule against poor transactions resulting from informational asymmetries. Thus, the kinds of question posed by regulatory studies become a meaningful style of interrogation of the basic rules of private law just as much as they can be applied to the rules promulgated by a regulatory agency.

Strategic Litigation

A third type of argument designed to emphasize the instrumental quality of legal reasoning adopts a sociological perspective on legal reasoning. It examines how legal rules are, in fact, made or interpreted in the courts. The process of making rules determinate and applying them in concrete situations involves litigation, where the parties seek to persuade the court that their view of the particular rule is correct. The study of this process reveals how powerful actors in the market use litigation about the relevant rules in order to try to persuade the courts to accept rules that protect the interests of those powerful actors. That is not to say that these powerful actors such as large companies and the government always achieve their goal, but observation of litigation strategies suggests that, even if they fail in a particular case, they have the resources to return to the courts again and again with a view to securing favourable qualifications and adjustments to the regulation.

In the common law world, litigation about questions of law is a privilege of the rich. The leading cases decided by the higher courts of appeal, where questions of law tend to be settled, usually involve one powerful actor trying to secure a favourable outcome. To some extent this pattern of litigation is masked by the convention that the subrogated insurance company hides behind the name of the insured. But many of the leading cases on contract law will reveal, in the names of banks, large corporations, shipping companies, how appeals to the highest courts are part of strategic litigation for the purpose of obtaining favourable rules.

Consider, for example, the recent rash of litigation in England concerning the enforceability of security rights over a matrimonial home given by a wife in order to guarantee a loan to her husband's business. In such cases the wife tries to resist the bank's action for possession of the house when the husband's business fails to repay the bank loan on the ground that the husband had either lied to the wife about the loan or had exerted undue influence over her. The banks succeeded initially in obtaining a favourable rule that they would only be prevented from enforcing their security in the unlikely event that the husband had acted as the bank's agent in obtaining the wife's consent to the charge over the matrimonial home.[12] But in *Barclays Bank plc v O'Brien*,[13] the House of Lords developed a new rule that the bank would have constructive notice of the husband's misrepresentation or undue influence, if the wife apparently would receive no immediate benefit from the loan to the husband's company. With this constructive notice of wrongdoing, the bank could only enforce the charge if it took reasonable steps to ensure that the wife had understood the nature of the transaction and the risks that she was taking. The House of Lords suggested that these reasonable steps would require the bank to hold a private meeting with the wife, during which the risks of the transaction could be explained. Following this defeat, the banks engaged in extensive strategic litigation to challenge this ruling. Although the doctrine of constructive notice was conceded, the banks insisted that a private meeting with the wife should not be necessary. Indeed, the banks did not want to hold such private meetings for fear that, although such a meeting would avoid the taint of undue influence or misrepresentation, it might generate a new liability for negligent misrepresentation for inadequate or inaccurate advice. Eventually, in a consolidated appeal of eight cases, the House of Lords bowed to the pressure from the banks and accepted a watered-down version of the requirement of taking reasonable steps. The new rule, announced in *Royal Bank of Scotland plc v Etridge (No 2)*,[14] permitted the bank merely to write to the wife warning her to obtain independent advice from a solicitor, and to require a letter from the solicitor to confirm that such advice had been obtained. This trivial precaution could at minimal cost to the bank restore the reliability of security given over the matrimonial home, and shifted the risk onto the liability insurance companies for solicitors, who would have to pay compensation to the wife in the event of negligent advice from the solicitor.

This history of strategic litigation, with large companies acting as repeat players, in order to obtain more favourable legal determinations could be reported in many other instances.[15] The pattern reveals how the courts do not operate in a vacuum in which they can ruminate on the demands of justice in the abstract, but have to face repeated attempts to persuade them to modify their decisions in the light of powerful business interests. Although these repeat players do not always succeed, they rarely give up without a long and expensive fight, during which time they can use the threat of litigation to obtain more favourable settlements. These private law contract rules set by the courts, therefore, emerge in the heat of hard-fought, economically motivated, litigation, and that context sets the scene for Galanter's explanation of 'why the haves come out ahead'.[16]

---

[12] *Coldunell v Gallon* [1986] QB 1184, [1986] 1 All ER 429, CA.   [13] [1994] 1 AC 180.
[14] [2001] UKHL 44, [2002] 2 AC 773.
[15] e.g. S. Wheeler, *Reservation of Title Clauses* (Oxford: Clarendon Press, 1991).
[16] M. Galanter, 'Why the "Haves" Come Out Ahead: Speculations on the Limits of Legal Change', *Law and Society Review*, 9 (1974–5), 95; M. Galanter, 'Afterword: Explaining Litigation', *Law and Society Review*, 9 (1974–5), 347.

The courts are aware, of course, of the instrumental purposes for which the repeat players litigate before them. In reaching their determinations, they must consider the potential consequences to the powerful actors, and, therefore, refine the rule in ways that to the judges appears to provide a suitable consequential outcome for these actors. From this sociological perspective on legal reasoning, the setting of rules through judicial determinations, which is the hallmark of private law, is necessarily an instrumental task, in which the courts try to reconcile the competing interests of the litigants. The courts must develop a view about the consequences for the market that they wish to achieve, such as protection of the security of banks over the matrimonial home, and they can observe and adjust the consequences of their rulings in the light of the effectiveness of the rules to achieve their objective. The courts are, therefore, performing a similar function to regulatory agencies by determining goals and selecting rules to achieve those goals. For this reason, it becomes intelligible to examine private law rules from a regulatory perspective, such as to ask whether or not they are effective in achieving their goals.

Purposive Legal Reasoning

A fourth argument for insisting on the appropriateness of applying a regulatory perspective to the private law of contract requires us to examine the content of the reasons put forward by the courts for reaching their decisions. To support the idea of the autonomy of legal reasoning, the idea that legal reasoning is based upon discovery of a pre-existing scheme of rights, we would need to find that the courts rely for the most part on arguments about the meaning of rules, the weight of principles, and the protection of rights. Although judicial reasoning certainly displays those dimensions, even a superficial examination of the reasoning reveals other important elements that are put forward as justifications for decisions.

In the litigation concerning banks' enforcement of security rights over the matrimonial home, for instance, the leading judgments in the cases rely as much upon an open discussion of policy considerations as they do upon legal precedent. In *Barclays Bank v O'Brien*, for instance, no precedent supported the doctrine of constructive notice. The rule was developed rather as the outcome of a policy discussion in which the need for small businesses to obtain capital from banks relatively easily was weighed against the need to protect some wives against lies and pressure from their husbands. In that case Lord Browne-Wilkinson summed up the policy discussion in these terms: 'It is therefore essential that a law designed to protect the vulnerable does not render the matrimonial home unacceptable as a security to financial institutions.' The need for small businesses, the lifeblood of the economy, to have access to capital is repeated in the subsequent cases as the guiding thread in the determination of the enforceability of security rights against sureties.

This open discussion of policy, placed at a pivotal point in the judgments, explaining firstly why a new rule of constructive notice has been created, and then why it has to be modified, provides considerable support for the view that private law should be assessed like other regulatory interventions by reference to its effectiveness in the pursuit of its goals. But I would go further and suggest that what occurs in the legal reasoning in modern cases is not simply the bifurcation of legal reasoning into legal doctrine and policy discussion, but the generation of a new kind of legal discourse, which incorporates within it social and economic policies.[17] General rules of private law become refined into local, detailed regulation, informed by more precise distributive or welfare goals. The courts monitor the effects of this regulation through the imperfect and biased feedback loop of litigation, and revise the detailed rules to ensure closer correspondence with the policy objective. The judicial references to policy are not merely rhetorical justifications for the decision but serve as vital steps in the reasoning process leading to the formulation of the rule to be applied by the court.

This description of legal reasoning in contemporary private law cases renders it possible to ask the same kinds of question about the legal rules as those posed about rules promulgated by regulatory agencies. We can ask what policy objectives have guided the courts, what standards they have promulgated for securing those objectives, whether businesses have complied with those standards, and whether the enforcement of the standards appears to have secured the policy objective. That approach does not involve a denial that one of the policies always pursued by the courts is to attempt to devise a coherent private law system, but it removes the search for integrity from its pedestal as the sole and governing criterion to one consideration among many others, which often turns out to be the weakest concern.

THE REFLEXIVITY OF THE PRIVATE LAW OF CONTRACT

Having overcome the methodological issues raised in the first section of the discussion, and having accepted for one or more of the four reasons put forward in the previous section that the application of the regulatory lens on the private law of contract is an intelligible activity, we can proceed to examine questions such as whether or not the private law of contract provides an efficient and effective way of regulating markets.

In general, we should expect private law to prove efficient, in the sense that it costs a government little to produce the rules and to monitor their observance, because most of the costs are borne by the parties to the litigation. By the same token, however, we should expect private law to be less effective than other regulatory systems, because its standard techniques of monitoring, enforcement, and sanctions rely upon individuals bringing claims, and the sanctions are likely to be the minimal ones of either escape from a contract or the

---

[17] Collins, *Regulating Contracts*, ch. 3.

receipt of compensation for provable, unavoidable economic losses, with no punitive element usually permitted. But the regulatory perspective also enables us to ask other kinds of question about the general rules of contract law.

We may inquire, for instance, about mechanisms of democratic accountability, and whether its relative absence in what is often largely judge-made law can be justified on grounds such as benefits to the effectiveness of the system of regulation. In recent years regulatory studies have become particularly interested in whether or not the regulation is 'responsive' or 'reflexive'.[18] Although these concepts differ, a common thread is a concern that regulation should not distort or undermine the desirable features of the social practice that is being regulated. For instance, we may be concerned that legal regulation of medical malpractice may cause behaviour described as 'defensive medicine', which greatly increases the cost of health care with little benefit to the patients treated and longer waiting times for everyone else. The question I shall consider here is how far private law's general rules of contract law satisfy the aspiration of reflexivity.

The terminology of reflexivity derives from systems theory, in which it refers to the interaction between law (or some kind of regulation) and the social practices that it regulates. In systems theory, these social practices are understood as being organized under and conducted according to one or more communication systems. These communication systems or discourses provide the language and the way in which participants think about their social practice. Reflexive regulation tries to be sensitive to the ways in which the participants in a social practice think about their activity, with a view to producing regulatory outcomes that avoid as far as possible interventions that distort, devalue, or corrupt the social practice as it is viewed in its own socially grounded communication systems. For instance, regulation of contractual practice that encouraged participants to break their promises all the time might not be reflexive in the sense that it would tend to undermine a moral communication system based upon promise-keeping in which many contractual practices may be embedded.

In my earlier work I argued that general contract law could claim to be unusually reflexive as a regulatory mechanism.[19] By crafting general rules for the formation of binding contracts and their enforcement, private law refrains from detailed regulation of the content of contractual obligations. Instead, the parties construct their own regulation in the terms of the contract, which can reflect the social communication system in which they are operating. For example, the general rules of private law apply to all sales of goods, but the parties can in the detail of the contract adjust the rules applicable according to the particular kind of goods involved, the nature of the market in those goods, and the likelihood of contingencies arising that will render performance

---

[18] I. Ayres and J. Braithwaite, *Responsive Regulation: Transcending the Deregulation Debate* (New York: Oxford University Press, 1992); G. Teubner, 'Substantive and Reflexive Elements in Modern Law', *Law and Society Review*, 17 (1983), 239; G. Teubner, 'After Legal Instrumentalism? Strategic Models of Post-regulatory Law', in Teubner (ed.), *Dilemmas of Law in the Welfare State* (New York: Walter de Gruyter, 1988), 299.   [19] Collins, *Regulating Contracts*, 65.

inefficient for one or both parties. The legal enforcement of the self-regulation provided by a contract permits those engaged in the social practice of contracting to incorporate other non-legal standards such as customary trading rules as well as idiosyncratic features of a particular transaction. Furthermore, the private law system adds to its reflexivity by leaving control over remedies for breach of the regulation and self-regulation to the parties themselves. A person disappointed by a breach of contract can decide whether or not to pursue a legal claim against the party in breach, and, if so, there is a range of remedies which may be sought. In practice, what is likely to happen is that once a breach of contract has been acknowledged, the parties will negotiate a contract of settlement that adjusts their future obligations in the light of what has happened. Again, this system of enforcement of contract law is highly reflexive, for in effect the parties typically determine what kind of outcome will satisfy their interests in the event of breach of regulatory standards.

In my earlier enthusiasm to explore the reflexive qualities of general contract law, I expressed only two reservations about this capacity of private law as a regulatory mechanism. The first reservation concerned the use by businesses of standard-form contracts, especially in their dealings with consumers. There is an obvious danger that the standard-form contract will be highly reflexive with respect to the business's concerns, such as efficiency, innovation, and effective organizational management, but fail to accommodate the consumer's interests and expectations in the express terms of the document. I emphasized, however, that modern regulations, such as the Unfair Terms in Consumer Contracts Directive,[20] had empowered administrative agencies and courts to invalidate unfair terms that inadequately respond to the competing interests and expectations of consumers and employees.

The second reservation concerned futures markets and the operation of Exchanges. In futures and derivatives markets and stock exchanges, it is necessary for the contracts to provide a homogeneous description of the product such as cotton, so that the speculation in the financial market can be directed solely to future prices and not the quality of the product.[21] The parties are effectively trading contracts as an object of property, and what they require is certainty that the object has no subtle differences from others of the same type, so that it can be traded quickly without any investigation of the terms governing the relationship between the contractual entitlement and any underlying assets. These contracts must be able to function rather like banknotes, so that it can be safely assumed that one note bearing a value of £10 has exactly the same value as another note bearing a value of £10. An Exchange is an association that establishes a compulsory system of classifications in order to permit trading by speculating

---

[20] Directive 93/13.

[21] A. W. B. Simpson, 'The Origin of Futures Trading in the Liverpool Cotton Market', in P. Cane and J. Stapleton (eds.), *Essays for Patrick Atiyah* (Oxford: Clarendon Press, 1991), 179; L. G. Telser and H. N. Higginbottom, 'Organised Futures Markets: Costs and Benefits', *Journal of Political Economy*, 85 (1977), 969; Collins, *Regulating Contracts*, 212.

solely on future prices. Any reflexivity in permitting parties to vary terms in these standardized transactions would have defeated these arrangements, and hence the private law system had to be effectively excluded by compulsory membership of the association and conformity to its rules governing transactions.

The other key purpose of an Exchange is to exclude the reflexivity of private law with respect to settlements of contractual disputes. A crucial rule of all Exchanges is that no contract can be broken, but every contract must be performed, without exception. The mechanisms by which this result can be achieved vary, but one common technique is for the Exchange to become an intermediate party to every transaction and to demand deposits or 'cover' against default on any transaction from its members. The amount of the deposit or margin is calculated by reference to the risk of exposure to default. The evolution of Exchanges or club markets where these types of contract could be created and traded can be explained as an effect of the excessive reflexivity of private law. The private law system of maximizing reflexivity in settlements, so that the parties can adjust their relationship in the light of subsequent events, could not provide the necessary assurance of performance to permit speculation in financial markets.

On further reflection, I now think that I failed to recognize a more general impediment to reflexivity that lurks in the deep structure of the private law of contract. It is ironic that I overlooked this structural problem, because one of my central theses is that contractual practices involve simultaneously several communication systems.[22] The existence of multiple communication systems in contractual practices creates an obstacle to reflexivity for any kind of regulation of contracts, including the general rules of private law, because inevitably in the selection of regulation, choices will have to be made about which communication system should receive priority. Consider as a simple illustration the debate over 'efficient breach of contract'.[23] In connection with contractual practices we are likely to find in many instances the presence of two discourses or communication systems: one, a moral discourse concerning the good of keeping one's promises, and another, an economic discourse about making a profit through trade. The theory of efficient breach of contract, which suggests that the law should encourage parties to contracts to break them whenever they can increase their wealth while not diminishing the wealth of the other party to the contract, though making eminent sense from an economic perspective, seems to violate elementary principles in the moral understanding of contractual practices. In determining the judicial remedies for breach of contract, the general law cannot avoid making a selection or a compromise between these two interpretations of

---

[22] Collins, *Regulating Contracts*, ch. 6.
[23] This extensive debate includes: R. Posner, *Economic Analysis of Law*, 4th edn. (Boston: Little, Brown, 1992), 131; P. Atiyah, *Essays on Contract* (Oxford: Clarendon Press, 1990); D. Friedman, 'The Efficient Breach Fallacy', *Journal of Legal Studies*, 18 (1981), 1; L. Smith, 'Disgorgement of the Profits of Breach of Contract: Property, Contract and "Efficient Breach" ', *Canadian Business Law Journal*, 24 (1994–5), 121.

contractual practices. It cannot be completely reflexive to both communication systems simultaneously, for the moral view would point to the use of specific performance as the normal remedy for breach of contract, and the economic view would insist upon the invariable use of compensatory damages.

In practice, of course, the normal remedy for breach of contract is determined by the self-regulation of the contract itself. To some extent, that facilitation of self-regulation of remedies permits the parties to determine for themselves what discourse or framework for action should govern their post-breach negotiations. Yet private law systems invariably place constraints on the self-regulation of remedies that the parties may choose. For example, a rule against the use of penalty clauses prevents the parties from agreeing a fixed level of damages for breach that exceeds a genuine pre-estimate of the likely losses to the injured party.[24] The effect of the rule is to obstruct legal regulation from being reflexive in those cases where, in return for a higher price, the parties seek an additional assurance of successful completion of a contract by a particular date. The rule against penalty clauses privileges a discourse about contracts that views them from an economic perspective as opposed to one that places greater weight on fulfilment of the promised performance.[25]

This argument can be extended more broadly to apply to the common law's general rules about contract law. The tendency of these rules is to provide a highly reflexive scheme for commercial transactions where the objective is to increase wealth through an exchange of goods or services. When the contractual practices follow a different framework, in which other non-economic valuations of conduct are paramount, the law becomes less reflexive because it tends to restrict or undermine the parties' attempts to regulate their relationship in ways that express that dimension of their practices. To some extent, legal doctrine can evolve better to accommodate different frameworks of contractual practices. English courts have been developing new principles on which they may award damages for non-pecuniary loss,[26] as in the case of having a disappointing and stressful holiday, in order to respond to the consumer's expectations generated by the tour operator's brochures. Yet, it proves extremely difficult to devise general rules about the quantification of damages for breach of contract that can encompass the variety of contractual practices, so that the rules identify successfully those instances (and only those instances) when the meaning of the contractual practices includes an expectation of successful performance that will deliver more than purely economic benefits. Starting with the paradigm that contractual practices are dominated by discourses of economic interest, the

---

[24] *Dunlop Pneumatic Tyre Company Ltd v New Garage and Motor Co Ltd* [1915] AC 79, HL.

[25] Of course, an economic value can be attributed to the fulfilment of the promise, and on that basis it is possible to argue that penalty clauses, though deterring efficient breach of contract, increase the value of the contract to the parties: C. Goetz and R. Scott, 'Liquidated Damages, Penalties and the Just Compensation Principle', *Columbia Law Review*, 77 (1977), 554. My point is rather that the economic analysis tends to exclude other discourses by which remedies for breach of contract might be understood and evaluated.

[26] *Farley v Skinner* [2001] UKHL 49, [2002] 2 AC 732, HL.

general rules of contract law will always encounter difficulty in achieving an adequate level of reflexivity when they encounter contractual practices which give priority to other frameworks of communication.

Meta-regulation of Contract Law

My final topic is the adequacy (from a regulatory perspective) of the governance mechanisms that regulate private contract law. We have already observed several ways in which private contract law is controlled. Modern legislation frequently creates special exceptions for classes of contract, such as contracts of employment and consumer purchases, where particular regimes, often involving compulsory terms, are imposed on these market sectors. We have also observed that to some extent the terms of the contractual agreement itself can be used to confine the application of the general law of contract or particular social regulation. Here, I shall concentrate attention on how the private law of contract is regulated by its interaction with other branches of law, transnational law, and other governance mechanisms. To understand the significance of this topic, it may be helpful to sketch a rough history of contract law.

During the nineteenth century Western legal systems evolved sophisticated systems of private law for governing contracts. The civil codes and the common law were perceived to be autonomous branches of the law, embodying fundamental values of a liberal society such as freedom of contract and respect for property rights. These private law regimes were significantly altered in the twentieth century primarily by national legislation to create special rules for particular kinds of market transactions such as employment and consumer purchases. This regulation adjusted the private law rules in these particular instances by creating exceptions, without, therefore, abolishing the general rules of private law. Yet now, new forces appear to be questioning the autonomy of these national private law systems, and compelling a reconsideration of the values and methods by which they operate.

There are probably many reasons that are provoking this questioning of traditional private law systems. Changes in values influence the emphasis of private law principles all the time. In recent years, however, perhaps the most important cause of questioning concerns the reconfiguration of the role of the state in Europe. In new visions of the role of government, the state diminishes its reliance upon publicly owned assets for the delivery of public services, and rather tries to use privately owned companies to provide equivalent services to the public. To ensure reliability and fair access to public services, the state often creates an elaborate regulatory apparatus to control the operations of these private companies. This is the European model of the 'regulatory state'.[27] These complex systems, often involving independent regulatory agencies, can be

---

[27] G. Majone, 'The Rise of the Regulatory State in Europe', *West European Politics*, 17 (1994), 77.

criticized, however, for being no more efficient and effective than the publicly owned enterprises that preceded them. Sceptics argue for greater contractual freedom for the private companies that deliver services to the public. Provided that private companies operate in a competitive market, the pressures of competition will induce them to innovate and become more efficient, thereby improving the responsiveness of the service to the public without the stifling and sometimes counter-productive effect of elaborate regulatory regimes. On this argument, the regulatory state should develop a light touch, perhaps setting a framework for the provision of services to the public, such as a basic ground rule that everyone should have reasonable access to the service, but leave the task of identifying the cheapest and most innovative ways of supplying the service to the market.

To the extent that the preceding argument is accepted, and as a consequence we move towards what might be termed a 'post-regulatory state',[28] and one type of 'decentred regulation',[29] marked by greater reliance on markets and less faith in both judicial elaboration of private law and control mechanisms involving regulators, inevitably we place a new burden on the law of contracts. Once the general law of contract is called upon to contribute to the steering mechanisms of the post-regulatory state, the traditional respect paid to liberal values such as freedom of contract must be reconciled with the demands for social justice or welfare that motivated the institutions of the welfare state and the regulatory state. Using a combination of light-touch regulatory institutions and general contract law, governments have to steer the market to ensure that it produces outcomes that achieve acceptable levels of social justice and social cohesion, as well as fulfilling its traditional role of augmenting wealth. Contract law becomes part of a multi-layered system of governance. States endeavour to achieve their goals of welfare and social cohesion by delivering services through a mixture of public ownership, regulatory regimes controlling private companies, and contractual arrangements between private actors. The topic of regulating contract law can be conceived as an inquiry into how the law of contract can contribute productively to this multi-layered system of governance.

Here, the objective of meta-regulation should be to try to align general contract law with the state's welfare and social inclusion goals and to coordinate its regulation with other regulatory systems. This objective will often require the imposition of restraints on the reflexivity of private law, in order to ensure that individual rights or welfare goals are secured. In particular, the general law of contract needs to become more open in its reasoning processes to two kinds of normative influence. Firstly, it has to be able to incorporate in its reasoning reference to general abstract principles of justice such as those found in statements of fundamental rights of citizens. Secondly, private contract law must

---

[28] C. Scott, 'Regulation in the Age of Governance: The Rise of the Post-regulatory State', in J. Jordana and D. Levi-Faur (eds.), *The Politics of Regulation* (Cheltenham: Edward Elgar, 2003).

[29] J. Black, 'Decentring Regulation: Understanding the Role of Regulation and Self-regulation in a "Post-regulatory" World', *Current Legal Problems*, 54 (2001), 103.

find ways to align its standards with those produced by actors in the market when they cooperate through democratically accountable associations to create self-regulation of market sectors. In some instances, these new imperatives compete and create fresh dilemmas for regulating contract law as a governance mechanism in the regulatory state.

The first alignment with statements of fundamental rights of citizens becomes necessary in order to evolve a law of contract that conforms to the broader schemes of social justice and social cohesion that these statements of fundamental rights represent. One way of describing this problem is to say that the traditional private law of contract with its strong emphasis on freedom of contract embodied certain core constitutional principles such as freedom of association, respect for private autonomy of individuals, and respect for dignity. Other core constitutional principles were secured by different legal and social mechanisms in the welfare state. Once the law of contract is relied upon as a governance mechanism to secure a richer conception of social justice, however, it becomes important for this branch of the law to become open to the influences of other fundamental constitutional principles. Contract law cannot take a partial view of the constitution, if it becomes one of the principal vehicles through which the general scheme of constitutional values is implemented. In other words, ordinary contract law has to become a site where the demands of private autonomy are reconciled with the need to support social solidarity.[30]

The second problem of coordination concerns the interaction between the general law of contract and new types of governance mechanism that seek to secure social objectives through collective self-regulation. Agreements between representative associations can establish regulatory standards whereby a high degree of reflexivity with the aspirations and expectations of a variety of stakeholders is achieved, and at the same time the representative character of such associations secures a level of democratic legitimacy for these standards. For example, in the European Community co-regulation between employers' associations and trade unions through the 'Social Dialogue' can produce labour standards, which can become hard law in the form of Directives.[31] Similarly, in the European Community technical standards for products set by associations can become the effective product safety and quality standard in private transactions, either by express incorporation into contracts or as the default standard. General contract law needs to coordinate its regulation with these systems of co-regulation in a variety of ways, sometimes by regarding the standards produced by regulation as mandatory, at other times as default rules, and in other instances by permitting these standards to influence the evolution of legal doctrine. In other words, in their development of the general law of contract, the courts have to pay attention not only to traditional sources of private law

---

[30] M. W. Hesselink, *The New European Private Law* (The Hague: Kluwer, 2002), ch. 6.

[31] Treaty Establishing the European Community, Art. 139 (as amended); C. Barnard, 'The Social Partners and the Governance Agenda', *European Law Journal*, 8 (2002), 80.

and regulatory legislation, but also to new sources of norms such as those that have been developed by democratically accountable groups of stakeholders.

I have stated these problems of alignment and coordination at a rather abstract level, because I want to try to capture the sheer diversity of the possible ramifications for meta-regulation of the general law of contract. But we can illustrate the subtleties of these ramifications by reconsidering the earlier example of determining the proper level of compensation for disappointing holidays. The traditional perception of private law is that the legal issue here merely concerns a definition of what is required by corrective justice between the parties. Once one views private law as merely one of a number of mechanisms of governance in a post-regulatory state for achieving the social goals of the community, the issue of the appropriate levels of compensation takes on new dimensions. For instance, in the Nice Charter of Fundamental Rights of the European Union the right to a paid holiday is regarded as an essential element of well-being.[32] The Working Time Directive, itself a product of co-regulation between social partners, provides more detailed criteria for this right and explains that it forms part of a concern for the health and safety of citizens.[33] From this perspective the right to compensation for a disappointing holiday concerns the protection and vindication of an important social right, for which purpose a generous measure of compensation should be required in order to deter unscrupulous traders who might effectively defeat this right by providing a lousy holiday. In forming an element in a multi-layered system of governance for the achievement of social goals, legal reasoning in the general law of contract has to create methods through which it can render its outcomes compatible with and supportive of both the more general ambitions recited in constitutional documents of the protection of the liberties, social rights, and well-being of citizens, and the norms produced by democratically accountable stakeholders.

CONCLUSION

Gathering together the threads of my argument, the central claim is that contract law is now being called upon to play a more pivotal role in the governance mechanisms of the post-regulatory state. In that context, the sharp contrast once drawn between the functions of the private market and the functions of public intervention, either through ownership or regulation, no longer appears so convincing. Contractual practices, though not necessarily legally enforceable contracts, are being used to deliver services to the public and to control relations between different parts of government.[34] The use of contracts as part of the governance mechanism reveals both a faith in the disciplinary properties of competitive markets and a hope that contracts, as a paradigm of reflexive regulation, in the sense that the parties determine the rules or standards largely

---

[32] Art. 31.   [33] Directive 93/104.   [34] Collins, *Regulating Contracts*, ch. 13.

on their own, will avoid the pitfalls of traditional command and control mechanisms. But I have argued that contract law, as the instrument for state regulation of the self-regulation by the parties to contracts, now has to embrace more fully than ever before a stance that permits legal reasoning about contracts to engage with broader political and social values than those limited to the efficiency of markets and the protection of economic rights.

Although lawyers usually conceive of legal statements of those broader political and social values in constitutional documents as ranking higher in the hierarchy of legal norms, and, therefore, possessing the legal power to trump contract law, a more accurate description of legal reasoning seems to me to invoke the metaphor of a collision between legal subsystems, between public and private law, during which the private law of contract determines how far it will modify its own reasoning in the light of public law norms. In the case of the British Human Rights Act 1998, for instance, the crucial issue is whether the courts will permit the Convention rights to influence how private law principles evolve. Similarly, the issue for the European Court of Justice is the extent to which it will permit the broad range of civil liberties and social rights contained in the soft law of the Nice Charter of the Fundamental Rights of the European Union 2000 to influence its determinations of private law issues. By adding to the legal complexity of regulating contracts, these new tasks for the judiciary and legal reasoning in regulating contracts will surely pose major dilemmas.

2

Law and Regulation: The Case of Finance

JULIA BLACK*

INTRODUCTION

The aim of this book is to examine the interaction of law and regulation, and the Introduction identifies three main themes: the dialogue between legal and regulatory scholarship, the relationship between private and regulatory law, and the interactions between law and other forms of normative or regulatory ordering. This chapter critically examines each of these themes, and considers each in the context of UK financial services regulation.

The first section asks what, if anything, is the difference between legal and regulatory scholarship. The second section considers the relationship between regulatory rules and common law, and argues that for the most part, the two live in separate rooms with little direct interaction occurring. Nonetheless, there are examples of collisions between them and there are significant areas where they live in an uneasy coexistence, negotiating their relationship around one another. The third section raises a further issue, which is the relationship of the law itself to the regulatory system and market players, including the categorization of law as an operational 'risk' that market players have to manage. The fourth section draws on UK and international financial regulation to illustrate the practical significance of the third theme, the interaction of normative systems of ordering.

REGULATORY AND LEGAL SCHOLARSHIP: IS THERE A DIFFERENCE?

The premise of the Introduction is that the 'legal lens' and the 'regulatory lens' look at different things in different ways, and perhaps, for different reasons. The editors suggest that regulatory scholarship is concerned with impact and effectiveness, legal scholarship with legal doctrine. This section argues that, while there is some truth in this distinction, there are nevertheless, strong similarities between the two sets of scholarship, and while there are differences, they

* I am grateful to Dimity Kingsford Smith and the editors for comments on a previous draft of this chapter.

are, perhaps, other than the Introduction suggests. In conducting any 'compare and contrast' exercise of this nature there are risks, for both the legal and, in particular, the regulatory 'lenses' are in reality loose agglomerations of perspectives, characterizations are always based on simplifications, and the lines between the two sets of scholarship are extremely fluid. Nonetheless, following the 'lens' metaphor through, they can be broadly compared by asking five questions: what does each look at, what lens does each look through, where does each look from, what does each see, and what questions does each ask?

What Does Each Look At?

The Introduction suggests that the 'legal' lens focuses on legal doctrine, and, perhaps, the allocation of rights and responsibilities, while the 'regulatory' lens is empirical and instrumental, looking at the impacts of law, and assessing it against the criteria of whether it is effective, responsive, and coherent.[1] To an extent, this is an accurate characterization of each, but it is not a complete one.

It is a truism that lawyers look at law, regulationists look at regulation. But whether there is a difference depends on how each is defined.[2] Law is frequently defined in positivist terms, based loosely on Hart, as rules articulated and enforced by an institutionalized authority. Regulation may be defined as the intentional activity of attempting to control, order, or influence the behaviour of others.[3] On this basis 'regulation' is a broader social phenomenon than 'law' in that 'regulation' does not need to emanate from the state, and 'law' can thus be seen as one form of 'regulation', i.e. a particular set of ordering.

What legal and regulatory scholars look at largely coincides when a broad view of law is taken by lawyers, and a relatively narrow view of regulation by regulationists. In other words, when both focus on institutions of the legal system more broadly, namely, the operation of the core institutions (courts, legal procedures, legal aid, the profession, judges), other modes of dispute settlement and adjudication (tribunals, mediation, arbitration, etc.), the police and other law enforcement officials, and administrative bodies.

More fundamentally, and in contrast to the Introduction, both sets of scholarship focus on the issue of law's impacts and effects. Admittedly, not all legal scholars raise their eyes above doctrine, but many do. To say otherwise ignores the rise of the 'law in action' movement in legal scholarship in the 1960s and 1970s, the hallmark of which is to look far beyond legal rules and legal procedures to the way in which law operates in society. In this respect the

---

[1] C. Parker and J. Braithwaite, 'Regulation', in P. Cane and M. Tushnet (eds.), *Oxford Handbook of Legal Studies* (Oxford: Oxford University Press, 2003); Introduction to this volume.

[2] J. Black, 'Critical Reflections on Regulation', *Australian Journal of Legal Philosophy*, 27 (2002), 1.

[3] Ibid.; J. Black, 'Decentring Regulation: The Role of Regulation and Self Regulation in a "Post Regulatory" World', *Current Legal Problems*, 54 (2001), 103; D. Kingsford Smith, 'What is Regulation? A Reply to Julia Black', *Australian Journal of Legal Philosophy*, 27 (2002), 38.

relationship between legal, or at least socio-legal, and regulatory scholars is a close one.[4]

Nonetheless, there are significant areas of socio-legal scholarship which regulationists have tended not to focus on, and quite large tracts of regulatory scholarship with which socio-legal scholars have not engaged. Thus, while law and legal institutions are central to lawyers; regulationists are concerned with modes of governance including but not limited to law. More particularly, as regulatory scholarship matures as a (sub)discipline in its own right, there are certain dominant themes and questions that it is becoming conventional to address which have not been traditionally central to legal scholarship. These include the influences shaping regulation, patterns of decision-making, strategies of monitoring and enforcement, the design and deployment of regulatory tools, patterns of regulation and distribution of regulatory functions, and responses to regulation.[5]

What Lens Does Each Look Through?

Here drawing contrasts is more complex. The Introduction suggests that the 'regulatory' lens is instrumental, whereas the 'legal' lens is doctrinal. Whether or not that is so is addressed below. Beyond that, the Introduction does not address whether any particular disciplinary perspective is associated with either set of scholarship, though identifying a disciplinary perspective is arguably critical to characterizing the 'lens'. Further, given the multitude of writers in both law and regulation and the range of disciplinary perspectives that are brought to bear on both, it is hard to say that there is clearly a single 'legal' lens or a single 'regulatory' lens, or that one is instrumental and the other is not. Rather, there are multiple lenses, varying in part with the disciplinary perspective adopted, resulting in different questions, different methodologies, and different assumptions.

That said, while economics, sociology, psychology, political theory, and political science are evident in both 'law in action' legal and regulatory work, the disciplinary mix is perhaps slightly different in the former than the latter. In the former, economics (in the United States) and sociology (in the UK and Australia) dominate.[6] In contrast, writers on regulation can be found in departments of

---

[4] Indeed many of the key texts in UK and Australian regulatory scholarship are written by socio-legal writers and many have been published in the Oxford Socio-Legal Studies series, e.g. K. Hawkins, *Environment and Enforcement* (Oxford: Clarendon Press, 1984); B. Hutter, *The Reasonable Arm of the Law* (Oxford: Oxford University Press, 1987); B. Hutter, *Compliance: Regulation and the Environment* (Oxford: Clarendon Press, 1997); I. Ayres and J. Braithwaite, *Responsive Regulation* (Oxford: Oxford University Press, 1992); C. Parker, *Just Lawyers* (Oxford: Oxford University Press, 1999); N. Gunningham and P. Grabosky, *Smart Regulation: Designing Environmental Policy* (Oxford: Clarendon Press, 1998); N. Gunningham and R. Johnstone, *Regulating Workplace Safety* (Oxford: Oxford University Press, 1999).

[5] See e.g. R. Baldwin and M. Cave, *Understanding Regulation* (Oxford: Oxford University Press, 1999).

[6] e.g. R. Cotterrell, 'Why Must Legal Ideas be Interpreted Sociologically?', *Journal of Law and Society*, 25 (1998), 171.

political science, public administration, economics, accountancy, geography, and management as well as sociology and law, to name but a few, a fact which imposes a particular character of interdisciplinarity on the field.[7]

But even where the same disciplinary frame is used, the lenses will be as many and various as exist within that discipline itself. A 'sociological' perspective on either law or regulation will reflect where the writer stands in the debates on consensus–conflict, action–structure, positivism or interpretivism, and both sets of scholarship have been at the receiving end of poststructuralist and postmodernist critiques.[8] Regulationists, like legal theorists, assume different positions in those debates, with consequences for the questions they ask and the answers they find. For example, some take an interpretivist approach, and are concerned with the interpretation of actions and the meanings that individuals give to their own actions. Such studies emphasize the importance of decision frames, of shared communities of interpretation or understanding, in the operation of the regulatory system.[9] Others takes a more positivistic approach, and see the regulatory world as one to be observed from the outside, patterns of behaviour deduced and causations shown. Empirical studies in this tradition, for example, seek to compare which theories offer the best causal explanations for regulatory operations and outcomes.[10] Moreover, in the study of regulation, as in the study of law, the postmodern critique has prompted a shift in focus away from the state to alternative systems of ordering, and to the relationships between them. Thus, the distance between regulatory and legal scholars may be short where both share a disciplinary lens, certainly a subdisciplinary one, even though other aspects of their inquiry may differ. Indeed, they may be closer to each other than they are to branches of their own scholarship which use a different disciplinary perspective: sociological lawyers and sociological regulationists in many respects have more in common with each other than they do with the law and economics school and economic regulationists respectively.

What Vantage Point Does Each Look From?

Situational perspective is as important as disciplinary perspective in creating 'maps' of a legal or regulatory system. Here again drawing contrasts between the two sets of scholarship is complex, for there is no single vantage point that dominates in each. Within a legal order, Twining points out, there are different vantage points: 'those of a rule maker, adjudicator, enforcement officer, bureaucrat, claimant, advocate, deviant, good citizen, bad man, professional adviser,

---

[7] See e.g. Baldwin and Cave, *Understanding Regulation*.

[8] For a recent overview, see R. Banakar and M. Travers, Introduction, in Banaker and Travers (eds.), *An Introduction to Law and Social Theory* (Oxford: Hart, 2002).

[9] e.g. K. Hawkins, *Law as Last Resort* (Oxford: Oxford University Press, 2002); J. Black, *Rules and Regulators* (Oxford: Oxford University Press, 1997).

[10] e.g. C. Hood, H. Rothstein and R. Baldwin, *Government of Risk* (Oxford: Oxford University Press, 2001); D. Thatcher, *The Politics of Telecommunications* (Oxford: Oxford University Press, 1999).

expositor, and jurist'.[11] The same can be said of regulatory systems. Each participant experiences law or regulation differently. For limited inquiries, only the perspective of one or two may be relevant (e.g. enforcement officer, compliance officer, rule-maker), while broader understandings involve taking account of multiple standpoints. Further, gaining an understanding of the whole involves moving from the general to the increasingly particular, from the 'helicopter' to the 'worm's-eye view'.[12] Both sets of scholarship face the difficulty that the gulf between the theoretical debates and empirical work can become almost unbridgeable,[13] and again the differences within the different sets of scholarship can be greater than those between them, depending on whether a vantage point is shared (for example, in their studies of enforcement legal and regulatory scholarship are almost indistinguishable).

What Does Each See?

Turning to the question of what each sees, it is worth asking at a very general level what legal and regulatory scholars see when they look at law, or, more particularly, law's relationship to society. The Introduction suggests that legal scholars typically take an internal approach to law that focuses on the content of legal doctrine and its coherence. Regulatory scholars, in contrast, ask empirical questions about the proactive effects of law on the whole or a segment of society, and normative questions about how law and regulatory technique can be designed to be most effective at accomplishing social goals.

This is a tempting distinction: it is clear and simple, and suits a purpose. But it does not bear the weight put on it for several reasons. Firstly, as noted above, the rise of the 'law in action' movement put paid to any notion that legal scholarship was concerned exclusively with doctrine. Secondly, many legal scholars do see law as an instrument of social order. As Peter Cane argues in this volume, few would go so far as to agree with Weinrib's position that the only purpose of private law 'is to be private law'.[14] Indeed, there is no single understanding among legal scholars, or others, of law's relationship to society. Thirdly, not all who write in regulation see law as purely instrumental.

Lawyers' (and others') view of law is complex and contested. Legal and other scholars remain deeply divided as to law's relationship to society, and thus, in this sense, as to what a 'legal lens' might be.[15] Law is for some an instrument

---

[11] W. Twining, *Globalisation and Legal Theory* (London: Butterworth, 2000), 212.

[12] Ibid. 211.

[13] For this argument with respect to sociology of law and socio-legal studies, see A. Hunt, 'The Problematisation of Law in Classical Social Theory', in Banakar and Travers (eds.), *An Introduction to Law and Social Theory*.

[14] E. J. Weinrib, *The Idea of Private Law* (Cambridge, Mass.: Harvard University Press, 1995), cited in Cane, Ch. 10 in this volume.

[15] For a good introduction, see B. Tamanaha, *A General Jurisprudence of Law and Society* (Oxford: Oxford University Press, 2001), chs. 1 and 2 (though the characterizations used here do not match his precisely).

for governing complex social and economic relations and serving social and economic interests ('law as order'). For others, it is an expression of society's morality ('law as glue'). For others, it is a reflection of society's customs and usages ('law as mirror'). For yet others, it is a mechanism of state power and of capitalist, male, or white domination ('law as a selective mirror'). To the debate between the ghosts of Weber, Durkheim, and Marx, among others, is added the challenge of postmodernism to the modernist idea that steering, guiding, or regulating is possible. Of these, Tamanaha argues, it is the instrumentalist view of law which has dominated twentieth-century legal theory.[16]

On the other hand, the instrumental conception of law is not the only one which is of interest to those seeking to understand the operation of regulatory systems. Hawkins, in particular, has highlighted both the relevance of the moral content of law (or lack of it) and its symbolism in the operation of regulatory systems. In decisions to prosecute, Hawkins stresses the 'expressive' role of law. He argues that the act of prosecution is a symbolic device as well as an instrumental one. It is a means of expressing important values about right and wrong, as well as a means of securing compliance.[17] His argument is not that the symbolism of law has an instrumental role in improving compliance, or otherwise improving the effectiveness of the regulatory system. Rather, he argues that, by its nature, such a use of law cannot be evaluated for its effectiveness.[18]

What of regulationists' understanding of the relationship of 'regulation' to society? Most regulationists have not engaged with the question, or at least not explicitly, and this is not the occasion. Nonetheless, it is suggested, albeit tentatively, that parallels can be drawn between the conceptions of law's relationship to society with that of regulation, and not just because much regulation is law. Regulation as an instrument of order is clearly the dominant perception and is embedded in the definition used here. As such, it has clear parallels with the instrumental conception of law, and is susceptible to the same critiques as being hopelessly 'modern' and a fated instrument. The notion of regulation as a 'mirror' is an intriguing one, and, it is suggested, it is echoed in analyses which see regulation as being, or aiming to be, 'responsive' to the particular section of society which they seek to regulate. 'Responsiveness' is advocated usually for instrumental reasons (e.g. Teubner) but for some, for example, Selznick, it has a deeper resonance, an intrinsic value which extends beyond its instrumental effects. For such writers, if regulation is, perhaps, not quite glue, it is at least, supposed to have some bonding effect.[19]

[16] B. Tamanaha, *A General Jurisprudence of Law and Society* (Oxford: Oxford University Press, 2001), 45; R. Cotterrell, 'Subverting the Orthodoxy, Making Law Central: A View of Socio-Legal Studies', *Journal of Law and Society*, 29 (2002), 632.   [17] Hawkins, *Law as Last Resort*.
    [18] Ibid. 6.
    [19] P. Nonet and P. Selznick, *Law and Society in Transition: Towards a Responsive Law* (New York: Octagon Books, 1978); P. Selznick, *The Moral Commonwealth* (Berkeley: University of California Press, 1992).

What Questions Does Each Ask?

The Introduction suggests that even where they look at the same social activity, lawyers and regulationists would ask different questions. In particular, lawyers would ask about doctrinal coherence and the allocation of rights and responsibilities. Regulationists, in contrast, are interested in effectiveness, coherence, and responsiveness to social facts and norms, and in effect, these are offered as normative criteria for assessing regulation. Of these, the most important is effectiveness; in their view responsiveness and coherence have predominantly instrumental rather than intrinsic value.[20]

To an extent, this is true. But again, the perspectives are so diffused that it is difficult to say that all regulationists are interested in these questions and all lawyers are not. Not all work by regulationists is concerned with normative questions of policy and effectiveness. Studies of enforcement processes,[21] or rule-making,[22] or the internal processes of regulatory organizations,[23] for example, have sought simply to interpret social life, not to make suggestions for how to alter what they find. Similarly, many studies of regulatory policy-making seek to operate at the descriptive rather than normative level.[24]

It is suggested instead that regulatory questions are characterized by two things: complex mapping and multiple modes of evaluation. Broadly speaking, in seeking to describe a regulatory system or regime (namely, the 'complex institutional geography, rules, practice, and animating ideas associated with regulating particular aspects of social and economic life'[25]), a regulatory approach would typically consist of asking questions that would enable the drawing of one or more of the following 'maps': the physical geography (institutions, actors, techniques, capacities); the social geography (interrelationships, power, discourses, epistemologies, cognitive frames, cultures, behaviours, interests); and the economic geography (market failures, economic interests, financial resources).

In seeking to evaluate that regime, if any evaluation is used at all, one or more of three different groups of criteria are usually used. These are, firstly, economic criteria: an assessment of the system against the principles of, for example, welfare economics, cost–benefit analysis, and one or other measure of economic efficiency. Secondly, technocratic criteria, that is assessing the system in terms of, for example, effectiveness, sectoral expertise, appropriate deployment of regulatory techniques, and so on. Thirdly, legitimacy criteria, assessing the system in terms of its adherence to constitutional values such as accountability, due

---

[20] Parker and Braithwaite, 'Regulation', 126.
[21] e.g. Hawkins, *Environment and Enforcement*; Hutter, *The Reasonable Arm of the Law*.
[22] Black, *Rules and Regulators*.
[23] C. Hall, C. Scott, and C. Hood, *Telecommunications Regulation: Culture, Chaos and Interdependency inside the Regulatory Process* (London: Routledge, 2000).
[24] Recent examples include Hood *et al.*, *Government of Risk*; Thatcher, *The Politics of Telecommunications*.   [25] Hood *et al.*, *Government of Risk*, 9.

process, openness, proportionality, participation, transparency, responsiveness, and to 'rule of law' values such as coherence, certainty, and predictability.

Thus, a doctrinal text on UK financial services law would discuss the key EU legislation relating to financial services, the UK statutes and associated subordinate legislation, and a discussion of the structure and powers of the Financial Services Authority (FSA), and, if it were very fat, discussion of the FSA's rules.[26]

A book which offered a more 'regulatory' perspective, in the sense outlined above, would, in contrast, devote only a relatively small part of the discussion to the legal provisions, if indeed much at all. Rather, it would discuss the rationales of financial services regulation (which are invariably framed in terms of welfare economics), the market context, and the impact and operation of the rules, and a wider discussion of the international regulatory context, in particular, key players such as the Basel Committee. Moreover, the book might not be purely descriptive of the institutional and market structure; it might include a discussion of the key interest and epistemic groups in shaping the regulation, the dominant preoccupations, the regulator's own 'decision frame' and perspective on their task, and so on.

It might also be looking to advance a particular thesis: that the regulation was formed principally in accordance with the interests of sectors of the industry, or particular bureaucrats, or that its operation is an example of the use of different types of regulatory tool, or its enforcement patterns provide further evidence of 'compliance' approaches or 'deterrence' approaches, or its decision-making can be analysed using cultural theory, or institutionalist theories, or some other familiar theme in regulatory scholarship. It might even seek to evaluate it against one or more of the three sets of criteria: does the regulation correct market failures, does it comply with cost–benefit analyses (economic); does it use the right regulatory tools, has it understood the problem correctly (technocratic); and is the system sufficiently accountable, or legitimate, according to some other set of criteria (legitimacy)?

Summary

Legal and regulatory scholarship thus, certainly, do have differences, but they are not necessarily those which the Introduction suggests. Each set of scholarship is too complex and too diverse to be assembled under a single characterization. Not all lawyers are concerned with doctrine, and not all regulationists are concerned with effectiveness, coherence, and responsiveness. There are significant areas of overlap between the two sets of scholarship, and while there are differences, they are not organized around the poles of instrumentalism–non-instrumentalism or internal (doctrine)–external (social impacts). Thus, one might ask, what an 'instrumentalist' view of law might reveal, but this question is one which is as familiar to socio-legal agendas as it is to regulatory ones.

---

[26] Those that do run to volumes, e.g. E. Lomnicka and J. Powell, *Encyclopedia of Financial Services Law* (London: Sweet & Maxwell, 1987).

THE RELATIONSHIP BETWEEN 'PRIVATE LAW' AND 'REGULATORY LAW'

The second question that the Introduction seeks to address is how do 'private law' and 'regulatory law' interact. Before we can begin to examine their interaction, however, we need to find ways of identifying what each is in order to identify just what entities the interaction is between. This leads us into difficulties, for while the categories may have intuitive appeal, establishing criteria which differentiate them is not straightforward.

The argument is that the development of 'private law' is characterized by the hallmarks of judicial reasoning in which each decision is concerned with the allocation of rights and liabilities between the parties in dispute. The orientation of 'public' or 'regulatory law', on the other hand, is to policy and instrumental values in which the horizons of a decision are extended beyond the particular case in question.[27] There are a number of problems with this approach, however. Firstly, the two sets may coexist, rather than one being totally displaced by the other. Secondly, as noted above, instrumentalism cannot be the distinguishing characteristic of the forms of law, as there are instrumentalist conceptions of law (and thus, of private law), and non-instrumentalist conceptions of regulation.

Thirdly, drawing the line on the basis of the rationality or 'mentality' of implementation assumes that there is 'a' mode of judicial reasoning, and indeed, 'a' mode of regulatory reasoning. Instead, the 'hallmarks of judicial reasoning' can vary from the Herculean search for principles and coherence to the measuring of the Lord Chancellor's foot, depending on the theory of judicial rationality that one favours. Furthermore, it is not clear that there is a mode of 'regulatory rationality', at least at the point of the application of rules to particular instances. The application of rules by an enforcement officer has strong resonances with Collins's description of the application of contractual provisions between contracting parties: the process is one of negotiation shaped by the surrounding context of the parties' relationship.[28] The decision by a regulator to take formal action is often akin to the decision by one of the parties to a contract to sue. Once the formal action has begun in both cases, then legal principles come into play.[29] So there certainly is a 'regulatory', i.e. policy or instrumental, mode of decision-making in rule-making and compliance, and even at the point of deciding whether or not to take formal action for a breach. But once that action is commenced, then events and relationships are redrawn to fit the legal frame, as they are when one party to a contract decides to litigate.

It is perhaps preferable, therefore, to reframe the question simply in terms of the interaction of legal subsystems, rather than trying to identify just two forms of subsystem, private and regulatory. Thus, it could be said, there are subsystems of criminal law, company law, property law, competition law, and

---

[27] G. Teubner, 'Substantive and Reflexive Elements in Modern Law', *Law and Society Review*, 17 (1983), 239.

[28] H. Collins, *Regulating Contracts* (Oxford: Oxford University Press, 1999), ch. 6.

[29] Assuming, throughout this discussion, that what is at issue is the application of a legal rule.

commercial law, which themselves are complex combinations of statutory provisions and common law, and any attempt to draw a theoretically coherent distinction between 'private' and 'regulatory' law is unlikely to succeed. At best, we can distinguish between statute and common law, and between orientations or modes of reasoning, but we cannot expect that the lines between each of them will necessarily coincide.

Therefore, in this chapter a distinction will be drawn between the regulatory rules, by which is meant those provisions contained in statutes, statutory instruments, and the rules of the key regulatory agency, the FSA, and the common law and equity, which will have their normally understood meaning. The thesis which the Introduction seeks to examine is that where these two meet, the relationship will be one of 'productive disintegration'. That is, that the 'mentalities' of the two will collide, but out of this collision will come a new understanding.

The next sections will examine whether this has been the case in UK financial services regulation. Given the broad scope of the regulation, only a few examples are drawn on. However, it will be argued that for the most part the two exist in separate 'rooms', and rarely meet. However, where they do meet, where, for example, statutory provisions are introduced which have unintended impacts on the common law, then the statutory provisions can upset the common law, though not necessarily because there is a clash of 'mentalities'. Finally, while the two may coexist, they may do so in an uneasy relationship in which the exact protocols of their engagement are unclear. In the example drawn on here the relationship has so far been that each keeps a watchful eye on the other, using each to inform its own development.

Separate Rooms

The 'productive disintegration' thesis focuses on litigation: on the interrelationship of regulatory and private law in the context of adjudication. In any relationship structured by law, be it a contract, a property transaction, the operation of a company, or the running of a regulatory system, the legal process plays only a peripheral role. Parties conduct their affairs often in ignorance of their own contracts, as Collins illustrates, as firms do in ignorance of regulatory provisions. Further, just as parties to a contract rarely go to court when one party is in breach, regulatory officials rarely prosecute when a firm does not comply. Moreover, the decision to go to court for both involves similar considerations.

Thus, there is nothing unusual about the fact that for the most part a regulatory system will operate separately from the courts. However, there are additional reasons why the courts are rarely called on to adjudicate on regulatory rules in the UK financial services context, stemming from its particular institutional structure. The key statute, the Financial Services and Markets Act 2000 (FSMA), is a piece of framework legislation conferring wide rule-making and enforcement powers on the FSA (a private company limited by guarantee).

It sets up a fairly self-contained system of rule-making, enforcement, redress, and compensation, all separate from the courts. Thus, the FSA has wide powers to impose sanctions without needing to prosecute. In addition, the FSMA provides for the establishment of an ombudsman scheme to deal with claims by private investors against financial firms, a compensation scheme to give them compensation if the firm has gone out of business, an elaborate system of hearings and appeals for firms who have been disciplined, and a separate body for any person to complain to about the way the FSA carries out its functions.[30] There is provision for investors to seek redress in the courts against firms who breach the FSA's rules in their dealings with investors, but this is limited by statute to private investors, and, moreover, the FSA has the power to determine to which of its rules the right applies.[31] The few formal, institutionalized linkages between the courts and the regulatory system are, principally, where the FSA uses its powers of prosecution and the operation of public law: notably actions in judicial review, under the Human Rights Act 1998, and for breach of statutory duty. Otherwise, there is very little reason or opportunity for the regulatory rules to 'interact' with the common law in the sense of being subject to judicial interpretation. Thus, while the regulatory system is clearly constituted by law and operates in its frame, there is little formal interaction occurring in the courts between the provisions of one and the doctrines of the other. Indeed, it could be argued that the regulatory system, particularly in the UK, given the FSA's extensive rule-making powers, has removed the need, if not the ability, for common law to develop in this area: regulatory rules could thus be argued to stunt the growth of common law in this respect.[32]

Collisions

Nonetheless, there are situations where the regulatory provisions have had a direct and very unsettling effect on common law, calling into question traditional common law conceptualizations. A key example in the UK is the dematerialization of share transfers.[33] Share transfers have traditionally been effected by paper documents. Companies would receive transfer documents, which they would verify, register the transferee, and issue new documents. Changes in the financial markets, in particular the increased facility and speed of trading introduced as a result of technological developments, meant this system was increasingly cumbersome,[34] and in 1995 the law was changed to introduce uncertificated

---

[30] See, generally, W. Blair *et al.*, *Blackstone's Guide to the Financial Services and Markets Act 2000* (London: Blackstone Press, 2000).

[31] Financial Services and Markets Act 2000 (FSMA), s. 150.

[32] I am grateful to Dimity Kingsford Smith for this point.

[33] See E. Micheler, 'Farewell Quasi-Negotiability? Legal Title and Transfer of Shares in a Paperless World', *Journal of Business Law* (2002), 358; J. Benjamin, *Interests in Securities* (Oxford: Oxford University Press, 2001), 202.

[34] For discussion, see Department of Trade and Industry, *Consultation Paper on Dematerialisation of Share Certificates and Share Transfers* (London, 1988).

shares: shares for which there are no paper documents.[35] Uncertificated shares
are transferred through an electronic transfer system, CREST, to which all
companies listed on the London Stock Exchange must belong. The transferor
and transferee send their instructions to CRESTCo, rather than the company, the
system carries out the verification process, and then sends an instruction to the
company to amend its register. The company is required to register a transfer
within two hours of receipt of a CREST computer instruction. A person holding
uncertificated shares is not treated as a member of the company unless both the
company register and the CREST register show him to be holding shares in an
uncertificated form, although the Regulations do not provide which should
prevail where there is an inconsistency between the two.

The introduction of uncertificated shares (dematerialization) has called into
question the traditional principles on which a transfer of shares was thought to
be based. Shares are not negotiable instruments; in other words, they are not
transferable independently of the equities that have arisen under the original contract, and a bona fide purchaser for value does not acquire the right if the transferor did not have authority to sell. However, to facilitate transfer, the common
law developed two techniques, one of contract and one of estoppel, which led to
a similar effect as negotiability. The first, contractual technique, was to argue that
shares are transferred by way of novation. The second, estoppel technique, was
that share certificates are prima facie evidence of the title of the member in whose
name the certificate has been issued. If the transferee acquires shares relying
on the certificates issued by the company, the company is estopped from denying
title. Both techniques, however, involve the notion (however fictional in practice)
that the company plays an active role in the transfer process, either by consent-
ing to the transfer by accepting the offer of the transferee and agreeing to treat
him as a member, while releasing the transferee (novation), or by representations
made on the face of the certificate (estoppel). However, with dematerialization,
the company plays no role in the transfer process other than to respond to a computer instruction, and there is no certificate. As a result, Micheler argues, both
rules cannot be said to apply with any conviction, and the changes introduced by
the Regulations will have to force English law to reconceive its understanding of
the share transfer process, perhaps recognizing the full negotiability of shares.[36]

In addition, dematerialization has created a new legal risk, in that the risks
associated with unauthorized transfers of shares are allocated differently
depending on whether or not the shares are certificated or uncertificated. As
regards certificated shares, the legal owner is not bound by transfers which have
not been authorized by her, and the transferee may claim an indemnity from the
company, based in estoppel. As regards uncertificated shares, the legal owner is
bound by instructions sent to CRESTCo without her authority, though

---

[35] Uncertificated Securities Regulations 1995, SI 1995/3272, introduced under Companies Act
1989, s. 40; as amended by Uncertificated Securities (Amendment) Regulations 2000, SI 2000/1682.
[36] Micheler, 'Farewell Quasi-Negotiability?', 365.

CRESTCo is liable for damages arising out of forged transfer instructions up to a limit of £50,000. However, it is not clear whether the rules on estoppel, which are again based in the notion that the company has made a representation on the certificate, can operate in the case of uncertificated securities, and thus, whether the transferee has a remedy against the company in the case of unauthorized transfers. The risk of unauthorized transfers is thus greater for uncertificated securities than it is for certificated ones, and is placed on the person who arguably is in the least position to control it, the transferee.[37]

In essence, therefore, the rules that the common law created to facilitate the transfer of shares are themselves now being challenged by statutory provisions which are also created to facilitate share transfers. It is important to note, however, that both developments were clearly driven with instrumental considerations in mind, and for both the policy consideration was the same. As Micheler argues, 'The rules enhancing the transferability of shares did not develop because paper documents were used to transfer shares. They developed because shares are issued to circulate in an anonymous market.'[38] Thus, it is not that the different 'mentalities' of the law conflicted; the common law principles were clearly based on instrumental considerations, and, moreover, they were the same considerations as prompted the regulatory rules: namely, to facilitate the transfer of shares and thus, directly or indirectly, the development of the stock markets. Rather than the mentalities clashing, one has been outpaced by the other. The method introduced by the regulatory requirements has, inadvertently, undermined the fictions the common law invented to pursue the same aim.

Uneasy Coexistence?

Rather than clashing, the regulatory rules and common law may instead live in an uneasy coexistence. This is particularly a feature of UK financial services regulation as so much of the substantive regulation is contained in regulatory rules, rather than in statute. This contrasts with the position in Australia, for example, where the Corporations Act is the principal source of rules, and the regulator does not have wide rule-making powers. In the UK the issue arises either because the conduct required by one set of rules (at common law and equity) is higher or lower than that imposed under the other (regulatory rules); in which case compliance with one does not provide a safe harbour from liability under the other. Alternatively, and more problematically, the requirements of the two sets of rules might conflict, but it is not clear how that conflict should be resolved. Two significant areas where the issues have arisen in the UK are fiduciary duties and the laws of confidential information.

The potential for a clash between fiduciary duties and regulatory rules became a very live one in the late 1980s with the growth of financial conglomerates, that is firms which combine a number of investment functions such as banking,

[37] Ibid. 377.   [38] Ibid. 378.

corporate finance, fund management, financial analysis, and investment advisory services. This led to widespread concerns at the significant conflicts of interest which result, and for the protection of confidential client information. The market had its own solution: broad disclosures in contracts with clients (to the extent that contracts were agreed at all), and Chinese Walls, organizational arrangements which restrict the flow of information between different sectors of the firm or group.

Both of these techniques were sanctioned by the rules of the previous regulatory regime, and still are. However, when they were introduced there was considerable discussion as to whether the rules were consistent with fiduciary obligations. In other words, could a firm be simultaneously in compliance with its regulatory requirements but in breach of common law and equity? As well as illustrating the point that too much responsiveness to market practices might not be a valuable quality, this raised the issue of the relationship between the regulatory rules and common law and equity in the hierarchy of legal norms: did the former modify the latter, or did the two systems run alongside one another, with all the uncertainties that would result?

In 1990 a reference was made to the Law Commission to consider the issue. In its interim report the Law Commission concluded that the conduct required by regulatory provisions did not, in fact, meet the standards imposed under common law and equity, and that the potential for a clash was thus a very real one.[39] The issues were, in part, met by developments in case-law,[40] and, partly for this reason, the issue has fallen off the policy agenda,[41] although specific provisions were introduced in the FSMA to authorize the FSA to make rules permitting the control of information within firms (i.e. the erection of Chinese Walls).[42]

However, while the threat of a clash between the two sets of provisions has waned in some respects, it still remains a possibility.[43] Moreover, there is still some

---

[39] Law Commission, *Fiduciary Duties and Regulatory Rules: A Consultation Paper* (London: Law Commission, 1992).

[40] In its final report the Law Commission formed the view that subsequent developments at common law brought the legal position closer to that provided for in the regulatory rules, at least so far as managing conflicts through contractual provisions was concerned (*Kelly v Cooper* [1993] AC 205 and *Clark Boyce v Mouat* [1994] 1 AC 428), though concerns remained where the fiduciary relationship existed separately from the contract, and where in a relationship based in contract a firm put itself in a position where its own interest conflicted with that of the customer, or where it acted for competing customers in the same transaction: Law Commission, *Fiduciary Duties and Regulatory Rules*, Law Com No 236 (London: Law Commission, 1995).

[41] Interestingly, the FSA's two recent papers on conflicts of interest make no mention of the position at common law and equity: FSA, *Investment Research: Conflicts and Other Issues*, Discussion Paper 15 (London: FSA, 2002); FSA, *Conflicts of Interest: Investment Research and Issues of Securities*, Consultation Paper 171 (London: FSA, 2003).

[42] FSMA, s. 147. The FSA rules on Chinese Walls are set out in *FSA Handbook*, COB (London: FSA; available at http://www.fsa.gov.uk), 2.4.4.R.

[43] In addition, Colin Bamford has argued that such a clash might arise between directors' duties and the regulatory rules governing approved persons: 'Directors' Fiduciary Duties and the Approved Persons Regime', in E. Ferran and C. Goodhart (eds.), *Regulating Financial Services and Markets in the 21st Century* (Oxford: Hart, 2001).

uncertainty as to what constitutes an effective Chinese Wall both under the FSA rules and at common law. The issue thus remains a relevant one: what is or should be the relationship between common law and equity and the regulatory rules?

The control of information provisions aside, it is hard to see that the general rule-making powers that the FSA has been given constitute clear and unambiguous authority for those rules to modify common law. The position will thus depend on the presumption that statute does not alter the common law, although this presumption may be weaker where a statute lays down a coherent regulatory scheme.[44] How exactly the presumption would operate remains an open question. The Commission considered three possible options, which it termed a public law model, a private law model, and a hybrid model.[45]

Under the 'private law model' regulatory law would be subject to the general principles of private law unless the common law or equitable principles are necessarily overridden by statute expressly or by implication. Thus, there would otherwise be no authority to make rules altering private rights and obligations, and the fact that a person was acting in compliance with the regulatory rules would have no bearing on their position at common law or in equity.

Under the 'public law model' the absence of express powers would not be important in determining the scope of the rule-making powers; what is important is the nature and scope of the statutory scheme. Thus, the process of interpreting the scope of the rule-making powers 'would not start with presumptions about common law's survival'.[46] Rather, the court would assess the rules on public law principles, for example *Wednesbury* unreasonableness or illegality (for example, whether altering common law rights is contrary to the statutory purpose).

Thirdly, under a 'hybrid model' the court would give some recognition to the public law nature of the regulatory rules by allowing them to affect the content of common law and equitable obligations. Thus, under a process akin to that by which market and trade practices may shape the content of contractual or other obligations (e.g. the reasonableness of exclusion clauses, duties of disclosure, or the confidentiality of information), the shape of common law and equitable rights and duties is shaped by the valid and reasonable regulatory rules and practices, though the justification lies in the rules' public law character, rather than their notoriety or the intentions of the parties. A regulatory rule would be evidence or guidance as to the expectations of the parties and of market usage.

While the specific context in which the models were considered no longer exists in exactly the same terms, these models clearly have wider relevance either than the Commission's report or indeed than the financial services context itself, and, in principle, would apply to any situation where regulatory rules and common law and equitable principles appear to conflict. The Commission suggested that the

---

[44] Law Commission, *Fiduciary Duties and Regulatory Rules*, para. 5.4.4.
[45] Ibid., paras. 5.4.6–5.4.29.   [46] Ibid., para. 5.4.13.

courts were most likely to adopt a hybrid model, i.e. to use regulatory rules to shape or modify common law duties. If so, this would be in line with the 'productive' nature of the interaction between common law and public law provisions that Collins and Teubner discuss, though without involving any visible 'disintegration'. There are indeed a number of cases where regulatory rules have been used by the court to determine whether or not an obligation under the common law or in equity exists or has been broken, several of which involve the Panel on Takeovers and Mergers, a non-statutory (but public) body.[47]

In the recent cases on Chinese Walls there is also some suggestion that the courts looked to the regulatory rules in determining what an effective Chinese Wall would consist of if it were to provide a defence to a claim of breach of confidentiality.[48] The judgment of the leading case referred to the regulatory rules that existed at the time and to the Law Commission's report for examples of what these arrangements consisted of as evidence of best practice in the financial services industry, and drew on these to formulate the common law standard, namely, that there is clear and convincing evidence that all effective measures have been taken to ensure that no disclosure will occur.[49]

Following this 'hybrid' approach, the content of the regulatory rules may be used to inform the common law's own development in other areas. For example, it has also been suggested that the provisions in the Code of Conduct on Market Abuse governing the early or selective disclosure of information may inform the common law test for what constitutes confidential information.[50] On the other hand, common law duties could inform the content of the regulatory rules. For example, the rules provide that firms must treat customers fairly,[51] and that one way to do so is by a policy of independence, which includes requiring employees to disregard any material interest or conflict of interest when advising a customer or dealing in the exercise of discretion.[52] This may involve giving a specific undertaking and it has been suggested that the content of that undertaking could be informed by common law principles.[53]

What we can see, therefore, is that there may be a process of mutual learning occurring between the common law and the regulatory system, although there is no guarantee that this does and will always occur. This 'hybrid' approach, in effect, allows each system to leave its options open: where each finds the norms

---

[47] Law Commission, *Fiduciary Duties and Regulatory Rules*, paras. 5.4.24–5.4.29.

[48] *Prince Jefri Bolkiah v KPMG* [1999] AC 222 (HL); *Young v Robson Rhodes* [1999] 3 All ER 524. Alternatively, giving an undertaking not to disclose the information may also protect the defendant, but again only under quite specific conditions: *Koch Shipping v Richards Butler*, The Times, 21 Aug. 2002 (CA). See, generally, C. Hollander and S. Salzedo, *Conflicts of Interest and Chinese Walls* (London: Sweet & Maxwell, 2000); C. Nakajima, *Conflicts of Interest and Chinese Walls* (London: Butterworth, 2002).   [49] [1999] AC 222 at 237–8 per Lord Millet.

[50] *Koch Shipping v Richards Butler*, The Times, 21 Aug. 2002 (CA); A. Henderson, 'Confident about Confidentiality? Civil Claims for the Misuse of Price Sensitive Information', *Company Lawyer* (2003), 116.

[51] *FSA Handbook*, FSA Statement of Principles for Business, Principle 6, COB 7.1.3 R.

[52] COB 7.1.7 G.   [53] Henderson, 'Confident about Confidentiality?'

imposed by the other useful and relevant, it will use them; where it does not, it will not. This is not so much 'productive disintegration', however, as 'productive cherry-picking'.

THE EFFECT OF LAW

The Introduction focuses on the interaction between provisions of legal rules in framing its second theme. However, it is suggested that there is a further level of interaction which is related to the broader theme of understanding the interaction between law and regulation, and that is between the law itself and the regulatory system, and the perception the regulatory system and market actors have of law. By this is not meant the impact of judicial review or the Human Rights Act 1998 on the regulators, though these clearly have been and will continue to be important.[54] However, the impact of the legal system has more subtle effects on the regulatory system. There is clearly the pervasive effect of the role of lawyers within the regulatory system, both as advisers to regulatees and as legal officials within the regulator, although the extent to which lawyers in regulatory agencies shape agency policy and actions, thus 'mixing' knowledge of private law doctrines and canons of interpretation gained through their legal training with regulatory rules, has not yet been researched. Instead, the examples discussed will be, firstly, the impact of law on the nature of the rules that have been formed, secondly, its impact on the decisions to take formal enforcement action, and thirdly, the perception of regulators and market actors of law as a risk to be managed. The latter, in particular, challenges the instrumental view of law, and, perhaps, law's own view of itself.

The Nature of the Rules

The FSA has a wide range of rule-making powers which it has used to create a number of different types of rule. Such rules may have full legal status, or they may have evidential status only, that is that breach of or compliance with the rule may be relied on as 'tending to establish' the contravention or compliance of another rule.[55] The FSA also has the power to publish guidance consisting of information or advice with respect to the FSMA or its own rules, for the purposes of meeting its objectives, or with respect to any matters relating to the FSA's functions or as to which it appears necessary or desirable.

---

[54] In particular, the impact of the Human Rights Act was a key area of debate in the passage of the bill: Joint Committee on the Financial Services and Markets Act, *First Report* (Apr. 1999), Joint Committee on the Financial Services and Markets Act, *Second Report* (June 1999), and for discussion of the application of the Act, see D. F. Walters and M. Hopper, 'Regulatory Discipline and the European Convention on Human Rights—a Reality Check', in Ferran and Goodhart (eds.), *Regulating Financial Services and Markets*.   [55] FSMA, s. 149.

Crucially, the FSA has the discretion to determine which rules are subject to the right of private action, that is in respect of which rules breach of the rule will entitle a private investor (or where the FSA specifies, any other person) to bring a civil action.[56] It is this ability to decide which rules are litigable and which are not that has freed the FSA to make rules which are general and vague in their structure (principles). The provision limiting the right of action for breach of the rules has a long and significant history.[57] In the late 1980s and early 1990s the FSA's predecessor sought, for a range of reasons, to move away from the writing of detailed rules and to, instead, issuing ten broad Principles of conduct, and forty Core Rules.[58] However, the statute provided a right of private action for breach of the regulator's rules.[59] The prospect of the Principles being litigable in court posed a significant threat to the operative stability of the regulatory system, for neither the regulator nor the regulated firms could guarantee what the court's interpretation of the Principles would be. Deliberately to facilitate the formation of the Principles, the statute was amended to provide that a right of action did not lie for breach of a Principle, and, moreover, to reduce the prospect of litigation occurring by restricting the right to bring an action for breach of any other rule to private investors.[60] These provisions were in essence carried forward to the current regime.[61]

Thus, the very potential for litigation had a critical impact on the form that the regulatory rules could take. The removal of that right frees up the regulator to make rules which are more general in their nature, for they can do so relatively safe in the knowledge that understandings as to their meanings which develop during the course of the inevitable conversations that occur between regulator and regulated as to the meaning and application of the rule, and which confer certainty within the regulatory system, can continue without the threat of intrusion by the courts.[62]

This is not to say that the courts will never pronounce on the interpretation of the FSA's rules even where the private right of action does not lie. As noted, they may be called to interpret the rules in the context of an action for judicial review, and because the courts will approach the issue as one of determining whether or not the FSA's interpretation of the rule was correct, rather than simply reasonable, in the battle for interpretative control the courts retain for themselves the final determination.[63] Nevertheless, the threat of judicial review is far more remote than the threat of litigation between private parties, particularly powerful commercial actors. Thus, the removal of the right of action

[56] FSMA, s. 150.   [57] For discussion, see Black, *Rules and Regulators*, 85.
[58] Ibid. 97 and J. Black, ' "Which Arrow?" Regulatory Policy and Rule Type', *Public Law* (1994), 94.
[59] Financial Services Act 1986, s. 62.
[60] Financial Services Act 1986, s. 62A, inserted by s. 193(1) Companies Act 1989.
[61] FSMA, s. 150.
[62] On regulatory conversations, see further J. Black, 'Talking about Regulation', *Public Law* (1998), 77, and J. Black, 'Regulatory Conversations', *Journal of Law and Society*, 29/1 (2002), 163.
[63] J. Black, 'Reviewing Regulatory Rules: Responding to Hybridisation', in J. Black, P. Muchlinski, and P. Walker (eds.), *Commercial Regulation and Judicial Review* (Oxford: Hart, 1998).

completely, in particular from the Statements of Principle and Codes on approved persons and market abuse, has been critical in facilitating the formation of general, purposive rules.

The Decision to Enforce the Law

In his study of enforcement processes, Hawkins argues that prosecution means that a transformation occurs in the relationship between regulator and regulatee.[64] The private ordering by negotiation, which marks the compliance process, gives way to public law enforcement and adjudication. At the same time, the character of the legal response changes from one concerned with the repair of a problem to one concerned with deterrence or retribution.[65] The nature of the relationship between the parties is depersonalized, and often rendered irredeemably hostile. Significantly, Hawkins argues that prosecution involves a progressive loss of control by the regulators: 'reliance on regulation by the threat or application of legal penalties places the regulatory body in a position of curious vulnerability'.[66]

But the loss of control stems not only from the fact that it will be the courts who will decide whether or not a rule was breached and what sanction should be imposed: the decision to prosecute transforms the whole case. The events which surround the breach and which prompt the recourse to prosecution have to be reframed to fit the requirements of the law. As a result, events have to be substantially recast. Cases or incidents are taken out of their complex social context, facts selected, and interwoven events and causes transformed into individualistic criminal law conceptions of causation, responsibility, and sanctioning.[67] This has a significant and systematic impact on the enforcement activities of regulators. Only those cases which are legally strong will be prosecuted. However, there is not necessarily a good fit between a public policy conception of a 'good case' and a legal conception, in a number of respects. In particular, the legal process is far more suited to being reactive than proactive: to responding to 'bodies on the floor', rather than systems failures that might, but have not yet, led to such bodies being there.[68] Further, law focuses on the particular, the concrete, and the legally unproblematic, and does not cope well with the uncertain and the complex.

Hawkins argues that legal forms of understanding introduce their own patterns and distortions on regulatory enforcement activity. Those offences which are defined in relatively specific terms are favoured over more general statements; not necessarily because the former are more successful than the latter—they are not. Rather, the latter take up a greater amount of regulatory time in preparation. Thus, it is more straightforward matters that are prosecuted, rather than those which are more complicated or may be defended.[69] Further, once a decision has

---

[64] Hawkins, *Law as Last Resort.*   [65] Ibid. 422.   [66] Ibid. 423.   [67] Ibid. 409.
[68] Ibid. 437.
[69] In the health and safety field, the consequence is that safety cases tend to be prosecuted more frequently than threats to health: ibid. 404.

been made to prosecute, regulators move from using information to deal with a situation as effectively as possible to a position where information is assessed primarily for its use in prosecution.[70]

Thus, Hawkins concludes that 'The nature of the legal method is to create its own reality by particularizing, to allow the ready application of legal rules to produce an outcome, an answer to a question posed in legal terms.'[71] While there has not been a similar study of the enforcement processes of financial regulators, it seems a strong hypothesis that the legal frame has a similar impact on their prosecution activities, and indeed, because of the ability to challenge the FSA's other formal enforcement actions, on those actions as well. As with the nature of the regulatory rules, the effect of law on the regulatory process is again shown to be more indirect, and yet far more pervasive, than a focus purely on the interaction of doctrine would reveal.

'Law as Risk'

Finally, while law might regulate, it is also seen by the regulatory system as a risk. This is not simply a rhetorical statement; legal risk is a specific category of risk that banks are being required to manage under current proposals. For law to be seen as a 'risk' is significant, however, for it calls into question all the main formulations of legal theorists as to the relationship of law and society. Law is here neither a mirror, nor glue, nor order: it is a technical obstacle devoid of any normative content which is to be managed or overcome.[72]

The Basel Committee on Banking Supervision has proposed that banks should set aside capital to cover their operational risks.[73] Operational risk is in effect a new category of risk, and in defining it the Committee has drawn on common industry usage of the term, namely, that operational risk is 'the risk of direct or indirect loss resulting from inadequate or failed internal processes, people and systems or from external events'.[74] It includes legal risk. Legal risk is commonly understood to refer to the risk that legal liability will arise from the operations of the bank (e.g. through breach of regulatory or common law rules), and also to the risk that transactions that a bank has entered into will, in fact, be held to be legally ineffective. In other words, that actions that a firm has taken to reduce its credit or market risk will in fact expose it to legal risk.

Both forms of legal risk can be expensive for the firm. Findings of non-compliance can lead the firm to incur significant fines or orders for compensation.[75]

---

[70] Hawkins, *Law as Last Resort*, 409.   [71] Ibid.

[72] I am grateful to Dimity Kingsford Smith for helping me to think more clearly about this point.

[73] Basel Committee on Banking Supervision (BCBS), *Consultative Document: Operational Risk* (Basel: Bank of International Settlements, 2001); BCBS, *The New Basel Capital Accord: Pillar One* (Basel: Bank of International Settlements, 2003).   [74] BCBS, *Operational Risk*, para. 6.

[75] See e.g. D. Hoffman, *Managing Operational Risk* (New York: Wiley, 2002), p. xxix; C. Goodhart, *Operational Risk*, Financial Markets Group Special Paper 131 (London: London Stock Exchange, 2001), 23.

It is the risk that firms face in their transactions with other market counter-parties on which most of the attention is focused, however. It is a key concern to firms, particularly banks, as many of the risk mitigation techniques that they might adopt to reduce their market and credit risk involve the use of complex financial instruments designed to transfer risk away from the bank. Examples are requiring collateral for transactions, the use of credit derivatives, netting arrangements, and asset securitization. There is a significant risk that arrange-ments entered into will be found to be invalid, either because the law in a particular jurisdiction is uncertain and/or because the law is certain but banks are operating globally across a range of legal jurisdictions in some of which the arrangements may not be held to be valid.

The implications could be considerable. Issues which are of key concern to market participants include the legal issues surrounding cross-border collateral arrangements (collateral which consists of interests in securities issued in a num-ber of jurisdictions), on which the International Swaps and Dealers Association (ISDA), among others, has been pressuring the European Commission for law reform,[76] the provisions of set-off, and netting of positions on insolvency, on which the laws of different jurisdictions conflict. Globalization has also meant that rules which reduced the risks to parties in a transaction when they operated in a national context now expose parties to risk when they operate internation-ally. Thus, Benjamin argues that the equitable rules on mortgages, which are designed to protect the giver of a security interest (initially distressed mortgagors so that they did not lose their land to moneylenders), are restricting the ability of firms to rehypothecate collateral (i.e. use the collateral that they have received from A to collateralize their own exposure to C). If the parties are dealing exclusively in UK securities, this does not matter so much, as English law has always recognized outright transfer of collateral, and protected the collateral-giver by permitting set-off on insolvency (broadly that all the transactions between A and B (the insolvent firm) will be set off against the other, and the net position obtained to determine the balance outstanding between A and B). However, in many other jurisdictions, set-off and netting on insolvency is not permitted, which makes outright transfer of collateral in cross-border transactions a risky strategy. The more prudent course of conduct is rehypothecation, but the ability to rehypothecate is restricted under the equitable rules on mortgages. Thus, Benjamin argues that the equitable rules not only have outlived their usefulness but have become a burden.[77]

Thus, law itself is conceptualized by the market, and in turn, by the regulatory framework, as a source of risk. However, the notion of law posing a risk to mar-ket actors runs against the grain for those who see law as essentially facilitating

---

[76] ISDA Collateral Law Reform Committee, *Collateral Arrangements in the EU Financial Markets* (ISDA, 2000; available at http://www.isda.org); see now the Directive on Financial Collateral Arrangements 2002/47/EC.

[77] J. Benjamin, *Interests in Securities* (Oxford: Oxford University Press, 2001), 118.

market transactions, or indeed against a reflexive conception of law, in which law reflects market practices, and of course imposes further pressures on law to respond. As in the example of dematerialization, it is not necessarily because of a clash of 'mentalities', however, it is because developments in the market, in particular globalization, have outpaced the common law. It also calls into question the notion that law or regulation has a normative content which binds social actors, or which mirrors their normative ordering. Contrary to the view that social practices can be 'read off' law, the notion of 'law as risk' emphasizes that for market actors law is uncertain, unpredictable, and external: a source of risk, not a map of market life.

THE INTERACTIONS BETWEEN LAW AND OTHER FORMS OF NORMATIVE OR REGULATORY ORDERING

The third theme of the project is to examine the relationship between law and other forms of normative ordering.[78] There are a number of ways this issue could be addressed. The Introduction refers to the potential for law to accommodate the norms according to which private individuals conduct their lives ('responsiveness'). The discussion of the 'hybrid' approach to the relationship between regulatory rules and common law provides examples of this form of interaction at the level of the common law.

The Introduction suggests that the theme can also be addressed by looking at the extent to which a single area of social or economic life is governed by different sets of legal and non-legal rules and the relationship between them. The term 'meta-regulation' has been applied by regulatory scholars to refer to one manifestation of this, notably the state regulation of a firm's own internal regulation.[79] The complex interaction of different sets of ordering has also been conceptualized in somewhat different and more fluid terms by legal theorists in terms of legal pluralism, or 'interlegality'.[80]

Financial regulation provides examples which illustrate both. 'Meta-regulation' is evidenced at the national level in the FSA's monitoring of firms' own internal regulatory systems, in particular, the regulation of internal systems and

---

[78] Clearly, one's conception of law will affect the framing of the inquiry; for a legal pluralist the question would simply be the interaction of systems of normative ordering, all of which could be characterized as law. See e.g. S. F. Moore, *Law as Process: An Anthropological Approach* (London: Routledge & Kegan Paul, 1978); M. Galanter, 'Justice in Many Rooms: Courts, Private Ordering, and Indigenous Law', *Journal of Legal Pluralism*, 19 (1981), 1; J. Griffiths, 'What is Legal Pluralism?', *Journal of Legal Pluralism*, 24 (1986), 1; S. E. Merry, 'Legal Pluralism', *Law and Society Review*, 22 (1988), 869; B. de Sousa Santos, *Towards a New Common Sense* (Berkeley: University of California Press, 1995); G. Teubner, 'The Two Faces of Janus: Rethinking Legal Pluralism', *Cardozo Law Review*, 13 (1992), 1443; G. Teubner, ' "Global Bukowina": Legal Pluralism in the World Society', in Teubner (ed.), *Global Law without a State* (Aldershot: Dartmouth, 1997); B. Tamanaha, 'A Non-essentialist Version of Legal Pluralism', *Journal of Law and Society*, 27/2 (2000), 296.

[79] C. Parker, *The Open Corporation* (Cambridge: Cambridge University Press, 2001), ch. 9.

[80] De Sousa Santos, *Towards a New Common Sense*.

controls,[81] and internationally by the proposals to use firms' internal risk models for establishing capital adequacy levels.[82] At the international level, international bodies monitor national bodies' own regulatory systems, though in a far less systematic way.

More generally, however, financial services is characterized by a complex of interlocking rules at the international, regional (e.g. EU), transnational, state, and non-state levels[83] which may be characterized as key examples of legal pluralism, or, in regulatory terms, of decentred or multi-centred regulation.[84] At the international and transnational level, the rules applicable to international financial activities are soft law international instruments which relate principally to how national regulators should regulate within their own jurisdictions.[85] The bodies issuing them may be comprised of groups of particular countries,[86] or sectoral regulators,[87] address specific issues,[88] or comprise national regulators and the other international bodies.[89]

The number of different rules and codes issued is considerable. Indeed, the Financial Stability Forum publishes a non-exhaustive compendium of standards issued by these various bodies containing forty-three sets of international standards which national regulatory bodies are supposed to apply.[90] While all the standards are 'soft law' in that they do not create legally enforceable rights and obligations, they vary in their degree of precision, their normative force, and in the degree of institutional support that exists for their monitoring and enforcement. In many cases they are a distillation of experiences of the group of people who are sitting round the table drafting them, a combination of lessons learnt from worst mistakes and best practices. As Goodhart observes (not particularly charitably), 'the standard practice of financial regulators . . . in the absence of much theory, or evidence . . . is to "go and ask what best practice banks do, and then get everyone to do the same" '.[91]

---

[81] *FSA Handbook*, Senior Management Arrangements, Systems and Controls (SYSC).

[82] BCBS, *The New Capital Accord*.

[83] For a more comprehensive taxonomy, see W. Twining, *Globalisation and Legal Theory* (London: Butterworth, 2000), 139.

[84] For further discussion, see J. Black, 'Mapping Contemporary Financial Services Regulation', *Journal of Corporate Law Studies*, 2 (2002), 253.

[85] For an excellent discussion, see M. Giovanoli, 'A New Architecture for the Global Financial Market: Legal Aspects of International Financial Standard Setting', in Giovanoli (ed.), *International Monetary Law: Issues for the New Millennium* (Oxford: Oxford University Press, 2000).

[86] e.g. the G7, G10, G20, OECD.

[87] e.g. the BCBS, the International Organization of Securities Commissions (IOSCO), and the International Association of Insurance Supervisors (IAIS).

[88] e.g. the Joint Forum on Financial Conglomerates and the Financial Action Task Force (which examines measures to combat money-laundering and monitors implementation).

[89] For example, the membership of the Financial Stability Forum includes representatives of the IMF, the OECD, the World Bank, the BCBS, IOSCO, and IAIS, as well as individual national representatives from a range of countries.

[90] http://www.fsforum.org. The Forum was established in 1999 in the wake of the Asian crisis with the task of examining the different soft law provisions in place to coordinate the initiatives of the various international bodies, and to address the issue of implementation.

[91] Goodhart, *Operational Risk*, 6.

There is also a significant body of norms which govern the terms on which (wholesale) market participants interact issued by a swathe of international professional bodies and trade associations.[92] These include the International Accounting Standards Committee, which works towards the establishment of international accounting rules, the ISDA, which has developed global standard documentation for derivatives, and the International Securities Markets Association (ISMA), which, in conjunction with the Bond Market Association (BMA), has developed the PSA/ISMA Global Master Repurchase Agreement (GMRA), which is accepted as the international basis for repo transactions. The BMA has also worked with a consortium of international trade associations to develop the Cross-product Market Agreement, which acts as an umbrella master agreement, covering the master agreements relating to specific products in order to ensure the effectiveness of global cross-product netting provisions in certain events, thus aiming to reduce significantly inter-party financial exposure, and thus systemic risk. While, to a large extent, these standardized agreements constitute a system of 'proto' law which circulates separately from any particular national legal jurisdiction, they cannot be completely insulated from national laws. In particular, they depend critically on the insolvency laws of national jurisdictions for the effect of key provisions on set-off and netting to be implemented, and thus for the agreements to be able to mitigate this aspect of credit risk.

In Teubner's terms, the norms governing the international financial markets are examples of 'global law': their boundaries are formed by networks that transcend territorial boundaries; they are produced not in national legislatures but in the self-reproduction of specialized organizational and functional networks, they are closely dependent on their respective social fields rather than being insulated from them, and their pull towards universalization clashes with the endless variety of national legal systems.[93] They can also be characterized as paradigmatic examples of legal pluralism: the coexistence of multiple legal orders in the same time and space and which interact in complex ways. This broader perspective draws attention to the multiple levels and sources of normative ordering and their complex interaction, and in de Sousa Santos's terms, their 'interlegality', the interactions between coexisting legal (normative) orderings that are superimposed, interpenetrated, and mixed in both our minds and our actions.[94]

The interactions continue through the different 'levels' or geographical sites. At the EU level, there is an extensive system of EU law governing financial services, and a system of mutual recognition of member states' regulation. Those firms authorized in one EU member state are automatically permitted to conduct business in other member states (the 'passport'), while remaining subject to home

---

[92] See, further, Giovanoli, 'A New Architecture for the Global Financial Market', 27.

[93] Teubner, 'Global Bukowina', 7.

[94] De Sousa Santos, *Towards a New Common Sense*, 472; D. Kingsford Smith, 'Networks, Norms and the Nation State: Thoughts on Pluralism and Global Securities Regulation', in C. Dauvergne (ed.), *Jurisprudence for an Interconnected Globe* (London: Ashgate, 2003).

country control. (They may, however, have to comply with rules of the host country that have been formed for the 'general good'[95]). At the national and subnational level, normative orderings and institutional structures coexist and also interact in quite precise ways. There may be explicit coordination in writing rules.[96] Alternatively, the FSA may simply rely on another's rules in an area, rather than writing its own. For example, in its prudential regulation of life assurance companies the FSA relies on the Faculty and Institute of Actuaries' guidance on the duties of appointed actuaries in providing standards of conduct for actuaries.[97] In its rules on money-laundering the FSA rules provide that firms should comply with the guidance notes of the Joint Money Laundering Steering Group (a group of financial institutions) on the methods for carrying out identification of customers, and has no written rules on this issue.[98]

Coordination may have the effect of providing a complete safe harbour from the FSA's rules. For example, under the market abuse regime, compliance with some of the rules of the Takeover Panel provides a safe harbour from the market abuse regime.[99] Similarly, compliance with the London Metal Exchange's rules, governing the behaviour of long position-holders, will provide a safe harbour from the prohibitions on market distortion.[100]

Alternatively, coordination may have the effect that rules provided by other standard-setting associations provide evidence of compliance with the FSA's rules. For example, compliance with the Combined Code developed by the Committee on Corporate Governance (a non-state body) will be relevant in determining whether a firm has complied with the rules relating to internal systems and controls,[101] and compliance with the Code and associated guidance issued by the Institute of Chartered Accountants for England and Wales is relevant to determining whether or not approved persons have complied with the Code of Conduct for Approved Persons.[102]

Further, coordination can take the form of using other codes to inform the FSA as to the prevalent standards of conduct in the market. Thus, the FSA rules provide that while the FSA does not endorse any other market code, it may take their provisions into account in determining the standards and practices operating in markets for the purposes of applying the Principles for Business, and further that non-compliance with any of those codes may raise issues as to the integrity or competence of a firm relevant to the threshold conditions (whether or not the firm is 'fit and proper' to be authorized).[103] Finally, the adoption of

---

[95] See e.g. N. Moloney, *EU Securities Regulation* (Oxford: Oxford University Press, 2001).
[96] For example, the FSA has agreed with the British Bankers' Association (BBA) that the FSA's rules on a particular investment product will be the same as the BBA's rules, given their mutual jurisdiction on the issue.
[97] FSA, *The Regulation of Equitable Life from 1 January 1999 to 8 December 2000* (London: FSA, 2001) (Baird Report). [98] *FSA Handbook*, ML 3.1.4 G.
[99] Ibid., MAR 1.7.   [100] Ibid., MAR 1.6.19 C.
[101] Ibid., SYSC 3.1.3 E (taking reasonable care to establish such systems and controls as are relevant to a firm's business).   [102] Ibid., APER 3.1.9 G.
[103] Ibid., MAR 3.8.1 G.

the norms of another body can extend the jurisdiction and powers of both regulators, and again the Takeover Panel and the FSA is a good example.[104]

Market practitioners, professional bodies, and international groupings of national governments and national regulators have thus combined in various ways and through a multitude of regulatory conversations, or 'dialogic webs',[105] to produce multiple layers of regulation which are loosely coordinated through horizontal and vertical interrelationships.[106] These interrelationships may be characterized as an interaction between 'law' and 'other' forms of normative ordering, or seen as examples of 'interlegality', or as 'regulatory webs', or, more simply, as the interaction of normative orders (in which the legal status of some is immaterial).

There is a clear link here, however, between the Introduction's first and third themes. For both legal and regulatory scholars have a keen interest in these interactions, albeit for slightly different reasons. For legal scholars they provide examples of legal pluralism, and thus bring with them legal pluralism's challenge to law's understanding of itself. For regulatory scholars, they provide examples of fractured, decentred, or multi-nodal regulation, of patterns of normative ordering issuing from multiple sources and interacting to produce a system of regulation which is marked by conflict and coordination, and thus provide a challenge to conceptions of regulation as state-dominated command and control systems. For both, concerns of legitimacy are strong. Thus, while the conceptualizations and focus of the two sets of scholarship may differ in parts, regulatory and legal pluralism is an area of common interest and concern, and one in which a great deal of mutual learning could occur.

Concluding Observations

Thus, pursuing each of the Introduction's three themes can help to illuminate the relationship between law and regulation at a number of levels. Of these, the most specific is the second theme: the interaction of regulatory rules and common law. Here it has been suggested that, consistent with the Introduction's argument, there are examples of the regulatory rules posing challenges to common law conceptualizations, but that this is not because of a clash of mentalities of common law and regulatory rules. Similarly, where law now poses a risk to market operations, it is not because of a clash of orientation, but because the market has outpaced law.

---

[104] Financial Services Act, s. 143; FSA, *Endorsement of the City Code on Takeovers and Mergers and Rules on Substantial Acquisition of Shares*, CP 87 (Apr. 2001); FSA, *Policy Statement: Endorsement of the City Code on Takeovers and Mergers and Rules on Substantial Acquisition of Shares: Feedback on CP 87* (Oct. 2001); *FSA Handbook*, ENF 14.9.3G.

[105] J. Braithwaite and P. Drahos, *Global Business Regulation* (Cambridge: Cambridge University Press, 2000), 142.

[106] See also S. Picciotto and J. Haines, 'Regulating Global Financial Markets', *Journal of Law and Society*, 26 (1999), 351; J. Black, 'Perspectives on Derivatives Regulation', in A. Hudson (ed.), *Modern Financial Techniques, Derivatives and Law* (London: Kluwer, 2000).

Further, there are examples of mutual learning, or 'productive cherry-picking', where judges have observed the rules and operation of the regulatory system and decided to model their own standards on them. Finally, while the regulatory rules may impact on the common law, the law itself impacts on the regulatory system in ways that go beyond the normal influences of judicial review: it shapes the rules the regulators form and their decisions on whether and how to enforce the law, and law itself is cast by the regulatory system as a risk that firms are required to manage.

At the more general level, it has been suggested here that there are differences between regulatory and legal scholarship, though they are not necessarily those the Introduction suggests. They do relate principally to what each looks at and the questions each asks, but are not divided in terms of instrumentalism versus non-instrumentalism, or internal (doctrine) versus external (impact). Broadly speaking, legal scholars are ultimately concerned with understanding law, and law's understanding of itself. They do not confine their gaze to doctrine, how-ever, nor do they eschew instrumentalism. Regulatory scholars are concerned with understanding modes of governance including but not limited to law. There are differences between the two sets of scholarship, but at points they may be closer to each other than they are to other branches of their own disci-pline: socio-legal lawyers and sociological regulationists have more in common with each other than either does with their economic counterparts. In particu-lar, it has been suggested that the two may usefully converge in seeking to conceptualize and comprehend the webs of legal and regulatory orderings that characterize much of contemporary governance. Nonetheless, there are differ-ences in the questions each asks. Regulatory studies are marked by investiga-tions into the physical, social, and economic 'geographies' of the areas they examine; and the normative criteria range across the economic, the techno-cratic, and the constitutional. Not all regulationists will recognize that picture of themselves, and many legal scholars may argue it applies to them too. As noted, characterizations oversimplify; in any event the boundaries between the two sets of scholarship are fluid. Hopefully, however, their interaction can be productive for each without requiring the disintegration of either.

3

Regulating Corporate Governance

ANGUS CORBETT and STEPHEN BOTTOMLEY

REGULATION AND CORPORATE LAW

This collection is an invitation to reflect on the impact of regulation on law in general and corporate law in particular. The impetus for considering the impact of regulation on law is the growing importance of regulation.[1] There is a broad and general move in the community to manage or regulate risk. This focus on regulation and risk management is, in turn, part of a broader interest in using a range of governance mechanisms to directly and indirectly 'influence the flow of events'.[2] As in many other areas of law, this has found expression in corporate law.[3] There are now many areas of corporate law that are subject to analysis from a regulatory standpoint.[4] The content of the rules in each of these particular areas of corporate law has been reviewed and reformed according to their capacity to achieve specified public policy goals.

The intermingling of private interests and public concerns in the regulation of corporations is complex. Accordingly, our analysis focuses on one example: the regulation of directors' behaviour via the duty of care and diligence. The story about the emergence of this duty has been told before,[5] but our focus here is on the shifts and interactions between private and public forms of regulation which the story reveals. It is clear that private law notions, derived from contract law and equity, have ceased to supply a sufficient basis on which to enforce the emerging public interest in what corporations do and how directors

---

[1] C. Parker and J. Braithwaite, 'Regulation', in P. Cane and M. Tushnet (eds.), *The Oxford Handbook of Legal Studies* (Oxford: Oxford University Press, 2003), 119.   [2] Ibid.

[3] The law concerned with securities regulation, including financial services regulation, is sometimes also referred to as corporate law. In this chapter our focus is on a narrower definition of corporate law that includes those areas of law that deal with the creation and internal governance of corporations.

[4] *Corporate Law Economic Reform Program, Policy Framework* http://www.treasury.gov.au: 'The Corporate Law Economic Reform Program . . . involves a fundamental review of key areas of regulation which will affect business and investment activity. The objective of the Program, therefore, is to promote business and market activity leading to important economic outcomes including increased employment, by enhancing market efficiency and integrity and investor confidence. Corporate regulation will be revamped to provide a clear and consistent framework which reflects the contemporary business environment and encourages business to create wealth, prosperity and jobs.'

[5] The directors' duty of care has been the subject of more academic commentary than can be cited here. One indicative list can be found in P. Lipton and A. Herzberg, *Understanding Company Law*, 10th edn. (Sydney: Law Book Co., 2001), 348.

should behave. However, this is not a story of a simple transition from private ordering to public regulation. The standards of behaviour for directors, and the sanctions that follow when they are not met, have clear public and private elements. The current law relating to the directors' duty of care presents a more complex, hybridized picture in which aspects of public regulation sit along-side private ordering.

Our analysis of the impact of regulation on this particular area of corporate law is based on a very broad conception of regulation. For the purposes of this chapter, we define regulation as an activity that is aimed at 'influencing the flow of events'. This definition allows us to frame our analysis around the impact of the regulatory standpoint, that is, whether and how a particular body of law—in this case, the directors' duty of care and diligence—can be transformed when decision-makers begin to focus on the problem of using institutions, conduct, practices, and law to influence the flow of events.

Given this broad definition, this chapter does not deal with many other issues which are an important part of regulatory studies. We are not concerned with questions about the impact or effectiveness of particular approaches to regulation. Nor are we concerned with the problem of how to improve particular regulatory frameworks. Instead, we are concerned with analysing changes in our understanding of corporate law that are wrought by the high level of interest in regulation.

Our argument is that regulation is transforming our understanding of the content of corporate law. We argue that the category of law known as 'corporate law' is being transformed into a broader category of rules which we call corporate governance. It is well understood that corporate governance is a set of practices, processes, and structures relating to the governance of the corporation. Our claim is that it is useful to think of corporate governance as a body or category of law as well as a body of governance practices, processes, and structures.

This claim may appear to be too subtle and arcane to make in a volume that is concerned with much broader issues. This would, however, miss the central point of this chapter—that regulation is transforming the content and organization of a major category of law, that is, corporate law. This argument is a particular instance of what Hugh Collins has described as the 'productive disintegration of private law':

The change in the pattern of private law reasoning has resulted most immediately from an inevitable clash with the discourses of the economic and social regulation that were designed to address the inadequacies of private law as a form of distributive regulation caused by its lack of differentiation between the social contexts of contractual practices. The result of the collision between discourses has been the reconfiguration of private law reasoning, so that instrumental or policy concerns within its normative orientation become the dominant force of its evolutionary trajectory.[6]

---

[6] H. Collins, *Regulating Contracts* (Oxford: Oxford University Press, 1999), 53.

The importance of this idea is that regulation is changing not only the events that it seeks to influence but also one of the vectors—the law—which regulation uses to achieve its goals. This is important because it suggests that the ubiquity of regulation should lead lawyers to think about how law should be organized, how its categories should be defined, and, more broadly still, how it is possible to know and learn about the 'law'.

The 'productive disintegration of private law' has the potential to lead to a transformation of 'private law' into the discourses that guide the development of public policy. Ultimately, this means that private law would cease to have any particular identity and would become simply another instrument of public policy.[7] Our argument is that corporate law is being transformed into a new category of law: corporate governance. In this transition the law of corporate governance demonstrates a capacity to integrate the goals and objectives found in other regulatory schemes. Put another way, we argue that the law of corporate governance is emerging as a coherent body of law that has the capacity to avoid being trapped by the third arm of the 'regulatory trilemma'.[8]

LAW AND REGULATION

In order to understand the regulatory perspective on corporate law, it is necessary to understand that regulators and decision-makers have many ways—direct and indirect—of influencing 'the flow of events'. This viewpoint requires a description of the field or space in which institutions, conduct, and laws seek to 'regulate' events. The activity of endeavouring to influence events requires an understanding of the complexity of regulatory space, that is, the relationship between the events being regulated and the mechanisms used to regulate those events.

Regulatory scholars have emphasized the complexity of relationships within this regulatory space. Colin Scott has argued that

The chief idea of the regulatory space metaphor is that resources relevant to holding regulatory power and exercising capabilities are dispersed and fragmented. These resources are not restricted to formal, state authority derived from legislation or contracts, but also include information, wealth and organisational capacities. The possession of these resources is fragmented among state bodies, and between state and non-state bodies. The combination of information and organisational capacities may give to a regulated firm considerable informal authority, which is important in the outcome even of a formal rule formation or rule enforcement processes. Put another way, capacities derived from the possession of key resources are not necessarily exercised hierarchically within the regulatory space, regulator over regulatee.[9]

[7] H. Collins, *Regulating Contracts*, 54.   [8] Introduction to this volume.
[9] C. Scott, 'Analysing Regulatory Space: Fragmented Resources and Institutional Design', *Public Law* (2001), 329.

This characterization of the problem of using regulation to achieve desired goals has some profound effects on our understanding of law. 'Regulatory space' is defined by reference to the events or conduct being regulated. There are two important features affecting the role of law in this space. Firstly, law is just one of the mechanisms which have the potential to influence events. This emphasizes the point that law is much more than an instrument which regulators can use to achieve public policy goals.[10] Secondly, and more importantly for this chapter, this space is full of many different laws that directly or indirectly influence events occurring in this space. This broad patchwork of laws includes, for example, statutory provisions which seek directly to influence the activities of corporations by imposing obligations on directors and officers. But this space also includes other areas of law which support and create corporations, and the transactions which those corporations enter into. In a broader sense, it also includes various areas of public law which support the activities of regulators such as the Australian Securities and Investments Commission.

There are many different categories of law that interact with this space. These include those that are concerned with regulation, for example, corporate law or financial services law. It will, though, also include other categories of law, for example, tort law, the law of contracts, and the particular bodies of commercial law which support ordinary commercial transactions. Any given regulatory space (e.g. the activities of corporations) will include a very complex interaction between public law and private law, statutory law and common law. There will be many points of intersection as these laws and categories of law interact with each other in some complex and unpredictable ways. The regulatory space metaphor is a useful tool for understanding the impact of regulation on law because it directs our attention to these points of intersection between laws and categories of law. It encourages analysis of how laws, and categories of law, interact. It suggests that more is required than merely an analysis of the content of particular categories of law.

The central focus of this chapter is on the way that law, and categories of law, are affected by the way in which they interact with each other. Rather than viewing corporate law as a discrete category of law, we are concerned with the way in which corporate law interacts with other categories of law. This focus allows us to analyse the content of corporate law rules without being restricted by the assumption that corporate law is a closed, self-referential body of law.

A One-Dimensional Model of Law

Lawyers commonly learn about or use particular categories of law independently of the way in which these categories interrelate with each other. This is

[10] C. Shearing and J. Wood, 'Nodal Governance, Democracy and the New "Denizens": Challenging the Westphalian Ideal', *Journal of Law and Society*, 30 (2003), 400.

more than a heuristic that allows lawyers to focus on one particular area of law without having to consider other related areas of law. Many categories of law, such as corporate law, are constructed as if they are formal bodies of knowledge built around a self-referential system of rules. Hugh Collins has described the law of contract as a self-referential system of rules:

> Private law discourse is self-referential in the sense that it evolves its own doctrinal concepts of what counts as a legally enforceable contract and its own rules governing the bargaining process. In turn, these concepts and rules are further defined by more detailed legal concepts and rules. As this communication system achieves ever greater complexity in its operational rules, it distances itself from the foundational normative criteria such as the political ideal of freedom of contract. The rules of private law may be described as autonomous in the sense that they can be deployed for the most part independently of other normative systems such as morality and custom.[11]

This self-referential system of rules is also a closed system in the sense that it directs 'legal examination of the facts of a dispute with strict criteria of relevance. Some facts will be relevant to legal reasoning, because they need to be established in order to satisfy the legal rule, whereas others will be irrelevant to the legal enquiry.'[12] This closed, self-referential system of rules produces a form of legal reasoning that is both formal and autonomous. For the purposes of the argument in this chapter it is not necessary to establish that all categories of law are as strongly self-referential and closed as the law of contract. It is sufficient to argue that many bodies of law are constructed as if they were a closed system of self-referential rules.

The significant point about self-referential categories of law is that they are one-dimensional. They are one-dimensional in the sense that, seemingly, it is possible to know and make use of rules in each self-referential category without reference to other related bodies of law. The legal system from this perspective is the result of these bodies of law bumping into one another. Where there is conflict between rules in related categories of law coherence and order within the legal system is the result of choices about which particular rule should prevail in any particular instance.[13]

A Multidimensional Model of Law

Regulation has diminished the usefulness of a one-dimensional model of law. When viewed from within regulatory space, categories of law are not merely self-referential systems of law. It is not just that there is within regulatory space difficulty in isolating the operation and impact of particular bodies of law. There are many different rules and sets of rules that interact with each other

---

[11] Collins, *Regulating Contracts*, 38. [12] Ibid. 53.
[13] For an example of this approach to the construction of the legal system, dealing with the problem of drawing boundaries between tort and contract: S. Deakin, A. Johnston, and B. Markesinis, *Markesinis and Deakin's Tort Law*, 5th edn. (Oxford: Clarendon Press, 2003), 7.

and with other formal and informal forms of conduct to produce outcomes. For example, there are many different regulatory schemes which affect the conduct of directors and the systems of corporate governance adopted by corporations.

It is not merely this diversity of law which diminishes the integrity of a one-dimensional model of law. At a more profound level, the primary challenge to the construction of law as a one-dimensional system is that the content and organization of law is affected by the way in which different bodies of law interact. The content and meaning of any given rule is dependent upon the particular legal context in which it is operating. The content of a particular rule is dependent upon the way in which it interacts with other bodies of law. In the context of corporate governance this means that the content of the duty of care imposed on directors is affected by the interaction between this rule in corporate law and several other regulatory schemes—in particular, the provisions regulating the disclosure of information by companies.

This approach to the construction of law and legal categories of knowledge is multidimensional in the sense that at any point in space and time the content of a rule or set of rules is dependent upon its relationship with other categories of law. This introduces a form of 'relativity' into our understanding of law: the meaning of law is always relative to the particular context in which it is operating.

A multidimensional model of law is not one in which the meaning of rules is 'purely' relative. That is, the meaning or content of a rule is not completely dependent upon the broader legal context. Rather, a multidimensional model of law is one that looks to the way in which particular rules accommodate or integrate competing, and perhaps complementary, public policy goals that find expression in other rules or bodies of law. The process of reasoning involves analysis of how laws, and bodies of law, interact by accommodating or integrating those competing goals or purposes.[14]

To summarize our argument so far, we maintain that regulation is changing the organization of categories of law in general, and of corporate law in particular. This is the result of the emergence of a multidimensional capacity in corporate law, by which we mean the capacity of corporate law to accommodate and integrate public policy goals that form part of other regulatory schemes. In other words, the meaning of particular rules of corporate law is dependent upon the way in which those rules interact with other bodies of regulation.

As mentioned previously, our focus is on the duty of care that directors and officers owe to their corporations. The changes that have occurred in this area

---

[14] I. Ayres and J. Braithwaite, *Responsive Regulation Transcending the Deregulation Debate* (New York: Oxford University Press, 1992), 17, use the term 'multidimensional' in reference to their regulatory programme. The use of this term in this chapter has a similar connotation, although the context in which it is used is different. For a multidimensional analysis of tort law, see A. Corbett, 'The (Self) Regulation of Law: A Synergistic Model of Tort Law and Regulation', *University of New South Wales Law Journal*, 25/3 (2002), 616, 622–8.

of corporate law are a good example of the emergence of a law of corporate governance. In particular, we argue that the changes in the obligations imposed by the duty of care are concerned with accommodating and integrating purposes and goals from other areas of law. This is indicative of the emergence of a multidimensional capacity in corporate law in general, and the creation of the law of corporate governance in particular.

The law of corporate governance has emerged in two distinct steps. The first step involved the regulation of directors' activities by the creation of a more stringent duty of care. This phase was the result of a series of decisions by the courts. The second step was a more protracted one that involved reform of corporate law by the Australian Parliament. This second step, marked primarily by the introduction of the statutory business judgement rule, also reveals the difficulties associated with fully developing the potential of the emerging law of corporate governance.

THE EMERGING LAW OF CORPORATE GOVERNANCE

A More Stringent Duty of Care

The early history of the duty of care and diligence in Anglo-Australian corporate law is well known to corporate law students and scholars. For around one hundred years from the late nineteenth century, corporate law regarded the relationship between a company's members and its directors as essentially a private concern. The control of directors was a matter for the members (and only the members). Examples of directors' misbehaviour or failure to act were generally treated by the law as internal company problems—the members should bear the consequences if they made poor choices in appointing their directors.[15] This attitude persisted well into the twentieth century and was associated with a general judicial reluctance to be seen to be involved in managing the internal affairs of companies. It was also tied to a judicial perception—easily found in cases from the late nineteenth century and early twentieth—of directors as 'gentlemen amateurs'.[16]

As late as 1956 the prevailing judicial attitude was still that a company must put up with a 'set of amiable lunatics' as its board members if that is who the members appointed.[17] The legal standard of care and diligence that a director was expected to meet was imprecise and undemanding. Although couched in objective terms, it was applied according to subjective criteria. According to the courts, it was each director's own particular knowledge and experience that determined the parameters of the reasonable standard of behaviour expected

---

[15] e.g. *Turquand v Marshall* (1869) 4 Ch App 376.
[16] Honorable Justice Ipp, 'The Diligent Director', *Company Lawyer*, 18 (1997), 162.
[17] *Pavlides v Jensen* [1956] Ch 565, 570.

of them.[18] This judicial approach was not concerned with regulating or steering the conduct of directors, either individually or as a group. Instead, the legal principles were very much oriented towards the private ordering and processing of intra-corporate disputes.

This presumption in favour of the private management of corporate governance persisted even when the duty of care and diligence was translated into statutory form. Australia—and the State of Victoria in particular—was apparently the first jurisdiction in the English-speaking world to legislate this duty.[19] Section 107 of the Companies Act 1958 (Vic) stated that 'a director shall at all times act honestly and use reasonable diligence in the discharge of the duties of his office'. This provision was later duplicated in section 124(1) of the Uniform Companies Acts of 1961, which applied in all Australian states. This did not, however, signal a shift towards close public regulation of directors' conduct. It was widely accepted that these provisions were simply a statutory restatement of the common law standard described above.[20] This approach persisted into the 1980s under the national Companies Code.

In this 'first phase' of its history, therefore, the duty of care and diligence presented a relatively undemanding performance standard that was to be used by company members in private actions against directors. Not surprisingly, this weak private law standard was little used in the courts, usually in only extreme cases of managerial neglect.

In Australia, from the late 1980s, this state of affairs underwent a significant transformation. In this 'second phase' we see several interlocking shifts. Firstly, the duty of care and diligence began to move from its exclusively private law origins to encompass overtly instrumental concerns. The courts and Parliament each began to acknowledge that misconduct by directors frequently has consequences that extend beyond the relatively well-protected interests of the company's immediate shareholders. Secondly, the statutory duty of care and diligence came to prescribe a much stronger standard that was used not only to determine private corporate grievances against directors but also to discipline the behaviour of directors as a group.

In a 1997 commentary Justice Ipp, at the time a judge of the Supreme Court of Western Australia, began by observing that 'the public do not view company directors, as a group, particularly favourably'.[21] The interesting thing about this observation is not whether it is empirically correct,[22] but its acceptance of the fact that company directors, as a professional group, had now become subject to the public gaze. The public's view of directors, favourable or otherwise, now mattered. Although corporations and the people who direct and manage them were

[18] The classic case is *Re City Equitable Fire Insurance Co.* [1925] Ch 407.

[19] W. Paterson and H. Ednie, *Australian Company Law*, 2nd edn., ii (Sydney: Butterworth, 1972), para. 124/2.   [20] See *Byrne v Baker* [1964] VR 443.

[21] Honorable Justice Ipp, 'The Diligent Director', 162. Justice Ipp delivered a number of influential decisions on the duty of care and diligence in the early 1990s.

[22] Justice Ipp does not cite any empirical evidence for his claim.

still regarded fundamentally as private arrangements, it nevertheless came to be expected that as private actors they should be responsive to public concerns.[23]

This change originated in a series of cases brought by company creditors against directors, using the insolvent trading sections in the corporations legislation. Those sections created a legislative mechanism whereby a director could be made personally liable to a creditor for the company's debt if the director had unreasonably allowed the insolvent company to enter into that debt. An important step in this change was the dissenting judgment of Justice Kirby in the New South Wales Supreme Court decision of *Metal Manufacturers v Lewis*. In a passage that signals a shift from the judicial view that a director's indolence or incompetence is only a matter of concern for shareholders, Justice Kirby observed that

The obvious purpose of the legislation is not only to provide a means of redress to creditors, lifting the veil of incorporation, where parliament has deemed it appropriate to do so, it is also aimed, by proper concern lest such proceedings subsequently be brought against directors personally, to instil in them, during times of insolvency or economic difficulty in the corporation, to take particular care in the incurring of debts by the corporation with third parties.[24]

Interestingly, His Honour then went on to state that 'The time has passed when directors and other officers can simply surrender *their duties to the public* and those with whom the corporation deals by washing their hands, with impunity, leaving it to one director or a cadre of directors or to a general manager to discharge their responsibilities for them.'[25]

In a spate of decisions Australian courts began to echo these ideas with much more stringent and detailed enunciations of the standard of care and diligence required of company directors, particularly concerning their duty to be informed about the activities of their companies. In one of the more strongly worded decisions, *Commonwealth Bank of Australia v Friedrich*, Justice Tadgell noted that

As the complexity of commerce has gradually intensified (for better or for worse) the community has of necessity come to expect more than formerly from directors whose task it is to govern the affairs of companies to which large sums of money are committed by way of equity capital or loan. In response, the parliaments and the courts have found it necessary in legislation and litigation to refer to the demands made on directors in more exacting terms than formerly; and the standard of culpability required of them has correspondingly increased.[26]

The courts quite clearly now perceived that they had a role in guiding market behaviour.

---

[23] e.g. Ayres and Braithwaite, *Responsive Regulation*, 3. See also C. Parker, *The Open Corporation: Effective Self-regulation and Democracy* (Cambridge: Cambridge University Press, 2002), 29: 'Regulation within the new regulatory state is aimed as much at reinventing regulation within private "regulatory space", such as corporations, as at reforming external regulatory agencies.'   [24] (1988) 13 ACLR 357, 359.
[25] Ibid., 360, emphasis added.   [26] (1991) 9 ACLC 946, 956.

An Emergent Multidimensional Capacity

It was in this series of decisions that the outlines of the law of corporate govern-ance began to emerge. We argue that these decisions set the framework for the development of a complex multidimensional capacity in corporate law. There are two parts to this argument, which we develop in the remainder of this chapter. The first is that the 'regulation' of directors' conduct by imposing extra obligations was not wholly a judicially inspired development. Rather, the courts sought to upgrade the rules concerning the duty of care by reference to the changes in the statutory regulation of disclosure of information by companies to their shareholders.

Secondly, and consequently, in constructing the rules defining the duty of care the courts endeavoured to balance two public policy goals. On the one hand, the courts sought to implement the disclosure of information obligations imposed on directors by corporations legislation. On the other hand, the courts recognized the centrality of the decision-making processes within corporations. These decision-making processes give responsibility for making business judge-ments to directors and managers. We argue that the courts set up a framework of rules defining the duty of care which had the capacity effectively to integrate these two potentially competing sets of regulatory goals.

The Role of Changes to Disclosure Rules in Duty of Care Cases

In recognizing the responsibility of directors to be informed about the activities of their companies, the courts consistently referred to changes in the law relat-ing to disclosure to justify the added obligations that their decisions imposed on directors. At the same time as these cases were being decided, legislators were considering, and then enacting, wide-ranging reforms to the disclosure of cor-porate information.[27] The principal argument behind this increased emphasis on disclosure was the promotion of market confidence and the protection of investors generally. In other words, companies came to be recognized as public actors whose actions have significant public consequences.[28]

As noted above, in his dissenting judgment in *Metal Manufacturer Ltd v Lewis* Justice Kirby argued that directors could not simply 'surrender their duties to the public . . . by washing their hands' of their responsibilities.[29] Immediately following this passage Justice Kirby referred to sections 269 and 270 of the Companies (New South Wales) Code. These provisions required directors to

---

[27] e.g. Companies and Securities Advisory Committee, *Report on an Enhanced Statutory Disclosure System*, Sept. 1991; Corporate Law Reform Bill (No. 2) 1992.

[28] See also Chief Justice Street in *Re Castlereagh Securities Ltd* [1973] 1 NSWLR 624, 638.

[29] *Metal Manufacturer Ltd v Lewis* (1988) 13 NSWLR 315, 318. Although in the minority, in the decision in this case Justice Kirby's conclusion were to find support in later cases, e.g. *Morley v Statewide Tobacco Services Ltd* [1993] VR 423, 442. The decision of Justice Ormiston at first instance was affirmed by the Full Court of the Supreme Court of Victoria in *Morley v Statewide Tobacco Services Ltd* [1993] VR 451, 458.

attach a directors' statement to their company's annual accounts. In this statement directors were required to address a range of matters concerning the affairs of the company. After referring to these provisions, Justice Kirby continued by stating that

In these circumstances, the terms of s.556 [the insolvent trading section at the time] must be understood to be part of an integrated legislative scheme. That scheme requires of (relevantly) directors (of whom there must be at least two) higher levels of attention to the affairs of the corporation and its dealings with the outside world than was the case in the past.[30]

The explicit connection between changes in the rules relating to mandatory disclosure, and the higher obligations imposed on directors in section 556, was also referred to by Justice Ormiston in *Morley v Statewide Tobacco Services Ltd.* After acknowledging concerns about imposing obligations on directors that were 'too rigorous an application' of section 556, Justice Ormiston argued that

On the other hand, the interpretation which has been here applied is, in my view, the obvious consequence of the re-drafting of the provision which is now s.556. If I may say so, it was a view formed by me when I happened to be a part-time director of a small company for a short time after the Code came into effect and that section, as well as s.269(9), in the context of the new Code appeared then, as now, to require a degree of attention to the affairs of a company, especially its financial affairs which had not previously been expected.[31]

There are similar references to the relevance of rules concerning mandatory disclosure in the context of the obligations to be informed about the affairs of the company in the leading duty of care cases. In *AWA Ltd v Daniels* Justice Rogers accepted the reasoning in the line of insolvent trading cases and specifically referred to *Commonwealth Bank v Friedrich.*[32] In *Daniels v Anderson* the Court of Appeal specifically referred to the connection between the obligation to be familiar with the business of the company and the obligation to review information provided in financial statements.[33] More recently the courts have applied the same considerations to board chairpersons, for whom the information set is expanded even further.[34]

The Elements of the Duty of Care

The duty of due care and diligence owed by directors and officers to their companies arises from three sources. There is a statutory duty of care in

---

[30] *Metal Manufacturer Ltd v Lewis* (1988) 13 NSWLR 315, 319.
[31] *Morley v Statewide Tobacco Services Ltd* [1993] 1 VR 423, 443.
[32] (1992) 10 ACLC 933; *Commonwealth Bank v Friedrich* (1991) 5 ACSR 115, 125–6. Justice Tadgell followed the reasoning of Justice Ormiston in *Morley v Statewide Tobacco Services Ltd* [1993] 1 VR 423 by referring to the importance of the provision in s. 269 of the Companies Code to support the proposition that directors be required to gain an understanding of the affairs of their company.
[33] *Daniels v Anderson* (1995) 37 NSWLR 438, 503–4.
[34] *ASIC v Rich* [2003] NSWSC 85.

section 180(1) of the Corporations Act, and there are common law and equitable duties. There seems to be support for the view that the statutory duty and
the common law duty are 'essentially the same'.[35] There is also some support
for the view that the content of the equitable and common law duties of care
will be the same. There is some suggestion that the quantum of damages may
be different in common law and equity.[36] The following analysis deals only with
the content of the duty of care and for this purpose we will treat the three duties
of care as if they are substantially similar.

In deciding whether a director or officer has breached their duty of care to the
company, there are two broad questions. The first relates to the issue of what
knowledge the director either had or should have had regarding the affairs of the
company. The second is concerned with defining the standard of care for deciding
whether a director, with the relevant knowledge, breached the duty of care. These
broad questions are described in a number of ways but a leading text characterizes the distinction as a standard of skill (knowledge) and a standard of care.[37]

The issue of deciding what knowledge the director had, or should have had,
about the affairs of the company is made up of three elements. The first is an
objective element and specifies that the directors should be 'familiar with the
business of the company and how it is running'.[38] The second element is that
the director has an obligation 'to take reasonable steps to place themselves in a
position to guide and monitor the management of the company'.[39] The third
element is that a director with special skills or expertise is expected to exercise
reasonable care and must keep abreast of the affairs of the company even outside his or her area of expertise.[40] There are, in addition, separate requirements
concerning when functions can be delegated and when directors can rely on the
judgement, information, or advice provided to them by a delegate.[41]

As we see it, these requirements specify the 'information set' which provides
the framework for determining whether a director has breached their duty
of care. The delineation of this information set—determining what a director
knew or should have known—is a crucial step in the process of deciding
whether there has been a breach of duty. This inquiry takes on added significance because it is likely that the 'information set' against which the director's
actions and decisions will be judged will not be the same as the director's
subjective knowledge of the affairs of the company.

---

[35] *ASIC v Adler* (2001) 41 ACSR 72, 166 (Santow J).
[36] H. Ford, R. Austin, and I. Ramsay, *Ford's Principles of Corporations Law*, 11th edn. (Sydney:
LexisNexis Butterworths, 2003), 359–60.   [37] Ibid. [8.330].
[38] *Daniels and Anderson* (1995) 37 NSWLR 438, 500 (Clarke and Sheller JJA). Ford *et al.*, *Ford's
Principles*, 362 (analysis of the element of 'skill').
[39] *Daniels and Anderson* (1995) 37 NSWLR 438, 501 (Clarke and Sheller JJA). Ford *et al.*, *Ford's
Principles*, 364 (analysis of the element of 'diligence'). For a recent summary of these two elements
of the duty of care, see *ASIC v Adler* (2001) 41 ACSR 72, 167 (numbered sub-para. '(8)' in [372]).
[40] *Daniels and Anderson* (1995) 37 NSWLR 438, 504–5 (Clarke and Sheller JJA). See also Ford
et al., *Ford's Principles*, 365 (analysis of the element of 'diligence'). For a recent summary of these
two elements of the duty of care, see *ASIC v Adler* (2001) 41 ACSR 72. 167 (numbered sub-para.
'(9)' in [372]).   [41] Ford *et al.*, *Ford's Principles*, 368.

As to the second question, there are a number of ways of expressing the standard of care used to decide whether a director or officer is in breach of their duty of care. One test is that proposed by Justice Pidgeon in *ASC v Gallagher*:

the test is basically an objective one in the sense that the question is what an ordinary person, with the knowledge and experience of the defendant, might be expected to have done in the circumstances if he was acting on his own behalf.[42]

This test was a reformulation of that first proposed by Lord Hatherly in *Overend & Gurney Co v Gibb* in 1872, namely, whether

they [i.e. the directors] were cognisant of circumstances of such a character, so plain, so manifest, and so simple of appreciation, that no men with any ordinary degree of prudence, acting on their own behalf, would have entered into such a transaction as they entered into.[43]

In considering whether a director is in breach of this standard of care in any particular instance, it is necessary to balance 'the foreseeable risk of harm against the potential benefits that could reasonably have been expected to accrue to the company from the conduct in question'.[44]

Another approach to defining the standard of care is found in *Daniels v Anderson*. In that case Justices Clark and Sheller in their joint judgment rejected the test proposed by Lord Hatherly in *Overend & Gurney Co v Gibb*.[45] In its place Their Honours sought to apply ordinary principles of negligence:

It turns upon the natural expectations and reliance placed by shareholders on the experience and skill of a particular director. The duty is a common law duty to take reasonable care owed severally by persons who are fiduciary agents bound not to exercise the powers conferred upon them for (a) private purpose or for any purpose foreign to the power and placed . . . at the apex of the structure of direction and management.[46]

This test seems to be more concerned with integrating the directors' duty of care within the ordinary principles of negligence than with any stated preference for changing the relatively undemanding standard of care.[47] This test does not appear to have been generally adopted by either the courts or text writers.[48]

---

[42] *ASC v Gallagher* (1993) 10 ACSR 43, 53. This test was applied in *Vrisakis v ASC* (1993) 11 ACSR 162, 182 (Chief Justice Malcolm adopted this part of Justice Ipp's reasoning), 185 (Justice Rowland), 212 (Justice Ipp). A recent case adopting this test is *ASIC v Adler* (2001) 41 ACSR 72, 166 (numbered sub-para. '(4)' in [372]).

[43] *Overend & Gurney Co v Gibb* (1872) LR 5 HL 480, 486–7. This is the standard of care referred to by Ford *et al.*, *Ford's Principles*, 362.

[44] *Vrisakis v ASC* (1993) 11 ACSR 162, 212 (Justice Ipp).

[45] *Daniels v Anderson* (1995) 37 NSWLR 438, 502.   [46] Ibid. 505.

[47] For example, the application of this test to decide whether the non-executive directors of AWA Ltd were in breach of their duty of care: *Daniels v Anderson* (1995) 37 NSWLR 438, 514. In applying the test in these circumstances Justices Clark and Sheller reverted to the older form of the test when they stated that it 'was not unreasonable for the non-executive directors to have accepted the statement as very reassuring indeed' (p. 514). The use of the double negative indicates that Their Honours were applying an undemanding standard of care.

[48] e.g. *ASIC v Adler* (2001) 41 ACSR 72, 166 (numbered sub-para. '(4)' in [372]); see also Ford *et al.*, *Ford's Principles*, 362.

The *Gallagher* test expresses what can be loosely referred to as a test for gross negligence.[49] In order for a director to be in breach they must make a decision which an ordinary person, encumbered with the relevant 'information set', could not reasonably make. It is generally accepted that this relatively undemanding standard of care reflects deference by courts to business judgements and decisions made by directors. This deference is founded on two separate considerations. Firstly, the recognition that it is directors who have responsibility for ensuring that the 'business of the company is . . . managed by or under' their direction.[50] Secondly, there is an awareness that courts are not in a position to second-guess business judgements of directors.[51]

It is crucial to delineate clearly between these two elements of the duty of care. It is crucial because the increased interest in regulation of corporate governance, in general, of the behaviour of directors, in particular, has not affected both of these parts of the duty of care in the same way. The higher standards imposed on directors have dealt with the amount and quality of information and knowledge which directors are presumed to have as they conduct the affairs of their companies. There has been no attempt, conscious or otherwise, to increase the standard of care that is used to decide whether a director, with the relevant 'information set', has actually breached the standard of care. What appears to be the generally accepted test for determining whether a director has breached their duty of care is a reformulation of the test proposed by Lord Hatherly in *Overend & Gurney Co v Gibb*.

These decisions accommodate and integrate the policies and objectives of two parts of the system regulating corporate governance into the rules defining the duty of care. On the one hand, there is the recognition of a perceived need for greater levels of public accountability for companies and directors that finds expression in the increasing levels of information companies are required to disclose to markets and shareholders. On the other hand, there is the recognition of the perceived need to uphold the capacity of directors to make decisions on behalf of companies and their shareholders without courts or regulators interfering in the exercise of business judgements.

The decisions in these cases do not simply revolve around attempts by courts to impose greater levels of accountability on directors. The regulatory space for corporate governance is more than just a balance between the need for certainty on the one hand, and the need for accountability on the other. The regulatory space is bounded by the interaction between different subsystems of law that are related to the activities of companies. The strength of the leading cases in this field is that they provide a method for integrating and accommodating both of these policies within the law defining the duty of care.

[49] *Re City Equitable Fire Insurance Co Ltd* [1925] Ch 407.
[50] Corporations Act 2001, s. 198A(1).
[51] Ford *et al.*, *Ford's Principles*, 318.

THE ROLE OF PARLIAMENT IN THE EMERGENCE OF
THE LAW OF CORPORATE GOVERNANCE

The response by the Australian Parliament to these changes in the duty of care
has revealed the complexity of the project of the developing law of corporate
governance. Initially, Parliament responded to these changes by standing back,
and allowing the courts to develop the law dealing with the duty of care. After
the expression of some concern about the direction taken by the courts,
Parliament moved to reform the elements of the statutory duty of care and to
introduce a business judgement rule.[52] This was the point at which lawmakers
recognized the need affirmatively to define the space within which directors
must make decisions. The attempt to define the outlines of this space is the
explicit recognition of the emergent law of corporate governance. It is also
evidence of the difficulty of fully comprehending all of the consequences of the
developing law of corporate governance.

Parliamentary Deference to the Courts

Prompted by the more openly instrumental stance being taken by the courts, the
legislators also began to re-examine the role of the statute in relation to the
conduct of directors. That corporate governance and directors' duties had
become a matter of public regulatory concern became evident between 1989
and 1991 with the publication of two reports by the Australian Parliament on
directors' duties and corporate practices.[53] The 1989 Senate inquiry into the
social and fiduciary duties and obligations of company directors recommended
that the companies' legislation should specify an objective standard of care for
directors.[54] That is, a director's conduct should be judged according to what
a reasonable person would have done in the situation, and not mainly by reference to that particular director's knowledge and experience. An objective standard gives the courts the scope to substitute their determination of what is
appropriate behaviour for that of the directors.[55] The report (known as the
Cooney Report) argued that this change was warranted because 'if the modern

---

[52] At the workshop at which this paper was first presented, Paul Finn and Suzanne Corcoran gave
a paper addressing a similar problem, and arguing that the complexity of modern commercial relations often outstrips the capacity of fiduciary and trust law, triggering the creation of new statutory
forms of regulation.

[53] Parliament of the Commonwealth of Australia, Senate Standing Committee on Legal and
Constitutional Affairs, *Company Directors' Duties: Report on the Social and Fiduciary Duties and
Obligations of Company Directors* (Canberra: Australian Government Publishing Service, 1989) (the
Cooney Report); House of Representatives Standing Committee on Legal and Constitutional Affairs,
Corporate Practices and the Rights of Shareholders (Canberra: Australian Government Publishing
Service, 1991) (the Lavarch Report).

[54] At the time the statute provided that 'An officer of a corporation shall at all times exercise a
reasonable degree of care and diligence in the exercise of his powers and the discharge of his duties.
Penalty $5,000' (Companies Code, s. 229(2)). Initially, this was copied into the Corporations Law
of 1991, s. 232(4).

[55] L. Sealy, 'Directors' Duties Revisited', *Company Lawyer*, 22 (2001), 79.

company director wants professional status, then professional standards of care ought to apply'.[56] In other words, the affirmation of an objective standard of care was prompted by a perception that directors now had a publicly significant role that could not be adequately determined by the interests of shareholders alone.

At the same time, these reports revealed one of the persistent tensions in the regulation of the conduct of directors and of corporate governance. The reports recommended that, as a counter-balance to the introduction of an objectively defined standard of care, the corporations legislation should give directors a 'safe harbour' in the form of a 'business judgement rule' that would protect directors from liability for the consequences of properly made decisions that nevertheless went wrong.[57] The main impetus for a statutory business judgement rule was a perception that the courts were not sufficiently responsive to the risk-taking context in which directors' decisions are made, coupled with a concern to put limits on the extent to which courts should be able to substitute their views for the informed judgements of directors.

The recommendation for an objective duty of care was accepted by the Australian government and included in the major reforms proposed in the Corporate Law Reform Bill of 1992. In support of these reform proposals, the government argued that the law governing directors was no longer merely a matter of private ordering: 'The law relating to the duties and obligations of company directors is one of central importance, affecting as it does the interests of shareholders, directors, creditors, employees and the general community.'[58] Nevertheless, the government rejected the idea of enacting a business judgement rule, emphasizing instead the importance of providing directors with 'the clearest guidance' about the standard of care and diligence that is required of them. In other words, the role of the legislature was to steer directors towards appropriate patterns of conduct, rather than simply imposing sanctions for failure to meet legal standards.

The 1992 reform proposals aimed to provide this guidance in the form of a list of factors that would be relevant in determining whether a director had contravened the objective standard of care and diligence.[59] The factors in the list included: determining the number of board meetings the director attended, what information the director acquired about the company's affairs, and what the director did to ensure that the company's managers were honest, competent, reliable, and properly monitored. The list read like, and was intended as, a general 'how to' guide for all company directors. While it was proposed that the list would be used by the courts to assess the legality of a director's actions

---

[56] Cooney Report, para. 3.25.

[57] Ibid., para. 3.35. Similar recommendations were subsequently made by the Companies and Securities Law Review Committee, *Company Directors and Officers: Indemnification, Relief and Insurance*, Report No. 10 (Melbourne, 1990), and in the Lavarch Report.

[58] Commonwealth of Australia, Attorney-General's Department, *Corporate Law Reform Bill 1992: Draft Legislation and Explanatory Paper* (Canberra: Australian Government Publishing Service, 1992), para. 91. [59] Ibid., proposed s. 232(4AA).

in a particular instance, it would also be consulted by directors as a general guide in planning their actions. The 1992 proposals presented a striking change from the then prevailing approach, being overtly concerned with regulating and guiding general patterns of corporate behaviour in addition to providing a response to individual instances of misbehaviour.

Not surprisingly, the 1992 proposals were criticized. In particular, the proposed guidance list was regarded by directors and some lawyers as too prescriptive, emphasizing compliance over 'good business practice', and giving priority to questions of form and procedure rather than substance.[60]

In the same year a further dimension was added to this debate about the appropriate form and content for corporate governance rules, with the influential decision of Justice Rogers in the Commercial Division of the Supreme Court of New South Wales in *AWA v Daniels*.[61] As with other contemporary decisions, Justice Rogers defined the context of the case in terms of community expectations and the role of directors as stewards of a company's resources. The decision reaffirmed the higher standard laid down in cases such as *Commonwealth Bank of Australia v Friedrich*, but differentiated between what was expected of executive and non-executive directors. This differentiation was praised by those (principally directors) who were concerned that the courts had raised the bar too high for non-executive directors. It was argued that this decision had finally 'got it right', attuning legal standards to the realities of corporate practice.[62]

When it was finally enacted, the 1992 bill did redefine the duty of care and diligence in overtly objective terms.[63] The amended section now required a director to exercise the degree of care and diligence that a reasonable person in a like position in a corporation would exercise in the corporation's circumstances. However, the proposed guidance list did not survive into the legislation, nor was a business judgement rule enacted. Instead, the government argued that the development of the law in this area was best left to the courts. Indeed, the expressed intention of the new section was to confirm the position expounded by the courts in decisions such as *Commonwealth Bank of Australia v Friedrich* and *AWA v Daniels*.[64]

Simultaneously with this debate about the formulation of the statutory duty of care and diligence, consideration was also being given to the nature of the sanctions that applied to a breach of the duty. Prior to the 1992 reforms the directors' duties sections in the corporations legislation had a strong emphasis

---

[60] See Parliament of the Commonwealth of Australia, Joint Statutory Committee on Corporations and Securities, *Summary of Evidence Presented to the Committee on the Draft Corporate Law Reform Bill 1992* (Canberra: Parliament House, 1992), 14.   [61] (1992) 10 ACLC 933.

[62] See e.g. R. Baxt, 'The Duty of Care of Directors—Does it Depend on the Swing of the Pendulum?', in I. Ramsay (ed.), *Corporate Governance and the Duties of Company Directors* (Melbourne: Centre for Corporate Law and Securities Regulation, University of Melbourne, 1997), 92.

[63] Corporations Law, s. 232(4).

[64] Parliament of the Commonwealth of Australia, House of Representatives, *Corporate Law Reform Bill 1992: Explanatory Memorandum* (Canberra, Nov. 1992), paras. 86–9.

on criminal sanctions, in addition to the possibility of damages or compensation. The 1989 Cooney Report had recommended that criminal liability be applied only in cases of 'genuine criminality' involving fraud or dishonesty, and that civil penalties, determined on the civil standard of proof, should apply in all other cases.[65] This recommendation was supported by the Lavarch Report, which noted that greater emphasis should be placed on administrative action and civil litigation, rather than criminal prosecution.[66] These recommendations were enacted by the 1992 reforms, and commenced operation in February 1993. Under the civil penalty regime a director who failed to meet their statutory duty of care and diligence (for example) faced the prospect of paying a non-criminal penalty of up to $A200,000 plus the possibility of being disqualified from acting as a director as well as having to pay compensation. Alternatively, where the contravention was serious (that is, involved intentional or reckless action aimed at dishonesty, deceit, or fraud), criminal action could have been taken.

The civil penalty system was a response to the perceived unwillingness of the courts to utilize the full force of the criminal sanctions that were available. The legislators responded by grafting aspects of the private law system of remedies to a public law system of penalties and disqualifications. The result, in theory, is an escalating set of sanctions that can be applied against directors, ranging from warnings or enforceable undertakings, through non-criminal monetary penalties, to disqualifications and, ultimately, criminal prosecution. As interpreted by the courts, the rationale for exercising the power of disqualification is explicitly public: the protection of the public from the harmful or improper use of corporate structures, as well as protecting individuals who have direct dealings with companies.[67]

An important consequence of this change was that the Australian Securities Commission (now the Australian Securities and Investments Commission) was given a formal role in monitoring and enforcing the law governing directors' conduct. Standing to apply for a civil penalty order is now restricted, in most cases, to the Commission. While shareholders may still use the general law,[68] the costs and complexities of such actions usually deter smaller shareholders.

We see, then, that within a relatively short time frame the courts and legislators both began to examine the public role of the law governing the directors' duty of care. This change in orientation was mandated not only by a growing awareness that directors' actions affect non-shareholder interests (especially those of creditors and employees), but also by the growing significance of indirect shareholdings, via superannuation and managed investment funds.

In May 1995 the Full Court of the Supreme Court of New South Wales handed down its decision in *Daniels v Anderson*,[69] the appeal from the 1992 *AWA* case. The Court affirmed the direction taken by Justice Rogers at first

[65] Cooney Report. This has echoes of the wider debate about the distinction between 'real crime' and 'mere' regulatory offences; see Lacey, Ch. 7 in this volume.   [66] Cooney Report, 211.
[67] *ASIC v Adler (No. 5)* (2002) 20 ACLC 1146, 1159.
[68] See Corporations Act 2001, s. 185.   [69] (1995) 13 ACLC 614.

instance and established in cases such as *Commonwealth Bank of Australia v Friedrich*. It confirmed that the duty of care owed by directors is based in both equity and the common law of negligence. In doing this, the Court rejected the categorical distinction that Justice Rogers had drawn between executive and non-executive directors.

For the purposes of our analysis, there were two noteworthy aspects to this decision. Firstly, the majority judgement makes a lengthy prescription of what is required in the decision-making processes of modern company directors. In many ways this aspect of the judgement is reminiscent of the list which had been proposed for enactment in the original 1992 legislative reforms. While its prescriptions do not go into specific detail, the judgement is, nevertheless, far more detailed than the approach of earlier cases in the history of the duty of care. Secondly, the response to the judgement (as with the judgement at first instance) was concerned not with the particulars of the case but with whether its prescriptions could be implemented in corporate boardrooms. In other words, the case stands as a clear example of how judicial decisions were now assessed according to how effectively the courts had reconfigured the space for corporate governance; in particular, how effectively the decisions of the courts integrated and accommodated the requirements of the law regulating the disclosure of information by companies into the duty of care.

Corporate Governance and the Business Judgement Rule

What does the history of the duty of care up until this point tell us about the emerging shape of the regulation of directors and corporate governance? It shows a convergence of judicial and legislative concerns towards the overt goal of 'steering' (to use Collins's term) the behaviour of directors, with directors now being regarded generally as a group of regulatory subjects.

From a legislative perspective our story shows how parliamentary concerns (specifically, about information disclosure) influenced judicial formulations of the duty. From the courts' perspective, it shows how judicial pronouncements had shaped the extent to which the legislation sought to regulate directors' conduct. The approach of the courts, which influenced the process of legislative reform, favoured the promulgation of broad standards over specific rules and guidelines. This approach was summed up in a paper by Chief Justice David Malcolm of the Supreme Court of Western Australia:

there is no magic form of words which will capture for every case the precise scope of a particular director's duty of care. There is no doubt that the bar has been raised in accordance with changing expectations, both in the community and in the commercial world. However, it remains the fact that the question of liability can only continue to be worked out on a case by case basis.[70]

---

[70] Chief Justice Malcolm, 'Directors' Duties: The Governing Principles', in Ramsay (ed.), *Corporate Governance and the Duties of Company Directors*, 60.

The substantive content of the rules defining the boundaries of the duty of care had been supplemented by legislative changes to the regimes for sanctions and penalties. To that extent, we see that the approach of the general law had become integrated into the fabric of legislation over the course of time.[71] We see—at least in relation to the duty of care and diligence—that the regulation of directors' conduct was most commonly depicted as a combination of self-regulatory codes of best practice and the threat of civil penalties and/or disqualification. However, the primary responsibility for defining the space in which directors and other officers operated when carrying out their roles lay with the courts. The next step in the story relied more on the use of legislation to regulate the public and private elements involved in the application of the duty of care.

This most recent instalment occurred between 1998 and 2000 with the proposal and enactment of another major set of reforms to the corporations legislation. Again, the intention behind the changes to the statutory duty of care and diligence was to provide guidance and education for directors—the idea was 'to make it easier for company officers to know what is expected of them'.[72] The key component to achieving this aim was the introduction of a business judgement rule.

The rationale for a business judgement rule was the need to create a space for boardroom decision-making. This would permit reliance on forms of private monitoring and self-regulation. Indeed, at the same time as the debate commenced about the need for a business judgement rule, directors and other industry bodies in Australia began to demonstrate a more overt interest in modes of self-regulation. In 1990 a self-appointed task force that included the Australian Institute of Company Directors, the Business Council of Australia, and the Australian Stock Exchange, chaired by Henry Bosch, the outgoing head of the National Companies and Securities Commission (NCSC),[73] published a code of conduct for company directors that could be adopted voluntarily by individual companies. This reflects an international trend: voluntary corporate governance codes are now commonplace in industrialized countries.[74]

As enacted in Australia, the business judgement rule states that a director is taken to have complied with their statutory and general law duty of care

[71] This sentence deliberately inverts Collins's claim about the relationship between common law and legislation; see Collins, *Regulating Contracts*, 60.

[72] Commonwealth of Australia, Department of the Treasury Corporate Law Economic Reform Program, *Commentary on Draft Provisions* (Canberra: Australian Government Printing Service, 1998), 76.

[73] The NCSC was replaced by the Australian Securities Commission, which later became the Australian Securities and Investments Commission.

[74] For examples: in Australia, in addition to the Bosch Code, ASX Corporate Governance Council, *Principles of Good Corporate Governance and Best Practice Recommendations* (2003), available at http://www.asx.com.au/about/CorporateGovernance_AA2.shtm; in the United Kingdom, the Committee on Corporate Governance, *The Combined Code* (London: Gee, 1998); in the United States, the American Law Institute, *Principles of Corporate Governance: Analysis and Recommendations* (1992); and the OECD, *Principles of Corporate Governance* (Paris: OECD, 1999).

and diligence if, when making a business decision, they act in good faith for a proper purpose, have no material personal interest in the decision, they appropriately inform themselves about the decision, and they rationally believe it to be in the company's best interests.[75] This rule has three interesting features. Firstly, it is quite generalized, being framed—for the most part—in terms of other duties owed by directors. Secondly, and consequently, it is non-directive, providing only a general process framework for directors. Thirdly, in its references to informed and rational decision-making, to lack of personal interest, and to proper purposes, it has striking parallels with the ways in which public decision-making is regulated by rules of administrative law.[76]

With its focus on the process of decision-making, the enactment of the business judgement rule recognizes the emerging law of corporate governance. The business judgement rule marks the development of a multidimensional capacity in corporate law because it is an affirmative move to define the space for decision-making by directors and senior managers in corporations. It is recognition of the need to integrate and accommodate the concerns of bodies of law regulating corporations into the heart of corporate law. In this sense the business judgement rule symbolizes an important turning point in the development of corporate law.

However, the enactment of the business judgement rule marks only the first tentative steps in the emerging law of corporate governance. It embodies the requirement that directors and officers should appropriately inform themselves about the subject matter of the decisions they are making. Importantly, this requirement merely reproduces the driving force which led the courts to reinterpret the nature of the duty of care. The statutory business judgement rule gives no indication about *how* to integrate the requirement to be informed into the process of decision-making by directors and officers. In addition, the business judgement rule makes no real attempt to integrate the impact of broader areas of regulation, such as trade practices or environmental regulation, into the processes of decision-making by directors. This is why we emphasize the symbolic, rather than the instrumental, significance of the business judgement rule.

One clear way in which these other bodies of regulation will contribute to the emerging law of corporate governance is by encouraging, or mandating, the introduction of compliance systems within corporations. These compliance systems are designed to ensure that information about non-compliance with regulatory requirements is brought to the attention of the board and of senior managers.[77] The extension of the 'information set' against which the actions of directors are assessed to include information generated by compliance systems has the potential to affect profoundly the operation of the duty of care.[78] A multidimensional analysis of the duty of care shows how the obligations

---

[75] Corporations Act 2001, s. 180(2).

[76] See M. Aronson and B. Dyer, *Judicial Review of Administrative Action*, 2nd edn. (Sydney: Lawbook Co. Information Services, 2000), ch. 6.   [77] Parker, *The Open Corporation*, 17.

[78] e.g. *In re Caremark International Inc. Derivative Litigation* 1996 WL 549894 (Del.Ch.).

created by 'compliance-oriented' regulation can be integrated into the rules defining the duty of care.

CONCLUSION

The impact of regulation on corporate law is of fundamental importance. Corporate law may, in the past, have been described as a one-dimensional body of law concerned with regulating the interests of investors, managers, and directors. The impact of regulation has been to transform this body of law into an emerging law of corporate governance, which seeks to integrate the policies and concerns of broad areas of regulation into corporate law. As we have argued, this involves using law to reconfigure the space within which directors and managers make decisions for their corporations.

The emerging law of corporate governance that we have described is in its very early stages of development. The steps taken have been tentative and the steps yet to be taken involve significant changes in our understanding of the role and function of corporate law. But there is already evidence of receptiveness to such changes. A prominent example can be found in Justice Owen's three-volume report on the Royal Commission of Inquiry into the collapse of HIH Insurance.[79] Early in his report Justice Owen expresses his disquiet about the widespread use of the phrase 'corporate governance' where it is tied to a 'tick the box' approach to corporate regulation. As we read it, Justice Owen's concerns centre on the lingering presence of a narrow and outdated 'command and control' mentality in corporate regulation. His Honour seems to sense that the emerging regulatory framework for corporate governance has—or should have—more dimensions than this. As he describes it,

Corporate governance—as properly understood—describes a framework of rules, relationships, systems and processes within and by which authority is exercised and controlled in corporations. Understood in this way, the expression 'corporate governance' embraces not only the models or systems themselves but also the practices by which that exercise and control of authority is in fact effected.[80]

There is one further concluding remark about these developments. This concerns the role of the traditional judicial techniques in the emerging law of corporate governance. There has been a great deal of legislative reform of corporate law in recent years. Indeed, for some, the impact of regulation on law is the impact of legislation on the legal system. The core of the argument that we have developed is that traditional judicial techniques have the capacity to integrate and accommodate the interaction between bodies of law and regulation. It is this capacity, when combined with legislative reform, which has the potential to transform our understanding of corporate law and regulation.

---

[79] The HIH Royal Commission, *The Failure of HIH Insurance* (Canberra: Commonwealth of Australia, 2003). [80] Ibid., vol. i, p. xxxiii.

4

Regulating Families

JOHN DEWAR

INTRODUCTION

The regulation of families through law is most obvious in the rules governing marriage, divorce, parenthood, cohabitation, and their consequences. These rules, and the procedures associated with them, are usually referred to as 'family law'.[1] Rules governing these basic aspects of human life are a feature of almost every legal system.[2] However, there are many other ways in which families are regulated, directly or indirectly, through law (such as laws relating to child support and social security, laws regulating the workplace, education, superannuation, and pensions, to name a few); and there are many non-legal modes of family regulation.[3]

In this chapter the 'regulatory lens' will be applied primarily to family law in the sense stipulated above. Before doing so, however, it is worth noting an unusual feature of family law in this context. This is that family law is not a coherent body of law in the sense that contract, tort, or trusts law are. It is chiefly the product of legislation, and, thus, of political processes, rather than the working-out of conceptual premises through application to new instances. This means that family law is more permeable, more open to external change or interference, than the more normatively closed areas of private law. At the same time, these statutory rules have been applied and interpreted, by lawyers and the courts, and so have acquired some of the appearance of stability and normative closure of other areas of law. Family law is still law in the sense that it is applied by courts and is governed, more or less, by precedent. This combination of the destabilizing input of legislative change coupled with the stabilizing effects of doctrinal techniques lends family law a hybrid quality that, it will be argued, is significant when viewed from a regulatory perspective.

---

[1] For example, see R. H. Graveson and F. R. Crane (eds.), *A Century of Family Law* (London: Sweet & Maxwell, 1957), an edited volume celebrating the centenary of the Matrimonial Causes Act 1857. 'Family law', as currently understood, was taken by the authors to have been inaugurated by the 1857 Act.

[2] For the purposes of this chapter, however, 'family law' should be understood as referring to the Anglo-Australian versions of it. The text will alert the reader to jurisdictionally specific aspects of what is being discussed, where relevant.

[3] N. Rose, 'Beyond the Public/Private Divide: Law, Power and the Family', *Journal of Law and Society*, 14 (1987), 61, arguing that while liberal notions of privacy set limits to the ability of the state to regulate families, e.g. through law, the family, nevertheless, remains intensively governed; cf. J. Donzelot, *The Policing of Families: Welfare versus the State* (London: Hutchinson, 1979).

Two other features of family law relate to this hybrid quality. One is that family law did not pre-exist regulatory interventions by the state. Laws relating to families, and to the welfare of family members, have for some time been a complex mix of doctrinal and regulatory, or public and private, elements. For example, family relations had been central to much Poor Law provision of the earliest manifestations of the welfare state, so to the extent that law 'saw' families at all, it was initially through the lens of public, rather than private, law. As we have seen, it could be argued that the family only emerges as a coherent legal phenomenon in private law in the late nineteenth and early twentieth century. In this context, the appearance of the family in private law at all was itself the *effect* of a regulatory impulse: first, to control the effects of informal marriages on property and the devolution of inheritance; later, to sanction and punish marital misdemeanours, especially against women; and more recently, to manage the financial and political consequences of serial partnering and blended families. In other words, rather than 'colliding' with a pre-existing body of stable doctrinal law relating to families, family law has always been an unstable mix of doctrinal and instrumental elements: the 'inter-penetration' of one by the other has been present from the start.

The next part of this chapter will explore this aspect of family law in more detail by looking at how that regulatory impulse present in family law has changed over time. It will be argued that the objectives sought to be achieved through family law, the assumptions made about the human subjects on which law operates, and the techniques used to achieve regulatory objectives, have all profoundly altered during the course of the twentieth century—not once, but twice; and that we are still in the throes of working out the implications of the second of those changes. This has meant that family law has passed through three distinct regulatory eras: the formal, the functionalist, and the complex.

Another feature of family law related to the notion of hybridity, but this time confined to more recent eras of its development, is that it can be understood as operating at two different normative levels. The normative content of family law speaks simultaneously to individuals whose disputes are to be resolved, and at the same time to a much wider audience who will settle their own differences, and who, in doing so, must self-apply the relevant rules.[4] Family law is now a mass dispute settlement system, and the system must speak to those who may never see the inside of a lawyer's office or a court building. Much of family law has this dual aspect of immediate dispute settlement on the one hand, and the large-scale steering settlement behaviour on the other—i.e. the characteristics often associated with doctrinal and regulatory law respectively. In this context, family law's hybridity can be explained by the fact that the family law system is one of 'wide reach and low intensity'. What this refers to is the fact that while many people will think of their family problems as being legal ones, requiring some form of legal assistance, most people will only seek low levels of legal input

[4] J. Dewar, 'The Normal Chaos of Family Law', *Modern Law Review*, 61 (1998), 467.

into solving those problems.[5] The legal system has evolved many low-intensity interventions designed to assist people to self-apply the normative framework; which in turn has led to the system becoming highly dispersed, fragmented, and horizontalized.[6] These features of family law will be explored later in the chapter through the perspectives of effectiveness, responsiveness, and coherence.

HOW FAMILY LAW HAS ALWAYS BEEN INSTRUMENTAL:
FROM FORMALISM TO COMPLEXITY

It was suggested above that family law has for some time been characterized by hybridity, in that it has over time displayed features of both doctrinal and regulatory law. It was also suggested that the regulatory impulses driving this ensemble of rules, practices, and procedures have changed significantly since the first introduction of statutory divorce. In particular, the regulatory object-ives, the assumptions made about those being regulated, and the techniques employed, have all shifted dramatically during that period.

Dewar and Parker have suggested[7] that the history of family law during this period can be understood as a period of transition between eras—from the first *formal* era to the second *functionalist* era in the middle decades of the twentieth century; and from the second to the third *complex* era, over a period starting in the late 1980s and continuing today. Each era, we argued, can be understood as characterized by a different set of balances struck between four dichotomies: rights–utility, form–substance, principle–pragmatism, and public–private. By rights–utility, we intended to contrast two different modes of ethical reasoning in decision-making, the former, characterized by an emphasis on fixed entitle-ments enforceable by remedy, the latter, by an emphasis on maximizing the benefits of the decision irrespective of whatever fixed claims or entitlements there might be.[8] By form–substance, we intended a distinction between what is considered relevant to an outcome—formal categories and technical rules, or a broader search for evidence and expert opinion. By principle–pragmatism,

---

[5] H. Genn, *Paths to Justice: What People Do and Think about Going to Law* (Oxford: Hart, 1999). Genn's study of different areas of commonly encountered legal need found that those with fam-ily law problems had higher rates of advice-seeking than all other types of legal problem—92 per cent compared to 78 per cent for employment, 69 per cent for personal injuries, 49 per cent for housing, and 36 per cent for consumer problems. Similarly, a far higher proportion of family cases were resolved by court proceedings than any other type of matter, although that figure would include court orders made by consent.

[6] W. Murphy, *The Oldest Social Science: Configurations of Law and Modernity* (Oxford: Oxford University Press, 1997), ch. 6; P. Goodrich, 'Social Science and the Displacement of Law', *Law and Society Review*, 32 (1998), 473.

[7] J. Dewar and S. Parker 'English Family Law since WWII: From Status to Chaos', in S. Katz, J. Eekelaar, and M. Maclean (eds.), *Cross-currents: Family Law and Policy in the US and England* (Oxford: Oxford University Press, 2000). This section is substantially derived from that chapter.

[8] See S. Parker, 'Rights and Utility in Anglo-Australian Family Law', *Modern Law Review*, 55 (1992), 311.

we intended a distinction between different forms of justification; and by public–private, we intended a distinction between different ways of proceduraliz-ing a family law system—i.e. between one in which decision-making is public, and one in which it is not.

We suggested that these successive eras in family law can be analysed by look-ing at which of the two poles in each of these dualities is emphasized. In the first era the first is emphasized, in the second era the second is emphasized. In the third era matters become more complex. The point of adopting this analysis for these purposes is that it illustrates the longevity of the doctrinal–regulatory mix in family law, and enables us to identify more precisely what the regulatory tasks were thought to be.

The Formal Era

This era refers to the period from 1857 (the introduction of civil divorce) to the introduction of the divorce reforms in the late 1960s and 1970s (although in practice it had been petering out from the end of the Second World War). The marital relationship was seen basically as a form of contract, albeit a contract of adhesion, because the terms were not freely negotiable. It was more accurately a contractually acquired status, with the terms of that status set out by law.

In terms of the dichotomies set out above, there was a strong emphasis on spouses as right-holders, using rights in the sense of claims that need no other justification for their enforcement. Rights had correlative duties. Breach gave rise to a remedy in the other, or the forfeiture by the guilty party of relief. Marriage was dissoluble only by showing breach, in the form of a matrimonial offence that had not itself been condoned, connived at, or conduced.[9] A wife's entitlement to maintenance was affected by her 'guilt' or 'innocence';[10] and decisions about the custody of children were resolved either by reference to the assumed superiority of the father's right to custody[11] or, latterly, by reference to moral evaluations of the parties' conduct.[12]

This era was also formal, in the sense that family law was made up of fixed categories that gave rise to predictable legal consequences. There were grounds of

[9] See M. Finer and O. MacGregor, 'The History of the Obligation to Maintain', in *Report of the Committee on One Parent Families*, vol. ii (London: HMSO, 1975), app. 5; C. Gibson, *Dissolving Wedlock* (London: Routledge, 1994), ch. 4, for accounts of the development of the law of divorce during this period.

[10] See J. Barton, 'The Enforcement of Financial Provisions', in Graveson and Crane (eds.), *A Century of Family Law*; J. Eekelaar and M. Maclean, *Maintenance after Divorce* (Oxford: Oxford University Press, 1986) for a discussion of the development of the law of maintenance and financial claims.

[11] At common law a father had the right to the legal custody of his legitimate children, subject to limited exceptions: see *Re Agar-Ellis* (1883) 24 Ch.D 317. This common law principle was gradu-ally displaced during the late 19th and early 20th centuries by the principle that custody was to be resolved by reference to the 'welfare of the child' as the paramount consideration: see Guardianship of Infants Act 1925.

[12] For an analysis of the moralistic case-law on child custody, decided under the auspices of the 'welfare principle', see C. Smart, *The Ties that Bind: Law, Marriage and the Reproduction of Patriarchal Relations* (London: Routledge & Kegan Paul, 1984).

divorce and other relief, coupled with technical bars to relief. The analogies with classical contract law, and even tort and criminal law, were close. Discretionary powers addressing the substance of the relationship were anathema, just as judicial variation of a contract was anathema to the common lawyer.

Running through all of this was a coherent, albeit patriarchal, set of principles. The lack of reciprocity in the grounds of divorce available to men and women,[13] the limited and conditional availability of maintenance, and decision-making about children, all pointed to a legal edifice founded on patriarchal assumptions: the sexual double standard, the assumed economic dependence of women, and the idealizing of motherhood. The ecclesiastical origins of secular law had a continuing influence and reflected many centuries of principled development, expressed in such ideologies as the doctrine of unity of husband and wife, and of *consortium vitae* (the legal elements of a shared marital life, entitlement to which could, in some circumstances, be enforced). These doctrines had far-reaching consequences for the civil status of married couples, especially in relation to property ownership, contractual capacity, tortious liability, and the protection of the criminal law from physical harassment or abuse.[14]

Finally, proceedings took place in public and there were clear public policy goals about deterring misconduct through punishment, stigma, and public shaming.[15] The frequently humiliating and intrusive nature of divorce proceedings was one of the factors leading to demands for a change in the law.

In one sense, the formal era, with its emphasis on detailed and technical rules and procedures, appears more normatively closed and doctrinal than overtly regulatory. Yet, it could be argued that there was a coherent regulatory objective, namely, the deterrence of divorce by imposing strict legal and procedural requirements, by restricting the availability of effective legal relief to women, and by ensuring the public humiliation of divorcees.[16] Yet, by the 1960s the objective of supporting marriage and the family was seen to require a quite different approach.

The Functionalist Era

In the middle decades of the twentieth century changes were evident in the conception of marriage itself, and of the role of marriage and the family in the wider society. A growing ideological belief in personal individualism was

[13] Under the Matrimonial Causes Act 1857 a husband could divorce his wife for adultery alone (subject to the statutory bars to a decree), whereas a wife could divorce her husband only on proof of adultery coupled with another 'aggravating' offence, such as incest, bigamy, cruelty, or desertion. The grounds were equalized in 1923 and extended in 1937.

[14] Many of the consequences of these doctrines outlasted the end of the formal era. For example, a husband's common law immunity from prosecution for raping his wife was abolished only as recently as 1991: see *R v R* [1991] 4 All ER 481 (HL).

[15] It is instructive to read some old accounts (such as H. E. Fenn, *Thirty-Five Years in the Divorce Courts* (London: T. Werner Laurie, n.d.)) to remind oneself of the theatrical nature of divorce proceedings.

[16] C. Smart, 'Divorce in England 1950–2000: A Moral Tale?', in Katz *et al.* (eds.), *Cross-currents*.

taking place, catching up with earlier beliefs in economic and political individualism.[17] There was an increased faith in the power of social science to explain, predict, and control human behaviour. Legislation for the purpose of deliberately bringing about social change became an accepted part of government, with a consequent growth of an administrative state, and, later, a welfare state, with a broad range of utilitarian functions. At the same time, there was increased recognition that the concept of matrimonial fault drew the courts into issues that were either impossible or inappropriate to resolve judicially, or just irrelevant. If adjusting to the future was what mattered, the concept of fault hardly seemed to fit.[18]

Through a mix of case-law and statutory reform from the mid-1940s to the mid-1970s a new family law was put into place that emphasized the second pole of the dichotomies. The new laws, by largely eliminating concepts of fault, removed the basis for seeing family law as an apparatus for the enforcement of rights. Instead, the task of the legal system was to assist the parties to an optimal outcome, defined in terms of welfare and other broadly defined standards. A functionalist view of the law prevailed, according to which the tasks of the law were adjustive, supportive, and protective—that is, to assist couples and their children to adjust from one status to another, and to protect and support them in the process.[19] Similarly, the approach was substantive and pragmatic, rather than formal or principled, in that it was believed that a case-by-case treatment, subject to a broad-ranging judicial discretion, was the best way of fine-tuning outcomes to circumstances. This era entailed a more privatized model of decision-making in that the 'privacy' that was preserved by the functionalist era was one concerned to keep the matrimonial history out of the public eye, while preserving the central role of the legal process to determine the future consequences of the divorce itself. Thus, the point at which state intervention in matters of social policy was, arguably, at its peak marked the high-water mark of individualized, privatized decision-making—albeit aimed at achieving explicitly functionalist objectives. These objectives included the preservation of marriage as an institution, in turn thought to require the decent burial of individual marriages that were dead, so that the parties to it could then remarry. As Carol Smart has put it, 'The main purpose of the new divorce law. . . was to facilitate remarriage . . . [so as] to ease the redistribution of men, women, and children around units that were capable of legal recognition.'[20]

Looking back, family law seemed appropriate to the political times. Technocratic decision-making, implementing future-oriented utilitarian policies,

[17] See S. Parker, *Informal Marriage, Cohabitation and the Law, 1750–1989* (London: Macmillan, 1990).

[18] For a brief account of the background to the Divorce Reform Act 1969, see C. Gibson, *Dissolving Wedlock* (London: Routledge, 1994), ch. 7; and L. Stone, *Road to Divorce: England 1530–1987* (Oxford: Oxford University Press, 1990), 401.

[19] See e.g. J. Eekelaar, *Family Law and Social Policy* (London: Weidenfeld & Nicolson, 1978) for this view.

[20] C. Smart, 'Regulating Families or Legitimating Patriarchy? Family Law in Britain', *International Journal of the Sociology of Law*, 10 (1982), 129 at 141.

promised to make the world a better place. There was a form of egalitarianism at work, but it was of the 'equal but different' kind. Men and women had their functions and roles in 'the family'. The family had its functions in society. Given continued economic growth and high-quality administration by governments, all would be well.

The Complex Era

Since the late 1980s there has been a sense that the functionalist model is not working. Firstly, there has been a continued anxiety at the seemingly inexorable rise in the rate of divorce and at the levels of family instability this seems to indicate. The blame for this is often laid at the door of no-fault divorce, which is said to make divorce too easy and to set up incentives to divorcing behaviour. At any rate, there is now scepticism surrounding the claim that no-fault divorce is the answer to family instability.

Secondly, governments keen to reduce state expenditure have been alarmed at the inexorable rise in the costs to government of marriage and relationship breakdown. These arise from state welfare payments made to single parents, and from the cost of providing a legal system and associated legal services through legal aid budgets. Governments have sought to contain those costs, by defining and enforcing post-separation child support obligations more forcefully and by seeking alternatives to conventional legal processes for resolving family disputes.

Thirdly, there is a growing sense that neither women nor men have done well out of no-fault divorce. For women, it is argued that they suffer financially from marriage and divorce, and that the heavily discretionary regime of financial adjustment accompanying no-fault divorce is inadequate to the task of protecting women's economic investments in marriage.[21] For men, the increasing emphasis on parental obligations of financial support has refocused attention on post-separation parenting, and, in particular, on the perceived inequalities of custody and access arrangements.

Fourthly, there has been a growing willingness to invoke rights arguments in debates about family law. This is evident in constitutional discussion in the United States and is an increasingly common feature of other jurisdictions, driven in part by new international declarations of rights (such as the UN Convention on the Rights of the Child) or by new bill of rights instruments (such as the Human Rights Act 1998 in the UK). At any rate, the discretionary techniques of the functionalist model have come under sustained scrutiny from this constitutional and rights-based perspective. This has often been allied with a suspicion of technocratic elites and a more or less overt policy of controlling the discretion available to judges.[22]

---

[21] I. M. Ellman, 'The Theory of Alimony', *California Law Review*, 77 (1989), 1; G. Sheehan, 'Financial Aspects of the Divorce Transition in Australia: Recent Empirical Findings', *International Journal of Law, Policy and the Family*, 16 (2002), 95.

[22] See J. Dewar, 'Reducing Discretion in Family Law', *Australian Journal of Family Law*, 11 (1997), 309.

Finally, the privileged position of marriage (and divorce) in the functionalist model is called into question by the growing diversity of family forms. Marriage is no longer the only arena in which family life is played out and legislative techniques need to be more responsive to the ways of life that it is sought to regulate. Thus, non-marital relations become more visible in law, as well as relationships centred on parenting—in particular, parenting across households post-separation, and step-parenting.

So how does all of this play out in terms of the second transformation of family law in the late twentieth century, from a functionalist to complex era? We can identify a number of trends and patterns flowing from the factors just described which, taken together, amount to at least a significant revision, or, perhaps, a complete rejection, of the features of the functionalist no-fault model just described. Yet, the changes described below do not always sit easily together—indeed, may be directly contradictory. This is why the term 'complexity' is used to characterize the era in which we now find ourselves.

Firstly, marriage has been displaced as the central concept linking law to families. Instead, legislation increasingly 'recognizes' other relationships, such as unmarried cohabitation, or attaches greater significance to existing ones, such as parenthood. Some jurisdictions have gone further and have created new forms of marriage or legal partnership to accommodate those who cannot enter marriage in its conventional sense. Secondly, there has been a retreat from the discretionary legislation that was a centrepiece of the functionalist model. Increasingly, family law legislation is drafted in more specific, rule-like, terms. For example, child support legislation, whether drafted as judicial guidelines or as legislation creating a separate agency charged with assessment and enforcement of child support, is drafted in terms of fixed entitlements, rather than discretionary awards. Rules on property adjustment are similarly debated increasingly in terms of clearer rules, rather than broad discretions;[23] while legislation on post-separation parenting often includes statements of principles of equality between parents, or of rights of children, in mandatory, rather than discretionary, terms.

The explanation for this lies in a number of factors: governmental concern to control the costs of family breakdown to the welfare state and the legal system; an increased tendency to conceive of parties in family law disputes as bearers of rights, rather than as objects of welfarist interventions; and a perceived need to offer a clearer set of principles for law in this area, so that parties are more easily able to arrive at their own agreements, rather than having to litigate. This is not to suggest that family law has become a seamless code of rules—rather, that new techniques are steadily being superimposed on old. In any case, the question of which technique is best, and of the costs and benefits of each, is yet to be settled. Indeed, it has been suggested that 'the continuing search for the third way between discretion and rules is a key feature of modern family law'.[24]

---

[23] G. G. Blumberg, 'The Financial Incidents of Family Dissolution', in Katz *et al.* (eds.), *Crosscurrents.*

[24] G. Douglas, *An Introduction to Family Law* (Oxford: Oxford University Press, 2001).

Thirdly, there is a greater emphasis on family autonomy in decision-making, through promotion of binding prenuptial agreements, and non-judicial forms of dispute resolution for those who have no ready-made agreements to fall back on. Once again, this trend is informed by a wish to remove family disputes from costly judicial fora as far as possible, while at the same time drawing on the language of individual empowerment, responsibility, and autonomy as self-sufficient justifications for parties to agree without court or professional involvement. Indeed, it seems that the role of law itself, at any rate of lawyers, is sometimes in question, even though research relating to lawyers' work in family law generally paints a positive picture.[25]

A final shift of emphasis has been in the area of post-divorce parenting. Under the functionalist model, the emphasis was on assisting parties to move on from one relationship, and household, to the next. The language was that of the clean break, of 'looking to the future'. In this context, little prominence was given to the issue of how ongoing relationships were to be maintained or managed between children and their non-resident parent. That issue has now moved to centre stage, with policy-makers increasingly concerned to respond to demands from non-resident parents, often framed in terms of fathers' rights, for greater participation and involvement in the lives of children. Indeed, much attention is now focused on how best to manage post-separation relationships centred on children, including (and, perhaps, especially) those relationships characterized by high conflict.

The reasons for this change of emphasis are complex, and include a revival of fatherhood claims in law, possibly linked to enhanced child support obligations that usually fall on men;[26] psychological evidence pointing towards the harm caused by the loss of relationships with fathers, which has, in turn, fuelled official concerns with preserving contact or access arrangements;[27] and a recognition that family instability and fluidity is a permanent feature of the landscape and has to be managed, rather than ignored—in short, that a complex of parent–child relations, often within and between households, has to be allowed for and, indeed, encouraged.

The Doctrinal–Regulatory Mix

From this brief survey of over 150 years of legislative history and policy, it should be apparent that family law has sought to provide a normative framework within which individual disputes can be resolved, while simultaneously seeking to achieve, more or less consciously, some larger-scale regulatory purposes. The precise configuration of those purposes has shifted, along with assumptions made

[25] M. Maclean, J. Eekelaar, and S. Beinart, *Family Lawyers: The Divorce Work of Solicitors* (Oxford: Hart, 2000); R. Hunter, *Legal Services in Family Law* (Sydney: Law Foundation of NSW, 2000).

[26] R. Collier, *Masculinity, Law and the Family* (London: Routledge, 1995).

[27] C. Smart, B. Neale, and A. Wade, *The Changing Experience of Childhood: Families and Divorce* (London: Polity Press, 2001), ch. 2, for a summary.

about the phenomenon being regulated, and the techniques employed to achieve them. As a result, it is difficult to identify a stable or coherent normative system enduring through these successive phases. The law of divorce, for example, was almost completely reinvented in the 1970s, with very little of the previous fault-based rules and doctrine surviving in any form. This brings us to the question of whether the responsiveness of family law to its environment has affected either its effectiveness or its coherence; and whether there are, nevertheless, normative limits to that responsiveness.

Effectiveness, Responsiveness, and Coherence

Effectiveness

The question of effectiveness immediately begs the question of what family law's purposes are. These are sometimes described on a grand scale: it is not uncommon, for example, to hear the introduction of no-fault divorce being blamed for the increase in single-parent families, juvenile delinquency, and male suicide. This line of argument often concludes in calls for the reintroduction of fault as the conceptual basis of the law[28] or ensuring a greater role for fathers after separation. On this view, the function of law is no less than that of sustaining social cohesion around family groups and marital ties. However, for the most part, there is now generalized scepticism about the social objectives that can effectively be pursued through law. So, attempts made previously to ascribe even modest functions or purposes to family law, such as Eekelaar's triptych of adjustment, support, and protection,[29] are no longer taken very seriously.

There are three reasons for this. The first is that there has been a loss of faith in our capacity to know in advance what the effects of particular legislative or policy interventions are likely to be.[30] Studies that have been conducted of the impact of new family law legislation often reveal more about unintended consequences flowing from change than about intended objectives being achieved. For example, recent Australian research suggests that new legislation concerning post-separation parenting, which was intended to reduce levels of parental conflict by placing more emphasis on the rights and safety of children, has, in fact, led in some cases to heightened levels of conflict between parents, and to children being placed in more dangerous situations than previously.[31] These studies often paint a picture of an exceedingly complex system of actors and

---

[28] L. Wardle, 'Divorce Reform at the Turn of the Millennium: Certainties and Possibilities', *Family Law Quarterly*, 33 (1999), 783. [29] Eekelaar, *Family Law and Social Policy*.
[30] K. O'Donovan, *Family Law Matters* (London: Pluto Press, 1997).
[31] H. Rhoades, R. Graycar, and M. Harrison, *The Family Law Reform Act 1995: The First Three Years* (Sydney: University of Sydney/Family Court of Australia, 2000); J. Dewar and S. Parker, 'The Impact of the New Part VII FLA 1975', *Australian Journal of Family* Law, 13 (1999), 99. It has also been argued that in these respects the legislation effectively achieved the (undisclosed) objectives of its proponents.

institutions, in which the correlation between inputs and outputs is so heavily mediated by factors such as professional practice and the policies and practices of court and legal aid administrators, that any linear relationship between legal change and changes in outcome disappears.

Allied to this, has been a theoretically derived scepticism about the capacity of law to achieve welfare outcomes of any sort. Drawing on an autopoietic perspective, Michael King and others have argued that, as a system, law encodes or interprets its environment in its own terms.[32] In the case of law, that interpretative code is a simple binary one of legal–illegal. As a consequence of this inability of law to reconstruct information from other disciplines except in these oversimplified terms, law distorts the messages, or inputs, from other disciplines (such as child psychology); and goes off in pursuit of questions (such as fault, causation, or blame) that have little bearing on what family members, and especially children, 'really' need. This is an important argument, especially in the context of a legal system that commits itself to promoting the child's welfare or best interests as its paramount concern. If a child's needs are ultimately unknowable by law, then the objective of promoting them through law is, arguably, pointless.

Secondly, the idea that a privileged set of official purposes can or should be ascribed to the law, or provide a benchmark against which it can be measured, has come under sustained scrutiny from critical scholars working in what I have called the 'constructionist' school of thought.[33] This body of thought, which draws heavily on feminism, postmodernism, and Foucauldian conceptions of power, is concerned with the way in which law, together with other regulatory or normalizing discourses, plays a part in constructing the social reality and lived experience of the family. Analysing law in this way allows the further argument to be made that the family so constructed is limited and exclusionary, and privileges some forms of relationship (heterosexual ones, for example) at the expense of others.[34] There is a sense in which this body of scholarship has regulatory concerns as its focus, since it suggests that normalizing discourses of law have some sort of empirical effect on behaviour (although these are rarely investigated by empirical means); yet it has problematized the question of effectiveness by putting in doubt our capacity to identify in advance what the regulatory effects of law are likely to be, and by suggesting that the sources of power are multiple and, therefore, beyond the control of any single agent.

Thirdly, a strong political tendency has been to downplay the role of law in family law, to see the involvement of law and lawyers as uniformly bad. Although this has been driven in part by a belief that lawyers are expensive, and

---

[32] See M. King and C. Piper, *How the Law Thinks about Children*, 2nd edn. (Aldershot: Arena, 1995), 136; M. King and J. Trowell, *Children's Welfare and the Law: The Limits of Legal Intervention* (London: Sage, 1992).   [33] Dewar, 'The Normal Chaos of Family Law'.

[34] Collier, *Masculinity, Law and the Family*; O'Donovan, *Family Law Matters*; A. Diduck, 'A Family by Any Other Name, or, Starbucks™ comes to England', *Journal of Law and Society*, 28 (2001), 290.

that non-adversarial alternatives are cheaper, there is also a widespread suspicion of the motivations of lawyers and their willingness to uphold professional values over financial self-interest. As a result, it is only rarely that serious thought is given to the proper role of law and legal processes in family law. The Australian Family Law Pathways Advisory Group's report *Out of the Maze* is a rare example of sustained attention being applied to this.[35]

There has thus been a curious coming-together of official policy and much critical and empirical thinking in family law that has made the question of effectiveness a difficult one to address. Both have led to suspicion of the capacity of law to achieve its officially set objectives or, more generally, to contribute anything positive to family life, or to family adjustment, at all. This means that there have been few attempts to understand this complexity, to seek to discern patterns in it; and almost no attempt to defend the role of lawyers or the legal system. Yet I want to argue that if we draw the tasks of law more modestly, it should be possible to engage in research that will enhance effectiveness, and to articulate more clearly what law and lawyers are good for, and what not.

I have argued elsewhere[36] that family law's tasks could be described as the provision of a normative framework that can express and promote agreement about the terms of family life within the community and between individuals.[37] We need to recall that family law is an outlier in terms of people's willingness to frame their problem as one requiring a legal solution;[38] yet, at the same time, most of those who progress to a legal outcome do so with relatively low levels of involvement by the legal system. In short, the role of family law could be characterized as 'wide-reach, low-intensity' with respect to family law disputes. Family law, in other words, speaks to a wide range of individuals, not just those in a formal court setting or lawyer's office. Research conducted for the Family Law Pathways Advisory Group suggested that levels of client satisfaction with the family law system were affected by (*a*) the availability, early in the process, of clear and accessible information concerning procedures and 'entitlements', and (*b*) the timeliness of dispute resolution, level of conflict between parties, degree of coordination in service delivery, and access to 'clear and honest' advice.[39] This suggests that well-drafted laws, capable of being understood and self-applied by individuals in a range of settings, can assist parties to arrive at their own agreements by setting out clear expectations, obligations, entitlements, principles, etc.

This raises the question of whether it is possible, by adjusting the normative framework of family law, to enhance the capacity of parties to reach agreement.

---

[35] Family Law Pathways Advisory Group, *Out of the Maze: Pathways to the Future for Families Experiencing Separation* (Canberra: Commonwealth Attorney-General's Department, 2001).

[36] J. Dewar, 'Is Law Good for Families?', Keynote Address, Family Centre Annual Conference, Brisbane, Feb. 2002.

[37] This part of the argument, not directly relevant here, draws on Sunstein's concept of the 'incompletely theorized agreement'. [38] Genn, *Paths to Justice.*

[39] B. Fehlberg, G. Sheehan, and F. Kelly, *Family Law Pathways and Processes: Case Studies* (Melbourne: Australian Institute of Family Studies, 2000).

The 'norm-form' project set out to test this hypothesis, by isolating one variable in the process of negotiations: the form of the relevant legal norms applicable to the parties' problems. The hypothesis being tested was that wide-ranging discretions, commonly encountered in family law, make it harder for parties to settle disputes than if the relevant norms were couched in a more rule-like form. The findings suggest that there is no evidence that norm-form plays a significant role in lawyers' negotiating behaviour; power, personality, and attitudes to risk are more significant factors, and conventions matter more than formally expressed rules. Instead, legislators and drafters should emphasize clarity and purpose of legislation to maximize compliance and correct interpretation: as the conclusions of the study put it, 'there is a case for assisting parties to bargain in the *light* of the law rather than its shadow'. The factors most conducive to settlement were found to be 'comprehensibility to the lay person and predictability of result to the lawyer'. This is not necessarily correlated with norm-form as such, although it may be strategically more effective to start at the rule end of the spectrum.[40]

Responsiveness

The issue of responsiveness can be addressed at two levels: the normative and the institutional. In both cases, it will be argued that family law exhibits a high level of responsiveness to changing patterns of family life, and a high level of incorporation of formal and informal dispute resolution mechanisms. It would be surprising if it were otherwise—family law cannot ignore the realities of family life and structures, just as a 'wide-range, low-intensity' system cannot fail to recognize a variety of dispute settlement fora. Yet, it could still be argued that some groups remain marginalized or excluded, either from the legal family itself, or within dispute settlement processes. The latter is dealt with in more detail in the next section, entitled 'Coherence', which looks at the fragmentation of the family law 'system' and its consequences.

Perhaps the largest conceptual shift to take place in family law over the last 150 years has been the demise of marriage as the conceptual centrepiece, linking legal obligations to family members.[41] In its place, increased significance has been attached to unmarried cohabitation and, more importantly, to parenthood. In one sense, this is an inevitable response to the decline in marriage as a social practice, which has required other concepts to be pressed into service; but it also reflects changed perceptions of the relative importance of parental

---

[40] M. Harvey, M. Karras, S. Parker, J. Dewar, T. Wright, and S. Bottomley, *Negotiating by the Light of the Law*, Working Paper (Melbourne: Law Faculty, Monash University, 2002). See also M. Garrison, 'How Do Judges Decide Divorce Cases: An Empirical Analysis of Discretionary Decision-Making', *North Carolina Law Review*, 74 (1996), 401; M. Garrison, 'The Economic Consequences of Divorce: Would Adoption of the ALI Principles Improve Current Outcomes?', *Duke Journal of Gender Law and Policy*, 8 (2001), 119.

[41] See J. Dewar, 'Family Law and its Discontents', *International Journal of Law, Policy and the Family*, 14 (2000), 59.

versus children's rights. The more the latter have come to predominate, the more marriage has faded into the background. The best example of this is the child support legislation, which imposes significant financial obligations on individuals, and does so without invoking the concept of marriage. Indeed, it could be argued that the greatest challenge facing family law and policy is to manage the post-separation.

Yet, there are limits to the extent to which individuals or relationships are recognized for legal purposes. For example, transgender people have only recently been recognized as able to marry as a member of their 'new' gender,[42] while marriage itself remains firmly heterosexual. Same-sex couples are often prevented from accessing fertility services. To that extent, legal provisions may reflect a majority view of what relationships are legitimately recognized as marital, or parental, ones. Less obviously, there are ways in which Western kinship structures are invisibly embedded in the legal relationships of parent and child. Thus, legislation assumes that children have only two parents, usually identified by a genetic link; yet when applied to indigenous cultures, this assumption quickly proves inadequate to capture the complexities of kinship practices.

In other areas, family law is cognitively open to other disciplines. For example, actuarial and accounting knowledge is increasingly central to settling property disputes, especially now that superannuation is available for distribution. Child welfare expertise is systematically made available in disputes involving children— although, as we have seen, there is some scepticism as to the legal system's ability to manage that information without distorting it.

Coherence

In this section I want to address the question of coherence by asking, What are the consequences of a 'wide-reach, low-intensity' legal system, characterized by high levels of normative and institutional responsiveness, for conventional understandings of legality and normative hierarchy?[43] I will suggest that the system has become highly fragmented, and that this has led to the same law being given different interpretations, or different tactical weight, at different points within it. This, in turn, challenges assumptions we make about the meaning of legal norms, and the sources of those meanings; and about the capacity of a legal system to ensure fair treatment for those who pass through it. This discussion suggests that there are normative limits to a system's responsiveness, or a point at which our ability to say that there is a coherent system in place at all is in doubt. However, I will conclude by suggesting ways in which this problem of coherence can be addressed through a better understanding of how different normative types can assist individuals, in whatever setting they find themselves, to self-apply legal norms—in short, how coherence may be reinstituted at a normative level.

[42] *In re Kevin (Validity of Marriage of Transsexual)* [2001] FamCa 1074.
[43] This section is based on Dewar, 'Family Law and its Discontents'.

I begin by describing the causes and effects of this fragmentation of the system. The examples in this section are drawn from Australia, but there is no reason to think that similar examples could not also be found in most Western legal systems.

Private Ordering

Australian family law, both in policy and in practice, places heavy emphasis on encouraging parties to settle their own differences without going to court. There are a number of ways in which parties can be assisted to do this, including referral to mediation or counselling, or through negotiations between lawyers. The Family Court also has its own procedures for encouraging parties to settle. The success of these various methods is evident in the fact that 95 per cent of matters settle without requiring a full trial in front of a judge.[44] In these cases, the parties will usually formalize their agreement in a court order, which is then approved by the court as a consent order. Another method of private ordering that will shortly be available is for parties to make binding prenuptial agreements that would oust the jurisdiction of the court altogether.

How does this relate to the question of coherence? The answer lies in the fact that private ordering of disputes takes place in a growing range of arenas, including solicitors' offices, legal aid conferences, counselling, and mediation inside and outside the Family Court, as well as at formal stages on the Family Court's case management pathway. Yet, the meaning attached to legal provisions may vary according to the arena in which they are being invoked. The meanings given to law in one arena may be determined in ways that may be quite autonomous from meanings that would be given in other parts of the system.[45] For example, empirical research suggests that negotiations between lawyers may take place on the basis of assumptions about the meaning of legal provisions that may bear only a tenuous relationship to 'official' interpretations of legal provisions (for example, by judges);[46] and that these inter-lawyer negotiations may form an independent source of conventions and assumptions about legal interpretation that are just as powerful in practice as those that come from 'above'.[47] Similarly, counsellors or mediators may seek to place

---

[44] Family Court of Australia, *Response of the Family Court of Australia to the Attorney-General's Department Paper on Primary Dispute Resolution Services in Family Law* (Canberra: Family Court of Australia, 1997), p. xvii.

[45] J. Wade, 'Forever Bargaining in the Shadow of the Law: Who Sells Solid Shadows? (Who Advises What, How and When?)', *Australian Journal of Family Law*, 12 (1998), 256.

[46] For a striking example of this, see J. Dewar and S. Parker (with D. Cooper and B. Tynan), *Parenting, Planning and Partnership: A Study of the Impact of the Family Law Reform Act 1995* (Nathan: Griffith University, 1999) and the discussion of the 'reverse effect' of the Full Court decision in *B and B: Family Law Reform Act 1995* (1997) 21 Family Law Reports 676 (discussed above). Professional understandings of legal meaning, especially when translated into concrete strategies, may be at odds with judicial interpretation. For another example of the gap that might exist between 'official' divorce law and professional culture, see C. Archbold, P. McKee, and C. White, 'Divorce Law and Divorce Culture: The Case of Northern Ireland', *Child and Family Law Quarterly*, 10 (1998), 377.

[47] 'Negotiation between solicitors is a "semi-autonomous" process which takes place in the shadows of, and itself casts shadows on, other such processes': R. Ingleby, *Solicitors and Divorce*

interpretations on legal provisions that either suit their own professional frame of reference (e.g. as trained social workers or psychologists) or serve their own objectives in the counselling or mediation process.[48] In other words, the forum in large part determines the meaning of legal rules—which will, in turn, affect the type of bargaining positions they confer. The heavy emphasis on alternative, or 'primary', dispute resolution in family law is likely to continue, and so increase the diversity of interpretive fora.[49]

Legal Aid

Another threat to coherence, and one that is related to the immediately preceding discussion, relates to the impact of legal aid policies on the operation of the family law system. Legal aid is of crucial significance in family law: it is the largest single head of government expenditure on legal aid in Australia, and many family law litigants are able to access the system only with its assistance. The overall shape of legal aid policy is, therefore, crucial in determining the shape and functioning of the family law system.

For present purposes, we need only note that if someone is dependent on legal aid, it is increasingly likely that they will be in a different strategic position from a privately funded litigant. Depending on local legal aid policies, they will either find that their grants of aid are 'capped' at a certain level, so that once that level has been reached all forms of aid will be withdrawn; or they will find that legal aid is not available at all for certain aspects of proceedings; or they will find that they will be eligible only for limited forms of assistance, such as legal aid conferencing (a form of mediation).[50] The net result of this is that legally aided and privately funded litigants are not equal in their abilities to access the core of the family law system. So, what we have here is fragmentation, not of interpretations, but of an individual's ability to access the core of the system (the court) for authoritative determinations of the parties' rights and entitlements. This ability is increasingly unevenly spread, so to the extent that being able to get to court is necessary to make good the bargaining positions conferred by law, those bargaining positions are themselves unevenly spread.

Entry Points

A third threat to coherence relates to the way in which litigants enter the family law system in the first place. Research has shown that this can have a significant

(Oxford: Clarendon Press, 1992), 155; see also M. Melli, H. Erlanger, and E. Chambliss, 'The Process of Negotiation: An Exploratory Investigation in the Context of No-Fault Divorce', *Rutgers Law Review*, 40 (1988), 1133.

[48] C. Piper, *The Responsible Parent: A Study in Divorce Mediation* (New York: Harvester Wheatsheaf, 1995).

[49] A good example of this is the introduction of arbitration.

[50] J. Dewar, J. Giddings, and S. Parker, 'The Impact of Legal Aid Changes on the Practice of Family Law', *Australian Journal of Family Law*, 13 (1999), 33.

effect on the way in which matters are subsequently resolved.[51] To begin with, the entry point may determine whether a party regards their case as raising an issue that can or should be resolved by legal means. If the first point of contact is with a lawyer, then there is a higher likelihood that a legal solution will be sought, and that the nature of that legal solution will be different, than cases in which the first point of contact is with someone other than a lawyer. Of course, a party's choice of first contact may itself reflect their own predispositions as to how they want their matter resolved: there is evidence, for example, that while some parties want their lawyers to take an aggressive, partisan approach, others want their lawyers to be more conciliatory in style, or may not want a lawyer at all, and their choice of first contact will reflect those predispositions.[52] Initial entry point is not, therefore, an independent variable; but once that choice is made, it has observable consequences. This is particularly so where the litigant is unrepresented (as many in the Family Court now are[53]). In such cases, the extent to which a litigant operates within the shadow of the law *at all* is likely to vary from person to person. Again, the shadow(s) cast by law will not be the same for everyone.

Implications?

So, what are the consequences of these different threats to the coherence of the system? At a theoretical level, one consequence is that the traditional 'top-down' model of law, in which legislators and judges have hierarchical superiority in the production of authoritative legal meaning over all other parts of the system, may have to be reconsidered. Instead, there are multiple sites of legal interpretation, each operating side by side and interacting with each other in a variety of ways. Instead of a single shadow cast by law, there are many shadows, with no single shadow covering the whole system. This could be thought of as a *horizontal* rather than *hierarchical* view of the system.[54] This suggests a need for some sort of meta-regulation of these different regulating systems, a point to which I will return.

   Does any of this matter in a practical way? It will be suggested that it does, and that it is possible to take a positive or negative view of how and why. On

---

[51] Dewar and Parker (with Cooper and Tynan), *Parenting, Planning and Partnership*; H. Jacob, 'The Elusive Shadow of the Law', *Law and Society Review*, 26 (1992), 565. Jacob argues that the role of law in divorce negotiations is contingent on a range of variables, such as the client's initial 'framing' of their problem as one that does or does not require a legal resolution.

[52] G. Davis, *Partisans and Mediators* (Oxford: Clarendon Press, 1988).

[53] B. Smith, *1998 Study of the Effects of Legal Aid Cuts on the Family Court of Australia and its Litigants*, Research Report No. 19 (Canberra: Family Court of Australia, 1999), 20; J. Dewar, B. Smith, and C. Banks, *Litigants in Person in the Family Court of Australia*, Research Report (Canberra: Family Court of Australia, 2000); R. Hunter, A. Genovese, A. Curzanowski, and C. Morris, *The Changing Face of Litigation: Unrepresented Litigants in the Family Court of Australia* (Sydney: Law and Justice Foundation of New South Wales, 2002).

[54] For further elaboration of the notion of 'horizontalization', see Dewar and Parker (with Cooper and Tynan), *Parenting, Planning and Partnership*; and see Murphy, *The Oldest Social Science*; Goodrich, 'Social Science and the Displacement of Law'. See D. Luban, *Lawyers and Justice: An Ethical Study* (Princeton: Princeton University Press, 1988), chs. 11 and 12.

a positive view, it could be argued that what I have referred to here as fragmentation is, in fact, an example of how the law is facilitating private choice, and of being responsive to individual difference. It is consistent with the view that private law in general should develop so as to permit 'many autonomies', rather than operating in a traditional 'top-down' way, by imposing one set of values and ideas on everyone.

Yet, on a negative view, it could be said to mark the decline of an important aspect of legalism, namely, the idea that all are equal before the law. Instead, the abandonment of litigants to their 'many autonomies' is a form of the 'reprivatization' of family law, in which the state withdraws from guaranteeing the fairness of outcomes when judged against an objective benchmark and assumes instead that parties are equally capable of defining and defending their own view of what is fair. As such, it overlooks inequalities in bargaining power and entrenches those inequalities in legal policy. The increased emphasis on private ordering and the steady withdrawal of legal aid for court proceedings may simply alter the terms of bargaining in favour of the more powerful—who are often men rather than women.

There is a sense in which the positive and negative views of fragmentation merely give expression to a more deeply seated tension in our modern understandings of legality. On the one hand, there is a conventional understanding of what it means to live in a liberal democracy under the rule of law, in which equality before the law, and equality of access to law, are cornerstones of conceptions of citizenship and the bedrocks on which the legitimacy of our system of government is based. On this view, courts and related institutions are crucial arenas of social integration, and law a central framework for making sense of our social and institutional life.[55] On the other hand, there is the need to respond to and accommodate individual difference, and to guard against the danger that conventional liberal legalism does not become a byword for majoritarianism, or the imposition of the values of the many on the many 'others'. On this view, law is merely instrumental, a way of facilitating exchange and setting the tone or background noise for private exchanges.[56]

Applying a regulatory lens to this dilemma offers us a new language in which to resolve it. Employing that language, the problem being posed is that of the normative limits to responsiveness, and the potential for the disintegration of a highly responsive system and the values that support it. Is there a way in which we can preserve coherence and responsiveness simultaneously? I would suggest that there is, by exploring further the possibilities of more clearly expressed norms that individuals can self-apply to their own disputes. As we have seen, one of the consequences of a 'wide-range, low-intensity' legal system is that legal norms need to be applied by a range of actors in a range of settings. Legal

[55] C. Greenhouse, 'Nature is to Culture as Praying is to Suing: Legal Pluralism in an American Suburb', *Journal of Legal Pluralism*, 20 (1982), 17.

[56] Cf. G. Teubner, 'After Privatisation? The Many Autonomies of Private Law', in M. Freeman (ed.), *Legal Theory at the End of the Millennium* (Oxford: Oxford University Press, 1998).

norms, therefore, have to speak to a variety of audiences, only some of whom have a legal training. Drawing on the insights of the norm-form project, and of the Australian Family Law *Pathways* research, I would argue that more could be done to remove the context-dependent variability in the meanings ascribed to legal norms by making them clearer as to intent and likely outcomes. In short, we need to explore whether an institutionally fragmented system can be reconstituted at the normative level, to achieve a form of meta-regulation of the different subsystems at work.

Conclusion

This chapter began by suggesting that family law consists of a number of hybrids: of normative closure and openness, of doctrinal and regulatory components, and of dispute settlement and behaviour-steering impulses. I have suggested that the high level of responsiveness displayed by family law—to its political and economic environment, as well as to the varying needs of individuals—poses a potential threat to its coherence. I have also explored the difficulties associated with measuring effectiveness, in the light of widespread disagreement about what the purposes of the law are, and scepticism about the ability of law to achieve intentional effects.

I have also argued that the language of regulation, and of regulation by a meta-system of different internal subsystems, may prove to be a fruitful way forward. In practical terms, that means thinking harder about how the normative messages are expressed and communicated in family law systems. Family law is an attempt to create a normative framework for settling private disputes, and in this respect, I suggest, there is much still to learn about how its effectiveness can be enhanced. The possibility that there is, indeed, a connection between the three horns of the regulatory trilemma certainly deserves further investigation.

5

Regulating Work

RICHARD JOHNSTONE and RICHARD MITCHELL*

INTRODUCTION

The purpose of this chapter is to examine the regulation of 'work': principally the circumstances in which labour is engaged and the conditions attaching to the work relationships which are consequently formed and carried on. Fundamentally, this is the subject area labelled 'labour law' in modern-day legal, academic, and professional discourse. Curiously, while this field is, obviously, an area ripe for examination within the general area of 'regulatory analysis',[1] with the exception of occupational health and safety, and manpower planning, labour seems to have been largely ignored in the regulatory literature.[2] This chapter, thus, presents us with an opportunity for opening an exploratory discussion about how some issues in the regulatory literature impact upon this field.

One of the central arguments in this chapter is that instrumental regulation in the field of labour law is not a relatively modern phenomenon.[3] Rather, our reading of the historical literature pertaining to labour under earlier economic and social conditions shows that the instrumental regulation of the labour market by the state and its courts has been the dominant form of law in this field for centuries. Thus, while the private law of obligations and of wrongs (contract and tort) has had a role to play in regulating work, to conceive of this role as being fundamentally invaded or overturned by a twentieth-century 'regulatory' state is to misrepresent the historical position. Consequently, throughout we have largely adopted a historical narrative, with a view to establishing the longevity of state instrumental regulation in labour matters and the relative lack of relevance, in any substantial regulatory or dispute settlement sense, of the doctrine of contract seen as private law. In the course of this narrative we look at labour law 'though a regulatory lens', address some issues of 'collision'

---

* The authors thank their colleague Harry Glasbeek for helpful comments on an earlier version of this chapter.

[1] For example, labour law was singled out as one of the early culprits in the 'over-regulation' of social fields: see S. Simitis, 'Juridification of Industrial Relations', *Comparative Labor Law Journal*, 7 (1986), 93.

[2] See II. Collins, Book Review, *Comparative Labor Law and Policy Journal*, 20 (1999), 523; but see G. Teubner (ed.), *Juridification of Social Spheres: A Comparative Analysis in the Areas of Labor, Corporate, Antitrust and Social Welfare Law* (Berlin: Walter de Gruyter, 1987).

[3] Cf. 'Tax administrations aside, nearly all of the important regulatory agencies emerged in the nineteenth and twentieth centuries': C. Parker and J. Braithwaite, 'Regulation', in P. Cane and M. Tushnet (eds.), *The Oxford Handbook of Legal Studies* (New York: Oxford University Press, 2003), 119.

between instrumental public regulation and private law doctrine, and examine the contemporary drift from state-imposed standards to 'self-regulation' which labour law shares in common with other regulatory fields. We argue that labour law has always been concerned with the regulation of the labour market, with a view to accomplishing the social goals of production and distribution, accompanied by a secondary 'protective' purpose which has achieved greater prominence from the beginning of the twentieth century onwards.

In the context of the historical narrative that we present, our argument observes the interaction of custom, common law, statute, and state administration in the regulation of work over many centuries. However, the fact that continued instrumental state regulation of labour since the thirteenth century has left little scope for the free operation of contract doctrine in relation to the purchase and sale of labour, has also meant that major 'collisions' (which we take to mean the recasting of one form of regulation in light of pressure from the other) between the purposes of 'regulatory law' and 'private law' in this field have been rare. In short, our view is that common law doctrine and state instrumental regulation present two different outlooks upon the employment relationship, and while there is frequent incidental legal interaction between these perspectives, they have remained largely separate regimes in Britain and Australia.

The major consequence of this has been that the key instrumental regulatory regimes established by the state in Britain and Australia have, on the whole, scarcely reshaped the common law of employment. This is particularly surprising in the Australian case, at least. Here judges and arbitrators in courts and statutorily created tribunals under the Australian compulsory arbitration system have been major figures in regulation, setting standards of conduct for fair and equitable employment conditions, and labour market arrangements, widely throughout industry.[4] Yet, these obviously powerful regulatory bureaucrats appear to have had little impact upon the deliberations of common law courts on employment matters.

That said, of course, it is also necessary to take into account two important points of qualification. Firstly, modern state instrumental regulation was constructed upon an emerging idea that employment was inherently contractual, although, as we shall see, it was largely the instrumental state device of regulation in the twentieth century which gave the contract of employment its shape as we know it today. As a result, the common law was undoubtedly important, in so far as it legitimized certain assumptions about the employment relationship, which are common both to the common law notion itself and also to statutory regulation (for example, matters concerning consensual agreement, managerial prerogative, and control) and, indeed, to the very commodification of labour. Thus, we find, to take the Australian case in particular, tribunals which were invested with the statutory authority to determine employment

---

[4] The classical account is given in M. Perlman, *Judges in Industry: A Study of Labour Arbitration in Australia* (Melbourne: Melbourne University Press, 1954).

rights and conditions on the basis of 'good conscience' and 'equity' nevertheless subjugated these powers to the common law understanding of the managerial rights of the employer to control and dismiss employees more or less at will.[5] Secondly, while there are recent examples of resistance to influence between the common law and statutory regimes, there are also reasons for arguing, as we do later in this chapter, that there are some indications of a contrary trend in the impact of instrumental regulatory design upon the common law of the contract of employment.

We are conscious, however, that these are only casually observed examples of the interface between statutory regulation and common law, and that more work needs to be done on the major issues arising from the treatment of private law as a source of public regulation in labour law.[6]

FOUR ERAS OF LABOUR REGULATION

Regulating Work in the Pre-modern Regulatory State

The regulation of labour in England, including the obligation to serve and to be paid, precedes modern labour law by many centuries. Going back into the thirteenth century, at least, even before the first recognized statutory intervention, labour was regulated through social ordering, custom, town, and guild by-laws, and by manorial courts. Such regulation applied with respect to the principal institutions of the state, the landed estates and townships, and to the labour force, which, through various forms of relationship and status, was bonded to serve. The main sources of labour were household servants, farm labourers, and craftsmen (the last constituting about 5 per cent of the workforce by the fourteenth century).[7]

Sources of regulation at this time included custom: bonded people were required to serve, and even non-bonded labour by custom was required to serve at particular times (for example, at harvest time). Further, towns under corporate charter were empowered to make and enforce their own by-laws, and frequently did so on matters of labour regulation—for example, requiring labour supply. Craft guilds regulated work done in the various skilled handicrafts. Matters regulated included rates of pay, entry to the craft, labour supply, working hours, holidays, methods of work, and apprenticeship training periods. The ordinances of these guilds could be confirmed by the lord of the particular manor or by the town members themselves.

---

[5] Deakin describes these in the British context as the contract concept 'permeating' statutory employment law: S. Deakin, 'Private Law, Economic Rationality and the Regulatory State', in P. Birks, *The Classification of Obligations* (Oxford: Clarendon Press, 1997), 283, 297.

[6] See, in particular, the issues raised in H. Collins, *Regulating Contracts* (Oxford: Oxford University Press, 1999), chs. 3 and 4.

[7] G. Unwin, *Industrial Organisation in the Sixteenth and Seventeenth Centuries* (Oxford: Clarendon Press, 1904); T. Rogers, *Six Centuries of Work and Wages* (London: Swan Sonnenschein, 1901).

Historical accounts indicate that this fairly stable set of communal arrangements and relationships was severely disturbed by the Black Death of the late 1340s, which is estimated to have killed more than one-third of the population. Labour available to work on the estates was in acute short supply, and competition for workers led to the bidding-up of wages and absenteeism of servants. The immediate response to this set of circumstances was the introduction of the Ordinance of Labourers in 1349, followed by the Statute of Labourers in 1350. These provisions are generally regarded as the first known instances of statutory ordering and regulation of labour in the common law world, but it is important to recognize that their major object was to do no more than preserve the traditional arrangements inherent in the social and economic systems of the times. Hence, they largely built upon existing customs, and town and guild regulation, to fix the supply and price of labour. All persons without independent support (i.e. those who were not independent peasant farmers or merchants) were obliged to serve within their own town or locality, and could be imprisoned or compulsorily repatriated (to their place of origin) for breach. The statutes also fixed price controls on food and drink.

These early state interventions were followed by a series of similar statutes to the same effect, setting differential wage rates between classes of labourers and craftsmen, and obliging service according to those conditions. The list of pre-Elizabethan statutes—passed in 1349, 1350, 1360, 1388, 1389, 1414, 1423, 1427, 1429, 1444, 1494, 1496, 1514—tells us something of the state's persistent intention to regulate labour, but at the same time, clearly indicates the ineffectiveness of the regulatory endeavour. In a highly unstable set of economic and labour market circumstances, these statutes essentially were attempting, but also failing, to make old customs adhere.

This regulatory system may be seen as both serving a protective function, and at the same time ordering the supply of labour and its control. Its emphasis was undoubtedly the latter, but the provision for customary wages and price controls on food and drink clearly imposed a 'fairness' or 'reasonableness' element on the arrangements, which, along with the obligation to serve, took them out of the realm of private 'agreements' and into that of instrumental state regulation.

Such was the extent of the labour problem by the mid-sixteenth century that there was a major attempt to completely revamp the whole system. All previous legislation was repealed and a new set of provisions (the Statute of Artificers or Statute of Apprentices of 1563, sometimes known as the Elizabethan Code) introduced.[8]

Under this new system justices of the peace and magistrates of cities and towns were able to fix wages for particular areas, based on a sliding scale determined by the price of food. It also determined that many crafts and tradesmen

---

[8] For general accounts, see Unwin, *Industrial Organisation in the Sixteenth and Seventeenth Centuries*; Rogers, *Six Centuries of Work and Wages*.

could only be engaged for a minimum period of one year; and that all persons between the ages of twelve and sixty who were not apprentices must work as agricultural labourers unless they were otherwise legitimately occupied. All those employed by the day or by the week for wages had their working times fixed, including mealtimes and starting and finishing times.[9]

The more detailed regulation of apprenticeship in this legislation is a further indication of the interconnection between customary regulation and statute at this time. The Elizabethan statute extended the existing custom on apprentices in the London locality by nationalizing the seven years apprenticeship rule. It also continued earlier statutory practices, attempting both to ensure the supply of labour for agricultural purposes and at the same time to protect the crafts against oversupply. For example, the statute contained a provision that no child of a husbandsman whose parents' income was less than twenty shillings per annum could become an apprentice in a craft. In many trades it was required that a journeyman must work until he was at least twenty-four years of age before becoming a master craftsman, and many trades also imposed a ratio of the numbers of apprentices to journeymen. A further example of the labour control element is found in the requirement that servants who changed their work location needed the approval of their master in the form of a certificate.

The effectiveness of this nationalized system of general employment regulation has been the subject of much debate, but there is general agreement that it had more or less fallen into disuse by the mid-1700s. Nevertheless, the core of the system of regulation was continued, and its scope extended, by the Masters and Servants Acts introduced during the eighteenth century and into the nineteenth century (1747, 1758, 1766, 1823, and 1867).[10] In addition to this regulation, there was a growing propensity on the part of the state to introduce specific regulation for particular industries considered to be in difficulties owing to severe disturbances between masters and workmen. These statutes included not just powers to regulate wages; they were increasingly associated with extending to justices of the peace and to magistrates' courts powers to settle industrial disputes over work issues.[11]

Consequently, by the late 1700s and early 1800s there existed many continuing industry, wage, and other regulations applying to labour control and supply. The notion of master and servant still had vital resonance, but feudal ties were

[9] See, further, R. K. Kelsall, 'A Century of Wage Assessment in Hertfordshire, 1666–1762', in W. E. Minchington (ed.), *Wage Regulation in Pre-industrial England* (Newton Abbot: David & Charles, 1972); E. A. McArthur, ' "The Boke Longying to a Justice of the Peace" and the Assessment of Wages', *English Historical Review*, 9 (1894), 305; E. A. McArthur, 'A Fifteenth-Century Assessment of Wages', *English Historical Review*, 13 (1898), 299; E. A. McArthur, 'The Regulation of Wages in the Sixteenth Century', *English Historical Review*, 15 (1900), 445.

[10] See S. Deakin, 'Legal Origins of Wage Labour: The Evolution of the Contract of Employment from Industrialisation to the Welfare State', in L. Clarke, P. de Gijsel, and J. Janssen (eds.), *The Dynamics of Wage Relations in the New Europe* (Boston: Kluwer, 2000), 32.

[11] See C. R. Dobson, *Masters and Journeymen: A Prehistory of Industrial Relations 1717–1800* (London: Croom Helm, 1980); C. Fisher, *The English Origins of Australian Federal Arbitration: To 1824* (Canberra: Australian National University, Research School of Social Sciences, 1986).

all but destroyed legally, and thus labour was increasingly seen as 'free' in at least this one sense. Around the same time we also notice the beginnings of a continuous trade union movement, accompanied by a more explicit recognition of the need to resolve formally disputes between labour and capital.

Regulating Work in the Nightwatchman State

In 1813 the wage-fixing aspects of the Elizabethan Code were repealed, and by this stage employment relationships, no doubt, increasingly began to take on the appearance of contracts.[12] For example, there were voluntary elements in the engagement of labour, in that people were no longer tightly bound to serve a particular master, at least theoretically, or bound to work in a particular occupation, and the wages that they received for working were open to negotiation. On the other hand, the master and servant laws established by general statute in the wake of the Elizabethan Code and other specific-industry statutes (such as those introduced in the eighteenth century) continued the pattern of control over the conduct of the employment relationship according to notions of master and servant status.[13]

Accordingly, during this period there was no substantial development of the employment relationship under the private law of contract, when it came to the rules governing the content of the relationship and its termination.[14] In short, to quote Deakin, 'the transformation in the employment relationship that occurred in the course of the first half of the nineteenth century did not consist solely, or even primarily, of its "contractualisation" '.[15] The state still invested the employment relationship with substantial doses of the criminal law, and thus the employer remained in control of both the obligations and the duration of the relationship through the old rules of master and servant law, as administered by the magistrates' courts and justices of the peace. Misconduct, disobedience, absconding from work, and refusal to complete tasks were all offences capable of being sanctioned under the criminal law for the great bulk of the workforce. Almost throughout the entire nineteenth century, relationships under which work was performed by one for another were largely conducted according to notions of service, obligation, loyalty, and control, and courts infused 'agreements' for work with 'implied terms', which embodied those ancient obligations and values.[16]

Here, then, we find a collision of sorts between instrumental regulation and contract, but one in which emerging ideas of private law in employment are struggling to accommodate centuries-old instrumental regulation. This was

---

[12] O. Kahn-Freund, 'Blackstone's Neglected Child: The Contract of Employment', *Law Quarterly Review*, 93 (1978), 508.

[13] Deakin, 'Legal Origins of Wage Labour'; A. S. Merritt, 'The Historical Role of Law in the Regulation of Employment—Abstentionist or Interventionist?', *Australian Journal of Law and Society*, 1 (1982), 56.   [14] Ibid.

[15] Deakin, 'Legal Origins of Wage Labour'.

[16] See ibid.; Merritt, 'The Historical Role of Law in the Regulation of Employment'.

achieved, but only under sufferance of the pretence of agreement and the patent invention of 'implied' terms supposedly drawn from the apparent 'intention' of the parties. Only in the case of a 'middle class' of salaried workers, managers, clerks, and the like (occupations not governed by the Masters and Servants Acts) did purely contractual notions of the employment relationship begin to emerge by the mid-nineteenth century.[17]

The period between the abandonment of the masters and servants laws (bringing to a close the formal criminal regime in work regulation) and the commencement of new regulatory regimes was, generally speaking, very short—probably only twenty to thirty years. Even with the repeal of the Masters and Servants Acts in Britain in 1875, most workers continued to be subject to the supervision of the magistrates and county courts under the terms of the Employers and Workmen Act of 1875, while in Australia the Masters and Servants Acts remained in operation, in some cases well into the twentieth century. Thus, it was only with the emergence of modern-day industrial relations systems (collective bargaining in Britain and compulsory arbitration in Australia) that the legal notion of a formal contractual equality between employer and employee took hold.[18]

What that contract might consist of, and the elaboration of its implications, had scarcely begun to develop beyond the adoption of a few fundamental implied terms based upon statute and custom.[19] Thus, the nineteenth century is linked not with the *development* of a new regulatory framework based on the contract of employment but with its 'atrophy', in that the underlying developmental basis of labour law continued to be through its public statutory regulation, kept juridically separate and distinct from the contract of employment.[20] There was, therefore, during this period no prospect of major collision between the objectives of public regulation and the development of contract doctrine through private agreement in employment. Outside of a relatively confined section of the workforce, the contract of employment remained largely conceptually underdeveloped, and almost entirely subordinated to public instrumental regulation. Put another way, 'the lingering influence of the master and servant model . . . retarded the application of general contractual principles to the service relationship'.[21] But what were the consequences of this separation in the context

---

[17] See Deakin, 'Legal Origins of Wage Labour'.

[18] See S. Deakin, 'The Evolution of the Contract of Employment, 1900–50', in N. Whiteside and R. Salais (eds.), *Governance, Industry and Labour Markets in Britain and France* (London: Routledge, 1998), 212; J. Howe and R. Mitchell, 'The Evolution of the Contract of Employment in Australia: A Discussion', *Australian Journal of Labour Law*, 12 (1999), 113.

[19] See Deakin, 'Legal Origins of Wage Labour'; Merritt, 'The Historical Role of Law in the Regulation of Employment'.

[20] 'With this development [the law failing to recognize employment as essentially a contractual relationship] I am inclined to link what I call the atrophy of employment in nineteenth century England. What I mean by this is that the bulk of labour law, and especially the bulk of legislation for the protection of workers, developed until our own century and still partly develops outside the frame of the contract of employment . . . This separation of statutory and contractual rights is in the Blackstonian tradition. It has had momentous consequences': Kahn-Freund, 'Blackstone's Neglected Child', 524.   [21] Deakin, 'Legal Origins of Wage Labour', 38.

of the emergence of the new regulatory regimes which characterized the development of twentieth-century labour law?

The Twentieth-Century Regulatory State, 1900–1980s: Public Regulation through State Agencies and Institutions

The period that we have labelled 'the twentieth-century regulatory state' is one of consolidation in labour market regulation. It is the period of the emergence of the 'modern' system of labour law as we know it today, its general orientation from about the onset of the twentieth century through to the 1980s being fundamentally similar across a broad range of industrialized market economies. A number of points may be noted about these developments.

Firstly, the idea that the state itself should be principally responsible for the ordering and regulation of the labour market continued to hold sway. Industrial relations and work relationships were regulated to produce a stable supply of labour, rewards for labour, and a disciplined workforce. There was, however, a substantial shift in the orientation of labour regulation at this historical juncture. Labour law in this period was largely influenced by theories which sought to stabilize the employment relationship in the context of rapidly growing capitalist economies and global trade. Labour law became much more specifically protective in outlook. It provided minimum standards, wages, and conditions, protected trade unions, and ensured procedural safeguards.

In Australia and New Zealand industrial tribunals were established with compulsory powers to intervene and settle industrial disputes by prescribing, in the form of industrial awards and agreements, terms and conditions of employment and otherwise ordering aspects of the labour market.[22] Judges and arbitrators, exercising powers in the courts and tribunals established under these systems, were invested with very broad regulatory powers over work relationships, which invite straightforward comparisons with the older forms of regulation discussed earlier in this chapter.[23] In Europe and Britain, and eventually in North America, state regulation sought legally to support regimes in which industrial parties attempted to self-order employment relationships through collective bargaining agreements. For the purposes of this discussion we treat these bargaining regimes as essentially 'instrumental', notwithstanding the state's less direct role in the regulatory process. Even in these less prescriptive systems, states tended to intervene more directly in times of national crisis (for example, Britain introduced compulsory arbitration of industrial disputes during the First and Second World Wars). There were, however, certain common elements to all of these systems. Trade unions were legitimized and incorporated into the regulatory process, and collective regulation of employment conditions was promoted through state-based agencies and institutions and through legislation.

---

[22] S. Macintyre and R. Mitchell (eds.), *Foundations of Arbitration: The Origins and Effects of State Compulsory Arbitration, 1890–1914* (Melbourne: Oxford University Press, 1989).

[23] Deakin, 'The Evolution of the Contract of Employment'; Howe and Mitchell, 'The Evolution of the Contract of Employment in Australia'.

Secondly, it was during this period that employment status was consolidated into two principal categories as courts and tribunals strove to determine which groups of workers should obtain the benefit of protective social and industrial legislation (such as workers' compensation and the minimum wage). Workers previously identified by many different labels, and accordingly assumed to have often quite different labour market statuses, became identified as 'employees' covered by 'contracts of employment', or, in the alternative, another type of labour market participant generally labelled as 'independent contractor'. This was a fairly drawn-out process, but was largely completed in Britain and Australia by the 1930s.[24]

Thirdly, no matter what the mode of state involvement, the contract of employment remained of only marginal importance as a regulatory instrument. Whereas the contract was the clearly recognized standard legal form identifying the juridical nature of the relationship, the content of that relationship was largely determined by regulation external to it (i.e. through statute, industrial award, and collective agreement). It is true that the common law contract did contain the notion of 'service' incorporated from the earlier customary and statutory regulation of master and servant relations, but otherwise, it offered little to the content of the employment relationship.

The curious point about this is that despite the complete dominance of state instrumental regulation (and, as noted above, we include the regulation of the labour market through collective bargaining between unions and employers as a form of state regulation), the contract of employment still remained a crucial juridical construct in the regulation of employment. Generally speaking, only persons engaged under such contracts were the subject of instrumental labour law, and, at least in the case of Britain, it was only through the contract of employment that the terms of the great bulk of external regulation were enforceable legally.[25]

Nevertheless, despite these important interfaces between instrumental regulation and the contract of employment, it remained the case that the private law of contract largely failed throughout the twentieth century to reach an understanding of employment as a complete legal construct embodying the ideas of both common law and state-based instrumental regulation.[26] As a result, there were two different understandings of the employment relationship, one contractual and the other statutory-based and, as Kahn-Freund noted, the complexities arising out of the interrelationship of these coexisting concepts were, and still are, very substantial.[27] For example, contract law has not systematically recognized the right of employees to recover adequate damages for the unlawful termination of employment, nor has it acknowledged the obvious need for a remedy to return an employee to employment when that might be the only

---

[24] See the discussion below.   [25] See the discussion below.
[26] '... the traditional legal analysis of the common law could be criticised as missing the essential attributes of the field': H. Collins, 'The Productive Disintegration of Labour Law', *Industrial Law Journal*, 26 (1997), 295.   [27] See above, n. 20.

appropriate remedy.[28] We also find similar stresses evident in the relationships between contracts of employment and instrumental regulation, where courts have been loath to draw the externally derived norms into the agreement unless there is a basis for doing so according to the various ways in which contracts may be varied between the parties.[29]

These problems have given rise to some very artificial concepts trying to harmonize the aims and tools of instrumental regulation with the purity of contract doctrine. Because public regulation through collective agreements has not, with some short periods of exception, been statutorily enforceable in Britain, British courts have had to rely principally on the invented notion that such agreements are 'impliedly incorporated' into the individual employment contract in order for the public regulation to take legal effect.[30] The difficulties of applying these, and other, concepts are evident in situations where, for one reason or another, there have been attempts to give legal effect to public regulation through the contract of employment in Australian courts.[31]

On the whole, Australian courts have been content to maintain the separation between contract and associated instrumental regulation, perhaps because the latter has been statutorily enforceable. For eighty years the relationship between the industrial awards of the Australian industrial tribunals and the contract of employment was largely ignored as a legal issue in employment relations. While it is uncontroversial that the existence of a contract of employment is a prerequisite for the operation of an award obligation, and that employers and employees can negotiate terms and conditions beneficial to the employee which are in excess of minimum award conditions (colloquially known as 'over-award payments'[32]), until the late 1980s the courts had not ruled decisively on whether some or all of the terms of an award were incorporated into the contract of employment of an employee covered by that award. There were several reasons for this, but principally most disputes over legal entitlements in the employment relationship were pursued through the industrial tribunals and by unions and inspection services, rather than litigated through the common law. However, with the introduction of unfair dismissal clauses in federal awards in 1984,[33] the opportunity of obtaining awards of compensation which far outstripped those available through the system of industrial regulation arose.

---

[28] It is possible that the common law is in transition towards rectifying these omissions, as we discuss later in this chapter.

[29] See H. Collins, 'Market Power, Bureaucratic Power and the Contract of Employment', *Industrial Law Journal*, 15 (1986), 1; G. J. Tolhurst, 'Contractual Confusion and Industrial Illusion: A Contract Law Perspective on Awards, Collective Agreements and the Contract of Employment', *Australian Law Journal*, 66 (1992), 705; R. Mitchell and R. Naughton, 'Collective Agreements, Industrial Awards and the Contract of Employment', *Australian Journal of Labour Law*, 2 (1989), 252.

[30] See S. Deakin and G. S. Morris, *Labour Law*, 3rd edn. (London: Butterworth, 2001), 259.

[31] See *Gregory v Philip Morris Ltd* (1987) 77 ALR 79, (1988) 80 ALR 455; *Ryan v Textile Clothing and Footwear Union Australia* [1996] 2 VR 235.

[32] See B. Creighton and A. Stewart, *Labour Law: An Introduction*, 3rd edn. (Sydney: Federation Press, 2000), 226.

[33] In the *Termination, Change and Redundancy Case* (1984) 8 IR 34, (1984) 9 IR 115.

If it could be shown that award terms 'became part of the contract of employment', then employees would be placed in a very advantageous position in the event of an unfair dismissal occurring. In particular, dismissed employees would be able to claim damages for any loss they might have suffered, resulting in substantial damages claims potentially going well beyond the limits of the usual damages flowing from a claim for 'wrongful' dismissal.[34] At the highest level, the High Court of Australia,[35] accepting the fact that the award largely characterized the employment relationship between the parties, nevertheless held that, as a matter of common law reasoning, the award governing the employment relationships did not become part of the contract of employment, and that the private law remedy was not available to enforce the award.

A key strand of the High Court's reasoning was that, in the circumstances of the case, the parties had not satisfied the elements of the common law tests required to give rise to an implied term in fact, and therefore, that they had not impliedly agreed that the terms of the award be incorporated into the contract of employment. In this case, the Court held that it was not necessary to imply such a term to make the contract of employment effective, and some of the judges considered that the term was not so obvious that it 'went without saying' and that there was no evidence that the term had been implied by established custom and practice. The Court also held that the governing legislation yielded no intention to give contractual force to awards, nor to found an action for breach of statutory duty.[36]

As an illustration of the interaction between private contract law and regulatory law, this decision has two aspects to it. First of all, it is an example of the continuing preoccupation of the courts with maintaining the internal coherence of contract doctrine. Its decision adopted a narrow, highly formalistic line of reasoning,[37] demonstrating no interest in the policy elements in the issues before them.[38] The second aspect is that the decision is at the same time a pragmatic response to the practical consequences of incorporating awards into the contract of employment. At the time of the decision there was considerable disquiet about the advisability of merging industrial awards with the contract of employment, among other things, because of the implications that might flow from extending contractual remedies to the full range of regulatory norms typically contained in such awards.[39]

---

[34] See A. Brooks, 'Damages for Harsh, Unjust or Unreasonable Dismissal: The Implications of *Gorgevski v Bostik (Australia) Pty. Ltd.*', *Australian Journal of Labour Law*, 8 (1995), 41.

[35] *Byrne v Australian Airlines* (1995) 185 CLR 410.

[36] See Creighton and Stewart, *Labour Law*, 222, 307.   [37] Ibid. 227.

[38] Many of which had been extensively canvassed in the secondary literature; see Mitchell and Naughton, 'Collective Agreements, Industrial Awards and the Contract of Employment'; Tolhurst, 'Contractual Confusion and Industrial Illusion'; J. de Meyrick, 'The Interaction of Awards and Contracts', *Australian Journal of Labour Law*, 8 (1995), 1.

[39] Mitchell and Naughton, 'Collective Agreements, Industrial Awards and the Contract of Employment'; Tolhurst, 'Contractual Confusion and Industrial Illusion'; de Meyrick, 'The Interaction of Awards and Contracts'. Similarly, English courts generally have taken the approach

Equally notable in the application of common law doctrine to employment relationships is the judicially developed distinction between the *contract* of employment and the *relationship* itself.[40] Such a distinction is maintained by the courts in order to reconcile two principles: firstly, that a party to a contract cannot unlawfully bring it to an end without acceptance of that termination by the other party, and secondly, that an employer who has unlawfully dismissed an employee is nevertheless not liable to pay wages under the ongoing contract.[41] The common law rule that the payment of wages is only due for work performed under an ongoing employment *relationship*, which, in the normal course of events, the unlawful dismissal brings to an end, rules out the obligation of the employer to pay wages until the contract is lawfully terminated, is plainly an issue of policy. Thus, for example, in the Australian case of *Automatic Fire Sprinklers v Watson*,[42] the managing director of a company had been dismissed in violation of wartime Manpower Regulations introduced by the Australian government to control employment decisions in a range of prescribed industries and occupations. Though it was found that the dismissal did not legally bring the contract to an end by virtue of the Regulations, the managing director was not entitled to wages for the period in which he made himself available for work under his admittedly extant contract. In such cases the obligation to pay wages (as distinct from damages) would only legally continue if the externally derived instrumental regulation had made it clear that wages continued to accrue under an existing, but not performed, contract of employment. Some Australian cases have, sometimes successfully, explored this possibility.[43]

The post-1945 period saw a continuation of earlier-established regulatory concepts, but at the same time a proliferation in the institutions of regulation and the volume of regulation, particularly as measured by the sheer number of regulatory norms applicable to employment relationships. With the consolidation of the Keynesian welfare state committed to full employment and mass production, a broader set of labour-oriented regulations and protections were introduced during this period. These included state-based employment services, state-based provision of unemployment benefits, and, with the re-emergence of long-term unemployment in the 1970s, larger-scale job creation schemes and labour market programmes.

Other developments which typified the regulation of work in this era included new occupational health and safety (OHS) regulatory systems,

---

which sees instrumental social legislation 'superimposed' on the contract of employment rather than forming part of it: see Deakin, 'Private Law, Economic Rationality and the Regulatory State'.

[40] Criticized as inconsistent with the general law of contract: see *Association of Professional Engineers, Scientists and Managers Australia v Skilled Engineering Pty. Ltd.* (1994) 122 ALR 471 (per Gray J at 480).   [41] Creighton and Stewart, *Labour Law*, 243.

[42] (1946) 72 CLR 435.

[43] See e.g. the 'no work–no pay' cases pursued under Australian regulatory regimes. In certain circumstances courts might treat awards and/or statutory regulation as an 'exclusive code' governing payment, and thus the common law rule would be excluded: see Creighton and Stewart, *Labour Law*, 237.

an emphasis on the protection of labour market participants against various forms of discrimination, and the extension of particular rights to individuals, rather than trade unions, including protection against unfair dismissal and redundancy. These developments showed an increasing spread of norms regulating the workplace, and a further proliferation in the number of regulatory agencies bearing on work. In some cases the administration of these increasing bodies of norms was confined to existing labour market institutions, such as collective bargaining arrangements or industrial tribunals. On the other hand, some led to the construction of new regulatory agencies, such as anti-discrimination bodies and state-supported agencies for administering unemployment benefits and employment placement services.

These statutory developments also provided at least one good example of the way in which the common law has had a notable influence over instrumental public regulation in the domain of OHS. Our sketch of the four stages in the development of labour law above omitted any reference to OHS regulation. From 1844 the British Factories Acts included detailed technical standards specifying particular safeguards that mill-owners initially, and then subsequently employers and occupiers in other industries, had to adopt in order to ensure the health and safety of their workers. These provisions were adopted by the Australian jurisdictions from 1885 onwards, and prevailed until the 1970s and 1980s. Because these specification standards were developed as detailed and ad hoc responses to safety issues raised by technological developments, they were criticized for their proliferation, excessive detail, unnecessary complexity, and failure to induce employers to develop their approaches to OHS to exceed minimum standards.

The response of the British Robens Report of 1972 was to recommend that there should be a single OHS statute, that it should 'contain a clear statement of the general principles of responsibility for safety and health',[44] and that this 'clear statement' be the statutory codification of the common law duty and standard of care in negligence and also implied into the contract of employment.[45] This is an obvious example of how the 'conceptual structure'[46] of the common law is from time to time utilized by regulatory law. These 'general duties' are owed by employers (to employees and to persons other than employees), by the self-employed, by persons in control of premises, by suppliers, designers, manufacturers, and importers of plant and substances, and by employees. The general duties are the pivotal provisions in the modern OHS statutes, and are supplemented by regulations and codes of practice.[47] Clearly, this is an instance in which judicial developments in the common law standard of care will impact

---

[44] Lord Robens, *Safety and Health at Work*, Report of the Committee (1970–2) (London: HMSO, 1972), para. 161(a).   [45] Ibid., para. 127.
[46] We have borrowed this term from Deakin, 'Private Law, Economic Rationality and the Regulatory State', 298.
[47] See R. Johnstone, *Occupational Health and Safety Law and Policy* (2nd edn. Sydney: LBC Information Services, 1997), ch. 6.

upon the instrumental regulation of the state through the interpretation of the general duties, although the courts will also be careful to acknowledge that differences in interpretation may result from the different contexts in which the common law and statutory duties appear.[48]

The post-war period, then, continued and intensified the importance of public regulation in the labour market. There was, moreover, very little indication that the incongruence between the associated concepts of the employment contract and the state instrumental regulation of the employment relationship was moving towards a resolution. In other words, there were, and are still, two paths to an understanding of the employment relationship and these continued to throw up substantive and procedural difficulties for the courts and users of the legal system. But at the same time, changes occurring during this period raised the possibility of new challenges to the relative position of contract doctrine and instrumental regulation. For example, as business organizations responded to the proliferating requirements of statutory regulation, described earlier, by engaging workers under 'independent', rather than 'employment' contracts,[49] the response of the courts was in the main to adhere to their restrictive common law notion of the employment contract, rather than expanding their understanding of the substance of employment relationships in order to give greater effect to the instrumentalist designs of statute.[50]

While most attention has been focused on the need for what Deakin has termed 'statutory innovations on the issue of labour classifications',[51] in which instrumentalist state regulation has sought to expand the definitions of the types of 'employee' and other worker covered by instrumentalist regulation, these developments have also presented the courts with opportunities to develop contractual doctrines governing 'independent' work relationships, and increasingly brought into relevance other areas of instrumental regulation, such as commercial law and competition law.[52] This problem of the limited scope of common law regulation does not appear, however, to be a collision arising because of differing regulatory purposes inherent in the private law of contract and the instrumental law of public regulation. Rather, it appears to be one consequence of the fact that the common law outlook towards the employment contract is formed separately from, and developed independently of, the regulatory strategy of the state towards work relationships and the labour market. This, in turn,

---

[48] See Johnstone, *Occupational Health and Safety Law and Policy*, 220.

[49] H. Collins, 'Independent Contractors and the Challenge of Vertical Disintegration to Employment Protection Laws', *Oxford Journal of Legal Studies*, 10 (1990), 353.

[50] A. Stewart, ' "Atypical" Employment and the Failure of Labour Law', *Australian Bulletin of Labour*, 18 (1992), 217.

[51] S. Deakin, *The Contract of Employment: A Study in Legal Evolution*, Working Paper No. 203 (Cambridge: ESRC Centre for Business Research, University of Cambridge, 2001).

[52] See e.g. P. Davies and M. Freedland, 'Employees, Workers and the Autonomy of Labour Law', in H. Collins, P. Davies, and R. Rideout (eds.), *Legal Regulation of the Employment Relation* (London: Kluwer Law International, 2000), 267.

seems to have been a consequence of the historical evolution of the employment relationship, as we noted earlier.[53]

A further important development saw the slow, but steady, emergence of a greater elaboration of common law principles governing the employment relationship. This arose principally out of the engagement of courts and tribunals with establishing grounds for permissible conduct in terminating employment relationships according to new statutory regulation governing unfair dismissals. In response to these provisions courts and tribunals have had to give renewed consideration to the breaches that might be committed by either party to the contract in so far as that may or may not justify the dismissal of a worker. For the first time on a sustained basis, and over a lengthy period of some twenty years from the early 1970s, courts began to explore seriously the common law nature of the contract, the basis of the mutual obligations between the parties, the limits of express terms, and the relationship between express and implied terms. In particular, the courts have had to consider what wrongful behaviour on the part of the employer would justify an employee's leaving the employment and qualifying that action as an unfair dismissal (otherwise called a constructive dismissal).[54] In this context the courts have opened up a number of new responsibilities of the parties. For example, they have found that the parties have an implied duty in law not to breach the relationship of trust and confidence between them,[55] and a similar duty to cooperate with each other in carrying out the purpose of the agreement.[56] What is notable is that these kinds of duty have been developed by the courts using classical doctrinal tools, such as implied terms.[57] Not surprisingly, these developments have had wide-ranging implications for the construction of the agreement, the conduct of its affairs and concerns, and for the parties' remedies upon breach, many of which are still in the process of being worked through.[58]

As Deakin has pointed out, these developments exhibit very clear mutual interactions between the common law and instrumental regulation, where in 'a series of loops the philosophy and perspectives of the legislation feed back

---

[53] It is necessary to note, however, that some of the contemporaneous new developments in this area of instrumental regulation were extending the reach of labour law beyond the limits of the narrow 'employment contract' relationship. Much of the legislation governing OHS and equal opportunity in particular directed its provisions at a far greater array of workplace relationships and statuses: see e.g. R. Johnstone, 'Paradigm Crossed? The Statutory Occupational Health and Safety Obligations of the Business Undertaking', *Australian Journal of Labour Law*, 12 (1999), 73.

[54] For the importance of this connection between common law doctrine and regulatory legislation, see Deakin and Morris, *Labour Law*, 330, 446; also see Deakin, 'The Contract of Employment: A Study in Legal Evolution'. On constructive dismissal in Australia, see Creighton and Stewart, *Labour Law*, 324.

[55] In Britain, *Malik v Bank of Credit and Commerce International S.A. (in liquidation)* [1997] 3 All ER 1. An Australian instance is *Burazin v Blacktown City Guardian Pty. Ltd.* (1996) 142 ALR 144.   [56] See Deakin and Morris, *Labour Law*, 328.

[57] See Collins, *Regulating Contracts*, 45.

[58] See D. Brodie, 'Beyond Exchange: The New Contract of Employment', *Industrial Law Journal*, 27 (1998), 79; D. Brodie, 'Mutual Trust and the Values of the Employment Contract', *Industrial Law Journal*, 30 (2001), 84.

into the common law and vice versa'.[59] However, while this clearly represents a breach in the central argument that the common law rules of contract and statutory regulation are separate, distinct, ways of ordering employment relations, it does not signal the demise of the separation between the two regimes. Labour law is still characterized by the 'separation' of contract and statute rather more than by the 'intermingling'[60] of these concepts. For example, as we noted earlier, the great weight of regulation in the Australian award and statutory agreement system barely seems to have impacted upon the way that the common law contract of employment has evolved in Australian courts.

The further development of the common law does, however, heighten the prospect of collision between the instrumental regulation of the state and the stated norms of the employment contract. These collisions, furthermore, potentially arise in different ways. For example, past encounters between common law and instrumental regulation might lead us to expect that a common law approach will be cautious and less likely to extend unqualified support to contentious instrumental collective regulation, if there are ways for courts to avoid doing so. It is also possible that the evolution of a common law notion of the employment contract as embodying ideas of mutual responsibilities is inconsistent with the aims and regulatory techniques of instrumental regulation, principally designed to extend protection to 'dependent' labour and to assign as much risk as possible away from labour to the employer. Or, put another way, the development of a common law contract of employment based on notions such as 'good faith', 'trust and confidence', and heightened mutual responsibility might be principally allied to the purpose of promoting greater competitiveness and efficiency through human resource management policies and 'high performance workplace systems' and with spreading risk between employers, employees, and independent contractors acting, at least theoretically, as equals in the market rather than with labour protection.[61]

We must also allow for the possibility that the development of doctrine on the contract of employment will drive the common law in the opposite direction to state policy, if the state is *seeking to withdraw* from a particular instrumental approach, or, indeed, from any regulation of the labour market at all. It is interesting to note that the recent emergence of judicial engagement with the employment contract has coincided with the partial, but steady, withdrawal by the state from its long-standing, historically based, assumed function of ordering and regulating the key aspects of the labour market. This is not to say that the willingness of the courts to explore the content of the contract more closely has been in response to the state's withdrawal, but neither can that possibility

---

[59] Deakin, 'Private Law, Economic Rationality and the Regulatory State', 298.
[60] Ibid. 296.
[61] H. Collins, 'Regulating the Employment Relation for Competitiveness', *Industrial Law Journal*, 30 (2001), 1; R. Mitchell and J. Fetter, 'Human Resource Management and Individualisation in Australian Labour Law', *Journal of Industrial Relations*, 45 (2003) 292.

be ruled out. Although a 'socialized',[62] contractualist approach is unlikely to be able to fill the gap left by a retreating regulatory state, the potential 'collision' of purpose which might arise as the common law takes up the regulatory space is self-evident.

Work and the New Regulatory State, post-1980

The 'new regulatory state' describes a position in which governments are increasingly relying on non-governmental institutions (market and civil society) to accomplish policy objectives and to deliver previously state-delivered services.[63] Labour market regulation has responded accordingly. Both in Britain and in Australia the post-1980 period has undoubtedly been marked by a withdrawal of the state from its regulatory function in favour of the market, and, as a consequence, state-based agencies have been withdrawn or given a diminished regulatory role or function. For example, the Australian federal government and some Australian state governments have moved decisively either to abolish or to reduce the sphere of operation of industrial tribunals and awards, to provide increased opportunities for individual agreement-making, and, at the same time, to reduce the influence of trade unions as labour market regulators.[64] While in Britain the role of the state was always traditionally less direct, there have been similar tendencies to 'deregulate' the labour market by reducing the support for collective arrangements and trade unions.[65]

We need to be careful, however, of what the implications of this deregulation are for the relationship between the common law and instrumental regulation. As we noted earlier, these changes open up the possibility of a greater instrumental role for the common law courts in regulating the employment relationship, though it is unclear to what extent this will be exploited. Until recently Australian courts, at least, have been reluctant to develop the general common law of contract to afford individual employees adequate protection in cases beyond the reach of state instrumental regulation.[66]

What *is* clear, however, is that the withdrawal of public regulation by the state does not necessarily reduce the sheer amount of 'regulatory' public law.[67] Occasionally, governments have repealed most of the external regulation in labour law, leaving a regulatory vacuum.[68] In some instances, however,

[62] D. Chin, 'Exhuming the Individual Employment Contract: A Case of Labour Law Exceptionalism', *Australian Journal of Labour Law*, 10 (1997), 257.

[63] The state is 'reinvented to do less rowing and more steering': see Parker and Braithwaite, 'Regulation', 123.

[64] See R. Mitchell, 'Juridification and Labour Law: A Legal Response to the Flexibility Debate in Australia', *International Journal of Comparative Labour Law and Industrial Relations*, 14 (1998), 113.

[65] For an account of the deregulation of the labour market in Britain, see Deakin and Morris, *Labour Law*, 32.   [66] See Chin, 'Exhuming the Individual Employment Contract'.

[67] See Parker and Braithwaite, 'Regulation'.

[68] As, for example, in the State of Victoria following the introduction of that state's Employee Relations Act 1992.

the return to market-based, or 'private', arrangements has been accompanied by a marked increase in regulatory instruments, norms, and agencies.[69]

It is also the case that as part of the shift in emphasis from state-based to market-ordered regulation, there has been a move towards the facilitation of private arrangements in labour law, although, as we noted above, this shift may be strongly regulated in line with the continuing instrumental objectives of the statutory law.[70] This, in turn, opens up the possibility of both interaction and conflict between various forms of agreements, to the extent that the relationship between the statutory contractual arrangements and their common law counterparts may be best described as a 'regulatory stew'.[71] For example, in addition to facilitating two major forms of collective agreements, the Australian federal Workplace Relations Act 1996 also makes provision for certain categories of employer to conclude Australian workplace agreements (AWAs) with one or more of their workers. These AWAs must satisfy a 'no disadvantage' test, requiring the terms of the AWA to be measured against any relevant or designated awards, and must be approved by an employment advocate. They also 'possess many of the characteristics of an individual contract of employment, but are enforceable in public law, in essentially the same manner as an award'.[72] At the same time, however, AWAs and the contract of employment are, apparently, quite separate legal instruments and the Workplace Relations Act does not preclude employers and employees from framing their legal work relationship (or at least those parts of it not already covered by award or statute) in a contract of employment in addition to an AWA and/or a certified collective agreement.[73]

In all of this mix, the exact nature of the relationship between AWAs and the contract of employment is far from clear. While it may be the case that the Act makes the pre-existence of a contract of employment a prerequisite for the creation of an AWA, once the AWA is made, it does not necessarily displace all the terms of the contract of employment upon which it is predicated.[74] On the other hand, the reasoning in *Byrne v Australian Airlines* suggests that the provisions of an AWA are not part of the contract of employment. The questions thrown up in this complex set of interrelating common law and statutory norms are both extensive and formidable. For example, it is unclear whether an AWA

---

[69] This was, undoubtedly, the experience with the Industrial Relations Reform Act 1993 (Cth) and the Workplace Relations Act 1996 (Cth), both of which were 'deregulatory' in orientation at least.

[70] See, generally, R. McCallum, 'Australian Workplace Agreements—An Analysis', *Australian Journal of Labour Law*, 10 (1997), 50.

[71] Some of the various interpretative possibilities are opened up for discussion in A. Stewart, 'The Legal Framework for Industrial Employment Agreements in Australia', in S. Deery and R. Mitchell (eds.), *Employment Relations: Individualisation and Union Exclusion* (Sydney: Federation Press, 1999), 18, 31.   [72] See Creighton and Stewart, *Labour Law*, 46.

[73] See e.g. the Workplace Relations Act 1996 (Cth), s. 3(c).

[74] See Creighton and Stewart, *Labour Law*, 228; Stewart, 'The Legal Framework for Industrial Employment Agreements in Australia', 31.

will contain its own implied terms,[75] or be found to contain the usual implied terms of a common law contract of employment. Equally, it is unknown whether contractual principles pertaining to vitiating factors in the formation of contracts (undue influence, duress, unconscionability, and the like) apply to AWAs, particularly given the availability of provisions in the Workplace Relations Act providing for relief where AWAs are made under duress.[76] These issues seemingly present prospects for both interaction and collision in what is a conglomeration of common law and highly ordered instruments of self-regulation in the form of statutory agreements.

CONCLUSION

We have noted that there are historical points of engagement between the public, instrumental regulation of work and the private or customary ordering of work relationships. As we have seen, historically long-standing customary norms have found their way into general statutory regulation; and subsequent statutory regulation of the master and servant relationship has come to be accepted as part of the general common law of employment. On the whole, though, the major thrust of our argument has been that private ordering of employment relations through contract law has remained largely subdued and subordinated to the more or less continuous regulatory involvement of the state in this field since the thirteenth century. The regulatory control of labour pursued through the masters and servants legislation and implemented by magistrates and county courts was not effectively brought to an end until virtually the turn of the twentieth century, when it was almost immediately replaced by completely new schemes of industrial regulation. As a result, contract doctrine generally has developed without the necessity of adjusting itself to the special peculiarities of employment relations. Consequently, the common law has not found it necessary to respond in a systematic way to changes in the organization of work, and when it has had to respond it has often found it difficult to do so through the cumbersome tools provided by the common law of contract.[77]

---

[75] In a recent decision, the Federal Court of Australia found that an agreement between an employer and a union certified under the Workplace Relations Act 1996 (Cth) could contain a term implied *in fact*: see *Automotive, Food, Metals, Engineering, Printing and Kindred Industries Union v Skilled Engineering Ltd.* [2003] FCA 260.

[76] See the Workplace Relations Act 1996 (Cth), s. 170WG. Also S. McCrystal and R. Gross, 'Duress and Australian Workplace Agreements: The *Schanka* Litigation and Other Developments', *Australian Journal of Labour Law*, 15 (2002), 184.

[77] An excellent example being found in the legal gymnastics engaged in, by legal scholars in particular, in attempting to explain the incorporation by courts of terms of collective agreements into contracts of employment: see Mitchell and Naughton, 'Collective Agreements, Industrial Awards and the Contract of Employment'. It is not clear whether Kahn-Freund's suggestion that collective agreements constituted a form of 'crystallized custom' which were, thereby, incorporated into employment contracts (O. Kahn-Freund, 'Legal Framework', in A. Flanders and H. Clegg (eds.), *The System of Industrial Relations in Great Britain: Its History, Law and Institutions* (Oxford: Blackwell, 1956),

It follows, therefore, that what the examples of 'interface' or 'collision' demonstrate is that there are firm limits to the willingness of common law courts to abandon a 'pure' understanding of contract doctrine in regulating work and to take on the logic of state regulation. In other words, the common law still favours 'coherence' over what Collins refers to as 'disintegration'.[78] This reluctance is abundantly confirmed in the decision of the House of Lords in *Johnson v Unisys Ltd*[79] not to extend the common law right to sue for damages for wrongful dismissal on the basis of a breach of the common law duty of trust and confidence. In a decision which echoes the sentiments of the Australian High Court in *Byrne v Australian Airlines Ltd* (noted earlier) the law lords held that to permit the extension of the common law in this way was inconsistent with the public regulation of the employment relationship through unfair dismissal legislation, signalling the continued separation of the two regulatory systems.[80]

We conclude this chapter with some reflections on the interrelationship in labour law between private law doctrine and instrumental regulatory law. Our argument tends to repudiate any view that instrumental regulation of the labour market began principally in the twentieth century with consequent severe implications for the private law of the contract of employment at that time. On the contrary, our view is that instrumental law regulating work largely pre-dated any contractual notions of the employment relationships. Furthermore, while it is true that the amount and depth of regulatory norms grew substantially with the advent of the twentieth-century regulatory state, this growth has persisted even with the advent of a supposedly less directly interventionist 'new' regulatory state in the final two decades of the century.

We have also noted that the rise of explicitly regulatory law is not to any great degree noticeably influencing courts to adopt regulatory styles of reasoning in developing private law doctrine in labour law. Rather, in our view, the impact of regulatory law on the contract of employment has been generally fairly muted apart from the infiltration of master and servant rules into the contract of employment via the implied-term device in the latter part of the nineteenth century. It is true, of course, that there are some signs in the evolution of contract doctrine, particularly in the development of new implied terms, that matters of employment protection, fairness, and potentially even efficiency and productivity in employment relationships are, perhaps, finding their way into judicial reasoning, albeit without much explicit engagement with these employment values. But we cannot predict with any certainty whether these trends will become more explicit, or even follow a clear trajectory.

We close with one final note. Throughout we have stressed the existence of 'regulatory law' as a historical mix of custom, legislation, and judicial activity.

42, 58, was ever formally adopted by any British court, but the idea has been specifically rejected by the Australian authorities: see *Byrne v Australian Airlines Ltd.*

[78] Collins, *Regulating Contracts*, 53.   [79] [2001] 2 WLR 1076.

[80] Early indications are that this ruling will be followed in the Australian courts: see *Aldersea v Public Transport Corporation* (2001) 183 ALR 545 (Supreme Court of Victoria).

Inevitably, we feel, the historical role of courts in labour market ordering (albeit principally local and regional courts) must give rise to doubts about any straightforward distinction between the supposed legal 'autonomy' of the common law as expressed by courts and the instrumental, purposive approach of regulatory legislation. As our editors indicate, such a distinction is too simple and liable to mislead.[81] The history of 'regulating work' is a case in point.

[81] See the Introduction to this volume.

6

Regulating Torts

JANE STAPLETON

The editors of this volume assume that all law can fruitfully be seen as 'regulation' and invite us to consider what it means to see tort law as a form of regulation, as a governance mechanism for steering and controlling behaviour, and as something that is itself regulated by other forms of regulation. As a stranger to regulatory studies the first step I needed to take, having accepted this invitation to view tort law through a 'regulatory lens', was to identify what meaning attached to key terms used in this field of inquiry. This was not an easy task. In some areas I decided simply to adopt one of a competing number of definitions. For example, I will follow the editors and define regulation in the way suggested by Julia Black: as 'the intentional activity of attempting to control, order or influence the behaviour of others'.[1] In other areas I found that I had to identify the terrain that I would regard as being designated by an otherwise ambiguous term. For example, I will assume that 'private law' doctrine includes both common law doctrines and statutory liability rules and that, by contrast, 'public' regulation means statutory, administrative, and organizational rules that set out entitlements from the state (or an organization) or mandate norms of behaviour with sanctions directed to the non-complying party, regardless of whether injury to or complaint from another private party has resulted from that non-compliance. In this definitional framework, then, 'public regulation' includes government compensation schemes such as the Criminal Injuries Compensation Scheme, as well as the behavioural standards set out in the criminal law and in regulations such as those applying to health and safety at work. Nevertheless, in the case of some key terms in the regulatory study of central interest to the editors, that of Hugh Collins in *Regulating Contracts*,[2] the task of pinpointing a workable and consistent definition has proved intractable. Chief among these troublesome terms is the notion of 'private ordering'.

---

[1] J. Black, 'Critical Reflections on Regulation', *Australian Journal of Legal Philosophy*, 27 (2002), 1.
[2] H. Collins, *Regulating Contracts* (Oxford: Oxford University Press, 1999), on which, see J. Gava, 'The Limits of Modern Contract Theory: Hugh Collins on Regulating Contracts', *Adelaide Law Review*, 22 (2001), 299.

COLLINS, CONTRACT, AND THE REGULATORY LENS

Scope and Methodology

Collins[3] notes that the scope of his regulatory perspective's inquiry into the subject of regulating contract law requires an inclusive view of 'law' that encompasses all the governance mechanisms that serve to regulate or steer contractual behaviour. He holds that before we can examine how the different types of law, 'soft law', and other institutional mechanisms interact and contribute to the steering of social behaviour, it is methodologically necessary to use a social, rather than a legal, perception of what should be regarded as a 'contractual practice'. He says we need an independent theory for determining what kinds of meaning attributed to events by the participants should be regarded as amounting to a contractual meaning, in other words which social phenomena should count as a 'contractual practice'.

Even in the contractual setting, these statements are hard to understand. Citizens without legal training often have no clear fixed concept of what a contract is. How many would describe getting on a bus as a 'contractual practice'? It seems more plausible that the social perception of what should be regarded as a 'contractual practice' is dependent on the legal perception. Like accident victims, who tend to allocate blame to those that they believe the law would blame,[4] it seems more plausible that citizens would identify arrangements as contractual by referring back to what they know of legal definitions. Moreover, if the regulatory lens requires an 'independent' theory by which it picks and chooses which social meanings are to count as 'contractual meanings', have we not come full circle and ended up with a legal meaning?

In any case, how can any of this translate to the field of torts? It gives the tort lawyer no guidance as to the limits of the 'regulating torts' inquiry because in tort law there are no central 'practices'. Tort law can bite on any form of behaviour, even nonfeasance. What constitutes a 'tortious practice' is a wholly legal construct.

Is it Intelligible to View Private Law as Regulation or a Governance Mechanism or a Part of the State's Regulatory Structure?

Collins correctly notes that an area of law can only be analysed as regulation if it is motivated by an identifiable goal. He says that contract lawyers conventionally do not see the private law of contract as purporting to control business behaviour by reference to enforceable standards in the pursuit of a particular goal, but rather regard it as essentially facilitative. Collins gives four reasons why contract law must be about more than this facilitation of freedom of association.

---

[3] Except where otherwise stated, all references to Collins herein are to Collins, Ch. 1 in this volume.
[4] S. Lloyd-Bostock, 'Common Sense Morality and Accident Compensation', *Insurance Law Journal* (1980), 331.

Firstly, he observes that doctrinal choices carry different distributional *effect*, so that judges facing a choice of contract rules cannot avoid 'taking a stand' on the consequences of the rules on the distributive outcomes of markets. He deduces from this that contract law necessarily embraces a distributive goal so that it becomes intelligible to ask whether it is effective in achieving this regulatory goal. The tort lawyer finds this a very dubious deduction. Merely because a decision-maker appreciates that a particular doctrinal choice has a particular distributional effect does not mean he or she must embrace such effects as goals. For example, courts are well aware that the rules of assessment of tort damages give a doctor a strong economic incentive to rank the interests of a mother well above those of her unborn child: the damages for carelessly injuring a high-earning pregnant woman, even in a very minor way, far outstrip those for carelessly killing the unborn child. This perverse economic incentive of tort rules is known but not embraced as a goal of those rules. In short, pointing to the distributional impact of private law rules does not warrant the deduction that the application of the regulatory lens to it is an intelligible activity. We know the weather steers human conduct, but it does not fit regulatory rhetoric to say that the weather regulates or is a governance mechanism of human conduct.

Secondly, Collins correctly points out that legal reasoning cannot proceed according to a process for the reconciliation of individual rights without the need to employ consequential or policy arguments because there is no fixed scheme of individual rights. Collins, however, then jumps to the assertion that when courts resolve disputes they do so according to the foreseeable distributive consequences that the courts prefer. This being so, according to Collins, application of the regulatory lens to contract law is an intelligible activity because we can examine the legal rules with a view to assessing courts' objectives and whether those objectives are achieved. This analysis simply does not describe legal reasoning in tort cases. Just as the 'high' theorists of corrective justice are unable to generate the complexity of real-world legal reasoning in tort cases with their pure, autonomous, immanent tool of 'rights',[5] any other pure theory will similarly fail at a descriptive level. It is true that tort judges sometimes consider and may be influenced by the distributional consequences of a particular legal option, but I know of no case where this is the sole criterion by which the dispute was resolved. A comparable observation has long been a major criticism of lawyer–economists who claim that courts are solely influenced by wealth maximization.

Thirdly, Collins, again correctly, notes that courts are aware of the instrumental purposes for which repeat players litigate and that the setting of rules through judicial determinations is necessarily an instrumental task in the sense that courts try to reconcile the competing interests of the litigants. But, again,

---

[5] J. Stapleton, 'Comparative Economic Loss: Gary Schwartz and Case Law Focussed "Middle Theory"', *UCLA Law Review*, 50 (2002), 531.

Collins then jumps to the assertion that courts must develop a view about the consequences for the market 'that they wish to achieve' and they can adjust the consequences of their rulings in the light of the effectiveness of the rules to achieve 'their objective'.[6] If this did, indeed, capture what courts do, they would, indeed, then be 'performing a similar function to regulatory agencies by determining goals and selecting rules to achieve those goals' so that application of the regulatory lens to contract law would be an intelligible activity.[7] But again, even if this is so in contract, which I doubt, the reasoning in tort cases does not support a parallel assertion. It is true that tort courts are aware that deep-pocketed litigants will return to court repeatedly, but this phenomenon is equally consistent with the importance to such parties of having the details of the rule clarified. Since *Hedley Byrne v Heller*[8] recognized that a negligent professional adviser might be liable to those who had suffered economic loss as a result of that negligence, litigation of claims against professional advisers has been intense as the exact basis and incidence of the liability has been fleshed out. That courts must resolve such cases does not warrant an assertion that they 'must' have decided a pattern of social consequences that they wish to achieve, let alone that such an 'objective' is the sole criterion by which a dispute between an individual adviser and advisee is resolved.

Collins's fourth and final argument as to why application of the regulatory lens to contract law would be an intelligible activity is that, though courts rely on arguments about the meaning of rules, the weight of principles, and the protection of rights, the leading judgments rely as much upon an open discussion of policy considerations as they do upon legal precedent. Collins believes that this open discussion of policy supports the view that private law should be assessed like other regulatory interventions by reference to its effectiveness in the pursuit of its goals. Again, the tort lawyer finds that this dangerously elides distinct features of legal reasoning. Tort cases are chock-full of discussions of general or, as I have termed them, systemic matters of concern to and influence with tort judges. If we construct 'menus' of these concerns,[9] we see that *some* might, indeed, be described as consequentialist 'policy', in the sense of a desired positive outcome (for example, that drivers halt at stop signs).

There are, however, two reasons why this does not warrant the conclusion that tort law should be assessed like other regulatory interventions. Firstly, where tort cases are litigated on points of law, and not merely on the facts, courts are typically confronted with a heterogeneous mix of legal concerns, *many of which are simply not amenable to description in terms of consequentialist 'policy' and thereby regulatory goals.* For example, our menus of tort concerns reflect the fact that when a surgeon was sued by parents for the upkeep of an unwanted baby born after a careless sterilization procedure failed, the

---

[6] Collins, Ch. 1 in this volume.   [7] Ibid.   [8] (1964) AC 465.

[9] J. Stapleton, 'Duty of Care Factors: A Selection from the Judicial Menus', in P. Cane and J. Stapleton (eds.), *The Law of Obligations: Essays in Honour of John Fleming* (Oxford: Oxford University Press, 1998), 59.

court ruled in the plaintiffs' favour, citing as influential concerns not merely the deterrence of careless surgery but also the law's concern that its rules do not positively encourage abortion. Later, when a pregnant woman was the target of litigation relating to the dangers posed to the foetus by her drug-using lifestyle, the court ruled in the defendant's favour *inter alia* on the basis that not to do so might result in the law positively encouraging abortion. These cases highlight a central feature of much of the private law of obligations which militates heavily against the view that it can, let alone should, be assessed like other regulatory interventions by reference to its effectiveness in the pursuit of its 'goals': namely, that many of the law's concerns relate to negative goals, rather than steering social arrangements to some positive objective.

Collins accepts that the legal reasoning in modern contract cases is heterogeneous, a 'hybrid' incorporating both doctrine and policy concerns, though, surprisingly to a tort lawyer, he identifies this as 'a *new* kind of legal discourse, which incorporates within it social and economic policies'.[10] The flaw in Collins's analysis here is that he does not identify the critical role in legal reasoning in contemporary private law cases that is played by legal concerns that are neither doctrinal nor sensibly described as 'policy concerns'. As a consequence, he too readily jumps to the conclusion that it is possible to ask what policy objectives have guided the courts, thereby allowing the deployment of the regulatory lens to the law.

The second reason why merely identifying non-doctrinal legal reasoning does not warrant the conclusion that tort law can and should be assessed like other regulatory interventions is that, even if we could isolate those tort cases in which the only systemic legal concerns relate to positive goals, *these need not pull in the same direction*. The negligence liability of public authorities is a well-known arena for this phenomenon, where the law's concern to protect the individual citizen from and deter losses due to carelessness exists in tension with the law's concern to support the public interest pursued by the public authority.

In short, while we might accept the reasons Collins gives as to why private law is about more than the facilitation of rights, the reasons do not warrant a deduction that legal reasoning in private law involves the instrumental pursuit of social aims, determinate results, or social policy goals, nor that application of the regulatory lens to it is an intelligible, let alone necessary, activity.

What Does Collins Mean by 'Private Ordering'?

It is not self-evident which patterns of social behaviour are 'private orderings'. Is the fact that most people would rescue a baby drowning in a puddle a pattern that we can call a private ordering? What about queuing at a bus stop? Are all social rules and conventions that have been created through repeated social interactions a species of private orderings?

---

[10] Collins, *Regulating Contracts*, ch. 3; emphasis added.

Collins's chapter for this volume (Chapter 1) suggests that, by private order-ing, he means reciprocal bilateral agreements to perform in ways not mandated by law (self-restraint chosen by the two parties), but that are enforceable by the parties (self-enforcement) in law only if the procedural legal requirements laid down by contract doctrine (procedural regulation chosen by the courts) are met. If so, most of Collins's arguments directed to matters of 'private ordering' simply do not speak to the subject matter of the law of torts, where the para-digm relationship between the litigants is that of strangers who have had no prior dealings, let alone have entered into any bilateral agreement to govern each other's conduct. In other words, there is not going to be much insight to be had into the 'operations of private ordering', as defined by Collins, by looking at that area of private law that is the law of torts.

Responsive Regulation and Contract

If we assume, for the moment, that we can apply the regulatory lens to tort law, we will be led to ask questions such as, do tort doctrines satisfy the regulatory or good-governance criteria of efficiency, effectiveness, and responsiveness? Ayres and Braithwaite[11] described 'responsive regulation' as a form of legal control that was sensitive to the possibility that regulatory goals might most efficiently be achieved by the targets of the regulation being allowed local leeway to decide on how in detail to arrange their practices to meet those broad goals. The idea is that by allowing this 'self-regulation' by the regulatory targets to be 'nested' within the overarching regulatory goal imposed by the regulator, the autonomy and special knowledge of the targets will be engaged in creating the most practicable and efficient methods for meeting the regulatory goals, while at the same time better securing cooperation and compliance.

But this model of responsive regulation does not even seem to apply con-vincingly to contract doctrine. When contracting parties make a deal, they are exercising an important freedom: to bind themselves in ways in which other-wise they would not be bound. The law of contract shapes the boundaries within which this one specific freedom can be exercised, by refusing to recog-nize and enforce certain agreements. Because freedom of contract is highly valued, most of the shaping that contract doctrine performs relates not to the content of the deal chosen by the parties but to the 'acceptability' of the pro-cedure by which the deal was struck. Only to a limited extent, in the modern era, has contract doctrine become more willing to regulate the substance of the deal when it impinges too severely on others.

A contract lawyer might initially be attracted to the notion that this freedom to make deals forms the central basis of our societies. But this freedom, though important, is merely one of a range of freedoms that characterize Western

---

[11] I. Ayres and J. Braithwaite, *Responsive Regulation: Transcending the Deregulation Debate* (New York: Oxford University Press, 1992).

democratic societies. Other important characteristics include: that we are free to criticize others, free to develop and use our land in any way we desire, free to own and vindicate title to property, free to refuse help to a stranger, free to go about our chosen activities much as we please. The law of torts is one of the forces within society that seeks to shape the boundaries within which these wide-ranging freedoms can be exercised. In contrast to tort law, the law of contract has one focal point—the bilateral agreement formed by the mutual and reciprocal exercise of an important freedom by the parties—and it is this focal point that provides the basis of legitimacy on which the law enforces such agreements.

So far so good. But Collins equates the parties' reciprocal agreement to engage in self-restraint with 'self-regulation' of the sort that is 'nested' within a regime of responsive regulation.[12] I do not find this a convincing characterization. Let us assume that the doctrinal constraints on freedom of contract reflect regulatory concerns of the law. Is it sensible to regard the whole specific contractual agreement that is enforceable by the law as merely the local means these particular parties have chosen to address those concerns? Those doctrinal constraints typically address only peripheral aspects of the deal, not its core contents. Collins's identification of the agreement with 'self-regulation' simply does not match the responsive regulation model where what the targets are left free to choose are the methods by which their conduct can meet the regulatory goals.

Say a deal has met the procedural (and any substantive) requirements of contract doctrine. It is simply not accurate to describe the substance of that deal, the detailed obligations of and performance standards of the parties, as setting the detailed local standards needed to promote the law's regulatory goals. It is true that the peripheral aspects of the deal, such as its procedural requirements, might be thought of in that way, but not the entire substantive commitments of the contract (for example, that C1 will deliver a new merchantable green compact car to C2 on Tuesday morning in return for C2 paying C1 £20,000 cash). In general, the substantive choices the parties made within the agreement are not the concern of the law of contract. By its silence contract law allows me just as much freedom to commit myself to the purchase of a new green compact car as it does to the purchase of a used red semi-trailer. Contract does not have *regulatory goals* about where, when, and how to exercise my freedom of contract, it merely sets a *few limits* thereon. The huge variety of enforceable bilateral agreements of contracting parties, their reciprocal choices of what self-restraint they promise to undertake, is testament to the *absence* of legal regulation at the core of the phenomenon of contractual deals. Little of the reciprocal self-restraint set out in these agreements can be seen as self-regulation in the responsive regulation sense. Nor, in my view, can Collins's approach be sensibly salvaged by inverting this conception of contract doctrine to say that, by its silence, it has the positive regulatory goal of promoting freedom of private ordering.

---

[12] Collins, *Regulating Contracts*, 63–8.

A more realistic, Diceyan, way of seeing the rules of contract law is as minor negative restraints on freedom of action. Contract doctrine does not 'row' or 'steer' freedom of private ordering. It merely lays down minimum construction requirements for the canoe that the coxless pair will use! It follows that the values reflected in contract doctrine can tell us little more about our society than a few of society's baseline values. This is true even where legal concerns and rules constrain the substance of agreements in pursuit of concerns, such as the protection of vulnerable consumers.

Responsive Regulation and Tort Doctrines

My foregoing argument applies, *a fortiori*, to tort doctrines. Tort law cannot and does not focus on mutual reciprocal exercises of the freedom to make commitments. Rather, the law of torts addresses itself to a wide range of individual human conduct that a defendant may have unilaterally engaged in. Tort law seeks to provide boundaries within which the defendant is to be free to engage in that conduct despite the objection of another party. In some torts, such as negligence, there will be no curtailment of the defendant's freedom, unless his conduct has injured another in a particular way. Even when this injury is present, the law will examine the 'appropriateness' of the substantive choice of behaviour by the defendant. It may be, for example, that a person is free to drive past a school at 30 mph in a compact car but not in a semi-trailer fully laden with barrels of sulphuric acid. Moreover, identical conduct may be penalized in one context but not another. A parent who does not feed their child for a week will be tortiously liable for the child's deterioration. A distant neighbour who also did not feed the child for a week will not be.

Tort law addresses the acceptability of the unilateral choice made by a defendant in how he conducts himself. Tort entitlements are created by the law between people that may never have met, let alone swapped commitments to each other. At its most characteristic, then, tort law evaluates the acceptability of defendant conduct by considerations that have nothing to do with the relationship or any prior dealings, let alone private orderings undertaken by the parties. No benchmark of legitimacy agreed beforehand by the parties provides the basis on which the law recognizes and enforces tort entitlements. In contrast to contract, the source of tort entitlements and of the legitimacy of their legal enforcement is typically from the law's own response to an amalgam of legal concerns: social, moral economic, and institutional. In contrast to contract, where the prior reciprocal commitment of the parties provides the legitimacy on which the law may enforce a promise to achieve a specific result, *tort entitlements never impose a strict obligation of affirmative action to achieve a result.*

A realistic way of seeing tort doctrines is as minor negative restraints on freedoms of action. Tort doctrine does not row or steer our freedoms of action. It merely lays down minimum construction requirements for the single scull we use to pursue them! To look at tort through a regulatory lens in the way Collins

looked at contract, presumably, we would need to postulate that the vast freedoms of action left untouched by tort law are just local ways that the targets of
tort liability are allowed to structure their conduct in line with the 'regulatory
objectives' of tort law. In my view, this is not a helpful way of refocusing our
attention. Nor does it fit the reasons courts give when crafting those doctrines.
Tort law does not have regulatory goals about where, when, and how to
exercise my freedoms of conduct, it merely sets thereon a few limits reflecting
diverse matters of concern to the law.

Reflexive Regulation and Tort Doctrines

According to Collins, 'reflexive regulation' is sensitive to the ways in which the
participants in a social practice think about their activity, producing regulatory
outcomes that avoid, as far as possible, interventions that distort the social
practice. In other words, regulation works best when it 'speaks' the language of
those it addresses. Collins now acknowledges that, even in the practice of contracting, the parties may not speak the same language in the sense of thinking
about their activity in the same way: where there is such a gap, the regulation
must give one 'communication system' priority, risking distortion to the social
practice.[13]

If this makes sense for contract law and sets a limit on its performance as a
regulatory mechanism, how much greater is the problem for promoting tort law
as a viable regulatory mechanism with an adequate level of reflexivity. As we
have seen, the paradigm tort disputes involve complete strangers, so the possibility that they do not see their interaction in the same light is even greater.
A citizen may have one concept of a police officer's obligations to that citizen,
while the police officer may have a fundamentally different one.

TORT LAW

Effects: Impact of Tort Doctrines on Behaviour

Let me now tone down the scepticism and consider the effects of tort doctrines.
These effects do not necessarily coincide with any goals that the law might seek
to achieve when it places peripheral restraints on conduct. For example, one
well-known effect of the doctrine of vicarious liability is to shield the tortfea-
sor, a real-world effect that could hardly be a goal of torts.[14] Similarly, the
imposition of liability by tort doctrines has the effects that the claimant receives
compensation and the defendant class may be deterred from similar conduct in

---

[13] Collins, Ch. 1 in this volume.
[14] For other examples, see W. A. Bogart, *Consequences: The Impact of Law and its Complexity*
(Toronto: University of Toronto Press, 2002), 118; P. A. Bell and J. O'Connell, *Accidental Justice:
The Dilemmas of Tort Law* (New Haven: Yale University Press, 1997).

the future. But neither could be a goal of tort law, otherwise no claimant would fail to recover.

There are good grounds to suspect that tort doctrines have contributed to certain specific effects on social practices. Over their lifetime most of today's pensioners have witnessed a remarkable increase in the amount of information about risks that medical professionals disclose to patients before treatment. This shift in social practice might well be associated with the doctrinal expansion of the duty to inform and the rise in successful complaints in the tort of negligence framed in terms of careless failure to warn. Similarly, though there seem to be no thorough empirical studies of the impact of the tort doctrine of conversion on commercial practices, it seems highly likely that markets have been structured in ways to protect innocent commercial parties from the risk of being encumbered with strict liability under that tort. There are also some interesting, albeit isolated, examples of developments in private law tort doctrines in the common law that have specifically triggered a response in public regulation.[15]

Hard empirical evidence on the impact of tort is remarkably patchy. That which is available tends only to address the impact of tort doctrine on repeat players. In the United States, where there have been the most extensive empirical studies on the deterrent effect of tort law, the evidence has been judged equivocal.[16] In the Commonwealth, empirical studies on tort law looking at who was sued, who sued, and why, found torts' doctrinal norms played a relatively small role in these behaviours.[17] Yet, the reasons for this were typically quite different from the sort of reason that Collins asserts make the specific norms set by contract law marginal to contracting parties when a dispute arises. Unlike in many contracting situations, in most tort situations there is no desire to maintain a cordial ongoing relationship with the defendant, but problems accessing justice were a very significant deterrent on tort claims. This was particularly the case outside the areas where access to justice was facilitated by union or insurer support, work and road accidents, respectively.

In general, there is insufficient empirical evidence to conclude whether tort doctrines are influencing public regulation or social norms, such as the behaviour of the target population, either at the pre-tort stage or in how they react to the commission of a tort. The diversity of torts suggests that there will be some circumstances where tort doctrine will have moulded behaviour, as in the avoidance measures taken in relation to liability for conversion. Yet, there will be other

---

[15] The well-publicized English Court of Appeal rejection of negligence claims by asbestos workers in *Fairchild v Glenhaven* [2002] 1 WLR 1052 generated a public outcry that prompted the Labour government to extend the state no-fault workers' compensation scheme. Tort law developments, such as the recent recognition of the tort of harassment, can also help prompt a response in regulation by the criminal law: Protection from Harassment Act 1997, ch. 40.

[16] D. Dewes, D. Duff, and M. Trebilcock, *Exploring the Domain of Accident Law* (Oxford: Oxford University Press, 1996), 414.

[17] D. Harris *et al.*, *Compensation and Support for Illness and Injury* (Oxford: Oxford University Press, 1984); Lord Pearson (Chairman), *Report of the Royal Commission on Civil Liability and Compensation for Personal Injury*, 3 vols., Cmnd. 7054 (London: HMSO, 1978); Bogart, *Consequences*, 119.

areas, such as negligence and trespass, where social behaviour may appear to be tracking tort norms for a variety of reasons, and these cannot be unravelled because of the incremental nature of tort law development. Tort doctrines typically evolve incrementally. Even a landmark decision is often only appreciated as changing doctrine in a profound way when its authority is later applied to wider and wider circumstances. This incremental nature of the emergence of tort doctrine means that any impact that it has on social practices and public regulation is typically masked by the operation of other forces over time. For example, the increased disclosure of risks to patients may have also resulted from the changing appreciation by medical personnel of the intelligence and autonomy rights of patients, which, in turn, may have been largely prompted by social campaigns by an ageing electorate.[18]

Effectiveness: Goals of Tort Doctrines

So far, we have merely looked at the effect tort doctrines may have on social norms and public regulation. But if we are to address the editors' question about the *regulatory* effectiveness of those doctrines we must determine what are their *intended* norms, goals, and policies. One problem here is that most tort doctrines, because they are a creation of the common law, have no definitive stated purpose. So in looking for the goals of tort doctrines we are in the field of speculation.

Many North American tort law scholars have located themselves in various camps, each of which speculates that there is one central 'pure' goal for 'tort law' doctrine. The problem for these 'high theorists' of torts is that no one pure theory or model fits the acknowledged contours of tort doctrines and they are, therefore, of no use to practitioners and courts dealing with precedents based on those contours.[19]

The more convincing thesis is that the judges who create tort doctrines (and, to a lesser extent, the few legislatures that enact liability statutes) are motivated by a complex and diverse set of concerns, some of which may be in tension with each other in a particular fact situation.[20] These produce a richly textured and contextualized set of doctrinal norms that provide some of the legal boundaries within which we are free to act. As we have seen, for example, one such micro-concern that would rarely be triggered by the facts of a case is that tort doctrine should not positively encourage abortion.[21] Not unexpectedly, tort shares this concern with other areas of law and social norms. Another, more general, concern is that liability should not be indeterminate but sufficiently foreseeable for potential defendants to weigh up their conduct in its light. Courts craft the contours of tort doctrine so that liability operates within confines that control for this concern.[22]

---

[18] This is suggested by the empirical evidence that the level of disclosure increased to the same extent even where tort liability had not been expanded: Bogart, *Consequences*, 119.
[19] Stapleton, 'Comparative Economic Loss', 531.   [20] Stapleton, 'Duty of Care Factors', 59.
[21] Ibid.   [22] Stapleton, 'Comparative Economic Loss', 531.

Another set of concerns that influence the incidence of tort liability emerges when courts deal in a tort claim with parties that were or could have been linked by direct contract or indirectly through a contractual matrix.[23] On the one hand, the law of torts is averse to assisting a party that could have protected itself in an appropriate way, at least from pure economic loss. This means that where contractual bargaining between the parties was easy, tort doctrine is reluctant to help the aggrieved party. The viability of the contractual path of self-protection provides a reason for non-intervention by tort in the economic loss area. On the other hand, a core concern of torts is to protect the vulnerable from invasion of those interests protected by the relevant tort. This means that even where the parties were linked by, say, a contractual matrix, if that matrix contributed to the vulnerability of the claimant by preventing contractual protection, this contractual matrix can be a positive reason for the intervention of tort law. In other words, sometimes tort intervenes to assist the victim of what seems to be a contractual 'stitch-up' by much more powerful parties.[24]

Moreover, the context of an individual tort case does not reflect a single socially constructed area of concern such as the workplace, the family, the home, the environment, personal injuries, and so on. For each such social context there will be a specific set of public regulatory goals. But, typically, a tort claim cuts across a number of such contexts. For example, tort will entertain a tort claim from a wife (family context) who contracted mesothelioma (personal injuries context) after decades washing (home context) the work clothes of her husband laden with asbestos dust (environmental context) from his workplace (workplace context). This means that for each unique tort case the facts will trigger a unique set of concerns and it is the complex weighing of these that produce the complex boundaries imposed on our freedoms by tort law.

This, in turn, means that there is no one canonical list of tort concerns relevant to a case. This suggests that there will be no easy way empirically to assess tort doctrine's effectiveness in responding to such concerns. The problems here are compounded by the rich factual diversity of the torts doctrines themselves. In one tort, such as private nuisance, the law is centrally concerned with a particular invasion of interest, namely that of amenity. So, in nuisance the actionable harm typically concerns matters such as noises and smells. Such irritations are simply not actionable in the tort of negligence, which protects a somewhat different set of interests. Similarly, whereas in the tort of negligence courts are centrally concerned with the reasonableness of the conduct of the defendant that harmed the claimant, in the tort of conversion the reasonableness, indeed, the complete innocence, of the converter is irrelevant. In some torts, such as negligence, damage is the gist of the action, while in others, such as defamation, there is no need to show damage to the interest protected.

---

[23] Stapleton, 'Duty of Care Factors', 59.
[24] See e.g. *Smith v Bush (Eric S)* [1989] 2 All ER 514; *Henderson v Merrett Syndicates Ltd.* [1994] 3 All ER 506.

Another problem with seeing tort doctrines as regulatory, even once we concede that, like contract, they only operate as minor peripheral boundaries on our freedoms, is that it is plausible that those who construct torts doctrines are concerned that these boundary restrictions encapsulate certain *moral values*, regardless of whether the doctrines affect pre-tort behaviour or post-tort dispute resolution. In other words, there may be an important motivation that is quite separate from the 'instrumental mentality' that seeks to influence behaviour to accomplish particular social objectives. For example, in societies where there are high barriers to access to justice it is still plausible that the excluded would support the existence of, say, the tort of defamation because it reflects values that the excluded hold dear[25] including: the protection of the reputation of celebrities from cynical exploitation by the media; the truthfulness of published information; and the punishment of media who resort to defamation in order to boost sales and manipulate the public for profit. These symbolic aspects of defamation may be valued by the excluded even while they themselves defame others on a daily basis. It seems likely that this symbolic role for tort law is a main concern for judges. Two recent examples show courts deciding major tort cases explicitly on the basis of broad non-instrumental concerns of fairness.[26] In contrast to the hypothesis that tort doctrines have a public regulatory objective, the judicial importance accorded to such concerns is consistent with the absence of amicus briefs in tort cases, even where, as in one of these cases, huge sums turned on the case.[27]

What follows from the fact that the concerns of tort law are complex, diverse, sometimes in tension with each other, and by no means all perceived as instrumental by those that erect tort doctrines? It is that we are unlikely to be able to devise any feasible empirical study to evaluate the general 'regulatory impact', where this is taken to mean 'effectiveness', of tort doctrines on behaviour.

Responsiveness of Tort Doctrines to Other Regulatory Orders

Collins argues that two broad subsystems of legal reasoning, one associated with private law and, apparently, concerned solely with conflict resolution between private parties, and an instrumental one associated with public law and regulatory law which used empirical evidence to comprehend actual social practices, have begun to interact with each other.[28] This, he claims, has begun to produce a new form of legal reasoning whereby, for example, private law reasoning is beginning to accommodate instrumental reasoning and values.

---

[25] Compare E. P. Thompson, *Whigs and Hunters* (London: Penguin, 1977), 266: 'the forms and rhetoric of law acquire a distinct identity which may, on occasion, inhibit power and afford some protection to the powerless'.
[26] *McFarlane v Tayside Health Bd. (Scotland)* [2000] 2 AC 59, 82–3, 96; *Fairchild v Glenhaven Funeral Services Ltd & Ors* [2002] 3 All ER 305.
[27] The House of Lords decision in *Fairchild v Glenhaven Funeral Services Ltd & Ors* [2002] 3 All ER 305 will cost the insurance industry between £6 billion and £8 billion: J. Stapleton, 'Lords a'Leaping Evidentiary Gaps', *Torts Law Journal*, 10 (2002), 276.
[28] Collins, *Regulating Contracts*, 7–10.

Even if this account holds true for contract, few tort lawyers or judges conceive of tort doctrine as concerned solely with the conflict between the parties. Unlike contract doctrine, which typically operates on, and indeed is somewhat obsessed by, an agreement between the litigating parties, tort doctrines do not start with the requirement that the parties even knew each other. A stranger can be liable for running down a pedestrian he has never met; a person can be liable for unwittingly defaming a person of whom they have never heard; and a person can commit the tort of conversion of property without knowing the property was stolen, let alone who its true owner is. Indeed, tort obligations might in part be defined as ones that can apply between complete strangers. This means that many tort complaints emerge from social contexts that have, in the eyes of the law, no advance normative structure agreed between the parties, no 'private ordering' of entitlements providing the legitimacy for the intervention of private law.

This situation requires tort judges to use markedly open-textured reasoning as they carefully scrutinize the wider context in which the dispute arose, including relevant public regulations and market arrangements, to see whether tort *should* remedy the claimant's grievance.[29] As a result, tort analysis seems normatively more open than contract. For example, where the parties to a contract suit have had prior dealings, these will tend to be largely eclipsed in importance by the crystallization of their relationship in the agreement. In contrast, where the parties to a tort suit have had prior dealings, these will form an important part of the context in which the issue of tort entitlements will be considered.

It is a routine task of tort doctrine to supply, unilaterally, the relevant normative structure. As we saw in the last section, tort judges do this after an investigation of each thread of the factual context to determine which of its features raises matters of concern to the law and, therefore, which is relevant to the claim. We saw that these concerns range from policy concerns generated by the psychological, economic, and social context of the case, to moral evaluations, to administrative and institutional concerns. Far from bringing a 'closed' system of legal reasoning to bear on tort cases, tort judges have always been required to engage in a relatively open analysis. To the extent that elsewhere the law also takes account of such concerns (protecting the vulnerable from damage, the law not positively encouraging abortion, etc.) tort law is better seen as *sharing* values with, rather than responding to, these other forms of regulatory ordering.

Whereas Collins is critical of contract courts for allegedly underemphasizing the 'embeddedness' of the relationship of the parties,[30] tort courts are typically forced to *start* with such issues, including conventional and expected behaviours, and address 'all the circumstances' whether the tort obligation arises at common law or under statute. In tort, it is this very context and history of the

---

[29] For particularly fine recent examples, see *Caledonia North Sea Limited v British Telecommunications Plc (Scotland) and Others* [2002] UKHL 4 and *Perez v Wyeth Laboratories Inc.* 161 NJ 1, 734 A 2d 1245 (1999).   [30] Collins, *Regulating Contracts*, 25–8, 356.

parties that generates the tort obligation, which is itself a direct response to the social reality. Indeed, landmark tort judgments occur exactly when a judge sweeps away artificial factual distinctions that reflect no normative concern, 'striking through forms of legal separateness to reality'.[31]

Collins notes that, in the contractual context, parties embrace non-doctrinal values such as trusting and being trustworthy, and that these emerge from prior dealings between the parties.[32] In contrast, pre-tort reliance between parties typically comes not from prior dealings but from other more general social norms and phenomena. An awareness of tort obligations may not even be one of these: in general, people can be relied on to drive safely because they do not want to maim themselves or others,[33] doctors can be relied on to care for their patients for vocational reasons, and so on. Where, however, a party has changed his or her position in response to a specific undertaking by another, this special form of 'change-of-position' reliance may well trigger the protection of tort where breach of the undertaking causes injury to the first party.[34] Thus, far from being a factor that competes with doctrinal norms, in tort the notions of trust and trustworthiness can be central to how those doctrines generate tort entitlements.

Of course, tort courts are aware that any determined effort to discover meaningful sociological and psychological evidence to illuminate the concerns in a case will be prohibitively costly for many parties. These underlying institutional and personal limitations on the analysis rightly prompt limits to the types of evidence that are accepted as relevant and admissible in order to avoid disadvantaging a poor party who would not be able to marshal as compelling a case as a party with a deep pocket. It is widely understood, therefore, that much of the resultant legal reasoning emerging in judgments will be of an impressionistic nature.

The tight interrelationship of public concerns and rules with tort doctrines has been long acknowledged, and well before the emergence of the new regulatory state. Examples abound where tort doctrines have long ago been crafted to take account of local social practices and norms. We have seen earlier, for example, that courts are anxious to avoid setting up a dynamic through tort doctrines that might positively encourage abortion, a medical procedure that few in society would want positively to encourage in preference to other forms of contraception. Another example is where judges take account of the nature of the locality when determining whether a use of land constitutes a nuisance, a responsiveness that, in turn, earns the description of 'judicial zoning',[35] since

---

[31] As Justice Evatt expressed his admiration to Lord Atkin for the latter's judgment in *Donoghue v Stevenson* [1932] AC 562: G. Lewis, *Lord Atkin* (London: Butterworth, 1983), 66.

[32] Collins, *Regulating Contracts*, 27–8, 98–102, 110–14.

[33] For example, recent empirical work found that the introduction of no-fault auto insurance did not increase the accident rate by reducing drivers' incentives to drive carefully: D. Loughran, *The Effect of No-Fault Automobile Insurance on Driver Behaviour and Automobile Accidents in the United States* (Santa Monica, Calif.: RAND Institute for Civil Justice, 2001).

[34] Stapleton, 'Comparative Economic Loss', 541.

[35] W. Prosser, *Handbook of the Law of Torts*, 4th edn. (St Paul, Minn.: West Publishing, 1971), 600.

once the locality has been analysed by one judge, other judges are likely to follow his or her characterization of the area. Yet another example is set out in a 1914 decision[36] where the High Court of Australia departed from the English rule relating to a landowner's liability for fire that a camper allows to escape, on the explicit instrumental basis that such a liability would deter the social practice of open hospitality in the Australian bush.

But this long-standing dialogue between tort doctrines and public concerns and rules does not necessarily result in tort doctrines tracking those norms. For example, the relevance of compliance or non-compliance by an employer with public health and safety at work regulations to the standard of care required of him under the tort of negligence has long been settled. But, typically, the tort standard holds that mere compliance with public regulation is not determinative.[37] Similarly, tort standards, far from aiming to mirror industry practice, often reject it as inadequate, requiring parties to meet what are, in effect, pace-setting norms. There are other striking examples where tort obligations in the common law have clearly not matched social expectations or regulatory norms.[38] For example, in contrast to social norms, the law of torts in the Commonwealth did not, until recently, provide protection from harassment. It still provides no sanction against: a landlord for injuries to an entrant when he knowingly leases a tumbledown house; the plagiarist *simpliciter*; the party that carelessly or intentionally destroys the evidence which was crucial to a person's civil action. Indeed, the absence of injunctive relief for many types of tortious behaviour, such as negligence, no matter how likely it is to cause damage and no matter how extreme the injury threatened, also indicates that the tort of negligence does not seek to track the realm of public regulation.

We would not expect there to be a clear pattern in the response of tort doctrines to social norms and public regulation. Tort courts are influenced by a mix of concerns when crafting tort doctrines. Given the diversity of this area of law and the haphazard spread of issues reaching appellate courts, it is not clear how one could answer the question whether courts are recasting tort doctrine to be more 'reflexive' with or 'responsive' to other forms of regulatory ordering. Tort courts have always appreciated that their decisions will have larger social impact than merely on the parties. Indeed, they often speculate as to the ways their decisions might impact on the wider world. Sometimes this speculation influences a decision, sometimes it is given no weight, and sometimes[39]

---

[36] See *Whinfield v Lands Purchase and Management Board* (1914) 18 CLR 606, 616 (per Griffiths CJ), on which, see *Burnie Port Authority v General Jones Pty. Ltd.* (1992) 179 CLR 520, 566 (per Brennan CJ).
[37] But see the debate on the merits of the regulatory compliance defence in the United States: R. Rabin, 'Reassessing Regulatory Compliance', *Georgetown Law Journal*, 88 (2000), 2049.
[38] For example, although public regulations in New York mandate the wearing of seatbelts, statute provides that 'non-compliance with the provisions of this section shall not be admissible as evidence in any civil action in a court of law in regard to the issue of liability': N.Y. Vehicle & Traffic Laws §1229-c(8) (Consol. 2001).
[39] As in *Fairchild v Glenhaven Funeral Services Ltd & Ors* [2002] 3 All ER 305.

a decision is taken despite the acknowledged inevitability that it will have a profoundly unsettling impact on social or regulatory norms. Sometimes the court declines to address an issue that is critical to the decision of how parties respond to the judgment.[40]

Finally, we might take issue with what Collins characterizes as a public regulatory norm. For example, far from agreeing with Collins's characterization of consumer protection as a public regulation norm, tort lawyers, generally, appreciate that this protectionist impulse has old and complex origins. It was an impulse reflected in private law doctrines, albeit far from consistently, well before the rise of the welfare state and the post-war proliferation of statutory protections. We have seen that Collins describes legal reasoning being polarized between the formal stance of private law being focused on conflict resolution between private parties, and reasoning that is sensitive to the norms of policy-oriented public regulation in the consumer protection area. But tort law in this area has long provided a vivid illustration of why this polarized vision of Collins is inadequate. Not only can the same legal concern be packaged in terms of public issues (manufacturers should owe a duty to those who use their products) or private justice (Mr Stevenson must compensate Mrs Donoghue for the injury he carelessly caused her in violation of her rights), courts routinely express a single specific concern in both forms in the same case. Tort cases are rich with examples of how a private litigant can always be taken as the representative of a class of citizen. It would, in short, be very hard to establish that tort law has seen a recent shift from 'private' concerns within a 'closed' doctrinal discourse to accommodate concerns with 'other regulatory orderings'.

META-REGULATION

Coherence of Tort Doctrines Set within Complex Systems

The editors and Hugh Collins are not only interested in whether tort doctrines satisfy the regulatory or good-governance criteria of efficiency, effectiveness, and responsiveness. They also point to the levers of 'meta-regulation' that exclude, confine, or alter the law of torts (i.e. other branches of law such as statute and constitutional law, transnational legal orders, or non-state institutional arrangements, such as the terms of any prior arrangement between the parties). Collins, having noted the complex systems of interaction between private law, social norms, and regulatory norms, argues that practitioners and judges have little understanding of these complex interactions. He argues that were they to acquire a better understanding, they could achieve better 'coherence' in private law doctrines set within such complex systems.

[40] In *Fairchild v Glenhaven Funeral Services Ltd & Ors* [2002] 3 All ER 305 the Lords did not address the critical apportionment issue: Stapleton, 'Lords a'Leaping Evidentiary Gaps'.

The complex interaction of tort doctrines and social norms is nothing new or surprising. For example, it is well known to tort scholars that it was the perceived inadequacies of tort liability for work injuries that, at the end of the nineteenth century, gave rise to the addition of workers' compensation entitlements that, in turn, became a model for the Beveridge welfare state. While in New Zealand it was the perceived inadequacies of the workers' compensation system that led to the replacement of tort liability for personal injury by accident, and in the United States it was the poor levels of workers' compensation coupled with the sole-remedy doctrine (that prevents injured workers from suing their employers) that fuelled the boom in product liability claims as injured workers sought out parties that they were allowed to sue for tort-level damages.

As we have seen, though tort courts are alive to the complex interactions tort doctrines have with other social and public regulatory systems, they do not manifest a simple response to them. In some cases, courts are explicitly concerned with how the law they are developing fits with other areas of law. Some courts openly state that their new doctrine is needed to 'fill a gap'. Elsewhere, a doctrine may be defended on the basis that it reinforces other social or legal norms. Elsewhere still, courts state that their decision is made despite the possibility, even likelihood, that other legal and social relations will be disrupted thereby. In other words, courts sometimes assert that a doctrine is justified even though it clashes with some other social or public regulation. In my view, though judges are indeed sensitive to the complexity of interactions within and between social systems and are acutely aware of their limited understanding of these interactions, they are also rightly sceptical of being able to deduce the full impact any doctrinal development may have, let alone use their speculations in this regard to guide their legal reasoning. Even if the judges and we agreed on the mix of outcomes we wanted from private law, and we do not agree, judges seem rightly to appreciate that the system is too complex to allow great accuracy about predictions of how a doctrinal shift will work its way through it.

Finally, it is worth taking issue with the very pursuit of 'coherence' here, at least if what is meant by that goal is that the norms of tort doctrines should not conflict with but should complement other forms of regulation. There is an implicit and loaded assumption that underlies this approach. It is an assumption that Patrick Atiyah made in his landmark book on tort law and its role in society, *Accidents, Compensation and the Law*.[41] It is that if our system accommodates a plethora of schemes that deal with the same problem (or, more accurately, what is assumed to be the same problem) there is something wrong, something incoherent, about it that calls out for change. These schemes 'collide' and we should look for approaches, such as systems theory, to heal the duplications and dislocations that result.

---

[41] P. S. A. Atiyah, *Accidents, Compensation and the Law* (London: Butterworth, 1970).

But why is there an objection to complexity? After all, we do not regard a complex biodiverse ecosystem in dynamic flux as problematic. Quite the contrary. The plethora of systems we see may be an inevitable characteristic of the dynamic evolution of societal values. More importantly, this plethora may be a desirable, because nuanced, multidimensional response to the complex needs of the system. In other words, another way of looking at the existence of, say, the plethora of schemes that provide compensation for personal injuries is that each responds in a subtly specific way to different complex sets of concerns. The patchwork of avenues to compensation may well track an explicable and defensible patchwork of public policy concerns. For example, we might hold a particular view of the role of tort in this area but still be in favour of there being a separate additional no-fault compensation scheme in certain limited contexts because the scheme encourages very specific conduct that we believe benefits society as a whole. Vaccine damage compensation schemes and favoured treatment of veterans' health are two obvious examples.[42]

This also raises the question: Why is it problematic to Collins that contracting parties only resort to law as a sanction and not as a template for their behaviour? Parties get different things out of litigating, as opposed to negotiation or forbearance. Parties are provided with different options: is that a bad thing? Would Collins find a problem with parties preferring to ignore the expense, publicity, and adversarial posture involved with tort litigation? What, for example, might be objectionable with a doctor saying sorry and not getting sued, a dentist who had not met a standard of care paying an ex gratia sum to the injured party in settlement, a worker taking no-fault state benefits rather than suing? Similarly, may not the justification for tort doctrines be their symbolic role? Only a very small number of citizens invoke the law of defamation, but it is plausible that a large majority of the population support the existence of the doctrine because it enshrines important cultural values about truth-telling, especially by the powerful about the powerful. Judgments couched in consequentialist reasoning may rest on nothing more than speculation yet, nevertheless, fulfil a valued symbolic role which other avenues to compensation for, say, personal injuries do not provide.

Even in the private law area itself we see, and seem to accept, this rich phenomenon of doctrinal entitlements that respond to different concerns. Thus, depending on the facts of a specific case, one injured party may have no claim, another may have a claim under one doctrine, while yet another plaintiff may have claims under a number of doctrines. The same patchwork is seen when we look at private law remedies: I can apply for injunctive relief if you are creating a nuisance but not if your carelessness is threatening my life. But there are reasons for these differences that can be stated and evaluated. Another example is that tort makes little attempt to hold tort litigants 'accountable'. Successful plaintiffs are not monitored to ensure they spend their compensation wisely and

---

[42] J. Stapleton, *Disease and the Compensation Debate* (Oxford: Oxford University Press, 1986), 112.

on the heads of damage they claimed.[43] Defendants held liable for damages need
not change their behaviour or face inquiries into how their safety systems could
be successfully modified. But reasons for the lack of these forms of accountability can be found and evaluated. Tort law is not public law in disguise.

Of course, there will be cases of 'overlap' of features. For example, certain tort
norms have echoes in criminal law and contract law. But the role of the criminal
law cannot be completely met by tort, because its sanctions and concerns are
different. Even if criminal justice is bolstered by restorative justice procedures,
tort remedies are not an exact substitute for the conventional treatment of criminals because, for example, they fail to meet public pressure for retribution.
Similarly, contract cannot be a direct substitute for tort entitlements because
contract rights are only available to certain victims, and even these, generally,
have to pay for the protection. Tort entitlements are at large and are free.

Rather than being a problem in need of resolution, the complexity of tort
doctrines and their relationships with other forms of ordering may be valuable
and well grounded. In any case, the delicacy of these relationships is such that
we should not disturb them lightly. Least of all should we do so in pursuit of
some vague notion of coherence, simplification, or allowing other orderings
'more space'. Such a reform project will have systematic social impact that needs
to be acknowledged and justified.

Finally, there are constitutional issues to be noted. Firstly, we should remember that in some federal common law jurisdictions, such as the United States,
the federal legislature may have power to bar tort claims by virtue of the
pre-empting effect of regulatory legislation.[44] Similarly, it is possible that state
courts might decide that the rigours of a particular regulatory regime are such
as to justify a rule of law that regulatory compliance precludes tort liability.[45]
So far, both these phenomena are rare elsewhere.

From a constitutional point of view, perhaps the most alarming development
relevant to seeing tort law through a regulatory lens is the new phenomenon
in the United States which has been dubbed 'regulation through litigation'.[46]
Here, state politicians have initiated tort suits against target industries such
as tobacco, firearms, lead-based paints, and breast implants. This tort litigation
has been used as the financial lever to force companies to accept negotiated

---

[43] See e.g. the current 'havoc' in native Alaskan communities resulting from the fact that some
beneficiaries of the Exxon Valdez litigation 'have blown it all on impulse purchases': *Electronic
Telegraph*, 1 June 2003.

[44] See e.g. *Boulahanis v Prevo's Family Mkt., Inc.*, 583 NW 2d 509, 509 (Mich. Ct. App. 1998),
holding the claims of consumers who were made sick (one died) by beef infected with E. coli 0157
were pre-empted by the Federal Meat Inspection Act. Contrast: *Smith v Secretary of State for Health*
(QB, 15 Feb. 2002) (Morland J), available at http://www.lexis.com, concerning a negligence claim,
against the government agency which regulates medicines, by a child whose Reye's syndrome was
triggered by aspirin; and the $A5.6 billion negligence claim made by the liquidator of HIH Insurance
against the Australian insurance industry regulator: *Australian Financial Review*, 13 Nov. 2002.

[45] Rabin, 'Reassessing Regulatory Compliance'.

[46] W. K. Viscusi (ed.), *Regulation through Litigation* (Washington: Brookings Institution Press,
2002).

regulatory policies. Thus, as part of the package to end the litigation the defendants have agreed to arrangements that include a de facto tax on consumers,
and states have agreed to limit the access to state markets by new companies
that might seek to enter the market, unburdened by the settlement agreement.
But, as attested by the concern this phenomenon has aroused, regulation
through litigation of this sort bypasses the usual rule-making process that
involves a careful analysis by government regulatory agencies subject to their
legislative mandates. Thus, the settlements impose taxes and market limitation agreements that violate important competitive norms without legislative
mandate.[47]

CONCLUSION

I conclude with three points. Firstly, using a regulatory lens as a broad supple-
mental perspective can illuminate legal research in some ways. It gets us asking
fruitful questions; for example, why tort remedies are not twinned with
accountability regimes. The answers we find may be compelling and fully justify
the status quo. Nevertheless, the regulatory lens can distort the picture by tending to identify incorrectly the concerns that influence those who construct the
private law of torts: our judges and the counsel that address them.[48] Empirical
social science data are not likely to influence these groups. Because such data
are impressionistic and inconclusive when magnified to the level of generality,
they do not possess an essential characteristic that legal doctrine must have to
fulfil the minimum certainty requirements of the rule of law. Given its lack
of precision, it is understandable why such material remains unattractive to
the private lawyer who requires the 'evidence' to dovetail relatively straightfor-
wardly with the legal question in issue.

Secondly, there is a real danger that the regulatory lens will be used to
downgrade private law to the role of mere servant to a multi-layered system
of governance. For example, in addressing the meta-regulation question of the
adequacy of governance mechanisms that regulate private contract law, Collins
states that 'once one views *private law* as *merely* one of a number of mechanisms of governance for achieving the social goals of the community' the objective 'should be to try to align general contract law with the state's welfare and
social inclusion goals and to co-ordinate its regulation with other regulatory
systems'.[49] The foregoing chapter has attempted to show that the law of torts

---

[47] W. K. Viscusi (ed.), *Regulation through Litigation* (Washington: Brookings Institution Press,
2002). 351.
[48] On the general point, see also P. Cane, 'Tort Law as Regulation', *Common Law World Review*,
31 (2002), 305, arguing that the regulatory lens blurs the reality of tort law by concentrating on
sanctioned conduct at the expense of interests that are vindicated, and emphasizing forward-looking
behaviour modification goals at the expense of backward-looking responsibility-based values.
[49] Collins, *Regulating Contracts*, 63; emphasis added.

simply cannot play such a role. But we should also remember that there are strong normative reasons why we might not agree to such a relegation of tort law without a very rigorous debate.

Thirdly, in contrast to the claims Collins makes for contract law, in recent years tort law has not been called upon to play a significantly more pivotal role in the governance mechanisms of society than beforehand. Because tort law does not focus on one specific social practice but rather bites on all types of conduct including misfeasance, it has never been possible for it to draw a sharp contrast between the relationship of the parties *inter se* and their wider role as representative of wider classes in society. Perhaps for longer than most fields of private law, tort reasoning has had to engage directly with broader political and social values than those limited to efficiency and the protection of rights.

7

Criminalization as Regulation: The Role of Criminal Law

NICOLA LACEY*

The field of criminalization has long provided fertile terrain for the application of regulatory analysis: criminalization is, after all, quintessentially a related set of 'intentional activit[ies] of attempting to control, order or influence the behaviour of others'.[1] In the discipline of criminology, a central topic of debate has always been the role of criminalization in shaping social behaviour. And it is next to axiomatic in much criminal justice scholarship that the actors, agencies, and practices which form the object of study—policing, prosecuting, and punishing, in all their variegated institutional environments and cultural forms—are performing regulatory tasks, the effectiveness of which is, therefore, a primary research question. Among the many practices which interlock to produce the social field of criminalization, however, the creation and interpretation of the norms and doctrines of criminal law have received relatively little attention from scholars of regulation.

This claim must immediately be modified. The implementation of so-called 'regulatory offences' in areas such as licensing or health and safety have, of course, been the object of a great deal of empirical study.[2] Indeed, one might observe that, over the last thirty years, a division of labour has grown up among criminal lawyers and regulatory scholars. Criminal lawyers focus on the traditional sphere of 'real crime'—roughly equating to those offences requiring proof of 'mens rea' or fault—while treating regulatory offences of strict liability, often enforced by specialist agencies rather than the public police, as a marginal and, perhaps, embarrassing exception to the general method and principles of criminal law. Regulation scholars, on the other hand, have tended to focus their attention on the substance of regulatory norms and on empirical facts about

* My warm thanks to John Braithwaite, Valerie Braithwaite, Geoffrey Brennan, Peter Cane, Julian Le Grand, Philip Pettit, Colin Scott, and David Soskice for constructive comments on and discussion of the first draft of this chapter, and to Jim Jacobs and the other members of the New York University School of Law criminal law group for stimulating discussion of a later version.

[1] J. Black, 'Decentring Regulation: Understanding the Role of Regulation and Self-regulation in a Post-regulating World', *Current Legal Problems*, 54 (2001), 103.
[2] For a wide range of examples, see R. Baldwin, C. Scott, and C. Hood (eds.), *A Reader on Regulation* (Oxford: Oxford University Press, 1998); R. Baldwin, *Understanding Regulation* (Oxford: Oxford University Press, 1999).

their enforcement and effectiveness:[3] they, conversely, have paid relatively little attention to the terrain of 'real crime', such as serious offences against property or the person, and show little interest in the 'normative complexity' of liability doctrines which Hugh Collins, in *Regulating Contracts*, has identified as distinctive of legal modes of regulation.[4] While the 'regulatory offences' are, naturally, thought of in instrumental, means–ends terms, and, hence, standardly interrogated in terms of efficiency and effectiveness, the quasi-moral terrain of 'real crime' tends to be thought of in terms of intrinsic values, such as justice, fairness, right, and wrong: a distinction which also realizes itself in relation to contrasting—deterrent versus retributive—approaches to punishment.[5] There is a strong analogy between the quasi-moral, retributive justice view of criminal law and the non-instrumental commitment to principles such as reparation in private law doctrine noted by Peter Cane.[6]

In this chapter I shall focus my attention on the norms and doctrines of criminal law in order to ask three questions which echo those raised in Hugh Collins's *Regulating Contracts*. First, what contribution, if any, does criminal law make to the regulatory tasks of the criminal process as a whole and, assuming that criminal law is making some regulatory contribution, what is distinctive about criminal law's regulatory aspect? Secondly, how is criminal law itself regulated by other normative systems, and might substantive or procedural changes in criminal law enhance its regulatory contribution: might, as it were, criminal law itself be more effectively regulated? Thirdly, how, if at all, have the dynamics of regulation in late modern states affected criminal law and what contribution does or might criminal law make to the reflexive or responsive regulation of socially undesirable behaviour? My argument will proceed as follows. Firstly, I shall sketch out the theoretical framework which will shape my analysis, tracing its application to the various aspects of criminalization. Secondly, I shall apply this analysis to a number of key aspects of criminal law viewed in historical perspective, so as to tease out the regulatory aspects of modern criminal law in England and Wales. Thirdly, I shall address some of the questions raised in the introduction to this collection, so as to examine the regulatory and meta-regulatory actuality and potential of criminal law in the contemporary regulatory state.

Before proceeding, however, I should like to enter certain caveats about this project. From a regulatory perspective, I am not at all sure that it makes sense to take 'criminal law' as one's starting point: rather, one would surely start with

---

[3] See e.g. K. Hawkins, *Environment and Enforcement: Regulation and the Social Definition of Pollution* (Oxford: Oxford University Press, 1984); *Law as Last Resort: Prosecution Decision-Making in a Regulatory Agency* (Oxford: Oxford University Press, 2003).

[4] H. Collins, *Regulating Contracts* (Oxford: Oxford University Press, 1999), 32.

[5] Significantly, much of the regulation literature in the criminal justice field has concerned itself with crime and punishment in the corporate context: see e.g. B. Fisse, and J. Braithwaite, *The Impact of Publicity on Corporate Offenders* (Albany: State University of New York Press, 1983).

[6] Ch. 10 in this volume.

the distinctive forms of antisocial behaviour or wrongdoing which criminal processes seek to regulate. Indeed, this social-practice-led form of analysis is precisely the approach taken in the criminal law textbook which I co-author,[7] in which the substantive chapters are organized around social problems—public disorder, dangerousness, violence—or social values—property, sexual integrity—which criminal law claims to address or protect. This mode of analysis speaks to the argument which Collins makes when he talks about the desirability—particularly in terms of reflexivity—of a sector-specific approach to regulating contracts.[8]

Moreover, in training my attention specifically on criminal law, I should not be taken to imply that its operation can be understood in isolation from the norms, practices, and institutions of criminal justice which form its most obvious environment. My assumption, on the contrary, is that the significance of criminal law—including its distinctive regulatory dynamics—can only be understood in relation to the entire criminal process and, indeed, its social environment.[9] However, I believe that a recognition of the propriety of viewing law from a regulatory point of view does not entail a collapse into an entirely reductionist view of law, such as that espoused by Chicago-style law and economics scholarship or some versions of sociological research inspired by Legal Realism. Rather, I share Collins's commitment to treading a middle path between an internal, doctrinally focused legal analysis and an external, social analysis: a middle path which explores the distinctive institutional organization, techniques, and assumptions of the legal order, while investigating their implications for social systems beyond the law.[10] Law, then, 'provides one form of regulation', 'but it is only one of many types of social regulation, such as custom, convention, and organised bureaucracies'.[11]

To see all aspects of the distinctive regulatory significance of legal doctrines, however, we have to move beyond an understanding of regulation as 'any system of rules intended to govern the behaviour of its subjects',[12] or even the broader conception of regulation as 'the intentional activity of attempting to control, order, or influence the behaviour of others'.[13] For, as I shall argue, some of the most interesting and distinctive regulatory capacities of criminal law lie in the indirect effect of common law doctrines which have evolved incrementally over many years, and which it would be difficult to establish had been designed with

---

[7] N. Lacey, C. Wells, and O. Quick, *Reconstructing Criminal Law*, 3rd edn. (London: Butterworth, 2003).

[8] See Collins, *Regulating Contracts*, 360 and ch. 4. Sector-specific scholarship is also common in other areas of legal doctrine, for example, the law of torts: see e.g. P. Cane, *Atiyah's Accidents, Compensation and the Law*, 6th edn. (London: Butterworth, 1999); J. Stapleton, *Disease and the Compensation Debate* (Oxford: Clarendon Press, 1986).

[9] See, further, N. Lacey, 'Legal Constructions of Crime', in M. Maguire, R. Morgan, and R. Reiner (eds.), *The Oxford Handbook of Criminology*, 3rd edn. (Oxford: Oxford University Press, 2002), 264.   [10] Collins, *Regulating Contracts*, 6.

[11] Ibid. 7.   [12] Ibid. 7.

[13] Black, 'Decentring Regulation'; J. Black, 'Critical Reflections on Regulation', *Australian Journal of Legal Philosophy*, 27 (2002), 1.

directly regulatory intent.[14] Since my view is that it is, nevertheless, appropriate to inquire into their regulatory significance or impact, I shall adopt a definition of regulation as 'any practice which has the intention or effect of controlling, ordering, or influencing the behaviour'. I would concede, however, that substantial questions may be raised about the costs, in terms of both analytic integrity and fit with linguistic usage, of so broadening the concept of regulation.

My claim, then, is that while the regulatory reality and potential of criminalization—like that of any other regulatory field—depends fundamentally on the interlocking relationships between criminal justice and other regulatory systems operating in the same environment, in assessing the reality and potential of the regulatory system of criminalization the distinctive contribution of criminal law—its norms, its general doctrines, its mode of reasoning, its personnel—are, indeed, a proper object of discrete analysis. While keeping an open mind about the sector-specific regulatory dynamics of criminal law, I shall, therefore, approach my task equipped with a positive hypothesis about the regulatory aspects of criminal law. This is that the development and survival of key doctrinal and substantive aspects of criminal law is likely to depend (at least in part) on their direct or indirect contribution to the regulatory objectives of the criminal process. A key assumption which I shall make in exploring this hypothesis is that the conditions of existence of any regulatory system include not only material resources such as economic or physical power, information, and institutional infrastructure, but also what we might call symbolic resources such as legitimacy.[15]

REGULATORY RESOURCES: ACTORS, TASKS, MODALITIES, SUBJECTS

In developing my analysis of criminal law's regulatory aspects, I shall use an analytic framework which draws on a number of ideas developed in regulation scholarship. Following Colin Scott, I shall think of the field of criminalization as a 'regulatory space' populated by a number of distinctive regulatory actors, regulatory modalities, and regulatory tasks: the interaction between these various components constitutes, what we might call the *regulatory resources*—material and symbolic, coordinated and fragmented—within a particular regulatory space.[16] The *actors* in the regulatory space of criminalization include, I shall argue, not only legislatures, courts, governments, regulatory agencies, and

---

[14] On the indirect significance of non-intentional aspects of institutional design, see R. E. Goodin, 'Institutions and their Design', in Goodin (ed.), *The Theory of Institutional Design* (Cambridge: Cambridge University Press, 1996), 28.

[15] Cf. John S. Dryzek's analysis of the role of underpinning discourses within institutions: 'The Informal Logic of Institutional Design', in Goodin (ed.), *The Theory of Institutional Design*, 103.

[16] C. Scott, 'Analysing Regulatory Space: Fragmented Resources and Institutional Design', *Public Law* (Summer 2001), 329, in turn developing L. Hancher and M. Moran, 'Organising Regulatory Space', in Hancher and Moran (eds.), *Capitalism, Culture and Economic Regulation* (Oxford: Clarendon Press, 1989).

formal criminal justice agencies, such as police, prosecution, probation, and prison services, but also the full panoply of non-governmental collectivities, such as pressure groups, private security services, other corporations, and indeed, crucially, individual members of society. Drawing on the work of Lawrence Lessig, as adapted by Andrew Murray and Colin Scott,[17] I shall adopt a fourfold framework of *regulatory modalities* as consisting of hierarchical, normative or community-based, competition-based, or design-based methods of control, these four methods being deployed variously to three distinctive *regulatory tasks*: standard-setting, information-gathering or monitoring, and behaviour modification or enforcement.

Contemporary criminalization participates in each of the three regulatory tasks and deploys each of the four modalities just delineated. To take some examples, criminal law is involved both in standard-setting and in setting up (through the rules of evidence) the framework for information-gathering: criminal justice agencies, such as the police, are involved in information-gathering and monitoring; the overall goal of the system is behaviour modification—a task most vividly attempted through practices of punishment. Similarly, criminalization deploys a variety of modalities. The legislation of norms of criminal law is a hierarchical means of standard-setting; social pressure founded in community-based controls is central to the production of compliance with the norms of criminal law. The manipulation of penalties, informed by certain assumptions about the motivations and capacities of the subjects of regulation (see below), could be seen as analogous to competition-based forms of control. Systems of self-regulation backed up by ultimate criminal sanctions in the business area, for example, may create a situation in which standards of compliance and good practice become one aspect of firms' competitive advantage. Design, including not only behavioural regulation through architectural design of public spaces or buildings in pursuit of 'situational crime prevention' or the panopticon prison, but also normative regulation through the discursive and ritual design of the criminal trial, the choreography of the trial process through courtroom design and rules of evidence, plays various roles in pursuing the regulatory tasks of criminalization. Among these four modalities, however, I shall focus on the first two, hierarchical and community-based means of regulatory control, and on the interaction between the two.

It is, perhaps, one of the most persistent myths about criminalization that it operates, primarily, in hierarchical regulatory mode. This image of criminalization as a hierarchical system is strongly associated with the role of law in the overall regulation of crime. Collins puts it thus:

In scholarly examinations of regulatory techniques, a contrast is frequently drawn between 'command and control' styles of regulation and 'responsive' (or reflexive)

[17] L. Lessig, *Code and Other Laws of Cyberspace* (New York: Basic Books, 1999); A. Murray and C. Scott, 'Controlling the New Media: Hybrid Responses to New Forms of Power', *Modern Law Review*, 65 (2002), 491.

regulation. The former style of regulation approximates to criminal law. The rules are imposed by the regulator (or parliament): inspectors monitor compliance; and courts or specialist tribunals impose deterrent sanctions against breach of regulations. In contrast, responsive regulation seeks to achieve the collaboration and co-operation of those subject to regulation. In setting the standards, it favours the use of self-regulation, so that within a broad requirement fixed by legislation the participants can settle through negotiation the detailed rules to govern transactions.[18]

Like most myths, this idea of criminalization as hierarchical has a basis in truth. At the level of standard-setting, courts and legislatures play a leading role, bringing with them the centralizing and top-down aspects of the 'command and control' model. But this is only—indeed, less than—half the truth: an image which is itself a product of thinking about criminal law in isolation from the regulatory contexts in which it is interpreted and enforced. The basic point here can be summed up in the old rallying cry of the Realist and law in context movements: the law in the books is not the same as the law in action. Moreover, the difference between the two must be explained not merely in terms of limited enforcement resources or the interpretative influence of officials, but in yet broader terms. Take, for example, the fact that (in Britain) the overwhelming majority of suspected offences investigated by the police come to their notice through report by members of the public. It is well known that limited resources—as well as the fact that we would have political objections to living in a panoptically policed society—mean that the proportion of the total amount of social behaviour susceptible to formal criminalization which is actually proceeded against is tiny. What is less often remarked is that a primary gatekeeper between social behaviour which might be defined as criminal and the process of formal criminalization is the ordinary citizen. What this implies, among other things, is that where central, hierarchically defined criminal law standards depart from community standards—as, unfortunately, has often been the case in relation to the application of the law of assault to domestic violence, or, perhaps more positively, in relation to the social use of cannabis or, in the famous US instance of prohibition, alcohol—or where community standards are themselves contested, the enforcement and, on occasion, interpretation of criminal law will be fundamentally affected by its dissonance with the structures of informal, community-based control.

Lack of articulation with community-based control will, therefore, place limits on the effectiveness with which centrally determined and hierarchically imposed regulatory objectives can be pursued: in this sense, wider social norms themselves regulate formal criminalization. But this is not just a matter of constraint. There is also a story here about regulatory capacity. For, positively, it is the underlying bedrock of social support for criminal law that underpins the widespread voluntary compliance without which the hierarchical regulatory resources of the criminal process at the monitoring and enforcement levels would

[18] Collins, *Regulating Contracts*, 65.

be entirely incapable of delivering the most modest of regulatory objectives.[19] And this is due, at least in part, to the resonance (or, at the least, lack of dissonance) between the substantive norms of criminal law and prevailing social norms. In this context, the internalization of norms at the social level underpins criminalization in something like the way that trust can facilitate contracting. John Braithwaite's regulatory pyramid sets restorative justice, the preferred option, at the bottom of the pyramid: deterrence through the announcement of standards and threat of penalties in the middle; and incapacitative punishments the last resort at the top.[20] In terms of this analysis, one could say that the most important regulatory work in relation to criminalization in fact goes on below the bottom of the pyramid, consisting in the personal internalization of norms or generalized receptivity to peer pressure, which secures voluntary compliance, rendering resort even to the first level of the regulatory pyramid unnecessary. The pyramid, perhaps, is focused on the tasks of monitoring and enforcement, rather than that of standard-setting.

Finally, drawing on both John Braithwaite's regulatory pyramid, which integrates restorative justice with more coercive regulatory techniques, and Julian Le Grand's recent work on agency, motivation, and public policy,[21] I will add to the framework of regulatory actors, tasks, and modalities a further set of analytic distinctions having to do with the assumptions which each regulatory modality makes about *the subjects of regulation*: in the case of criminalization, individuals, and corporations. Firstly, what assumptions are made about their motivations: secondly, what assumptions are made about their capacities; and thirdly, what normative limits have the assumptions about their capacities been thought to place on the practice of criminalization?

Let us begin with the question of motivation. Are the subjects of regulation assumed to be egoists or altruists—knights or knaves, in Le Grand's terms: 'virtuous', 'rational', or 'incompetent' actors in Braithwaite's (a classification which, in fact, elides my first two categories of motivation and capacity)?[22] And how does criminal justice manage the fact that criminal conduct has multiple motivations, such as rational calculation, principled resistance, and sheer incompetence?[23] While criminal law and the threat of punishment address subjects

---

[19] T. R. Tyler, *Why People Obey the Law* (London: Yale University Press, 1990).

[20] J. Braithwaite, *Restorative Justice and Responsive Regulation* (Oxford: Oxford University Press, 2001), 32 and ch. 2; cf. Philip Pettit's argument for prioritizing 'screening' over 'sanctioning': *Republicanism: A Theory of Freedom and Government* (Oxford: Clarendon Press, 1999), ch. 7; P. Pettit, 'Institutional Design and Rational Choice', in Goodin (ed.), *The Theory of Institutional Design*, 54.

[21] J. Le Grand, *Motivation, Agency and Public Policy* (Oxford: Oxford University Press, 2003).

[22] Braithwaite, *Restorative Justice*, ch. 2.

[23] See R. A. Kagan and J. T. Scholz, 'The "Criminology of the Corporation" and Regulatory Enforcement Strategies', in K. Hawkins and J. M. Thomas (eds.), *Enforcing Regulation* (Dordrecht: Kluwer, 1984), 67; V. Braithwaite, 'Games of Engagement: Postures within the Regulatory Community', *Law and Policy*, 17 (1995), 225; V. Braithwaite, J. Braithwaite, D. Gibson, and T. Makkai, 'Regulatory Styles, Motivational Postures and Nursing Home Compliance', *Law and Policy*, 16 (1994), 361. The latter two articles also emphasize and give evidence for the link between social bonds and regulatory motivations.

assumed to be self-interested knaves,[24] community-based modes of regulation might be thought to address subjects assumed to be 'virtuous'—'knights'—in the thin sense that they will comply with the relevant norms even when it is not in their self-interest to do so.[25] By associating the three regulatory approaches with different conceptions of the regulatory subject—restorative justice with the 'virtuous actor'; deterrence with the rational actor; incapacitation with the incompetent or irrational actor—Braithwaite's regulatory pyramid implies that, within the regulatory space of criminalization, there can be a productive interaction between modalities with different assumptions about subjects' motivations and capacities. Braithwaite's assumption is that the incentive structure provided by subjects' awareness of the existence of the more coercive upper levels of the pyramid helps to underpin cooperation with non-coercive techniques, such as restorative justice (as well as voluntary compliance below the pyramid): on this view, the harder-edged forms of regulation, rather than being inimical to trust and other goods which facilitate informal or self-regulation, can, in fact, foster these things. This is plausible: yet it also seems important to ask some questions about the conditions under which this productive interlocking can occur. For it seems clear that it is sometimes damaging to the interlocking of coexisting regulatory modalities within one regulatory space that they approach their subjects on the basis of fundamentally different assumptions about their motivations and capacities. We have probably all experienced the onset of a 'work to rule' mentality when subjected to overenthusiastic practices of, for example, auditing in the workplace. Under what conditions, then, can we motivate people to behave as knights while treating them as knaves?[26]

A full consideration of this question lies well beyond the scope of this chapter. But I want to suggest that, at least in the field of criminalization, a part of the answer depends on the second distinction among assumptions about the regulatory subject: the regulatory system's approach to its subjects' capacities. This is, perhaps, yet more important than the issue of motivational assumptions for modern criminal law, which proclaims as one of its central doctrines that the subjects of criminalization are, in Le Grand's terms, 'queens': self-determining agents capable not only of rational choice but of taking responsibility for their choices, rather than 'pawns': passive objects of regulatory power. But can we treat the subjects of regulation as competent agents for some purposes but not for others—as pawns for the purposes, for example, of situational crime

---

[24] Albeit with some exceptions, generally associated with defences such as insanity.

[25] Both Braithwaite and Le Grand allow for multiple motivations: see Le Grand, *Motivation, Agency and Public Policy*, 31. I am leaving aside here the thorny question of whether all behaviour, including morally motivated action, is at some level self-interested: on this point, see ibid., ch. 3.

[26] Pettit, *Republicanism* and 'Institutional Design and Rational Choice', has argued that this problem can be avoided by (cf. Braithwaite, *Restorative Justice*) prioritizing 'compliance-centred' over 'deviance-centred' regulatory strategies, and by ensuring that, when sanctions have to be resorted to, they are designed on the basis of either neutral or optimistic assumptions about subjects' motivations. This seems right in theory but hard to achieve in the criminalization context, though, as I shall argue below, the commitment to principles of responsibility may go some way to ensuring the motivational neutrality of criminal law, if not so plausibly of punishment.

prevention strategies such as target-hardening, but as queens for the purposes of answering criminal charges or committing themselves to certain sets of norms? Does the threat of a draconian penalty which leaves the subject only a theoretical 'choice' treat her as a 'queen' or a 'pawn'? And does this depend on whether it is threatened or imposed with deterrent or retributive intent? Must—and should—particular regulatory modalities be consistent in their attitude to the moral or rational capacities of their subjects, or can different assumptions be drawn upon for different purposes?

The potential for effective regulation on the basis of differing assumptions seems to me less plausible in relation to capacity than to motivation. However, while different regulatory modalities may differ in treating us as knaves or knights, almost all of them (excepting, perhaps, physically determining features of design, but including retributive versions of punitive incapacitation and restorative justice) make a common assumption about our capacities for rational choice and self-direction.[27] Hence, on the basis of an assumption that regulatory subjects have the cognitive and volitional capacities of the rational agent, other-regarding or 'virtuous' motives can (as both Braithwaite and Le Grand conclude in relation to rather different cases and by rather different routes) be fostered within a regulatory system based on an assumption of rationally self-interested motivation under certain further conditions. Once again, the question arises of what these conditions are.

Some further clues about the conditions which foster the regulation of knaves without undermining the motivations of knights lie, perhaps, in our third point about the assumed subjects of regulation. As we shall see below, the salient doctrinal assumption that the subjects of modern criminal law are, *empirically*, responsible agents has brought in its train a distinctive set of *normative* principles having to do with the moral limits which respect for human agency places on criminalization.[28] In what follows, I shall consider the possibility that criminal law's normative commitment to treating its subjects as 'queens'—as responsible, choosing agents—may turn out to be of particular importance to its regulatory potential. My hypothesis is that it may be one of the conditions,

---

[27] One might even say that such an assumption is the bedrock of not only the modern project of governance but also 'post-regulatory' practices, such as self-regulation, 'government-at-a-distance', and Foucauldian 'technologies of the self'. In this context, I would question the idea that the delivery of restorative justice necessarily depends on a 'virtuous' as opposed to a rational subject. I would argue that when regulatory subjects' concerns for factors such as their reputations—and there is plentiful evidence that just such concerns constitute a primary motivation not only for individuals but for corporations—are taken into account, a sufficiently complex version of the deterrence–rational actor model provides a powerful template for assessing the potential effectiveness of all regulatory modalities. See R. Baldwin, 'The New Punitive Regulation', forthcoming (*Modern Law Review* 2004), and R. Baldwin and R. Anderson, *Rethinking Regulatory Risk* (London: DLA/LSE 2002); Fisse and Braithwaite, *The Impact of Publicity on Corporate Offenders*; B. Fisse and J. Braithwaite, *Corporations, Crime and Accountability* (Cambridge: Cambridge University Press, 1993); D. J. McBarnet and C. Whelan, *Creative Accounting and the Cross-eyed Javelin Thrower* (Chichester: Wiley, 1999).

[28] It has also had the effect, until recently, of rendering problematic the legal construction of corporate responsibility for serious crimes: see C. Wells, *Corporations and Criminal Responsibility*, 2nd edn. (Oxford: Clarendon Press, 2001).

at least in relation to the regulation of serious crime by human individuals, which facilitates synergies between regulatory modalities which treat us as knights and as knaves.

Having set out a basic set of theoretical tools and sketched their relationship to various aspects of criminalization, I now want to narrow my focus to concentrate on the distinctive regulatory aspects of criminal law. Once again, I shall pay particular attention to the interaction between hierarchical and normative or community-based regulatory modalities; but I shall focus first on certain features of modern criminal law.

The 'Special Part' of Criminal Law: Standard-Setting and Legitimation

In thinking about the distinctive contribution of criminal law to the regulation of behaviour seen as wrong or antisocial there are, according to the analysis of both modern scholars and modern codes of criminal law, two broad places to look. The first and most obvious is the panoply of criminal offences themselves: the primary, duty-creating rules of criminal law which proscribe certain forms of behaviour and which implicitly announce certain values. This is, in lawyers' terms, the 'special part' of criminal law. The special part is an obvious focus given that it is the substantive duties which criminal law creates which—depending on one's perspective—either themselves perform a standard-setting task or provide the framework within which the interpretative standard-setting activities of authorities such as courts, police, prosecutors and indeed citizens take place.

It is puzzling, then, that the overall content and changing contours of the special part of criminal law have formed a relatively rare object of scholarly study among either criminal lawyers or regulation scholars. Studies of the content of criminal law standards have—as in the areas of regulation, such as health and safety—been sector-specific. At the start of the twenty-first century the reason for this is not far to seek. The content of criminal law—its special part—is simply too various to admit of any general assessment or rationalization. There is, therefore, little to be said of a general, as opposed to a sector-specific, nature about the distinctive regulatory contribution of the special part of criminal law, other than that the legislative mechanism allows legislatures (and, in effect, in many systems, governments) to use the articulation of new criminal law standards in a hierarchical way for a very wide range of regulatory purposes. This, of course, is an oversimplification: the legislative enactment of a law of homicide would engage in standard-setting in a completely different way from, say, legislative enactment of a rule that henceforward traffic would be required to take the right rather than the left-hand-side of the road. In the former case, the criminal law's standard plugs into widely shared social norms, which constrain its articulation and will shape—indeed 'regulate'—its interpretation and enforcement. In the latter, the new standard acts as a decisive coordinating and signalling device. Different again would be the enactment of a criminal law extending the law of theft to cover a widespread commercial activity, such as insider trading: here, social norms being contested, we have a partly hierarchical, partly community-constrained piece of standard-setting in which the back-up of formal sanctions might well be more important than in the traffic case.

Nevertheless, in a world in which governments use the creation of new criminal laws as the quick fix for social ills ranging from graffiti through drugs to terrorism via dangerous dogs—and in which, hence, the 'coherence' horn of Teubner's 'regulatory trilemma' having to do with the disintegration of the internal logic of law might be expected to be well and truly felt[29]—it is hard not to feel the force of the reductionist law and economics or Realist approach. It is, perhaps, to be regretted that there is not more regulatory scholarship track-ing judges' and enforcement agents' interpretative practices in relation to spe-cific kinds of offence—exploring questions, for example, of whether such interpretations are affected by the belief that criminal law has strayed into inap-propriate terrain. But it is probably not surprising that the main regulatory research focused on the special-part of criminal law has primarily to do with the attempt (simple in theory but often difficult in practice) to track its effects in specific sectors. An interesting research question about distinctively legal constraints on special-part standard-setting arises, however, in systems in which judges have the legal responsibility to subject the content of criminal law to scrutiny based on constitutional or human rights standards. Early indications of the impact of the Human Rights Act in England and Wales suggest that this will not be a very significant factor.[30] I am not a sufficiently qualified comparativist to judge the position in other systems, but recent evidence about the attitude of US judges to post-11 September criminal legislation suggests that even a rather strong constitutional framework gives judges limited resources to defend any distinctively legal conception of constraints on the special part of criminal law.

Today, then, it is not in the special part that we find the distinctive normative complexity which Collins identifies as specific to the regulatory modalities of private law. It is crucial to remember, however, that it was not ever thus—and that it is not thus in every legal system. Let us take two salient examples from the modern history of English criminal law. First, as Jeremy Horder has noted,[31]

---

[29] G. Teubner, 'After Legal Instrumentalism: Strategic Models of Post-regulatory Law', in Teubner (ed.), *Dilemmas of Law in the Welfare State* (New York: Walter de Gruyter, 1988), 299 and 309.

[30] See A. Ashworth, *Human Rights, Serious Crime and Criminal Procedure* (London: Sweet & Maxwell, 2002); A. Ashworth, 'Criminal Proceedings after the Human Rights Act: The First Year', *Criminal Law Review* (2001), 855.

[31] J. Horder, 'Two Histories and Four Hidden Principles of Mens Rea', *Law Quarterly Review*, 113 (1997), 95; J. Horder, 'Rethinking Non-fatal Offences against the Person', *Oxford Journal of Legal Studies*, 14 (1994), 335; J. Horder, 'A Critique of the Correspondence Principle in Criminal Law', *Criminal Law Review* (1995), 759.

notions of criminal conduct, such as 'assault' or 'battery', are today regarded as technicalities which should be abandoned in favour of an articulation of offences against the person in terms of a simple hierarchy of severity of harm done by whatever means. Yet, these venerable concepts, as Horder argues, reflected rather specific, socially rooted understandings of distinctive wrongs, which it was one of the proper functions of a criminal law system accurately to label and proscribe. Whereas today the articulation of the special part of criminal law—particularly in the area of offences against the person—is increasingly organized around a hierarchy of unwanted outcomes, in early modern criminal law the essence of criminal law's method was to be quite precise about the specific modality of wrongdoing. Of course, contemporary criminal codes do continue to fulfil, albeit less consistently, this sort of 'labelling' function, distinguishing offences such as rape, homicide, different forms of assault, and a wide range of offences against property and trust. But, as a result of a range of social and legal changes which I shall discuss below, we no longer have—and can no longer have—confidence that the shape of criminal wrongs reflects a shared conception of 'manifest criminality'[32] recognizable to any member of the community, symbolized by the jury.

Secondly, let us take William Blackstone's famous *Commentaries on the Laws of England*, published in the second half of the eighteenth century.[33] In the volume on criminal law we find a confident and eloquent rationalization of the nature of criminal law as tied ineluctably to its content: to the special part. Criminal law is characterized in terms of the distinctive interests and values which it expresses and protects: the state, the person, property, God, and religion. As Blackstone—the supreme defender of the common law—was keen to point out, this was a structure which had been worked out gradually in the courts through the common law method, with statutory innovations geared to deliberate steering interstitial. Though judge-made law clearly counts as hierarchical, a very small group of judges moving regularly around the country to hear cases was, arguably, relatively well equipped, as compared with a legislator, to be responsive (where they deemed it appropriate) to social norms, whether or not this responsiveness was accomplished with self-consciously regulatory intent. Indeed, as Peter Drahos's chapter in this collection shows,[34] common law judges have on occasion shown themselves capable of remarkable institutional innovation in the service of responsive regulation. In criminal law the primarily common law development of the offences up to the middle of the eighteenth century doubtless fostered a certain coherence—albeit one which began to be more regularly disrupted by politically motivated (and often draconian) legislation in areas such as poaching and social disorder.[35] This

---

[32] Themselves closely articulated with evaluative offence requirements, such as the requirement that a wrong be committed 'maliciously' or 'feloniously'. On manifest criminality, see G. Fletcher, *Rethinking Criminal Law* (New York: Little, Brown, 1978).

[33] W. Blackstone, *Commentaries on the Laws of England*, iv (London: Clarendon Press, 1765).

[34] Ch. 8.   [35] See E. P. Thompson, *Whigs and Hunters* (London: Penguin, 1975).

story—of criminal law as a distinctive social response to the need to protect certain threats to society's most cherished interests or values—still, of course, works well enough with the 'quasi-moral' terrain of 'real crime': the ancient offences of homicide, rape, assault, theft, burglary, and so on. But it is incapable of rationalizing the content of the instrumental, 'regulatory' aspects of criminal law in areas such as health and safety that increased in relative importance from the middle of the nineteenth century.

What do these two examples tell us about the changing regulatory aspects of criminal law? Firstly, they suggest that even the most obviously hierarchical aspect of criminal law—its creation of duty rules as standard-setting devices— is closely articulated with community-based regulatory modalities, which either enhance criminal law's standard-setting capacity or regulate it in a constraining way. Changing ideas about the importance of sexual expression to the identity of the regulatory subject, for example, have gradually regulated formal crim- inalization in the area of homosexual conduct. Secondly, the examples generate the hypothesis that it is in the systems in which there is the closest articulation of the special part of criminal law with standard-setting in the community that legal regulation will be most responsive and least in need of its more coercive tools. As much empirical research shows, the correspondence between legal criminalization and changes in social behaviour is, to put it mildly, incomplete— the 'effectiveness' horn of Teubner's regulatory trilemma. In this light, the use of formal criminalization might be regarded as a highly uncertain regulatory process. Structural couplings between formal law and community norms, sometimes fostered by imaginative public campaigns (as in the case of drinking and driving) seeking concurrently to shape social norms, occasionally facilitate effective regulation.[36] Absent such couplings, and given limited enforcement resources, effects on behaviour are likely to be modest. Thirdly—and the point on which I want to concentrate—the examples suggest that the standard-setting function of the special part of criminal law may, under certain conditions, oper- ate not only as a hierarchical regulatory modality but also in two further ways. Firstly, it may be complementary (as in Braithwaite's pyramid) to the internal- ization of norms at the community level through effective convergence with those norms and even by helping to coordinate convergence in contested areas; secondly, it may be indirectly functional to the stability and effectiveness of the formal regulation of crimes through a legitimating effect. This legitimating effect may arise through structural coupling between formal and informal norms or, in democratic systems, through the democratic credentials of the law-making process (though, particularly in executive-dominated and strongly centralized parliamentary systems, this seems likely to be relatively weak).

To sum up: in a system in which the substance of criminal law articulates closely with bottom-up, normative or community-based modes of regulation,

---

[36] R. Homel, *Policing and Punishing the Drinking Driver: A Study of General and Specific Deterrence* (New York: Springer Verlag, 1988); J. Jacobs, *Drunk Driving: An American Dilemma* (Chicago: University of Chicago Press, 1989), particularly pt. III.

the special part of criminal law will command a level of political, moral, and cultural support which may be expected to contribute substantially to the overall legitimation of the system, notwithstanding its use of coercive power. Under conditions, however, where governments use criminal law pragmatically and sometimes indiscriminately for a huge range of regulatory purposes commanding very different levels of support within conventional social morality, and under conditions of social pluralism—of diversity within social morality—the potential for the special part of criminal law to contribute to the overall legitimation of criminalization is diluted. And these, of course, were precisely the conditions which began to obtain in the UK in the first half of the nineteenth century, when—to paint with broad brush strokes—democratization, urbanization, and industrialization complicated both the normative social infrastructure underpinning criminal law and the regulatory challenges confronting an increasingly centralized and internal-governance-oriented nation state.[37]

The General Part of Criminal Law: The Indirect Regulatory Contribution of Legitimation and Coordination

Criminal law's distinctive regulatory contribution may, therefore, lie not so much in hierarchical standard-setting—a process which, as we have seen, has often uncertain outcomes, and ones which depend crucially on articulation with community-based regulation—as in legitimation: an indirect contribution, but a crucial one on the assumption that legitimacy is one of the key symbolic resources of any regulatory system. Pursuing this thought, the following question presents itself: how can criminal law make a contribution to legitimation in a situation in which there are huge variations in the extent to which its content overlaps with the norms of a conventional morality (which may itself be contested), and in which popular attachment to democratic legitimation is an unreliable source, given both the perception that governments use criminal law pragmatically and—in the case of those common law jurisdictions with a powerful but unelected judiciary in particular—in which the judiciary has significant criminal standard-setting power?

To answer this question, we need to turn to the second aspect of criminal law: its so-called 'general part'. The general part of criminal law refers to a set of rules, principles, doctrines, and procedural values which apply across the whole or a substantial part of the substantive terrain of criminal law. It includes, for example, the general defences, underpinned by doctrines of exemption, excuse, and justification; the notions that both a conduct element and a responsibility or fault element should have to be proven, at least in the case of serious offences; the idea that criminal trials should respect certain procedural standards, such as

---

[37] A more detailed account of both the theoretical argument here and the historical evidence for it, is set out in N. Lacey, 'Criminal Responsibility and Modernity', *Journal of Political Philosophy*, 9 (2001), 249, and 'In Search of the Responsible Subject', *Modern Law Review*, 64 (2001), 350; see also P. Cane *Responsibility in Law and Morality* (Oxford: Hart, 2002).

a special burden and standard of proof; the broad procedural aspirations often summarized under the heading of 'the principle of legality' or 'the rule of law'. The general part encompasses, therefore, both technical normative and conceptual doctrines and broad procedural values. What is true of each of its features, however, is that they have to do with the *form* of criminal law and not with its *substance*: with the rules addressed to judges in relation to what must be proven, and how it must be proven, to convict someone of a crime, and not with the duty rules addressed primarily to citizens. And it is this focus on form which provides the general part with its legitimating potential in a world in which the substance of criminal law is expanding, and in which the social normative systems underpinning formal criminalization are themselves diversifying and mapping less and less completely onto the special part of criminal law.

My contention that criminal law's distinctive contribution to the regulation of crimes is its indirect legitimation of the criminal process, and that this legitimating effect is today accomplished primarily through the doctrines of the general part, rests on an interpretation of the historical development of English criminal law since the eighteenth century. In Blackstone's *Commentaries* the notion of a general part of criminal law is entirely absent: the rationalization of criminal law is around the substantive values which it protects. In particular, any modern criminal lawyer would be struck by the cursory attention given to what is today regarded as the jewel in the crown of criminal law doctrine: the requirement of proof of individual responsibility or fault. The genesis of the 'mens rea' principle is a long and complex story which spans, in my interpretation,[38] at least a century: but a review of the key elements of the story will suffice for the purposes of this chapter. The story has three key elements: firstly, changing conceptions of the subject of regulation; secondly, changes in the institutional framework for the delivery of criminal regulation; thirdly, changing conceptions of the substantive tasks of criminal regulation and of its importance relative to other normative regulatory systems.

To begin with the subjects of regulation: the emergence of the modern project of centralized governance brought with it a self-conscious attempt to shape the behaviour of subjects; and this attempt was framed in terms of those subjects' capacities as rational actors capable of responding to adjusted incentives. In the work of the early Criminal Law Commissioners, it is this instrumental—indeed regulatory—recommendation of the 'mens rea' principle which predominates: only those who have acted intentionally or wilfully would have been susceptible to the deterrent incentives of the criminal law.[39] But as democratization proceeds, with the normative implication that the regulatory subject *should* be treated not

---

[38] Lacey, 'Criminal Responsibility and Modernity' and 'In Search of the Responsible Subject'; Cane, *Responsibility in Law and Morality*.

[39] As H. L. A. Hart noted in his justly famous essay on negligence as a form of mens rea, this was never a very convincing argument: H. L. A. Hart, *Punishment and Responsibility* (Oxford: Clarendon Press, 1968), ch. 6. On the work of the Commissioners, see K. J. M. Smith, *Lawyers, Legislators and Theorists* (Oxford: Clarendon Press, 1998).

only as a rational chooser but also in some stronger sense as an agent—as someone who not only makes choices but has some deeper form of responsibility for those choices, as a queen and not a pawn—a non-instrumental attachment to the responsibility condition emerges. This, of course, had always had a strong resonance in the retributive philosophical tradition, notably in the famous Kantian maxim of treating persons as ends in themselves rather than as means to ends.[40] But in England, at least, this strong notion of moral agency and responsibility only came to underpin the 'mens rea' doctrine rather slowly. Indeed, notwithstanding the Criminal Law Commissioners' robust emphasis on the normative importance of 'mens rea', at the level of legal practice, it was arguably not until the early twentieth century that English criminal law finally moved, more or less successfully, from what amounted to an exculpatory to an inculpatory system: in other words, to a system in which the criminal trial was geared to providing a full case for the defendant's inculpation as individually responsible, rather than exploring the exculpatory arguments for a defendant functionally assumed to be guilty.

The idea, then, of proof of some level of moral responsibility as a powerful legitimating device for criminal law emerged early but took decades to be institutionalized. What inhibited its initial development and then allowed its gradual implementation? To understand this, we have to move to the second of our key elements: the changing institutional infrastructure of criminal law. At the start of the nineteenth century the criminal trial was very different in form as compared with a century later. Defendants in felony cases had no right to legal representation until 1836; the law of evidence was in its infancy; in the absence of systematic legal argument, judges and even juries took a proactive role, which would today be associated with inquisitorial rather than adversarial systems; there was no system of appeal or regular reporting of cases. The institutional conditions under which the trial could systematically investigate the defendant's individual responsibility for the crime—under which responsibility could become an object of legal proof—developed only slowly during the course of the century. Only with the enactment of the Criminal Evidence Act 1898 and of the Criminal Appeal Act 1908 were they fully in place.

But if my argument about the needs for legitimacy of the criminal law system, and about the legitimating functions of the 'mens rea' doctrine, are right, how did the criminal law do without a full instantiation of the doctrine until the early twentieth century: through an era, what is more, which saw an explosion of criminal law's regulatory tasks, along with procedural innovations such as the creation of the summary jurisdiction, designed to manage the new regulatory terrain of criminal law? The answer here, I would argue, is twofold. Firstly, although the creation of the regulatory offences was a massive substantive change—and one which presented the system with a split between its

---

[40] On the relationship between Kant's philosophy and the influence of the retributive tradition in criminal law, see A. Norrie, *Punishment, Responsibility and Justice* (Oxford: Clarendon Press, 2000).

quasi-moral and regulatory terrains which persists to this day—the substance of the older offences was undergoing a far less radical revision during the nineteenth century. While the century was one of ceaseless procedural and penal innovation, the project of codification was never achieved,[41] and changes in the law of offences against the person and property—the quasi-moral core of 'real crime'—were relatively modest. This entailed that the articulation between the (relatively restricted) terrain of 'real crime' and a range of relatively uncontested social norms remained quite strong, thus making the need to develop concrete doctrines of 'mens rea' less urgent. The special part's legitimating potential outlived, in other words, the social conditions which had originally produced it.

Secondly, and following on from this point, informal means of control and dispute resolution at the local level predominated as a method of 'criminal enforcement', particularly in rural areas, well into the latter half of the century.[42] In this context, Brian Simpson's fascinating history of the case of *R v Dudley and Stephens* (1884) is instructive.[43] The defendants were sailors who had practised cannibalism in order to survive a shipwreck: shortly afterwards they were rescued. On their return to England, they immediately told the authorities what had happened. Marine custom sanctioned cannibalism under certain circumstances, and the British newspapers had reported several such incidents in the years immediately prior to Dudley's and Stephens's case. The two men clearly had no expectation that they would be prosecuted. Simpson shows that the decision to prosecute them—indeed to pursue their prosecution to unprecedented lengths—was based on a deliberate and high-level legal and political decision about the need to assert the primacy of criminal law's authority vis-à-vis other informal systems such as marine custom. What is significant about this is not so much the fact of that assertion as the lateness of the date at which the authorities felt the need to make it: on Simpson's analysis, 'legal pluralism' was only coming under strain in the last decades of the century.

What, however, of the new regulatory offences—the immense expansion of the terrain of criminalization which constituted one of the major changes in the criminal law of the nineteenth century and which remains one of that century's most substantial legacies to English criminal law? If, as I have argued, the notion of individual responsibility for crime, and associated general part doctrines, were gradually developing so as to shift the legitimating effect of criminal law onto a normatively complex and sophisticated formal framework for the justification of liability, how were the regulatory offences—the vast majority of which were offences of strict liability—legitimated? Doubtless, part

---

[41] This is, of course, a distinctive and local story: the political resettlements in many countries of the continent of Europe made for widespread projects of codification in the late 18th and early 19th centuries, while Britain exported criminal codes to many of its colonial territories, notably India.

[42] C. A. Conley, *The Unwritten Law: Criminal Justice in Victorian Kent* (Oxford: Oxford University Press, 1991).

[43] B. A. W. Simpson, *Cannibalism and the Common Law* (Chicago: Chicago University Press, 1984); 14 QBD 273; [1881–5] All ER 61.

of the story here was simply in terms of popular support for the proper regulation of the new industrial and urban activities, many of them dangerous to life and health: a reminder of the legitimating potential of the special part under conditions of social approval. But there is an ironic twist to the story: one in which the *lack of* a 'mens rea' requirement in these offences served to enhance their legitimation. Bear in mind that a disproportionate number of the subjects of these new regulations were people from relatively privileged social classes: in other words, people who were not used to being criminalized. As Alan Norrie has shown,[44] the resistance of factory owners and other powerful interest groups to the new regulatory offences was potentially fatal to their success: in this context, the argument that these were not 'real crimes' to which 'stigma' should attach, but were rather in the nature of administrative regulations with non-stigmatizing penalties such as fines, helped to lower resistance.[45] The lack of a 'mens rea' requirement operated, in other words, as the doctrinal marker of these defendants' 'less than fully criminal' status from a social point of view.[46]

CRIMINAL LAW IN THE LATE MODERN STATE:
META-REGULATION AND REFLEXIVITY

In the previous section I have argued that criminal law, not only through its hierarchical standard-setting functions, but also through its articulation with community-based modalities of regulation, has long served distinctive (if limited) regulatory purposes, while the currency of other social normative systems itself regulates criminal law. Hence, the form which criminal law's regulatory contribution takes, and—though I have not attempted to make any empirical assessment—its effectiveness, depend, I suggested, on a wide range of circumstances, including, notably, the social, economic, political, and institutional environment in which criminal law operates and the institutional shape of the criminal process. I now want to move to the present day to assess the regulatory dynamics of criminal law in the face of what some regulation scholars have diagnosed as a shift in the overall style of public regulation in developed economies during the last decades of the twentieth century. It has been argued that while the 'nightwatchman state' of classical liberalism neither 'rowed nor steered' civil society, and while the interventionist early welfare state both

---

[44] A. Norrie, *Crime, Reason and History*, 2nd edn. (London: Butterworth, 2001).

[45] It should be borne in mind, of course, that, as much empirical research shows (Hawkins, *Environment and Enforcement*), at the level of enforcement, regulatory agencies tend to direct their prosecution resources to those who are seen as being 'at fault', in the sense of, at least, having been negligent.

[46] It might also be seen as marking a belief in what Tony Honoré has called 'outcome responsibility'—i.e. responsibility for the harms which we cause irrespective of whether or not we had the capacity to avoid them in a strong sense—but with outcome responsibility seen as less stigmatizing than capacity responsibility: T. Honoré, *Responsibility and Fault* (Oxford: Hart, 1999), 14.

rowed and steered, the new regulatory state aspires at most to steer but never to row.[47] To this end, a variety of indirect regulatory techniques, such as auditing and benchmarking, facilitate practices of self-regulation or—from a more sceptical point of view—government-at-a-distance, creating a diverse and decentralized set of regulatory institutions. In this context, some scholars have hypothesized that we should expect an increase in regulatory law; the increasing infiltration of a regulatory style of reasoning into legal doctrine; collisions between the logics of public regulation and of private law;[48] innovation in legal doctrine; and a growth of 'reflexive law'. In this section I shall try to assess the strength of these hypotheses in the criminal law field and, where the hypotheses seem to be borne out, briefly to evaluate the implications for criminal law's coherence, effectiveness, and responsiveness.

At first sight, it might be thought that criminal law—indeed criminal justice—would provide a poor case study for exploration of the form of the new regulatory state. The creation of criminal law and the administration of criminal justice are, after all, state-led, hierarchical, and relatively centralized: the state's power to move the frontiers of criminality through new criminal legislation and techniques of enforcement constituting a distinct capacity not only to steer but to row. In the criminal justice system, announcements of the death (or 'hollowing out') of the nation state are premature indeed, and its institutions often act in hierarchical and coercive mode. If 'regulation should be aimed at a fairer distribution of the "good" of self-regulation of disputes',[49] we would have to conclude—as Nils Christie did in his classic article published in 1977[50]—that criminal law is doing badly. Nonetheless, at the level of criminal justice practices—policing, punishment, prosecution, and so on—there are many signs of a more indirect and diffuse style of regulation emerging in the governance of the public authorities which carry out these activities and of the private bodies to whom many aspects of the activities are increasingly delegated.[51] And in areas such as business regulation, environmental protection, and health and safety, there have certainly been moves towards using criminalization as the peripheral or last-resort framework underpinning practices of self-regulation which include elements of standard-setting as well as monitoring.

---

[47] See C. Parker and J. Braithwaite, 'Regulation', in P. Cane and M. Tushnet (eds.), *Oxford Handbook of Legal Studies* (Oxford: Oxford University Press, 2003), 119.

[48] I shall refrain from taking up the question of whether criminal law is best understood as private or public law. Though an interesting issue, I do not think that anything turns on this classification in terms of the argument of my chapter: my assumption is that the key contrast here is not so much 'public–private' as 'regulation–law', and that criminal law, therefore, provides as valid a case study for Collins's hypotheses as does the law of contract.   [49] Collins, *Regulating Contracts*, 12.

[50] N. Christie, 'Conflicts as Property', *British Journal of Criminology*, 17 (1977), 1.

[51] See e.g. D. Bayley and C. Shearing, 'The Future of Policing', *Law and Society Review*, 30 (1996), 586; D. Garland, *The Culture of Control* (Oxford: Oxford University Press, 2000); N. Rose, *Powers of Freedom* (Cambridge: Cambridge University Press, 1999); see also some of the innovative proposals of the Patton Report: *A New Beginning: Policing in Northern Ireland. Report of the Independent Commission on Policing for Northern Ireland* (London: Stationery Office, 1999).

Experimentation with diversion to restorative justice and other forms of alternative dispute resolution has undergone a revival in the last twenty years, and the criminal process and the other regulatory institutions with which it interacts have, undoubtedly, been affected by the changing style and culture of public regulation.

What, however, of criminal law? Taking first the hypothesis of an increase in regulatory offences, since many of the new, diffuse, indirect regulatory systems ultimately depend—albeit somewhere down the regulatory line—on a criminal sanction, this may well be made out. But it is not obvious that, overall, the intensity of criminal regulation is markedly greater now than it was, say, twenty years ago. In this context, Teubner's comments on the 'instrumentalization of law for the purposes of the political system' seem apposite but somewhat out-dated, for in criminal law this development dates back to the mid-nineteenth century and, hence, pre-dates the 'modern welfare state'.[52] I doubt that the added impetus for criminal regulation in the 'new regulatory state' matches up to that witnessed in the early decades of the industrial state or, indeed, of the post-war welfare state. These questions, however, I have yet to research, and these assertions are speculative.

What I would assert with some confidence is that there is a more vivid—though, perhaps, theoretically less interesting—sense in which regulatory criminal law, at least in Britain, is on the increase: and this is in the sense that successive governments over the last twenty years appear to have decided that criminalization is the quick fix for almost any social problem. In the last decade, substantial pieces of criminal legislation have averaged more than one a year in England and Wales. Though the vast majority of their provisions have to do with procedure, evidence, policing, and penalties, most of the legislation includes a scattergun array of new offences—covering specific kinds of fraud, new ways of accessing pornography, newly perceived social problems ranging from over-loud 'raves' through joyriding to harassment, paedophile offences, and international terrorism. These legislative innovations may be uneven and reactive, but they certainly amount to attempts at steering, and ones which commit the state to devoting some resources to rowing as well.

The real effectiveness of these serendipitous pieces of formal criminalization is hard to assess, but seems open to doubt. And the doubt about effectiveness may well relate indirectly to a concern about the internal coherence of criminal law doctrine—another horn of Teubner's regulatory trilemma. As I have already argued, the special part of criminal law has long lost the sort of coherence which it had in Blackstone's day: but the quotidian practice of reactive, populist criminal legislation can reasonably be expected to exacerbate this feature of criminal law. Perhaps more interesting is the fact that many of these new offences—particularly

---

[52] G. Teubner, 'Juridification: Concepts, Aspects, Limits, Solutions', in Teubner (ed.), *Juridification of Social Spheres* (Berlin: Walter de Gruyter, 1987), 389, repr. in Baldwin *et al.* (eds.), *A Reader on Regulation*, 401.

the less serious offences in the area of what we could loosely call public or social order—may be blurring the already tenuous boundaries between 'real' and 'regulatory' crime by which criminal law's legitimation is fostered. It is, perhaps, significant, therefore, that in several recent cases we have seen the House of Lords engaging in vigorous reassertions of the importance of the 'mens rea' principle to serious crimes and further attempts to delineate the boundaries between 'real' and 'regulatory' offences.[53] In a world in which criminal law is used for almost any regulatory purpose, and in which techniques of 'blame and punishment' are harnessed to regulatory purposes to a degree to which it makes sense to speak in the apparently oxymoronic terms of 'punitive risk',[54] one has to doubt the success of this heroic but probably Canute-like judicial endeavour.

In this context, perhaps, the most interesting regulatory perspectives from a criminal lawyer's point of view relate to the tendency to apply regulatory reasoning to private law doctrines, and to collisions between public regulation and private law. Certainly, a case like *Meridian Global Funds*[55] is instructive in this respect. In this case, serious offences against securities regulations had been committed by a large multinational corporation's investment managers—people somewhere in the middle of the company's managerial hierarchy. According to the 'identification doctrine' in criminal law, an employee's actions, at least where the offence with which the employee is charged involves proof of 'mens rea', can only be attributed to the corporation if the employee is so high in its managerial structure as to be 'identifiable' with the corporation. This, of course, would have let the corporation in this case off the regulatory hook. Lord Hoffmann in the Privy Council was having none of this. Applying straightforward policy reasoning, pointing out that respect for the identification doctrine would entirely subvert the regulatory scheme of the legislation and would, moreover, have the perverse result of rendering small, centralized corporations more vulnerable to the regulatory system than powerful, diffuse multinationals, he swept the criminal law doctrine aside with no hesitation whatsoever. This, certainly, was a key example of collision between the logics of commercial regulation and criminal law. But such collisions are an inevitable side-effect of any criminal law attempt to regulate another social system which has its own distinctive imperatives, and this sort of regulation has, of course, been with us for over 150 years. Moreover, though cases like this may accentuate the lack of coherence in criminal law doctrine, it could hardly be claimed that they create any great crisis. After all, criminal law's doctrinal coherence (and this is perfectly consistent with its legitimating role) has always been more a matter of ideology than of fact, as Ashworth and Blake's research on the structure of criminal offences has shown.[56] Legal doctrine is a flexible and

---

[53] See e.g. *B v DPP* (2000) 1 All ER 833.   [54] See Baldwin, 'The New Punitive Regulation'.

[55] *Meridian Global Funds etc. v Securities Commissioner* [1995] 2 AC 500.

[56] A. Ashworth and M. Blake, 'The Presumption of Innocence in English Criminal Law', *Criminal Law Review* (1996), 306. See also Lacey *et al.*, *Reconstructing Criminal Law*, ch. 1.I.

adaptable creature, and the demands of coherence with legal doctrine are relatively unconstraining.[57]

As for doctrinal innovation, once again the interaction of criminal law with other systems in its environment, via its regulatory functions, doubtless does lead to doctrinal development. But, as the history of the corporate identification doctrine itself shows, such regulation-prompted innovation is far from new. In the 1920s the courts held that a corporation could never be guilty of an offence requiring proof of 'mens rea' because it had 'no soul to damn': the identification doctrine was invented by the courts in the 1930s to overcome this barrier. In the 1990s, as a result of the difficulty of applying the identification doctrine where responsibility is diffused and, hence, criminal law's incapacity to regulate various corporate disasters (such as the sinking of the ferry *Herald of Free Enterprise*), there has been further pressure for doctrinal innovation in terms of notions such as aggregate or distinctively corporate fault.[58] To take an older example, Jerome Hall argued in his classic historical study of the law of theft that the fifteenth-century English courts invented the doctrine of 'breaking bulk' so as to overcome the barrier posed by the doctrine of possessorial immunity to theft by carriers, hence extending the criminal law's protection to the increasingly important phenomenon of international trade.[59] In terms of current doctrinal innovation, probably the most significant issues on the agenda in England are procedural: the dilution of the right of silence so as to make trials more effective; and the reversal of burdens of proof so as to increase the effectiveness of fields such as drug criminalization or the regulation of terrorism. In the area of procedure, to a far greater extent than of substantive law, we are already witnessing an interesting confrontation between these regulatory adaptations and the demands of the new framework of human rights—something of a new show in town as far as legitimating techniques are concerned.[60]

What, finally, of responsiveness and reflexivity? If criminal law were to be judged according to Collins's template of a 'fairer distribution of the "good" of self-regulation of disputes', how would it fare? As evidence of the criminal law's actual and potential reflexivity we can certainly cite the use in substantive law of ideas like 'reasonableness', 'indecency', and 'dishonesty', all of which are defined as substantially questions of fact and, hence, open to the lay evaluation of juries (in the tiny proportion of jury cases) or lay magistrates. As the instance of dishonesty shows, such open-textured concepts have the potential to render

---

[57] A good criminal law example of this kind of flexibility is the way in which offences in which the 'mens rea' requirement runs only to a part of the 'actus reus' are, nonetheless, constructed as offences which satisfy the responsibility requirement: see Lacey *et al.*, *Reconstructing Criminal Law*. ch. 1.II.

[58] See N. Lacey, 'Philosophical Foundations of the Common Law: Social not Metaphysical', in J. Horder (ed.), *Oxford Essays in Jurisprudence*, 4th ser. (Oxford: Oxford University Press, 2000), 17, for further discussion of these developments.

[59] J. Hall, *Theft, Law and Society* (Indianapolis: Bobbs-Merrill, 1952).

[60] See Ashworth, *Human Rights*; A. Ashworth, 'The Human Rights Act: A Non-minimalist View', *Criminal Law Review* (2000), 564; Ashworth, 'Criminal Proceedings after the Human Rights Act'.

even the most technical areas of criminal law responsive to, for example, commercial practice within a particular sector. It could be argued that the relevant standard of dishonesty should be relative to a particular sector, just as the relevant standard of reasonableness in provocation cases has been held to be responsive to the experience, circumstances, and characteristics of defendants.[61] Overall, criminal law would, doubtless, fare rather badly on the reflexivity test, but it would not be without arguments in its own defence.

A further question is whether we always want criminal law to be responsive: or, to put it more carefully, what are the proper limits of criminal law's reflexivity?[62] Should we necessarily applaud developments which blur the boundaries between criminal law and civil law, as in the recently enacted antisocial behaviour orders, which apply a criminal sanction to a civil wrong;[63] or the resort to civil suits by crime victims dissatisfied with the outcome of criminal processes? Should sentencers be responsive to victims' demands for punishment, as in some US jurisdictions? Should legislatures be responsive to popular demands for increased penalty levels or support for the institution of capital punishment? Community norms can and often do regulate criminal law, but should they always be allowed to do so? Reverting specifically to the dishonesty and provocation cases cited as examples of doctrinal reflexivity above, some hard questions arise. For we may not think it appropriate that criminal law be too responsive to local practices where these engage in abusive or costly or otherwise wrongful conduct, which is precisely what criminalization seeks to proscribe. Indeed, any global commitment to responsiveness would abandon the important and democratically legitimated, even if modest, steering function which criminal law claims. If city executives can use local commercial practice as a reason for denying dishonesty, or if a homicide defendant can use their background as a basis for claiming the reasonableness of their capitulation to provocation, the regulatory capacities of criminal law may be compromised at not merely instrumental but also symbolic levels. For the pretension to generality and universality is among the most important legitimating doctrines of criminal law. Furthermore, the use of open-textured concepts such as reasonableness and dishonesty, which in effect delegate the decision about the content of the criminal law duty to the finder of fact, might be thought to buy responsiveness at too great a cost in terms of procedural values such as certainty.[64] In his ambitious argument for self-regulation through restorative justice to replace state retributive justice as the paradigm of regulating crime, John Braithwaite acknowledges these limits in his recognition, for example, of the importance of human rights values.[65] In criminal law, the value of reflexivity is normatively, as well as practically, circumscribed in interesting and complicated ways.

---

[61] Lacey *et al. Reconstructing Criminal Law*. ch. 4.II.a.ii.
[62] This point is also taken up in Stapleton, Ch. 6 in this volume.
[63] See Lacey *et al.*, *Reconstructing Criminal Law*. ch. 3.I.c.
[64] See e.g. the impassioned dissenting speech of Lord Hobhouse in *R v Hinks* [2001] 4 All ER 833.
[65] Braithwaite, *Restorative Justice*, chs. 1 and 8.

CONCLUSION

I am conscious not merely that this chapter raises more questions than it answers, but also that several of the answers it proposes are in the nature of speculations and hypotheses rather than firm conclusions. I would, however, like to conclude by drawing out the main points which I hope to have made.

Firstly, I have argued that criminal law does indeed have a distinctive regulatory aspect which, secondly, is, however, contingent on its interaction with other regulatory systems and on its institutional infrastructure. Criminal law, in other words, both regulates and is regulated by other normative systems within the social order. Thirdly, I have argued that, beyond the obvious (though variegated and easily overplayed) standard-setting function of its special part, the distinctive regulatory aspect of modern English criminal law has two dimensions. The first flows from the (uneven) articulation of criminal law standards with normative, community-based regulation. The second is indirect and symbolic, and lies in the capacity of the general part—in particular, its principles geared to addressing its subjects as moral agents—to provide legitimation to the system of criminalization more generally. I must concede, however, the difficulty of establishing this claim empirically. If, as Jane Stapleton notes in relation to the law of torts,[66] it has proved extremely difficult to establish the material regulatory impact of particular legal arrangements, it would certainly be far more difficult to do so in relation to their symbolic impact. The most promising methods for strengthening the hypothesis would be to multiply comparative case studies of the developments canvassed here in relation to modern Britain. Fourthly, I have argued that the dynamics associated with the 'new regulatory state' are making themselves felt more on criminal procedure and criminal justice institutions than on substantive criminal law. Finally, I have suggested that reflexivity or responsiveness is a circumscribed value in criminal law, because there are some good political and moral reasons to retain the latter's distinctive, if modest, standard-setting function. In arguing for these tentative conclusions, I hope at the least to have demonstrated the fruitfulness of subjecting criminal law to a regulatory analysis. It is a project that, like all socio-legal research, prompts criminal lawyers to look again at many of the legal arrangements which we take for granted, and to interrogate their various different kinds of social significance.

[66] Ch. 6 in this volume.

8

Regulating Property: Problems of Efficiency and Regulatory Capture

PETER DRAHOS

INTRODUCTION

Regulation and property have always had a close association. John Locke in *The Second Treatise of Government* (1690) observes that 'laws regulate the right of property'.[1] Elsewhere he argues that the power of governments to regulate property does not amount to an arbitrary absolute power.[2] The property rights that individuals have in the state of nature, and which they seek to preserve by entering into society, set limits on what government may do to those rights. Thus, property rights in Locke's political theory are regulated by government and, in turn, regulate government.

Contemporary regulatory theory allows us to uncover much more of the duality of property law as both the object and subject of regulation. Contemporary theory shifts regulation away from a top-down process that is based on the command of rules to a decentred conception.[3] In these accounts different kinds of actor are interconnected by networks and organizational nodes such as trade associations and government advisory committees.[4] Regulatory resources are no longer centralized but flow through these networks and nodes.[5] Actors located in different parts of the network, by pulling levers of influence that range from dialogue to coercion, regulate other actors and are, in turn, themselves similarly regulated.[6] Regulation is multidirectional, technologically diverse, and carried out by a plurality of actors.

---

[1] J. Locke, *The Second Treatise of Government*, ed. T. P. Peardon (Indianapolis: Bobbs-Merrill Educational Publishing, 1952), §§50.

[2] Locke, *The Second Treatise of Government*, §§137 and 138.

[3] J. Black, 'Critical Reflections on Regulation', *Australian Journal of Legal Philosophy*, 27 (2002), 1.

[4] For an account of nodal governance, see L. Johnston and C. Shearing, *Governing Security: Explorations in Policing and Justice* (London: Routledge, 2003), ch. 8.

[5] C. Scott, 'Analysing Regulatory Space: Fragmented Resources and Institutional Design', *Public Law* (2001), 329, 330.

[6] J. Braithwaite and P. Drahos, *Global Business Regulation* (Cambridge: Cambridge University Press, 2000), ch. 23.

This chapter analyses two aspects of the regulation of property. The first line of analysis begins by treating the technique of private law as a regulatory technique. It then moves on to ask whether the technique is efficient when it comes to regulating property and markets. Hugh Collins asks this same question of the private law of contract and concludes that it is full of structural weakness compared to other styles of regulation.[7] These structural weaknesses are based on the difficulties that courts face in being able to acquire, analyse, and disseminate information (for example, information about the workings of markets, information about relevant third-party interests, and information about the effects of their decisions). Contract and property are intimately linked and so it is natural to ask the same question of the private law of property. In answering this question I shall adopt Collins's characterization of the private law technique as a reactive process that, at the instigation of parties to a dispute, settles that dispute through the application of general rules.[8]

The second line of analysis discusses how courts, the principal agents of the private law technique, might themselves be the objects of regulation. The focus in this section of the chapter is on the possibility of regulatory capture of judges and courts. Theories and models of regulatory capture have been widely discussed and accepted within regulatory literature.[9] It is surprising then that so little attention has been paid to the possibility of judicial or court capture. Intellectual property rights, especially patents, have always been the sites of strategic litigation. The creation in some jurisdictions of specialist intellectual property courts and the fact that multinational companies with large intellectual property portfolios are frequent repeat players in these courts create the kind of conditions that lead to the evolution of capture. Judicial or court capture may, of course, have a form that is very distinct from other kinds of capture, but is capture nevertheless.

CLARIFICATIONS

To ask whether the private law of contract is an efficient technique of regulation might be to ask about the productive efficiency of a process, in this case the process of decision-making by ordinary courts.[10] This is not the issue that Collins wants to reach. Rather, his analysis is aimed at assessing the efficiency and effectiveness of the standards that the process produces, rather than asking whether the output of standards is optimal. This is also the line of inquiry in this chapter.

One could attempt to answer questions of efficiency and effectiveness by selecting a significant number of cases and through an analysis of them arrive

---

[7] H. Collins, *Regulating Contracts* (Oxford: Oxford University Press, 1999), ch. 4.

[8] Ibid. 59.

[9] I. Ayres and J. Braithwaite, *Responsive Regulation* (Oxford: Oxford University Press, 1992), 54.

[10] Ordinary courts are 'the crucial agency in setting private law standards'. See Collins, *Regulating Contracts*, 82.

inductively at some conclusions. The potential data set for this approach is, of course, large. Private law techniques that have generated standards of property and contract have been around since at least Roman times. Collins's analysis assumes that the private law is part of the structured complexity that Luhmann says characterizes modern legal orders.[11] Drawing on this systems analysis of the law, Collins sets about identifying the structural failures that a systems approach would predict of a private law system of contract that was aimed at the generation of efficient and effective standards for the regulation of contract and markets. His use of English case-law is designed to illustrate the instrumental difficulties that private law has when it comes to engineering new structural complexity within the social system.

A different method is used in this chapter. It does not make use of Luhmann's sociological theory of law or variants of that theory. In the hands of theorists like Luhmann and Teubner systems thinking, in effect, functions as something of a hypothesis-generator about structure. As Karl Popper observed long ago, the test of a theory is the availability not of verifying evidence but rather of falsifying evidence.[12] Falsification does not work in a simple way in the social sciences. Nevertheless, the goal of falsification should alert us to the need to look for counter-examples to theories of regulation that make sweeping claims about structure. If we find such counter-examples, this does not mean that the systems approach has been falsified, but rather that certain hypotheses become less general, in need of reformulation, or redundant. The structural problems of the private law technique may, for example, be more true of the civil law than the common law or the reverse may be true, or what may be true of contract may not be true of property. Regulatory theory, especially of the systems kind, needs as its partner a contextual empiricism and comparative methods such as those to be found in comparative law.

This chapter asks whether in fact the structural weaknesses that Collins identifies in respect of the private law regulation of contract also apply to the regulation of property. It draws on some examples from the history of property, as well as more recent developments in intellectual property, and argues that claims about the structural weaknesses of the private law technique are essentially contingent truths, rather than truths that can be read off a priori from a systems-based account of law's structural complexity. It is worth noting that there is some concordance between this argument and Collins's conclusion that 'the private law of contract has the capacity to overcome or diminish many . . . structural weaknesses in its system of regulation'.[13]

Finally, for reasons of space this chapter confines itself to a discussion of efficiency and the private law technique. There is a distinction to be drawn between efficiency and effectiveness. One meaning of 'effective' might be to say

---

[11] N. Luhmann, *A Sociological Theory of Law*, trans. E. King and M. Albrow (London: Routledge & Kegan Paul, 1985), 5.

[12] K. Popper, *The Logic of Scientific Discovery* (London: Hutchinson, 1959).

[13] Collins, *Regulating Contracts*, 93.

that a legal rule is effective if it achieves its intended purpose. If, for example, a law that bans the sale of de-encryption devices is passed and it in fact stops the trade in such devices, the law is effective.[14] The relationship between efficiency and effectiveness is an interesting one. A law, such as the one prohibiting the sale of de-encryption devices, may be effective but inefficient because it allows copyright owners, for example, to lock up information that would otherwise enter the public domain once the copyright term had expired. An ineffective law might be efficient. Historically speaking, patents have been difficult to enforce, thereby allowing for a greater free leakage of patented information than would otherwise have been the case. Once in existence, information is most efficiently distributed at zero cost and so such leakages could be said to be efficient. There may even be an economic case for arguing that an ineffective patent system contributes to innovation (dynamic efficiency) because the free flow of information is more important to innovation than the appropriability of that information.[15]

KINDS OF EFFICIENCY

Asking how good the technique of private law is when it comes to promoting efficient property standards leads into a question about what type of efficiency we have in mind. We can distinguish, at least, among productive, allocative, dynamic, and transaction cost efficiency. *Productive efficiency* requires extracting the most output from a given input or lowering input to achieve the same ouput.[16] *Allocative efficiency* is linked to the model of perfect competition. Large numbers of suppliers with perfect information and little market power compete to meet the demands of consumers.[17] Resources continue to be allocated to production until price meets the marginal cost of production. Under conditions of equilibrium the model of perfect competition is also Pareto optimal:[18] that is to say, no one can be made better off without somebody else being made worse off. *Dynamic efficiency* refers to the process of resource allocation to enable the creation or discovery of knowledge. A society needs to ensure that some resources are devoted to supporting the production of knowledge because, among other things, technological progress is a source

---

[14] States that are members of the World Intellectual Property Organization Copyright Treaty 1996 are obliged to regulate to prevent the circumvention of technological devices employed by authors to protect their works.

[15] For an economist who argues this case, see T. Mandeville, *Understanding Novelty: Information, Technological Change, and the Patent System* (Norwood, NJ: Ablex, 1996).

[16] R. Cooter and T. Ulen, *Law and Economics*, 3rd edn. (Reading, Mass.: Addison-Wesley Longman, 2000), 12.   [17] Ibid. 29.

[18] The Pareto criterion allows for the idea of an individual transaction being a Pareto improvement. Further refinement has led to the idea of changes in allocation being potentially Pareto superior or 'Kaldor-Hicks' efficient. In this case, some individuals are made worse off, but there are overall gains.

of economic growth.[19] Yet another type of efficiency arises out of *transaction cost* economics. This branch of economics recasts economic activity, such as vertical integration, in the form of a contracting problem.[20] It hypothesizes that parties in organizing an economic relationship will choose an arrangement that minimizes transaction costs among themselves. Economic agents, in other words, seek transaction cost efficiency.

Having distinguished these different kinds of efficiency, it is possible to make some observations about the difficulties that will confront a rule-maker wishing to pursue one or more kinds. To begin with, it is clear that when it comes to setting property rules, decision-makers will sometimes find themselves involved in trade-offs between different kinds of efficiency. One example of this comes from the intellectual property field. Often a court will have to make a decision about whether to allow a defendant access to information that is in existence and that is the subject of an intellectual property right. So, for example, a defendant might seek to make use of copyright material under the principle of fair use, or a third party may seek to gain the use of a patent by applying for a compulsory licence. Information, once in existence, can be transmitted at close to zero cost. Moreover, from the point of view of competition, it is desirable for information to be distributed widely (perfect information is one of the key assumptions of the model of perfect competition). When a court grants access to information it has to take into account the possible effects of the grant on future investment activity in the generation of new information. Too liberal a use of compulsory licensing or too wide an interpretation of the principle of fair dealing might discourage individuals from creating new information if others are able to gain free or low-cost access to it. Many cases in intellectual property law present judges with a choice about whether to tilt the property right in favour of dynamic or allocative efficiency. In order to be able to make this particular judgement private law decision-makers have to be in a position of full information. They need to know what the relevant allocative efficiency loss is likely to be, as well as the dynamic gains. This leads directly into the issue that Collins is raising: is the private law technique capable of acquiring the kind of information needed to make regulatory decisions about efficiency trade-offs?

Transaction cost efficiency has implicit in it the curious possibility that in some cases it will not matter what the private law decision-maker does when it comes to defining property entitlements. On one view of the Coase theorem, the initial distribution of property rights in a two-party situation does not matter from the point of view of efficiency, where one party is causing injury to

[19] The classical discussion of the failure of the perfect model of competition to allocate sufficient resources to invention is K. J. Arrow, 'Economic Welfare and the Allocation of Resources for Invention', in National Bureau of Economic Research, *The Rate and Direction of Inventive Activity* (Princeton: Princeton University Press, 1962), 609.

[20] See O. E. Williamson and S. E. Masten, Introduction, in Williamson and Masten (eds.), *The Economics of Transaction Costs* (Cheltenham: Edward Elgar, 1999), p. ix.

another.[21] If the parties are prepared to bargain cooperatively they may be able to reach an outcome that satisfies them both. What guides them in this process is their subjective utilities, rather than the initial assignment of property rights. For Coase, bargaining allows the parties to reshuffle rights 'that may bring about a greater value of production than any other'.[22] This result, however, is certain only for a world of zero transaction costs. The actual world is full of complex transaction costs. These costs may well prevent bargaining from taking place, thereby also preventing a productive exchange of rights from taking place. Multimedia producers, for example, sometimes find that they have to track down so many copyright owners to get the licences they need that they end up abandoning the project. The upshot is that the private law decision-maker (for example, courts, tribunals, legislatures) does make a difference to efficiency in vesting entitlements in one party rather than another. Given that the private law decision-maker is in a position to make a difference to efficiency, the question becomes, how does she or he make a difference in a world of complex transaction costs? One possible way for rule-makers to sidestep the costs of bargaining is to formulate rules that direct resources to those that value them most, thereby obviating the need for bargaining. Once again, this raises an issue about the capacity of the private law technique to acquire the information needed to arrive at the same efficiency as costless bargaining.

Thus far, it is clear from the discussion that the private law regulator of property has more than one kind of efficiency goal to aim at and in some cases must choose between efficiencies. These kinds of decision require, among other things, the capacity to acquire information about costs and benefits. On Collins's account the private law is structurally weak when it comes to making these and other regulatory decisions. In summary form his objections go like this. When it comes to setting standards the private law technique does not sufficiently take into account affected third-party interests.[23] It deals directly with the individual interests of the parties before it. Third-party interests are dealt with indirectly by treating individuals as proxies for group interests (for example, unions, consumers, tenants, etc.). The reliance of the private law technique on individuals bearing costs means that it largely fails to provide solutions to collective action problems. A deeper problem than the failure to incorporate third-party interests in the private law regulatory process is the inability of that process 'to investigate the operation of markets and their inability to comprehend such information and transform it into practical regulation'.[24] The inability of private lawmakers to acquire or disseminate the information necessary for efficient standard-setting is Collins's central criticism of the private law technique of regulation. Courts lack the capability of systematically acquiring

[21] For a discussion of the theorem, see R. Cooter, 'The Cost of Coase', *Journal of Legal Studies*, 11 (1982), 1.

[22] R. H. Coase, 'The Problem of Social Cost', in R. C. Ellickson, C. M. Rose, and B. A. Ackerman (eds.), *Perspectives on Property Law*, 3rd edn. (New York: Aspen Law & Business, 2002), 200, 206.

[23] Collins, *Regulating Contracts*, 70.   [24] Ibid. 74.

information about markets, as well as the effects of the standards they set in those markets.[25] The public diffusion of information about private law standards is imperfect. Feedback about those standards is litigation-driven, an information mechanism that is hardly comprehensive in its sweep.[26] There are other problems as well. The indeterminacy of legal reasoning lends courts too much regulatory discretion.[27] Most policy shifts can be justified through legal reasoning. Moreover, the mystique of legal reasoning itself shields the private law's regulatory shifts from public criticism. Finally, it also lacks the necessary range of sanctions needed to influence behaviour.[28] In the remainder of this chapter we shall see how these criticisms of private law regulation apply to the regulation of property from the point of view of efficiency.

EFFICIENCY, PROPERTY, AND PRIVATE LAW — A MACRO VIEW

'Why aren't', asks Douglas North, 'all the countries in the world rich?'[29] The answer has everything to do with economic organization.[30] Economic organization underpins economic growth in the form of innovation, economies of scale, capital accumulation, and so on. Efficient economic organization lures individuals into productive activity by raising the level of private return to meet the social return. Foundational to this process of equalizing the private rate of return with the social rate of return are well-defined and enforced property rights. The success and failure of countries in western Europe can largely be understood in terms of their capacities to evolve efficient property rights. The economic and development successes in the historical story told by North and Thomas, which ends in the eighteenth century, are England and the Netherlands. France and Spain are labelled the 'also-rans'.

Let us assume for present purposes that the historical story that North and Thomas tell is broadly right. This assumption allows us to focus on the role that private law regulation played in the creation of property rights in England. That role is generally thought to be important. In the seventeenth century under the leadership of Coke CJ the common law courts began to absorb and refine the principles of the earlier *lex mercatoria*.[31] In the twelfth and thirteenth centuries the practices of merchants in western Europe had given rise to a largely customary and transnational Law Merchant.[32] Commercial paper, such as promissory notes and bills of exchange, was adopted by merchants to pay debts and create credit. These practices were recognized by merchant courts operating at

[25] Ibid. 83, 86.   [26] Ibid. 85.   [27] Ibid. 80.   [28] Ibid. 90.
[29] D. C. North, *Growth and Welfare in the American Past*, 2nd edn. (Englewood Cliffs, NJ: Prentice Hall, 1974), 15.
[30] D. C. North and R. T. Thomas, *The Rise of the Western World* (London: Cambridge University Press, 1973), 2.   [31] Braithwaite and Drahos, *Global Business Regulation*, 49.
[32] L. E. Trakman, *The Law Merchant: The Evolution of Commercial Law* (Littleton, Colo.: Fred B. Rothman, 1983).

the great commercial trade fairs of Champagne, Lyons, Anvers, Genoa, and other places in Europe. In England in the seventeenth and eighteenth centuries a succession of common law judges, most notably Lord Mansfield, turned the uses of commercial paper into forms of personal property. The courts refined the transferability and negotiability of commercial paper. Parliament passed statutes that eliminated some forms of property and created new ones. The Statute of Monopolies of 1624, for example, eliminated the many monopolies that had been granted to individuals with the exception of patents on inventions, patents in certain trades, and charters to companies. The Act of Anne 1709 made great inroads into the power of the Stationers' Company to control the book trade. The rights of authors over the printing of their books were expressly recognized, as was the social interest in a public domain by limiting the length of the copyright term.[33] These and other forms of personal property innovation, such as shares and the company limited by liability, laid the basis for financial capitalism.[34]

These types of personal property innovation led to one or more of the efficiencies I identified earlier. The recognition of the principle of negotiability, for example, allowed merchants to settle their debts more easily and facilitated trade across borders (transaction cost efficiency and allocative efficiency).[35] The enforcement of patents on inventions, in theory at least, should have contributed to dynamic efficiency. Setting limits on the copyright term cut back allocative efficiency losses. But it could not be the case that the thousands of decisions produced by English courts from the end of the medieval period across the full range of personal and real property rules were all efficient in one or more of the ways I have specified. The most obvious argument to support this claim is that courts had inherited inefficient rules of property from the feudal period, rules that they tended to preserve by virtue of the fact that they were courts of law. As courts of law they were confronted and bound by a 'pervasive traditionality' of rule-making.[36] So, for example, they had to work within feudalistic structures of tenure like copyhold for hundreds of years, structures that in many respects were or became inefficient. Land held under copyhold could only be conveyed under a procedure involving the surrender of the land to the lord and the admittance of the new tenant. It could not be done by one deed and the land itself was the subject of varying customary rights that were difficult to ascertain. Copyhold, among other things, raised the complexity and cost of conveyancing. It was not abolished until 1926.[37] The respect for tradition within the private law is one of the most important sources of explanation for why inefficient rules survive and are transmitted from one generation to the next.

---

[33] P. Drahos, *A Philosophy of Intellectual Property* (Aldershot: Dartmouth, 1996), 23.

[34] L. Neal, *The Rise of Financial Capitalism: International Capital Markets in the Age of Reason* (Cambridge: Cambridge University Press, 1990), ch. 1.

[35] Braithwaite and Drahos, *Global Business Regulation*, 49.

[36] M. Krygier, 'Critical Legal Studies and Social Theory: A Response to Alan Hunt', *Oxford Journal of Legal Studies*, 7 (1987), 26.

[37] R. Megarry and H. R. Wade, *The Law of Real Property*, 5th edn. (London: Stevens, 1984), 32.

Property rights provide a very good example of the horns of the 'regulatory trilemma' that confront courts as regulators of those rights.[38] The regulatory trilemma suggests that regulatory interventions face, at least, one of three costs. The intervention may fail to change norms, it may bring about undesirable change, or it may have damaging effects on the coherence of regulatory law itself. By following precedent, courts help to create a stable property rights regime for investors and producers. This helps to make property law effective. Yet, at the same time, tradition and precedent carries with it potential costs in terms of responsiveness. By entrenching tradition, the courts may fail to achieve the right rate of adaptation of property law to economic and technological change, thereby hindering that change. However, if the courts take to responding too quickly to the forces of economic change they will threaten the overall coherence of property law's rule base, thereby subverting its function of offering stability. In the case of property rights, effectiveness may threaten responsiveness, responsiveness may threaten coherence, and coherence may threaten effectiveness.

The historical story told by North and Alexander suggests that at the macro level of economic growth the private law technique of regulation in England contributed profoundly to that growth.[39] At various points in history, in other words, it seems that the courts in England did find ways to resolve the regulatory trilemma. Central to resolving this trilemma is solving the problem of information.

Under the Coasean approach to property rights, clearly defined property rights help the process of bargaining, and bargaining is efficient because it allows those who value the resource the most to exploit that value.[40] However, as I mentioned earlier, real-world transaction costs can prevent bargaining from taking place or produce an inefficient outcome. Courts, when the opportunity arises, have the option of allocating the relevant right to the party who values it most. But this means they must have reliable information about subjective utilities and obtaining this information is costly and difficult. Seemingly, we are back to Collins's point about the information problem that confronts the private law regulator. Here, though, we can point to a historical example of the way in which the private law successfully dealt with this information problem in the context of regulating personal property rights.

The construction of medieval Law Merchant took place, at first, in merchant tribunals that operated at trade fairs. The great constitutive principle of Law Merchant was that disputes were to be decided, as much as possible, by reference to the practices of merchants. It was law by merchants, for merchants, and in the interests of merchants. The English common law recognized this

---

[38] On the regulatory trilemma, see G. Teubner, 'Juridification: Concepts, Aspects, Limits, Solutions', in Teubner (ed.), *Juridification of Social Spheres: A Comparative Analysis of the Areas of Labor, Corporate, Antitrust and Social Welfare Law* (Berlin: Walter de Gruyter, 1987), 3.

[39] This would follow from the North and Thomas analysis since the courts were centrally involved in the redefinition of property rights.

[40] A Coasean bargaining theory of property is developed by Cooter and Ulen, *Law and Economics*, ch. 4.

constitutive principle and implemented it by accepting evidence of merchant custom when hearing commercial disputes. Lord Mansfield, the principal architect of English commercial law, drew upon juries of merchants in commercial hearings so that he could more accurately determine the actual custom of merchants. By ascertaining and recognizing the customs of merchants, the common law came close to operating in a genuinely declaratory mode.[41] Through the declaration of custom, the common law courts went a long way to solving the problem of information asymmetry that confronted them when setting standards of property. In any individual case the plaintiff had incentives to exaggerate his losses and the defendant to minimize those losses. Courts, in having to define a property rule based on an individual case, were faced by the problem that they would be acting on incomplete or possibly false information. By obtaining evidence of custom the courts were increasing the probability of having access to reliable information. The reason lies in the fact that merchant custom is, by definition, information about the iterative bargaining practices of many merchants. Moreover, it is also information about bargaining practices that have taken place before the property rules relating to those bargaining practices have been the subject of a declaratory finding by a court. By following custom the courts were adopting a practice that the community of merchants had thought advantageous to them in terms of bargaining utilities. The courts, by targeting custom, were maximizing their chances of defining an efficient property standard, because the very fact that something had become custom conveyed information about its efficiency.[42]

The claim that mercantile custom was a reliable guide to efficient standards of property can be usefully illustrated by the nineteenth-century case of *Goodwin v Robarts*. Rothschild, acting as agent for the Russian and Austrian governments, had arranged for the issue of a form of commercial paper known as scrip that entitled the holder to the delivery of foreign bonds. The court had to determine whether scrip was negotiable, thereby allowing the defendant, who had received it as a security from a third party, to sell it and keep the proceeds. The evidence showed that a practice had evolved by bankers, money-dealers, and stockbrokers of buying, selling, and accepting scrip as security for loans. Not to allow the negotiability of scrip would, the court observed, 'materially hamper the transactions of the money market'.[43] By allowing the negotiability, the court facilitated bargaining over the scrip itself and helped to

[41] In *Goodwin v Robarts* (1875) LR 10 Ex 337 at 346 the court defined Law Merchant as 'the usages of merchants and traders in the different departments of trade, ratified by the decisions of Courts of Law'.

[42] For a theory as to why merchant norms would tend towards efficiency, see R. D. Cooter, 'Decentralized Law for a Complex Economy: The Structural Approach to Adjudicating the New Law Merchant', *University of Pennsylvania Law Review*, 144 (1996), 1643. For an analysis that suggests courts should not follow business norms, see L. Bernstein, 'Merchant Law in a Merchant Court: Rethinking the Code's Search for Immanent Business Norms', *University of Pennsylvania Law Review*, 144 (1996), 1765. The haphazard and idiosyncratic nature of much custom is discussed in A. Watson, *The Evolution of Western Private Law* (Baltimore: Johns Hopkins University Press, 2001), ch. 4.   [43] *Goodwin v Robarts* (1875) LR 10 Ex 337 at 353.

lower transaction costs in the money markets because the scrip could be used as form of payment or a source of credit.

The next step in our analysis is to ask whether the courts were best placed to ascertain mercantile custom, or whether the structural problems that Collins draws attention to mean that some other agency, such as Parliament, was better placed to solve this information problem. It is not clear that one can, from a systems analysis of the private law technique, read off a conclusion of inefficiency.[44] The answer has too great an empirical component for that. In the case of mercantile custom, much depended on the attitude of individual judges and their preparedness to innovate procedurally to solve information problems. Lord Holt, the chief justice of the King's Bench from 1689 to 1709, was not especially sympathetic to using merchant custom as the basis for decision-making.[45] It was Parliament, rather than Holt, that extended the principle of negotiability to promissory notes.[46]

The common law took a very different attitude to the customs of merchants under Lord Mansfield. From 1645 in the Court of the King's Bench, an irregular practice of using a jury of merchants to try merchant disputes had arisen. Mansfield took this practice and institutionalized it by training 'a corps of jurors as a permanent liaison between law and commerce'.[47] By using merchants on juries, Mansfield gained access to expert information about custom that was independent of the distortions of the adversarial trial. Not only was the information reliable, but the fact that Mansfield was able to consult with knowledgeable and experienced merchants meant that he acquired information about the workings and likely impact of his rulings. Mansfield also used the cases to make sure that his court rendered statements of legal principle that were formally reported, rather than remaining silent as his predecessors had done as to the legal basis of the decision. Litigation was used to promulgate principle that was refined through the feedback mechanism of further litigation. Presumably this would have been more efficient for merchants than having to go to Parliament to obtain, for example, a statutory ruling on the application of the principle of negotiability to every new form or new use of commercial paper. In Mansfield's hands the regulation of property law really did travel in both the directions identified by John Locke. Mansfield's court regulated standards of property, but the limits and much of the content of that regulation flowed from the community of merchants.

The argument in this section suggests that the efficiency of the private law technique for property is more contingent than structural in nature. It may be

---

[44] This is true, of course, for other models. Rubin's evolutionary model explaining the efficiency of the common law rests on the assumption that it is more likely that 'parties will litigate inefficient rules than efficient rules'. See P. H. Rubin, 'Why is the Common Law Efficient?', *Journal of Legal Studies*, 6 (1977), 51. This ignores the problem of well-resourced players engaging in rent-seeking litigation strategies.

[45] C. H. S. Fifoot, *Lord Mansfield* (London: Clarendon Press, 1936), 17.

[46] J. H. Baker, *An Introduction to English Legal History*, 4th edn. (London: Butterworth, 2002), 370.   [47] Fifoot, *Lord Mansfield*, 105.

that as private commercial law has deviated from custom it has become less efficient. Patrick Devlin, writing in 1962, argued that commercial law ought to be based on the conduct of merchants, but that the written contract had replaced custom as the primary source of information about commercial matters.[48] The evolution of a global and complex commerce may mean that the private law technique faces a radically different kind of information problem to the one it did in Mansfield's time.

CAPTURING PROPERTY RIGHTS

For both Coase and North, property rights are key to stimulating economic activity that is socially productive. Even in the hypothetical world of zero trans-action costs, property rights are needed. Property rights define the resources that individual bargainers control and they allow those bargainers to consume the economic benefits of newly bargained for rights. Similarly, for North, the state must, if it wishes to encourage productive activity, grant incentives to individuals to undertake such activity. Property rights are the best form of incentive for raising the rate of private return on activities that have a social return. Based on this line of analysis we can conclude that whenever there is a potential productive gain to be made, property rights are the single most important mechanism for realizing that gain. But it does not follow from this that the presence of property rights always signals the presence of productive activity. Property rights can sometimes cause social losses. For example, the extension of the patent term to patents already in existence prolongs the monopoly cost without a dynamic efficiency gain, because the relevant inventions are already in existence. The extension of the patent term in this case creates a windfall gain for patent owners.

There are strong incentives for individuals to seek unproductive property rights, especially if the property right in question confers a monopoly of some kind. For example, copyright owners in the United States during the 1990s successfully lobbied for a twenty-year extension of the copyright term for subsisting copyrights.[49] The effect of the extension was to continue the copyright protection of lucrative works such as Fitzgerald's *The Great Gatsby*, Gershwin's *Rhapsody in Blue*, and films such as *Gone with the Wind* and *Casablanca*. An amici brief filed by the Association of American Publishers and other copyright owners pointed out that an annual nationwide licence for a Gershwin song earns around the \$US250,000 mark.[50] The gain of the twenty-year extension to the owners of Gershwin songs is, therefore, considerable. From the point of view of efficiency it is hard to justify. The extension of the copyright term could have an

---

[48] P. Devlin, *Samples of Lawmaking* (London: Oxford University Press, 1962), 30.

[49] Copyright Term Extension Act of 1998.

[50] See Brief of Amici Curiae Association of American Publishers et al. in Support of Respondent, No. 01-618, In the Supreme Court of the United States, *Eldred v Ashcroft*, 29 n. 85.

incentive effect only on future works, not works that were already in existence. These works had already been socially purchased, as it were, by the copyright term that existed prior to the extension. Extending the copyright term inflicts allocative efficiency losses with no compensating incentive effects. The allocative losses are likely to be high because many of these works were about to enter the public domain in the United States, meaning that the cost of continued monopoly pricing has to be worked out in present values, rather than discounted future values. There are also dynamic efficiency losses. When a copyright work enters the public domain, other creators no longer have to face the transaction costs of locating copyright owners or having to pay for the use of the work. They are free to adapt and innovate with those works.[51] Famous copyright works that enter the public domain are, in effect, cultural standards for which there is high demand by both creators wishing to adapt them for their own projects and consumers who wish to see the final product. The effect of extending the copyright term for works, especially those in the category of cultural standards, is to restrict the supply of cultural invention compared to the supply had the works not been the subject of copyright protection. A good example of the kind of dynamic efficiency gains that occur when a famous work enters the public domain is H. G. Wells's *The Time Machine*. It entered the public domain in the United States in 1951, and aside from being continuously in print, has been the subject of five sequels, five films, two musicals, a ballet, video games, and comic books.[52] In Europe, where the novel has yet to enter the public domain, the creators of all these follow-on works would have had to have obtained licensing permission.

The problem of unproductive property rights is part of a more general problem of rent-seeking in modern economies.[53] There are a couple of reasons as to why the pursuit of rents through the creation of unproductive property rights is likely to intensify. Firstly, in those cases where the property owner already has a lucrative asset, the cost of replacing that asset is likely to be greater than the cost of extending its property protection. Pharmaceutical companies in the United States, for example, are sometimes caught out attempting to patent the same drug twice. If the drug is a blockbuster, as in the case of Prozac, it becomes rational to find ways to extend its protection. There is no guarantee that investing in research and development will produce another blockbuster. Better, one might say, to protect the drug in hand than search for elusive ones in nature. Patent litigation is very expensive, and technical and patent offices have neither the resources nor the inclination to examine the patent applications of their best corporate customers too vigorously. There is a reasonable chance that a large

---

[51] Copyright law recognizes the right of a copyright owner to make an adaptation of the work or the right to prepare a derivative work.

[52] See Brief of Intellectual Property Law Professors as Amici Curiae Supporting Petitioners, No. 01-618, In the Supreme Court of the United States, *Eldred v Ashcroft*, 2.

[53] 'Rent' refers to a 'payment that is not needed to elicit productive labour or the productive services of some other input': W. J. Baumol, S. Blackman, and E. Wolff, *Productivity and American Leadership* (Cambridge, Mass.: MIT Press, 1991), 274.

company will get away with rent-seeking practices like double patenting. As it happens, Eli Lilly did not, in the case of its patents on Prozac.[54] Many of the doctrines that have been introduced in patent law, such as the patentability of new uses of old drugs and the patentability of purified versions of substances discovered in nature, are, for the most part, forms of rent-seeking. The second reason for thinking that the pressure to create unproductive forms of property will continue to rise has to do with the logic of collective action. Certain intellectual property industries such as film, sound recording, and publishing are characterized by oligopolistic structures. Companies within these industries are part of media conglomerates such as Sony, Viacom, and News Corporation.[55] The potential gains to these industry players of nationally and globally coordinated lobbying that produces results, such as the extension of the copyright term, clearly outweighs the costs of that lobbying. Consumers of intellectual property products have to absorb the costs of increased protection, but the cost to any one consumer is not likely to be greater than the cost to that consumer of organizing lobbying to counter the campaigns of intellectual property owners. Although this is something of an oversimplification of the politics of intellectual property standard-setting, especially at the international level, where non-governmental organizations have become much more active, this basic logic of collective action does explain why intellectual property owners have been much more active than intellectual property consumers in the twentieth century.[56]

The argument of this section, then, is that there are some good reasons for thinking that individuals will continue to demand unproductive property rights. This is especially true of intellectual property rights, where the technical nature of the rights and the inability to define or demarcate the intangible subject matter of the right, makes rent-seeking sometimes difficult to detect. These demands will be made of bodies with standard-setting powers over property rights, including international organizations (for example, the World Trade Organization), legislatures, courts, and regulatory agencies such as patent offices. From the point of view of efficiency, it follows that regulators should strive to set property standards that increase productive value and avoid unproductive forms of property. My discussion of mercantile custom suggested that courts could, in cases where they had access to reliable information, set property rights that were productive. My argument in this section shows that access to reliable information is not enough from the point of view of efficiency. Regulators also have to be in a position to be able to resist the demands from powerful interest groups for unproductive forms of property. This leads to a question the answer to which we explore in the next section: are courts, the

---

[54] *Eli Lilly and Co v Barr Laboratories Inc.*, 251 F 3d 955 (2001).

[55] P. Drahos and J. Braithwaite, *Information Feudalism: Who Owns the Knowledge Economy?* (London: Earthscan, 2002), 178.

[56] For further discussion, see P. Drahos, 'Developing Countries and International Intellectual Property Standard-Setting', *Journal of World Intellectual Property*, 5 (2002), 765.

principal agents of private law regulation, in a better or worse position than other regulators to resist rent-seeking demands?

CAPTURING COURTS

Judicial independence is a central tenet to be found in the constitutional jurisprudence of all Western democracies. The details of the institutional expression of this shared tenet vary considerably from country to country, as well as between types of court in the same country on matters such as selection, appointment, promotion, and tenure. From the point of view of the economic theory of institutional design, the institutional arrangements for courts form an incentive structure that can be used to explain and predict the behaviour of judicial agents.[57] Clearly, a judge who has to be re-elected to office faces a different incentive structure from one who is appointed with life tenure, especially if, as in some US state court elections, the judges campaigning for election accept campaign contributions from those lawyers and clients who appear before them.[58] This line of argument leads to the proposition that the extent to which judges are likely to resist pressures from interest groups will be importantly affected by the structure of incentive and reward in which they operate. This is a complex empirical matter. It is also an empirical matter about which we know comparatively little because, as Fred Schauer puts it, the 'self-interested judge is largely an absent figure in the academic literature on the judiciary and judicial decision-making'.[59]

Clearly, it is not possible to conclude that courts have been better or worse at resisting demands for unproductive property rights merely from the fact that Western democracies are ideologically committed to judicial independence. The assumption that courts are virtuous rather than venal agents has been used to underpin an argument that courts ought to engage in robust judicial review of economic legislation, in particular in order to lessen the effects of rent-seeking legislation.[60] Aside from Schauer's point about how little we know about the impact of judicial motivation and incentives, the structure of litigation itself might restrict the capacity of courts to function as the most likely guardians of the public good. The same logic of collective action that explains why interest

---

[57] G. Brennan, 'Selection and the Currency of Reward', in R. E. Goodin (ed.), *The Theory of Institutional Design* (Cambridge: Cambridge University Press, 1998), 256.

[58] For a discussion of this and other problems related to judicial elections in the United States, see M. A. Behrens and C. Silverman, 'The Case for Adopting Appointive Judicial Selection Systems for State Court Judges', *Cornell Journal of Law and Public Policy*, 11 (2002), 273.

[59] F. Schauer, 'Incentives, Reputation, and the Inglorious Determinants of Judicial Behaviour', *University of Cincinnati Law Review*, 68 (2000), 615.

[60] Drawing on Madison's theme of control of factions, Cass Sunstein has argued that US courts should be more active in guarding against laws that increase private wealth and opportunities at the expense of the public good. See C. R. Sunstein, 'Interest Groups in American Public Law', *Stanford Law Review*, 38 (1985), 29. For a critical discussion of this line of argument, see E. R. Elhauge, 'Does Interest Group Theory Justify More Intrusive Judicial Review?', *Yale Law Journal*, 101 (1991), 31.

groups lobby legislatures also explains why they litigate. Money is both a barrier to entry in the litigation market and a barrier to success. Wealthy interest groups in the United States, such as big business, tend to win most of their cases.[61] Litigation by its nature places decision-making power about the direction of the process in the hands of litigants. Well-resourced litigants can embark on a strategy of 'precedent-purchasing', aiming for certain precedents, forum shopping to that end, settling cases when the outcome appears uncertain, or pursuing them when the time is right.[62]

The danger of regulatory capture for a court is a real one, as is the danger of structural manipulation. By way of example of the dangers, it is worth considering the work of the US Court of Appeals for the Federal Circuit (CAFC). Patent appeals from the Court of Federal Claims, the International Trade Commission and the US Patent and Trademark Office, and the US district courts (in most cases) are all funnelled to the CAFC, giving it centralized power over patent law principle. This power has become all the greater since the US Supreme Court rarely exercises its certiorari jurisdiction to review the CAFC's decisions. Created in 1982, when the US Court of Customs and Patent Appeals and the US Court of Claims were merged, the CAFC was charged with the task of increasing the doctrinal stability and unity of patent law. While the idea for a specialist patent court had been discussed in the United States since the end of the nineteenth century, it was 'a very small group of large high technology firms and trade associations in the telecommunications, computer and pharmaceutical industries' that brought it to fruition.[63] These industries patent heavily. Since the arrival of the CAFC, patent owners have improved their odds in litigation over the validity and infringement of their patents. During the 1940s and 1950s getting a court to find a patent valid was tough. So, for example, one study of patent decisions of circuit courts of appeals found that for the period 1940–4 the number of patents held valid was 17.6 per cent and for 1945–9 it was 22.25 per cent.[64] When the CAFC arrived on the scene in 1982, the odds changed dramatically in favour of the patent holder. In 1988, in Harmon's first edition of his book dealing with the CAFC's decisions, he observed that an 'accused infringer who loses below has less than one chance in fifteen of turning things around on appeal'.[65] By the fourth edition (1998) those odds had reduced to one in seven.[66] They remained, nevertheless, pretty good odds for the patent holder.

---

[61] In a study of federal litigation involving the biggest 2,000 US companies between 1971 and 1991, Dunworth and Rogers found that 'businesses win overwhelmingly, both as plaintiffs and defendants': see T. Dunworth and J. Rogers, 'Corporations in Court: Big Business Litigation in U.S. Federal Courts, 1971–1991', *Law and Social Inquiry*, 21 (1996), 497.

[62] For a discussion of these issues, see F. B. Cross, 'The Judiciary and Public Choice', *Hastings Law Journal*, 50 (1999), 355.

[63] A. Silverman, 'Intellectual Property Law and the Venture Capital Process', *High Technology Law Journal*, 5 (1990), 157.

[64] E. H. Lang and B. K. Thomas, 'Disposition of Patent Cases by Courts during the Period 1939 to 1949', *Journal of the Patent Office Society*, 32 (1950), 803.

[65] R. L. Harmon, *Patents and the Federal Circuit*, 4th edn. (Washington: Bureau of National Affairs, 1988), 382.   [66] Ibid. 980.

The CAFC has almost single-handedly created a multi-billion dollar patent litigation market in the United States. Just before the CAFC came into existence in 1981, 835 patent infringement actions had been filed in the courts. By 1998 the number was 2,218. In the same period the revenues from the licensing and litigation of US patents went from $3 billion a year to more than $100 billion per year.[67] Patenting is a rich company's game. Not many companies can wear the estimated $100 million bill that Polaroid and Kodak did in their patent dispute in 1989. Not many companies can build patent portfolios that stretch across the jurisdictions of the world. The big money in licensing comes from a vast web of patents. The kind of odds the CAFC hands out to alleged patent infringers increases the bargaining power of owners of large patent portfolios. It is a private bargaining power, used behind the curtain of commercial-in-confidence, making its effects hard to measure.

Capture in the case of courts is likely to work in a subtler way than in the case of legislatures, especially where judges operate with the security of life tenure. In the case of the CAFC, for instance, reputational drivers may explain much about the pattern of its decision-making. The CAFC is part of a broader patent community that consists of patent attorneys, administrators, patent office officials, inventors, and the large corporate users of the patent system that congregate around the patent system. These groups form a community by virtue of their technical expertise and general pro-patent values. This patent community in the United States might be the psychologically salient one for the CAFC. It is this group that can confer recognition upon the court for its work, publicly praising or criticizing it through informal and formal channels. The very technical density of patent law means that other groups are not in a position to participate in a reputational assessment of the court's work, even if they had the interest to do so. Patent trials, so far as the general public is concerned, are at the opposite end of the spectrum of interest occupied by the O. J. Simpson trial. In short, it is mainly the patent community that can deliver reputational rewards to the court. The CAFC operates as a 'de facto supreme court of patents', but without any of the general interest and recognition that characterizes Supreme Court decisions.[68] Under these conditions it becomes rational, if one is seeking reputational recognition, to look to the patent in-group, some of the members of which are enormously powerful economic actors, and display a concordance with the basic pro-patent values of the in-group. Capture is probably too strong a word to describe this kind of process, especially as in the judicial context other kinds of values such as judicial independence would continue to operate. Nevertheless, reputation is a primary driver of behaviour and it is an entirely plausible hypothesis that it operates in quite profound psychological ways to affect judicial behaviour.[69]

---

[67] See B. Grossman and G. Hoffman (eds.), *Patent Litigation Strategies Handbook* (Washington: Bureau of National Affairs, 2000), preface, p. xiii.

[68] M. D. Janis, 'Patent Law in the Age of the Invisible Supreme Court', *University of Illinois Law Review* (2001), 387.

[69] See e.g. the discussion of reputation in relation to the US Supreme Court by Schauer, 'Incentives, Reputation, and the Inglorious Determinants of Judicial Behaviour'.

The psychological process being suggested here should not be seen as an exchange relationship of the kind that, public choice theory suggests, characterizes relationships between interest groups and legislatures. Politicians and interest groups can do deals in the electoral marketplace without necessarily sharing the same values or attitudes on policy issues. Public choice tends to depict these deals as exchanges between rational agents in which one party swaps statutory or policy goods for votes or other contributions that can be turned into votes. Rather, judicial agents become part of a process of psychological association with the perceived core values of the relevant interest group. In the case of the patent community, this psychological association means linking to pro-patent values and not departing from fundamental axioms of interpretation that serve those values. The process of psychological association is not directly in play in the routine work of a court. It is not an association based on a relationship of exchange with individual litigants.

Where it becomes significant is in relation to decisions that constitute potential turning points in the evolution of the relevant body of law. Such cases are full of reputational cachet to be won or lost by members of the court in the eyes of the relevant community. It is in these cases that courts, which have become psychologically associated with a dominant rent-seeking group, are most likely to deliver rents to the group or some of its members.

In the case of the CAFC, one can plausibly argue that its decisions in the area of biotech patenting amount to the creation of unproductive property rights. The general trend of the CAFC's decisions in the biotech field has been to expand the scope of patentability, so much so that some analysts have argued that it has distorted patent law principles in order to serve the private sector better.[70] In terms of the regulatory trilemma, over-responsiveness has brought with it growing incoherence. With incoherence there has also been a lack of effectiveness in terms of the goal of efficiency. The expansion of patents to cover research tools and products has given rise to a form of inefficiency known as the anti-commons problem.[71] In essence, the anti-commons problem arises when the legal system produces too many exclusive property rights relating to the use of a resource, thereby raising the transaction costs for users wishing to gain access to the resource. The high transaction costs lead to an under-utilization of the resource. A company wishing to carry out research on, say, a molecule discovers that it needs a number of research tools and products that are themselves the subject of patents. The transaction cost of having to obtain permission from a large number of patent holders outweighs the benefits of carrying out the research and so the company decides not to proceed.[72]

---

[70] See P. G. Ducour, *Patenting the Recombinant Products of Biotechnology and Other Molecules* (London: Kluwer Law International, 1998), 3.

[71] M. Heller, 'The Tragedy of the Anticommons: Property in the Transition from Marx to Markets', *Harvard Law Review*, 111 (1998), 621.

[72] For a discussion of the problem in the context of biomedical research, see M. A. Heller and R. S. Eisenberg, 'Can Patents Deter Innovation? The Anticommons in Biomedical Research', *Science*, 280 (1998), 698.

Courts that operate in the intellectual property rights field in large markets such as the US market are very likely to be targets of intensive litigation, because, among other things, the size of the rents to be gained by interest groups is very large. US courts are also likely to be targets because their decisions have an international influence. The decision of the CAFC in the *State Street Bank & Trust Co. v Signature Financial Group*[73], in which the court took the opportunity to lay to rest the 'ill-conceived exception' to patentability of business methods, has triggered a discussion in Europe as to whether it should follow suit.

Conclusion

Treating, as Collins does, the private law technique as a regulatory technique and then asking whether the agents of the technique have been efficient standard-setters is a fruitful approach. It is especially fruitful in the case of the regulation of property, because it allows regulatory theory and approaches to be brought to bear on an issue that has occupied Marxists, institutional economists (both old and new), economic historians, and property theorists for some time: what has been (and is) the role of courts in economic growth?

Property law, like other areas of regulation, has to grapple with the regulatory trilemma. However, this discussion suggests that the technique of private law is not structurally condemned to a failure to resolve the trilemma. The discussion of mercantile custom showed that the courts in some circumstances may be able to obtain reliable information about the market, allowing them to set efficient standards of property. One important step towards the definition of productive and efficient property rights is to obtain information about how those rights are likely to work in market systems. How well or badly a court does this is a contingent matter. The Mansfield court, it seems, did it well. That court was, of course, unusual in that it consulted widely and deliberatively, functioning in some ways as a hybrid of public and private regulation. The route to productive property rights may well lie in models of this kind in which the regulation of property travels in both the directions that Locke specifies. The lesson of the CAFC seems to be that property rights are too important to be left to specialist courts. The conditions needed for regulatory capture are likely to be more strongly present in such courts. These courts, especially if they are in the thrall of a narrowly constituted epistemic community, are less likely to be able to obtain the information they need to solve the regulatory trilemma. They are more likely to define property rights that deliver rents to some groups, rather than ones that deliver social-welfare-enhancing efficiencies.

[73] 149 F 3d 1368, 1375 (Fed. Cir. 1998).

9

Regulating Competition

IMELDA MAHER*

INTRODUCTION

Competition law usually is placed in opposition to regulation as a form of market control. Black's definition of regulation—'the intentional activity of attempting to control, order or influence the behaviour of others'[1]—is, as the editors of this volume suggest, a fairly broad one that incorporates three basic requirements for a regulatory regime: standard-setting, monitoring compliance, and enforcement of standards.[2] Competition law[3] generally attempts to control, order, and influence business conduct (including commercial activity by the state) by setting down appropriate standards of behaviour, by monitoring compliance with those standards (e.g. by requiring prior approval of certain activities such as mergers), and through enforcement including the imposition of fines. To see competition law as a form of regulation marks a departure from the literature that sets them in opposition to each other.[4] In this dichotomy, competition policy is equated with enabling the market to operate as freely as possible of encumbrances on the basis that free competition (i.e. rivalry) between market participants will maximize welfare. Thus, it is seen as tending towards market liberalization and generic in nature. Regulation, on the other hand, in its classic manifestation is equated with 'command and control' and represents control of specific domains (health and safety, environment) or sectors (telecommunications, financial services).[5] Deregulation is thus equated with a move towards competition and away from regulation.

Following this traditional distinction, regulatory research on competition has mainly focused on sectors that previously operated as state monopolies

* Thanks to Frances Hanks, Giorgio Monti, Christine Parker, Colin Scott, David Soskice, and the participants at the Regulating Law Workshop, Australian National University, Mar. 2003, for their helpful comments.

[1] J. Black, 'Decentring Regulation: Understanding the Role of Regulation and Self-regulation in a Post-regulating World', *Current Legal Problems*, 54 (2001), 103.

[2] Introduction to this volume.

[3] Competition law here refers to rules prohibiting business practices restrictive of competition such as anti-competitive agreements, abuse of market dominance, and merger control.

[4] See e.g. P. S. Crampton and B. A. Facey, 'Revisiting Regulation and Deregulation through the Lens of Competition Policy', *World Competition*, 25 (2002), 25.

[5] R. Baldwin, C. Scott, and C. Hood (eds.), *A Reader on Regulation* (Oxford: Oxford University Press, 1998), 24; T. Daintith, 'Regulation', in *International Encyclopedia of Comparative Law* (Tubingen: Mohr-Siebeck, 1997), ch. 10, vol. xvii, ss. 1–21.

and where additional regulatory mechanisms are necessary in order to create a competitive market, for example, utilities and communications.[6] Competition law also has been subject to a regulatory perspective in relation to the effectiveness, responsiveness, and coherence of its enforcement and the consequences for regulatory compliance.[7] However, using Black's definition of regulation, it is clear that enforcement is just one dimension of competition and regulation. That definition reflects the extent to which regulation has moved on intellectually and practically from traditional notions of command and control, such that the conceptual split between competition policy and regulation is diminishing. It also suggests that the dichotomy between competition and regulation be better conceived of as a spectrum with command and control at one extreme and the ordinary workings of the market founded on property rights and contract law at the other extreme. Even then, the market is in fact regulated by private law since the contract and notions of property rights are central to the operation of any market.[8]

Applying a regulatory lens to competition law is useful for a number of reasons. It leads to a re-evaluation of the traditional distinction between regulation and competition. It also places competition law doctrine—and not just its enforcement—under a regulatory spotlight. In doing so, it highlights another (crude) distinction found in legal scholarship on regulation. A regulatory approach sees law as instrumental in nature—a tool of society designed to influence behaviour to accomplish particular social objectives. A rule-based doctrinal approach emphasizes the autonomy of legal reasoning, and thus sees law as distinct from society.[9] Both approaches can be found within competition law. A regulatory lens teases out this distinction within competition law itself and the doctrinal tensions that arise as a result of it. Finally, a regulatory lens will allow inquiry into how law interacts with other forms of normative ordering, in particular in the competition sphere, the interaction of law, and economics as discourses found in two different but linked social systems.

This chapter adopts a regulatory lens to explore the issue of 'productive disintegration' of competition law, a term coined by Collins in relation to modern contract law. He recasts contract law as a regulatory technique with instrumental purposes capable of standard-setting, monitoring, and enforcement. In doing so, he explores the innovations seen in doctrine as a result of the blurring of distinctions between public and private law. He argues that the collision of the private law of contract with public law regulation is leading to both the disintegration and reconfiguration of private law reasoning.[10] Because contract law is doctrinally robust, however, it can accommodate and translate

---

[6] e.g. C. Hall, C. Scott, and C. Hood, *Telecommunications Regulation: Cultures, Chaos and Interdependence inside the Regulatory Process* (London: Routledge, 2000).

[7] e.g. C. Parker, 'Evaluating Regulatory Compliance: Standards and Best Practice', *Trade Practices Journal*, 7/2 (1999), 62; B. J. Rodger, 'Compliance with Competition Law: A View from Industry', *Commercial Liability Law Review*, (2000), 249.

[8] H. Collins, *Regulating Contracts* (Oxford: Oxford University Press, 1999), 58.

[9] Introduction to this volume.   [10] Collins, *Regulating Contracts*, 46.

social and economic arguments into relevant legal discourse. Therefore, the reconfiguration of reasoning is productive—hence the term 'productive disintegration'. Private law remains distinctive and, while enriched by a more purposive approach borne out of harnessing the reasoning of economic and social regulation, the normative complexity of contract law is such that there are necessarily limits to its productive disintegration.

This chapter begins by exploring tension between a rule-based doctrinal conception of competition law, rooted in a private law conception of competition law, and an instrumental approach, emphasizing the public ordering role of competition law. It then examines how competition law remains doctrinally distinctive in the light of its collision with other legal doctrines. Next, it sets out the extent to which competition law tends towards doctrinal consistency across jurisdictions both in the development of multilateral principles of competition in the World Trade Organization (WTO) and as a result of American antitrust influence. Finally, the dependence of competition law on economic discourse is examined noting the limitations of that relationship. These limitations are due to the politics that underlies competition law and the choice of economic theory as well as the limited use made of quantitative economic analysis by courts. The approach of the Australian High Court in the *Boral* case[11] is analysed as an example of these limitations before concluding.

COMPETITION AND FREEDOM OF CONTRACT

There is a fundamental tension within competition law[12] that is linked to opposing theoretical bases. One emphasizes its roots in private law and the other takes a more constitutional orientation. The historical antecedent to statutory competition law in the common law world is the restraint of trade doctrine. Under this doctrine, provisions that unreasonably restrict a party's freedom to enter into future contracts are unenforceable, for example, unduly long or geographically over-broad non-compete clauses on former employees or on owners–directors in a sale of business contract.[13] The doctrine is ultimately concerned with preserving the individual freedom of contract of the parties. Freedom of contract is a necessary prerequisite for competitive markets but competition law restricts that freedom in so far as it unduly constrains competition. Thus, Gerber notes that one view of competition law focuses on how competition law constrains those subject to it.[14] From this perspective, competition law should intervene to a minimal degree in contractual arrangements—a liberal, if not libertarian, approach.

[11] *Boral Besser Masonry Ltd. v ACCC* (2003) 195 ALR 609, (2003) 77 ALJR 623, (2003) 24(3) Leg Rep 18, (2003) ATPR 41-915, [2003] HCA 5, 7 Feb. 2003.

[12] See G. Amato, *Antitrust and the Bounds of Power* (Oxford: Hart, 1997), ch. 1.

[13] See J. D. Heydon, *The Restraint of Trade Doctrine* (London: Butterworth, 1971); M. J. Trebilcock, *The Common Law of Restraint of Trade* (London: Sweet & Maxwell, 1986).

[14] D. J. Gerber, *Law and Competition in Twentieth Century Europe: Protecting Prometheus* (Oxford: Clarendon Press, 1998), 9.

The alternative perspective focuses on the effects more broadly in society of
not constraining freedom of contract. This perspective sees competition law as
a constraint on the exercise of private power to prevent the concentration of
undue economic power. The collision between these two perspectives is the competition law version of the collision Collins identifies between public regulation
and private law.

These conflicting perceptions are reflected institutionally in the way competition laws can be enforced. Competition law is enforceable by administrative
action either directly, where an agency imposes fines as in the EU, or indirectly,
where it initiates an action in the courts as in Australia. Competition law also
may be enforceable through private actions in the courts where, for example, the
enforcement of a contract can be challenged on the basis that it is illegal given
the competition rules. The private enforcement of competition law is in fact
encouraged and is commonplace in the United States, where over 90 per cent of
competition cases are private actions,[15] triple damages are available, and any
preceding successful government action can be relied on as prima facie evidence
of the unlawful conduct.[16] In Ireland the attempt to enforce competition law
only through private actions was a singular failure and rapidly led to the
introduction of administrative actions.[17] Private actions are also common under
the Australian Trade Practices Act 1974.[18] In the UK the English courts have been
slow to entertain a European competition law defence, looking to the maxim
pacta sunt servanda ('contracts should be honoured').[19] This reticence may,
however, change in the light of private actions for damages brought under the
UK Competition Act 1998, which, despite the lack of an explicit provision
allowing for private actions, allows findings of fact by the competition agency to
be used in private actions[20] and in the light of the *Courage* case.[21]

The *Courage* case is an example of the interplay of these two perceptions of
competition law.[22] It was a test case concerned with whether or not a party to
a contract in breach of Article 81 EC—the EC provision prohibiting restrictive
agreements—could claim damages from the other party. The defendant,
Crehan, held a lease for a public house that included an exclusive purchasing
arrangement whereby he had to purchase all his beer from Courage. As the lease
was a standard form agreement, the only term that was negotiable was the level
of rent. Along with many other tenants, Crehan withheld payment because
Courage charged substantially lower prices to publicans not subject to the
exclusive supply agreements, making it difficult for the tenants to compete.

---

[15] *White Paper on Competition Policy: A World Class Competition Regime*, Cm. 5233 (July
2001), para. 8.1 (UK).   [16] ss. 4 and 16(a) Clayton Act 1914.
[17] Competition Act 1991 and Competition (Amendment) Act 1996; see I. Maher, *Competition
Law: Alignment and Reform* (Dublin: Round, Hall, Sweet & Maxwell, 1999), 53.
[18] S. 80 (injunctive relief) and s. 82 (damages).
[19] R. Whish, *Competition Law*, 5th edn. (London: Butterworth, 2003), 288.   [20] S. 58(1).
[21] G. A. Cumming, '*Courage Ltd. v Crehan*', *European Competition Law Review*, 23/4 (2002), 199.
[22] *Courage Ltd. v Crehan (No. 1)* [1999] EGCS 85 (CA); C-453/99 *Courage Ltd. v Crehan* [2002]
QB 507 (ECJ), [2001] 5 CMLR 28, para. 23.

Courage sued for payment owed for beer supplied. Crehan counter-claimed for damages based on the difference between the prices he paid and the price he would have paid if he had not been party to the exclusive purchasing agreement. If the agreement were contrary to Article 81 it would be illegal. But under English law, a party to an illegal contract cannot recover damages.[23] The Court referred the case to the European Court of Justice to see whether, as a matter of EC law, it would be possible to claim damages.[24]

The European Court held that a party to a contract liable to restrict competition contrary to Article 81(1) could rely on breach of that provision to claim damages. The Court adopted an instrumental approach, noting that the effectiveness of the Article 81 prohibition would be put at risk if a party to an anti-competitive contract could not claim damages.[25] In fact, it argued that the existence of a right to sue for damages would discourage anti-competitive agreements, as dominant parties in particular would be discouraged from entering into them.[26] At the same time, damages would not be available to a party that had significant responsibility for the distortion of competition on the basis that no one should profit from their own wrongdoing. Specifically, regard should be had to the economic and legal context and the respective bargaining power and conduct of the parties to the contract. Thus, if a party is in a substantially weaker bargaining position that compromises their capacity to negotiate terms, they should have all legal remedies available to them, for example, where a contract is one of a network controlled by the other party as in this case.

By recognizing a right to damages to compensate for loss caused by an anti-competitive agreement even for a party to that agreement[27] the Court set aside the specific contractual relation in issue in order to ensure that the rights contained in Article 81 for individuals can be applied.[28] The decision emphasizes the role of competition law as a regulatory tool designed to enhance consumer welfare with contextualization and instrumentality as central to its application. The Court implicitly rejected the view of the English Court of Appeal[29] that the parties to a prohibited agreement are the cause and not the victims of the restriction of competition by qualifying the right to damages by reference to the extent to which a party is responsible for the anti-competitive aspects of the

---

[23] *Gibbs Mew plc v Gemmel* [1998] EU LR 588, 606.

[24] Under Article 234 the preliminary reference procedure that is akin to a case stated procedure.

[25] The case only discussed damages and not the right to a remedy in restitution; see G. Monti, 'Anticompetitive Agreements: The Innocent Party's Right to Damages', *European Law Review*, 27/3 (2002), 282.

[26] For a critique of the view that the availability of damages will in fact, improve the effectiveness of Article 81, see ibid.

[27] The basis for damages in English law is most likely to be an action in tort for breach of statutory duty (Article 81 constituting the statutory duty); see A. Jones and D. Beard, 'Co-contractors, Damages and Article 81: The ECJ Finally Speaks', *European Competition Law Review*, 23 (2002), 246.

[28] Article 81(1) is directly effective in that it creates rights for individuals that can be enforced before their national courts; see *Courage Ltd. v Crehan (No. 1)* [1999] EGCS 85 (CA); C-453/99 *Courage Ltd. v Crehan* [2002] QB 507 (ECJ), [2001] 5 CMLR 28, para. 23.

[29] *Gibbs Mew plc v Gemmell* [1998] EU LR 588, 606.

agreement. Nonetheless, a side benefit of the case is that it addresses unfairness in a contract arising out of unequal bargaining power. However, this is a consequence of instrumental reasoning rather than an overriding concern with fairness of contracts.

PRODUCTIVE (DIS)INTEGRATION

The extent to which competition law is doctrinally robust can be addressed on two levels: to what extent does it retain internal consistency when it comes into collision with other legal disciplines and to what extent does it (or should it) retain internal consistency across jurisdictional boundaries?

Competition Law and Other Legal Doctrines

Competition law can collide with other legal doctrines. For example, there can be clashes between constitutional norms and competition law. This can be seen in a test case in Ireland concerning barriers to entry to the retail ice cream market. Mars, a new market entrant, was seeking access to HB's ice cream freezers in retail outlets that it provided to shops for free. (HB was the main incumbent in the market and a subsidiary of Unilever.) The High Court judgment is a model of detailed economic analysis carefully weighing up the expert evidence provided by both sides in the light of the competition legislation and the retail market in issue. After a very long judgment, the judge, however, turns to the property provisions of the Constitution and concludes that the injunction sought could not be awarded, as it would be inconsistent with the constitutionally protected property rights of the incumbent. While this constitutional analysis is questionable, the case is an excellent example of how, irrespective of the economic analysis, other legal doctrines may come into play.[30] The case was one of several on the issue in Europe and was later considered by the European Courts.[31] It is a relatively rare example of a competition law case explicitly raising doctrinal issues that collide directly with constitutional law and where a constitutional right trumped economic analysis.[32]

Generally, competition law is seen as *sui generis*. The relatively closed nature of the competition law community of practitioners and academics means that while competition law is enforced in the light of constitutional values,[33] little

[30] *Masterfoods Ltd. v HB Ice Cream Ltd.* [1993] ILRM 145. The need for a mandatory injunction here was probably also problematic.
[31] C-344/98 *Masterfoods v HB Ice Cream* [2001] 4 CMLR 449, [2000] ECR I-11369; T65/98 *Van Den Bergh Foods Ltd v Commission* 23 Oct. 2003, Court of First Instance, not yet reported.
[32] S. O'Keeffe, 'First among Equals: The Commission and the National Courts as Enforcers of EC Competition Law', *European Law Review*, 26/3 (2001), 301.
[33] Values such as certainty, stability, accountability, transparency, procedural fairness and rationality, consistency, and proportionality; see K. Yeung, Securing Compliance: A Principled Approach (Oxford: Hart, 2004), 36.

notice is taken outside competition law circles of the extent to which these constitutional values may be compromised in the enforcement of competition law. In particular, the instrumental nature of competition rules can lead to procedures that collide with—and undermine—other legal doctrines such as the law of evidence, the criminal law, natural justice, and human rights.[34]

Competition law statutes while leaving intact the burden of proof in criminal cases may change the rules of evidence by introducing presumptions so as to make proof less difficult, for example, in relation to documentary evidence. For example, in the Irish Competition Act 2002, subject to some caveats, a statement in a document by one member of a cartel that another cartel member was engaged in or proposed anti-competitive activity can constitute proof.[35] Where competition law actions are often characterized as administrative, this is contentious given the punitive nature of the fines that can be imposed. For example, in the Australian Trade Practices Act care is taken throughout to refer to 'pecuniary penalties' rather than 'fines' so as to avoid any whiff of criminal sanction (and hence of the criminal law burden of proof).[36] In the UK context, the administrative proceedings before the Office of Fair Trading have been held to be consistent with the Human Rights Act 1998 with a fine balance struck between the competing demands of the two pieces of legislation. Thus proceedings under the Competition Act 1998 are criminal for the purposes of the Human Rights Act but a civil standard of proof applies although strong and compelling evidence is required for imposition of a fine.[37] Natural justice principles are also undermined. For example, in the EU the same agency both investigates and decides on liability. While there have been some improvements over the years in terms of both rights of the defence and the hearing of the case in the Commission by an official independent of those investigating the case, criticism remains.[38] Concerns about the power of the Commission to inspect homes of company directors as well as their business premises and their consistency with rights of privacy in the European Convention of Human Rights recently have been addressed in so far as the consent of a national court must be sought prior to such an inspection.[39] In all these procedural examples, the result orientation of competition enforcement combined with the goal orientation of

[34] The instrumental nature of regulation also may lead to clashes with the rule of law; see, generally, J. Freigang, 'Scrutiny: Is Responsive Regulation Compatible with the Rule of Law?', *European Public Law*, 8/4 (2002), 463.

[35] S. 13, Competition Act 2002. The caveats are that the document must pre-date the proceedings and all circumstances including credibility have to be considered.

[36] S. 78, Trade Practices Act 1974. See R. V. Miller, *Miller's Annotated Trade Practices Act*, 23rd edn. (Sydney: Lawbook, 2002), 1.76.10. For a discussion of the relative neglect of regulatory offences by criminal law scholarship, see Lacey, Ch. 7 in this volume.

[37] *NAPP Pharmaceutical Holdings Ltd v Director General of Fair Trading*, Case No. 1000/1/1/01 [2002] CAT I, [2002] Comp AR 13, [2002] ECC 177. See also Whish, *Competition Law*, 368.

[38] See House of Lords Select Committee on the European Union, Session 1999–2000, 19th Report, *Strengthening the Role of the Hearing Officer in EC Competition Cases*, HL Paper 125 (London: HMSO, 21 Nov. 2000).

[39] Article 22, Regulation 1/2003, on the Implementation of the Rules on competition laid down in Articles 81 and 82 of the Treaty [2003] OJ L1/1, 4 Jan. 2003.

the rules themselves lead to a bending of the rules and rights protected by other legal doctrines, in the name of competition.

Substantively, the relationship between competition law and intellectual property law is, perhaps, the most conspicuous and hotly debated. The traditional grant of monopoly to the owner of an intellectual property right to encourage innovation by ensuring a return on their creative efforts is at odds with classical competition law that is designed to promote competition. In the EU the potential for disintegration of a new and supranational competition law in the light of long-standing and deeply embedded national intellectual property rights was avoided by resort to legal formalism in the shape of block exemption regulations. These regulations in effect provide detailed rules as to what terms were legal and illegal under the competition rules in intellectual property licensing agreements. In practice, lawyers did all they could to bring agreements within the exemptions, or as close as possible, so as to avoid notifying the Commission at all or to facilitate clearance.[40] When the Commission proposed restricting the application of the technology transfer regulation by reference to market shares, lobbying was described as frenzied[41]—indicating how the certainty provided by the formal competition rules was favoured by industry. The fact that the Commission was willing to move away from formalism for bigger businesses shows a growing confidence in relation to the competition rules, which is reflected in the new draft regulation and guidelines on technology transfer agreements published for consultation by the Commission in 2003.[42] It is arguable that the effect on competition of exclusive provisions in intellectual property licensing is limited and instead the competition rules were being used as a tool to advance the market integration agenda of the EU, where intellectual property rights remained national in nature and could easily be used to foreclose national markets.[43]

Doctrinal Consistency across Jurisdictional Boundaries: The Antitrust Paradigm

There are two main features of competition law that create a momentum towards convergence of norms and practices—a form of productive integration across jurisdictions. Firstly, the emergence of an epistemic community of international competition lawyers (who advise the main subjects of competition law, multinationals) facilitates the exchange of ideas and practices and creates

---

[40] See J.-E. de Cockborne, 'Franchising and EC Competition Law', in C. Joerges (ed.), *Franchising and the Law: Theoretical and Comparative Approaches in Europe and the US* (Baden-Baden: Nomos, 1991).

[41] I. Saltzman, 'The New Technology Transfer Block Exemption Regulation', *European Intellectual Property Journal*, 9 (1996), 506.

[42] EC Commission, Communication on Competition Rules Relating to Technology Transfer Agreements, OJ C235/10, 1 Oct. 2003.

[43] I. Maher, 'The Evolution of EU Law', in P. Craig and G. de Búrca (eds.), *The Evolution of EU Law* (Oxford: Oxford University Press, 1999).

a climate where doctrinal consistency across jurisdictions is favoured and competition law is viewed as *sui generis*.[44] Also, networks of competition officials have emerged in response to the perceived increase in international business as a means of overcoming the territorial constraints of their own laws and powers, in particular through the international competition network. The EU, emboldened by its experience of national competition laws in Europe converging towards the EU norms, has been a consistent and enthusiastic advocate of a multilateral approach. The United States historically shied away from multilateralism, instead advocating bilateral agreements centred mainly on cooperation on enforcement.[45] This difference in approach was grounded in part in the hegemony of US antitrust that is the second and more significant reason as to why there is doctrinal consistency across jurisdictions in competition law. Even in the EU, while the model adopted is European, antitrust influence is still apparent in discussions in practitioner and academic competition journals and reference to American experience in case-law and Commission decisions. By advocating multilateralism, the EU Commission is creating the prospect of an alternative benchmark to that of American antitrust. The US, on the other hand, by emphasizing bilateralism and technical assistance programmes, where policy learning and policy transfer can be implicit or explicit, shores up the pre-eminent position of American antitrust.

The influence of American antitrust law is pervasive and, in effect, it acts as a benchmark for other competition laws. The common usage of the term 'antitrust' outside the United States is indicative of this influence, given that the term relates specifically to the form of corporate governance that was common in late nineteenth-century America that underpinned the anti-competitive behaviour the Sherman Act made illegal.[46] This is for a number of reasons. Firstly, with economic theory dominated by the US academy, once outside the highest levels of abstraction, the vast majority of 'real world' examples or references to the law draw on the American experience. The use of English also increases the influence of US economic theory and law. For example, while German competition law has a long history, with a powerful and highly respected enforcement agency, the fact that its decisions are not in English hampers its influence (even though the web site of the Bundeskartellamt now

[44] See L. McGowan and S. Wilks, 'The First Supranational Policy in the European Union: Competition Policy', *European Journal of Political Research*, 28 (1995), 141. For a discussion of such a community in the EU context, see F. van Waarden and M. Drahos, 'Courts and (Epistemic) Communities in the Convergence of Competition Policies', *Journal of European Public Policy*, 9/6 (2002), 913; Y. Dezalay, 'Between the State, Law and the Market: The Social and Professional Stakes in the Construction and Definition of a Regulatory Arena', in W. Bratton, J. McCahery, S. Picciotto, and C. Scott (eds.), *International Regulatory Competition and Coordination: Perspectives on Economic Regulation in Europe and the United States* (Oxford: Oxford University Press, 1997).

[45] A.-M. Slaughter, 'Governing the Global Economy through Government Networks', in M. Byers (ed.), *The Role of Law in International Politics: Essays in International Relations and International Law* (Oxford: Oxford University Press, 2000).

[46] R. J. R. Peretz, *Competition Policy in America, 1888–1992: History, Rhetoric, Law* (New York: Oxford University Press, 1996).

has a fairly large English language section[47]. Similarly, the relatively limited
number of papers available in English on the Ordoliberal School—significant in
the German context—hampers understanding and transfer of German ideas,
decisions, and legal practice.[48] The fact that US antitrust law is also based on
one of the oldest competition law statutes gives it a pedigree lacking elsewhere
in the common law world. This longevity combined with the emphasis on litigation (both private and administrative) provides a very rich vein of case-law on
almost every aspect of competition law. It would be surprising not to find a US
precedent for whatever aspect of competition law was under discussion. The
staying power of the US antitrust statutes, despite many shifts in interpretation
of the core provisions,[49] is important. In addition, US officials, with their 'missionary zeal' in relation to their own competition laws,[50] are active in and, given
the importance of the US economy and the resources available to such officials,
influential participants in the networks of competition enforcement agencies
that have emerged.[51] Such influence re-enforces the hegemony of antitrust law.

The influence of US antitrust can thus be seen as an integrating mechanism
facilitating doctrinal consistency where competition law(s) are jurisdictionally
fragmented. This productive integration based on US antitrust law where it
provides a benchmark for the interpretation of competition law highlights the
extent to which competition law is defined by function, where that function is
to maximize welfare through the protection of competition. Competition law
is self-referential with American antitrust law a main source of reference. This
is true even in the EU, where, as Gerber demonstrates, the basis for its competition law lies within the German ordoliberal tradition.[52] Thus, a number of
US doctrines have been embraced to a greater or lesser degree by the EU courts,
for example, the essential facilities doctrine[53] and the failing firm defence.[54]

---

[47] See http://www.bundeskartellamt.de.

[48] W. Moschel, 'The Proper Scope of Government Viewed from an Ordoliberal Perspective: The
Example of Competition Policy', *Journal of Institutional and Theoretical Economics*, 157/1 (2001), 3;
V. J. Vanberg, 'The Freiburg School of Law and Economics', in P. Newman (ed.), *Palgrave Dictionary
of Economics and Law* (London: Macmillan, 1998); I. Maher, 'Re-imagining the Story of European
Competition Law', *Oxford Journal of Legal Studies*, 20 (2000), 155.

[49] S. W. Waller, 'Market Talk: Competition Policy in America', *Law and Social Inquiry*, 22
(1997), 435.

[50] J. Braithwaite and P. Drahos, *Global Business Regulation* (Cambridge: Cambridge University
Press, 2000), 216.

[51] I. Maher, 'Competition Law in the International Domain: Networks as a New Form of
Governance', *Journal of Law and Society*, 29 (2002), 111; S. Picciotto, 'Networks in International
Integration: Fragmented States and the Dilemmas of Neo-Liberalism', *North-Western Journal of
International Law and Business*, 17 (1996–7), 1014.

[52] D. J. Gerber, *Law and Competition in Twentieth Century Europe: Protecting Prometheus*
(Oxford: Clarendon Press, 1998), ch. 9.

[53] Sealink/B & I—Holyhead—Interim Measures; [1994] OJ L15/8, [1995] 4 CMLR 84; and
C-7/97 *Oscar Bronner v Mediaprint* [1998] ECR I-7791, [1999] 4 CMLR 112.

[54] C-68/94 and 30/95 *Commission v France* [1998] ECR I-1375, [1998] 4 CMLR 829; and
Comp/m.2314 BASF/Eurodiol/Pantochim [2002] OJ L32/45, where the Commission expressly states
it is applying the same criteria to the failing firm defence as the US Department of Justice merger
guidelines.

Even if an American doctrine is ultimately rejected, there are extensive debates about its suitability with it providing a key reference point, for example, the American rule of reason.[55] American antitrust hegemony is seen not necessarily in the degree to which competition laws are converging or consistent throughout the world but more fundamentally in the extent to which it is a primary benchmark. As a benchmark, it also acts as a bridge between law and economics with judges looking to American case-law as a guide to, if not as a substitute for, economic analysis.

COMPETITION LAW AND ECONOMICS

One of the most distinctive characteristics of competition law is its dependence on the discourse of economics. Some commentators contend that it owes its very existence to economics.[56] Institutionally, the link between competition law and economics is acknowledged in legislation that allows economists to be members of tribunals or courts deciding competition cases.[57] How economic analysis is harnessed within competition law in order to ensure its productive integration is of fundamental importance to the consistency of that doctrine. Economics is the communicative bridge between the social subsystems of law and economy: competition law and markets. Competition law translates 'the deal' (which may not even be a contract) into a legal construct subject to legal scrutiny—in the language of systems theory applying the binary code which can render certain conduct legal or illegal.[58] To understand the deal, account is taken of the market within which it is formed. The articulation of the market requires an economic analysis that in turn is framed by theory—with different theories in the ascendancy at different times and in different jurisdictions.

Competition law is inextricably linked to the market—a link articulated through economic discourse. Thus, in order to answer the question 'Is this conduct illegal because it is anti-competitive?', the nature of competition must first be defined. While economics is privileged and necessary to answer the question whether particular conduct is anti-competitive, it is not sufficient. This is for two reasons. Firstly, competition law is not purely technocratic in nature but raises political issues such as the balancing of public and private (economic) power where competition law acts as a bridge. This balancing is elegantly addressed by ordoliberalism—an overarching theory that embraces economics,

---

[55] EC Commission, White Paper on Modernization of the Rules Implementing Articles 85 and 86 of the EC Treaty, Commission Programme 99/027 (28 Apr. 1999), 23.

[56] See D. B. Audretsch, W. J. Baumol, and A. E. Burke, 'Competition Policy in Dynamic Markets', *International Journal of Industrial Organization*, 19/5 (2001), 613.

[57] In Australia membership of the Competition Tribunal can include an economist; see s. 31(2), Trade Practices Act 1974. In New Zealand an economist may sit as a lay member of the High Court when it is considering competition law matters; see s. 77 Commerce Act 1986.

[58] G. Teubner, 'Substantive and Reflexive Elements in Modern Law', *Law and Society Review*, 17 (1983), 239.

law, and politics.[59] In its conception of an economic constitution there is a concern to ensure structural parallels between the political constitution and free trade.[60] It seeks to protect the liberty of action of the individual as well as government by seeing competition law both as distributing competences between the individual and the state and as a means of resolving individual conflicts. There is respect for both individual and state power but both are constrained through the operation of the rule of law, with ordoliberalism emphasizing rule-based decisions over the exercise of administrative discretion that can be subject to political lobbying.[61] This, to some extent, addresses Hayek's criticism of regulation that it is not possible for the regulator to know or effectively regulate complex markets.[62] Thus, this theory addresses the inherent tension in competition law between individual freedom and private ordering but can only do so by embracing law, economics, and politics—economic discourse on its own not being sufficient.

The balancing of the values and objectives of the market (as embodied in competition law) with other social values is transparent in specific sectors. For example, there can be a collision between the social value of media plurality and the efficiency concerns of the market[63] and between the social value of loyalty to and identification with particular sporting teams and the application of competition laws to player transfers, ticket sales, and viewing rights.[64] This balancing of values is present—albeit to a less obvious degree—in the general application of competition law because, as one EU Commissioner for competition put it, competition is politics.[65]

Secondly, the dependence of competition law on economic discourse is problematic because of the existence of different economic theories and the complexity of economic quantitative analysis in particular. Classic economic theory is premised on a static model of perfect competition. Under this model, pure competition arises where there is allocative efficiency, i.e. where resources are used most efficiently because only those businesses that can produce at marginal cost will remain in the market while the absence of control over price ensures that prices remain at marginal cost.[66] Consumers have perfect information about

---

[59] W. Moschel, 'The Proper Scope of Government Viewed from an Ordoliberal Perspective: The Example of Competition Policy', *Journal of Institutional and Theoretical Economics*, 157/1 (2001), 3. See, generally, Gerber, *Law and Competition in Twentieth Century Europe*, ch. 7.

[60] Moschel, 'The Proper Scope of Government', 8.   [61] Ibid.

[62] F. Hayek, *The Constitution of Liberty* (London: Routledge, 1960).

[63] The application of the competition rules to a newspaper merger in Ireland led to a protracted political debate and ultimately reform of the competition rules; see Maher, *Competition Law*, 244. See, generally, T. Gibbons, *Regulating the Media*, 2nd edn. (London: Sweet & Maxwell, 1998).

[64] P. Morris, S. Morrow, and P. Spink, 'EC Law and Professional Football: Bosman and its Implications', *Modern Law Review*, 59 (1996), 893; H. Fleming, 'Exclusive Rights to Broadcast Sporting Events in Europe', *European Competition Law Review*, 20/3 (1999), 143.

[65] See S. Wilks and L. McGowan, 'Competition Policy in the European Union: Creating a Federal Agency?', in G. B. Doern and S. Wilks (eds.), *Comparative Competition Policy* (Oxford: Clarendon Press, 1996), 254, quoting Commissioner van Miert.

[66] Where price exceeds the incremental cost of producing another unit (marginal cost) then another unit will be produced because revenue exceeds cost. Thus, production expands up to the point where

the product which is homogeneous as technology is taken as a given. Thus, competition is purely on price. As a static and abstract model, it is relatively simple and its influence is such that perfect competition is often taken to be synonymous with welfare maximization. Its simplicity, clarity, and abstraction (there is no suggestion that pure competition actually exists) make it an attractive form of communication between the reality of markets and competition law. The model is flawed as it takes no account of innovation, the fact that in some circumstances competition can be destructive (i.e. market failure even outside traditional monopolies), and the fact that firm capability (and thence market structure) can be important in relation to market performance.[67] Thus, industrial economics has moved from an emphasis on market structure in the 1950s and 1960s to more of a focus on conduct. Static models have been superseded as competition is viewed as a dynamic process operating in dynamic markets, with game theory encapsulating this realization.

Lawyers, regulators, and judges are now faced with a bewildering array of theories, mostly emanating from the United States. As well as the Chicago School and Ordoliberalism, lawyers can also look to the Austrian School (with its emphasis on competition as process and the importance of entrepreneurship); the theory of contestable markets (where the focus is on barriers to market entry and exit); and game theory (where relational issues and the importance of repeated transactions are emphasized). Thus, the first issue to be addressed by those enforcing competition law is which theoretical paradigm is to be applied. This choice is itself political[68] with decisions about which economic theory to adopt involving important value judgements as to the role of competition law in public ordering. For example, in assessing a conglomerate merger, does an agency apply portfolio theory, i.e. does it regard the merger as creating the potential for mixed bundling where stand-alone products are offered as a discounted package to the detriment of competition? The EU and US competition authorities came to different conclusions in relation to the GE–Honeywell merger mainly because of a disagreement over the application of that theory to mergers.[69] Even when the particular theory is accepted, the next issue is how economists apply the theory to the particular facts. For example, a mix of econometric analysis and modelling as well as simulations may be used to define the product and geographic market and the levels of competition within that market. Sweeney and Hay argue that historically in the

marginal cost meets price. See P. Areeda, 'Introduction to Antitrust Economics', *Antitrust Law Journal*, 52 (1983), 523.

[67] D. B. Audretsch, W. J. Baumol, and A. E. Burke, 'Competition Policy in Dynamic Markets', *International Journal of Industrial Organization*, 19/5 (2001), 613.

[68] T. Frazer, *Monopoly, Competition and the Law*, 2nd edn. (Hemel Hempstead: Harvester Wheatsheaf, 1992), 5.

[69] Honeywell/GE [2001] OJ C46/6 (CEC). See E. E. Holland, 'Using Merger Review to Cure Prior Conduct: The European Commission's GE/Honeywell Decision', *Columbia Law Review* (2003), 74; and M. Pflanz and C. Caffarra, 'The Economics of G.E./Honeywell', *European Competition Law Review*, 23/3 (2002), 115.

Australian and New Zealand context judges have been unwilling to engage with such quantitative evidence.[70] Instead, economic principles are rejected where they might lead to results which run counter to the judge's own intuition.[71] If judges are ill at ease with economic analysis, a refusal to receive it removes them from any obligation to analyse it or explain why their judgement differs from it.[72] Even where the judges engage with economic analysis, their approach may lead to legal developments which are designed to minimize uncertainty by closing off some lines of inquiry. Thus, in the Australian *Boral* case, Justice McHugh suggested that recoupment be a requirement for predatory pricing, in part because this would avoid having to engage in the 'messy area'[73] of cost analysis. Economic evidence is also sometimes rejected where courts see the experts as treading on the adjudicative function.[74]

This question of the role of economic experts and their fit with the rules of evidence is complex. One response to this complexity has been the introduction in Australia of what is known as the 'hot tub' approach, where economic experts give evidence one after the other, comment on each other's testimony, and are cross-examined by counsel. This is done after all the evidence has been received by the court and just before closing submissions. It allows for the issues in dispute to be quickly identified and debated,[75] but does not guarantee that the court will fully engage with the economic evidence. In particular, judges point to the need to have regard to commercial realities—a qualitative analysis. But as Sweeney and Hay point out, such a qualitative analysis does not preclude the quantitative economic data. Instead, that data can inform the commercial reality. The challenge in competition cases is to enrich the qualitative analysis needed to determine commercial reality through critical engagement with the quantitative data put forward by economic experts. This requires some understanding of the limitations of quantitative analysis. For example, results of techniques using inappropriate data should not be relied on. An assessment needs to be made of how representative the data set is of the whole competitive process under review, given that an ideal set of data is rare.[76]

---

[70] C. Sweeney and D. L. Hay, 'Quantitative Economic Evidence in Australian and New Zealand Courtrooms', *Competition and Consumer Law Journal*, 10 (2003), 284.

[71] K. Yeung, 'The Court-Room Economist in Australian Antitrust Litigation: An Underutilised Resource?', *Australian Business Law Review*, 20 (1992), 461. Sweeney and Hay cite, by way of example, the first instance decision in the Superleague case *News Ltd. v Australian Rugby Football League Ltd.* (1996) 58 FCR 447 (Burchett J).

[72] Sweeney and Hay, 'Quantitative Economic Evidence in Australian and New Zealand Courtrooms', pt. IV.

[73] *Boral Besser Masonry Ltd. v ACCC* (2003) 195 ALR 609, (2003) 77 ALJR 623, (2003) 24(3) Leg Rep 18, (2003) ATPR 41-915, [2003] HCA 5, 7 Feb. 2003.

[74] See Sweeney and Hay's discussion of the reasons for rejecting the evidence of the economic expert in *TPC v Arnotts* (1990) 93 ALR 657; ATPR 41-062.

[75] In *Boral* the process took about a day; see Sweeney and Hay, 'Quantitative Economic Evidence in Australian and New Zealand Courtrooms', sect. 6(f).

[76] S. Bishop and M. Walker, *The Economics of EC Competition Law: Concepts, Application and Measurement* (London: Sweet & Maxwell, 1999), 171.

Instead of such critical engagement with the quality of economic analysis, judges may resort to rich factual analysis. This, to some extent, reflects the emphasis on factual analysis within judicial decision-making. *In extremis*, the risk is that references to commercial reality mask recourse to the judge's own intuition. American antitrust with its rich body of case-law and proximity to the dominant economic theories can act as a bridge between economic discourse and law with that jurisprudence providing concrete examples of the application of economic theory and 'translating' those theories into legal discourse. The issue of the interplay of economic discourse, American antitrust and competition law in all its complexity can be seen in the recent Australian High Court decision in the *Boral* case.[77]

Boral Besser Masonry Ltd. (BBM) v ACCC

In *Boral*, a majority of the Court rejected the argument of the Australian Competition and Consumer Commission that BBM took advantage of its substantial market power for the purpose of eliminating a competitor by engaging in predatory pricing contrary to section 46 of the Trade Practices Act.[78] The Court had to decide what the relevant market was, whether BBM enjoyed substantial market power, whether it had the relevant purpose required under the legislation, what predatory pricing was, and whether BBM engaged in it. BBM produced concrete masonry products—blocks, bricks, and pavers—in Melbourne and was part of a large holding company operating in the building and energy sectors in Australia. At first instance, the judge defined the relevant product market broadly to include all walling and paving materials.[79] The wider the market definition, the less likely a finding of substantial market power, so the ACCC lost. On appeal, the Full Federal Court gave a narrower definition of the market as concrete masonry products and held BBM had substantial market power because it was able to conduct a price war to exclude competition, i.e. it had engaged in predatory pricing.[80] Substantial market power is the ability to raise prices above the supply cost without rivals taking away customers in due time.[81] The majority in the High Court was of the view that the power to raise prices had to be considered first, before examining

---

[77] *Boral Besser Masonry Ltd. v ACCC* (2003) 195 ALR 609, (2003) 77 ALJR 623, (2003) 24(3) Leg Rep 18, (2003) ATPR 41-915, [2003] HCA 5, 7 Feb. 2003.

[78] The relevant parts of s. 46(1) provide: 'A corporation that has a substantial degree of power in a market shall not take advantage of that power for the purpose of:

(a) eliminating or substantially damaging a competitor of that corporation . . . in that . . . market;

(b) preventing the entry of a person in that . . . market; or

(c) deterring or preventing a person from engaging in competitive conduct in that . . . market.'

[79] *ACCC v Boral Ltd* [1999] FCA 1318 (22 Sept. 1999).

[80] *ACCC v Boral Ltd* [2001] FCA 30 (27 Feb. 2001). Heerey J's much criticized conclusion on market definition was that 'a wall is a wall', at para. 130.

[81] *Queensland Wire Industries Pty Ltd v Broken Hill Proprietary Co Ltd* (1989) 167 CLR 177, 200; ATPR 40-925, 50015.

whether the firm had power to exclude competition, for example, through predatory pricing. It accepted the narrow market definition used by the Full Federal Court but it found that BBM did not have substantial market power as there was vigorous price competition between BBM and the other major player. Given this finding, it did not have to consider predatory pricing but did comment obiter.

This was the first time the Court considered predatory pricing and a substantial amount of evidence was submitted on it. The most contentious issue in defining predation is whether or not recoupment of losses incurred in price-cutting through later higher prices is necessary. Recoupment is required under US law but the position is less clear-cut under EU law.[82] The problem is to define predation in such a way that price competition by a dominant firm is still possible. Justice McHugh, following American jurisprudence, noted that a firm with substantial market power that engaged in price-cutting to remove competitors and then recouped its losses by raising prices would be in breach of section 46.[83] While he acknowledged significant differences between section 46 and the US legislation, no valid reason existed for not using that jurisprudence as an aid to development. Thus, he treated American antitrust as the default position with the case-law used as an interpretative device for the understanding of economic theory.

Chief Justice Gleeson and Justice Callinan were at pains to point out that the term 'predatory pricing' is not used in the Act and warned of the risks inherent in its usage—that it could take on a life of its own, independent of statute, and distract attention from the statutory language. They were sensitive to the need for doctrinal consistency, such that they warned of concepts imported from other legislative contexts and of the dangers of adopting principles from other countries uncritically and without regard to the context in which they were developed.[84] In short, they prioritized the internal consistency of Australian competition law doctrine as encapsulated in the Trade Practices Act over consistency with American antitrust. Thus, they did not expressly state that predatory pricing falls within section 46, and noted that while recoupment may not be legally necessary, it may be factually important to prove a breach of the section.[85]

Justice Kirby, in dissent, drew on economic theory and American jurisprudence and reflected on the history of recoupment in his discussion of predatory pricing. He warned of the risks for other jurisdictions of unconsidered application of antitrust analysis without attention to the difference in emphasis of the relevant legislative provision.[86] In this instance, the differences between US antitrust and section 46 were twofold. Firstly, the US statute refers to monopolization, while

---

[82] See *Brooke Group Ltd v Brown & Williamson Tobacco Corp* 509 US 209 (1993); C-333/94P *Tetra Pak International SA v Commission* [1996] ECR I-5951, [1997] 5 CMLR 662, para. 44.

[83] Para. 274.   [84] Para. 126.

[85] Para. 130. The issue was not discussed by Justices Gaudron, Gummow, and Hayne in their judgment.   [86] Para. 434.

section 46 does not. The judge noted that predation could lead to market exclusion even where there is no monopoly.[87] Secondly, the US legislation requires an effects test, while section 46 is based on a purpose test. This distinction was significant as a requirement that recoupment be certain or even highly probable implied an effects test. Instead, under section 46, the purpose of the firm to eliminate a competitor would be necessary but, given the dynamic nature of markets, the prospect of longer-term recoupment would be sufficient. It would not be necessary to wait to see if recoupment actually occurred. Thus, after consideration of economic discourse, American antitrust, and section 46, Justice Kirby advocates a new test for predatory pricing designed to take account of the purpose test and the absence of any reference to monopoly under section 46.

The main issue for consideration was whether or not BBM had substantial market power. Chief Justice Gleeson and Justice Callinan approached the issue through a very detailed factual analysis and limited engagement with economic discourse. Throughout, the emphasis is on the contextualization of the alleged conduct by reference to business practice. Their main focus was whether or not there was market power, in particular as evidenced through the ability to price independently. They concluded that there was no substantial market power on the part of BBM through detailed description of tenders and the price war surrounding those tenders during a period of recession in the Victorian building industry. In Chief Justice Gleeson and Justice Callinan's judgment, regard is had primarily to tendering during the fierce price war borne of over-capacity where customers (builders) could play suppliers off against each other to secure lower prices. The decision of the Boral group to retain a presence in the market and to bear the interim losses was seen as a rational business decision. Of course, the only reason BBM could remain was because it was a member of a corporate group that could afford to sustain losses that bankrupted a smaller operator. The justices rejected the argument that financial strength implied substantial market power even though considerable financial strength was required to remain in the market given the extent and duration of price-cutting. They also rejected the 'smoking gun' documentary evidence.[88] Indeed, they warn against confusing an explicit, aggressive intent about eliminating competitors with anti-competitive behaviour, quoting from a US case[89] that monopolists set prices according to costs while competitors set them according to the market. Justice McHugh, like Chief Justice Gleeson and Justice Callinan, emphasizes context through a detailed factual analysis. For example, while he discusses the tests for market definition (in Australian, US, and EU case law), he notes that the views and practices of business are most instructive in relation to market definition.

---

[87] Para. 416.

[88] Documentary evidence expressly referred to the aim of driving at least one competitor from the market and making it more difficult for new entrants to get a foothold in the market; see Justice Kirby at para. 393.

[89] *AA Poultry Farms Inc v Rose Acre Farms Inc* 881 F 2d 1396 (1989) US Court of Appeals, Seventh Circuit.

In contrast, American writings and case-law are used in the judgment of Justices Gaudron, Gummow, and Hayne. Thus, in analysing section 46, they discuss how the Australian provisions reflect propositions found in US law and take account of the caveats to those propositions found (again) in US decisions and writers. In fact, in rejecting the conclusions of Justice Finkelstein in the Full Federal Court, that exclusionary conduct is by itself proof of market power, the argument proceeds mainly on the basis of American writings and cases. Thus, they counter the American law journal article[90] on which Justice Finkelstein relied by reference to the oral expert evidence of the economist (formally an official at the US Department of Justice Antitrust Division) who proffered an alternative view using American academic writings and case-law to support his argument. Justice Finkelstein's approach may have influenced the approach taken by these High Court judges, as his judgment is an elegant essay on predatory pricing drawing mainly on law and economics authorities in American law journals and offering a critique of the Chicago School.[91]

Justice Kirby (in dissent) initially limits the scope of his review of the earlier judgments by looking for the appealable errors in the primary findings of the trial judge. He thus follows the Full Federal Court rejection to the challenge of the trial judge's findings of subjective intention that BBM did have the relevant purpose of eliminating a competitor. He further limits his overview by noting the greater experience of the Federal Court in competition matters and the fact that the court had more time to consider the case. It is thus not surprising that he supports the findings of the Full Federal Court. He adopts a different threshold from the majority for triggering a finding of substantial power, drawing on the history of section 46, noting that 'substantial' does not imply control of the market. Like Justice Beaumont in the Full Federal Court, he draws heavily on the history of section 46 and its amendment where the substantial control of the market was replaced by substantial degree of market power, implying a lower threshold for illegality. He rejects the widely used independence of action test for measuring market power applied by the other judges, saying it confines section 46 in a way that is 'unnecessary, inconsistent with the Act's history, incompatible with its language, conflicting with its stated and apparent legislative objects and out of line with its international counterparts as well as economic theory which informs this area of the law'.[92] His primary concern is to advance the purpose of the Act—the promotion of competition in order to enhance consumer welfare. The quotation is a wonderful rhetorical flourish, but even at that level it is noteworthy that a judge who, from the outset, privileges legal analysis still finds it helpful to invoke economic discourse and international competition law in this way. In finding substantial market power, he notes BBM's capacity to survive the price war. He supports the conclusion by looking

---

[90] T. G. Krattenmaker, R. Lande, and S. Salop, 'Monopoly Power and Market Power in Antitrust Law', *George Washington Law Journal*, 76 (1987), 241.
[91] *Boral Besser Masonry Ltd. v ACCC* (2003) 195 ALR 609, (2003) 77 ALJR 623, (2003) 24(3) Leg Rep 18, (2003) ATPR 41-915, [2003] HCA 5, 7 Feb. 2003, para. 236.   [92] Para. 369.

at the incumbents' conduct as a way of defining barriers to entry. He also rejects the view that deep pockets cannot be relevant, noting that it may be a marker of market power—though it is not conclusive in itself. Similarly, the vertically integrated structure of BBM could not be ignored. He warns against using threshold tests divorced from conduct and context—an implicit criticism of reliance on economic tests. Like Chief Justice Gleeson and Justice Callinan, he warns against importing overseas case-law or pure economic theory, arguing that while they may assist, the decision-maker still has to give meaning to the local law. Consistent with his purposive approach he argues against the application of the three-point test for establishing a breach of section 46, instead interpreting it as a whole. He does not privilege business practice, noting that anti-competitive conduct may well be rational in increasing profit. The competitive conduct of BBM was rational, but it just happened to be illegal as well. Given that he was willing to find market power and unwilling to interfere with the finding of impugned purpose by the trial judge, Justice Kirby found that there had been a breach of section 46.

The emphasis on economic discourse and antitrust law varies among the judgments, with Justices Gaudron, Gummow, and Hayne reflecting the position of Justice McHugh—that antitrust law is the default position unless there is good reason to depart from it. Justice McHugh, Chief Justice Gleeson, and Justice Callinan avoid engagement with economic evidence by grounding themselves firmly in a detailed factual analysis providing rich description of the market to assist in their holding as to market power. The detailed reliance on pricing practices is at the expense of engagement with economic analysis on pricing. Substantively, the case shows the difficulty, firstly, of proving market power in a concentrated market where there is price-cutting, and, secondly, of proving predatory pricing. The strict interpretation of the Act set a relatively high threshold for the finding of substantial market power, rendering section 46 redundant in most situations. This interpretation rejects the notion of 'bad' competition and takes no account of firm capability. The findings of the majority are consistent with the wording of the section—that conduct of a firm with substantial market power will only be illegal where it is used for certain purposes, but are inconsistent with the overall purpose of the Act of promoting competition. The case highlights the problem of a subjective purposive test linked to the elimination of a competitor when competition law is about protecting the process of competition and not protecting competitors. Freedom of contract (especially in relation to price) is preserved, with competition law unable to challenge aggressive competition in a concentrated market.

CONCLUSION

There is an inherent contradiction in competition law. It is both a constraint on the freedom of contract and a device through which such freedom is protected for the public good. An awareness of which aspect of competition law is being prioritized in any particular decision will make more explicit the policy decisions being made as to the balance between freedom of contract and public ordering. This, then, allows for a more effective harnessing of economic discourse. Competition law must necessarily engage with economic theory in order to make sense of the markets that it regulates. Such a collision of discourses is problematic and there is little prospect of equilibrium being found between the two. The objective, however, is not one of equilibrium. Competition law must be and should be informed by economic discourse as a means of understanding the operation of markets but will then translate that discourse so it is consistent with legal reasoning. What we are seeing in competition law is not what Collins terms 'productive disintegration' but, instead, 'productive integration'. Competition law is not disintegrating through its engagement with economic discourse— it could not exist without that discourse. Instead, the emphasis is on integrating that discourse in such a manner that productive use can be made of it, for example, by explaining what predatory pricing or market definition are. It is here that American antitrust becomes important. While economic discourse provides the bridge between law and markets, it is mediated through the many decisions in American antitrust law which have already concretized and legalized the concepts and analyses of economics. A robust competition law is thus one mediated through economic discourse and American antitrust.

10

Administrative Law as Regulation

PETER CANE*

My first plan for this chapter was to ask whether major developments in Anglo-Australian administrative law over the past thirty years or so (such as liberalization of standing and the doctrine of legitimate expectations) could be interpreted as reflecting, or as having been influenced or provoked by, a 'regulatory' approach to law. But as I thought about this question, I realized that I was not going to be able to answer it without having a better understanding of what a 'regulatory approach' to administrative law might entail. Aware as I was of Julia Black's masterly analysis of the many meanings and dimensions of regulation,[1] I felt uneasy making too many assumptions about how a regulatory story about recent developments in administrative law might go. So, the main aim of this chapter is to suggest what the project of taking a regulatory approach to administrative law ('the Project') might involve. My conclusion (in the section entitled 'The Legal and Regulatory Approaches Revisited') is that the Project can be interpreted in at least three different ways, each of which can illuminate our understanding of both regulation and administrative law. A first interpretation merely involves acknowledging that administrative law is goal-oriented. A second interpretation attributes to administrative law the goal of securing compliance with its norms, while a third sees its goals in terms such as promoting good decision-making or rational public deliberation. My suggestion will be that it is the third of these interpretations that most clearly distinguishes a regulatory from a legal approach to administrative law.

In the first section of the chapter the aim is to identify differences between a 'legal' and a 'regulatory' approach to administrative law. The next section addresses the question 'What is administrative law?' and, in the process, discusses Hugh Collins's analysis of the respective roles of public law and contract law in

* The topic I was originally asked to write about was 'Regulating Administrative Law'. The change of title is deliberate because, although I might now be able to address that topic, at the time I did not think I could. And so this chapter has nothing to say about it. I benefited greatly from comments of and discussions with participants at the workshop at which an earlier version of this chapter was presented. Particular thanks are due to Nicola Lacey, Jerry Mashaw, and Colin Scott.

[1] J. Black, 'Decentring Regulation: Understanding Regulation and Self-regulation in a "Post-regulatory World" ', *Current Legal Problems*, 54 (2001), 103.

regulating government contracts. A major task in this section is to establish the importance of distinguishing between goals and tools of regulation. The following section discusses goals of administrative law. The next takes a closer look at administrative law viewed as a regulatory tool; while the penultimate section discusses empirical research about the regulatory impact of judicial review on bureaucratic behaviour.

The Legal and the Regulatory Approaches to Administrative Law

The editors suggest a contrast between legal and regulatory approaches to law in the following terms:

> a regulatory perspective asks empirical questions about the . . . effects of law on society as a whole (or at least the target segment of society) . . . and normative questions about how law . . . can be designed to be most effective at accomplishing social goals . . . Legal scholars, by contrast, typically . . . [focus] on the content of legal doctrine and its coherence . . .[2]

According to this view, two types of questions can be asked about law: empirical questions and normative questions. Empirically, the legal approach is concerned with the substance of administrative law, whereas the regulatory approach is concerned with the social effects of administrative law. Normatively, the legal approach is concerned with the goals (or values) of administrative law, whereas the regulatory approach is concerned with the effectiveness of administrative law as a tool for achieving those goals. On this account, the regulatory approach takes the goals and values of administrative law for granted and asks empirical questions about the actual social effects of administrative law, and normative questions about how best to achieve those goals and promote those values. By contrast, the legal approach concerns itself not with the effects of administrative law but with its rules and principles and with the goals and values that do and should underpin them. Implicit in this contrast between legal and regulatory approaches is a distinction between legal norms (rules and principles and their underlying values) and the institutions that make and enforce those norms. The legal approach is primarily concerned with norms, whereas the regulatory approach focuses on institutions.

Adopting this understanding of a regulatory approach to administrative law, the Project requires us, firstly, to identify administrative law. Secondly, it is necessary to identify the goals of administrative law. Thirdly, we need to give an account of administrative law as a regulatory tool. The fourth task is to ascertain the effects of administrative law and, in the light of those effects, to assess the effectiveness of administrative law in relation to its goals.

---

[2] Introduction to this volume.

WHAT IS ADMINISTRATIVE LAW?

It is increasingly common for lawyers to think of administrative law as part of public law—its other major component being constitutional law. But I have not adopted this approach because Colin Scott's contribution to this volume (Chapter 11) is concerned with constitutions. Treated as a distinct body of law, administrative law is typically taken to be concerned with the executive branch of government. However, this can be no more than a starting point because one of the central questions in contemporary administrative law concerns the extent to which it does and should apply to the exercise of 'governmental' or 'public' functions by bodies other than 'core' agencies of executive government.[3] The interaction between institutional and functional approaches to defining the scope of administrative law has yet to be fully explored by courts and scholars. For present purposes, it is adequate to associate administrative law loosely with 'public tasks of governance'. The only 'institutions of public governance' whose activities are routinely excluded from the scope of administrative law are 'sovereign' legislators and superior courts. Of course, identifying administrative law as 'law about performance of public tasks of governance' leaves open the question of what those tasks are. In the present context it is, perhaps, enough to observe that many would consider 'regulation'—of commercial activity, at least—to be one.[4]

Laws that establish relevant institutions of governance are usually included under the rubric of administrative law. But, for present purposes, it is, perhaps, better to treat such laws as 'constitutional'. In light of the 'core' definition of regulation that is being used as the starting point for the Project[5]—namely, 'the intentional activity of attempting to control, order, or influence the behaviour of others'—it would seem most fruitful to understand administrative law as a tool for controlling performance of public tasks of governance consisting of what the editors describe as 'three basic requirements for a regulatory regime: the setting of standards, processes for monitoring compliance with the standards, and mechanisms for enforcing the standards'.[6]

There is more than a touch of irony in this conclusion. The regulatory approach is often identified with an instrumental, outcome-oriented mentality (or 'rationality'). But lawyers who are most likely to be attracted by the understanding of administrative law just outlined are those who stress non-instrumental values such as legitimacy, legality, and due process—in other words, those who (in terms of Harlow and Rawlings's now-iconic distinction) take a 'red light' approach to administrative law.[7] Lawyers of a more instrumental disposition—those who, in

---

[3] In the regulatory literature this phenomenon is sometimes referred to as 'decentring': e.g. Black, 'Decentring Regulation'.

[4] See e.g. J. Black, 'Constitutionalising Self-regulation', *Modern Law Review*, 59 (1996), 24.

[5] Introduction to this volume, p. 1.   [6] Ibid. p. 1.

[7] C. Harlow and R. Rawlings, *Law and Administration*, 2nd edn. (London: Butterworth, 1997), chs. 1 and 2.

Harlow and Rawlings's terms, take a 'green light' approach to administrative law—view the prime function of administrative law as being to facilitate, rather than to control and constrain, performance of public tasks of governance. In fact, this irony alerts us to the importance of the distinction between regulatory tools and regulatory goals. Central to the regulatory approach to law is the idea that law can be viewed as a regulatory tool. In this regard, the red-light approach and the green-light approach to administrative law are equally consistent with viewing law from a regulatory perspective. Where red-lighters and green-lighters differ is in their attitude to the law's goals. Values traditionally associated with administrative law, such as legitimacy, legality, and due process, may conflict with the promotion of 'social goals' such as clean air, efficient welfare services, and transparent financial markets. The difference between red-lighters and green-lighters lies in the way they tend to resolve such conflicts: red-lighters give greater weight to traditional administrative law values than do green-lighters. A corollary of this difference is that green-lighters tend to prefer performance of the tasks of governance to be regulated by non-legal tools (such as parliamentary scrutiny, auditing, and inspection), rather than legal tools, precisely because administrative law is so strongly associated with values to which they give relatively less weight.

The distinction between goals and tools is also central to an understanding of normative debates about the respective roles of public law and private law. This point is well illustrated by Hugh Collins's discussion of government contracts in *Regulating Contracts*. Public law principles (he says in a discussion of what he calls 'club markets'[8]) are principles 'normally applied to agencies of the state in order to ensure that they conform to their limited powers and follow fair procedures'[9]—i.e. principles of administrative law. Collins makes two important claims about public law. The first is descriptive: that whereas parties can agree that rules of private law will not apply to dealings between them, rules of public law cannot be waived.[10] In other words, whereas contract law facilitates *self*-regulation of consensual relationships, public law regulates them externally. The second proposition is prescriptive: that public law principles should apply to the activities of a group whose existence is based on agreement between private citizens only if that group is given regulatory functions by the state. In other words, the role of public law is to regulate the performance of public functions (or what I called earlier 'public tasks of governance'). By contrast, for Collins, a basic purpose of contract law is to contribute to the formation of markets and to support the market system.[11]

The main discussion of administrative law and contract law is contained in chapter 13: 'Government by Contract'. The analysis is rich and suggestive, and it is worth taking a little time to sort out its various strands. In this chapter

---

[8] H. Collins, *Regulating Contracts* (Oxford: Oxford University Press, 1999), 219–21.

[9] Ibid. 219.

[10] This is not universally true. For instance, a person can agree to forgo the protection of the rules of natural justice. It is certainly true of criminal law.   [11] Collins, *Regulating Contracts*, 5, 10.

Collins considers three types of contractual arrangement. Firstly, there are contracts for the provision of what he calls 'public services' to citizens (two modes of service provision are relevant: privatization and outsourcing). Secondly, Collins discusses large, complex contracts for the provision of goods or services to government (whether for its own or for third-party consumption). Thirdly, he examines 'quasi-contracts' such as NHS (National Health Service) contracts (for the provision of services by 'providers' to 'purchasers' within the NHS in the UK) and 'framework documents' that govern relations between ministries and quasi-autonomous administrative agencies. Collins asks whether contract law provides the best regime for regulating each of these types of arrangement, in the sense that it best 'assimilates'[12] the arrangement to the model of competitive market exchange and consumer choice. 'What kind of legal regulation can best assist governments in the use of markets to deliver services to the public?' he asks.[13]

In relation to the provision of public services through outsourcing, Collins detects a 'structural' problem in using contract law to facilitate consumer choice, namely, that the citizen consumer is not a party to the contract, and so can neither participate in the negotiation of its terms (directly at least) nor enforce it. Similarly, in the case of provision of goods and services by privatized utilities to the public, the terms of supply will often be decided by negotiation between the provider and an industry regulator without any direct input from consumers; and in some cases there may not even be a legally binding contract between the provider and the consumer. It is worth noting that these 'structural problems' are not confined to government outsourcing contracts. Many everyday contracts involve the purchase of goods and services for consumption by third parties who have no control over the terms of the contract or their enforcement (dependants, for example); and the terms of many everyday contracts are effectively imposed on consumers, rather than negotiated bilaterally. In this light, the point apparently being made is that, as consumers of *public services, citizens* should have a meaningful say about the terms on which those services are provided, and an effective opportunity to enforce those terms. Contract law cannot achieve this because it does not distinguish between government outsourcing contracts and ordinary commercial contracts, or between public services and ordinary commercial services.

So far as concerns large, complex contracts for the provision of goods or services to government, Collins finds two structural problems that cast doubt on the regulatory efficacy of contract law. One arises where the contract allows the government to vary the provider's obligations unilaterally, without making adequate provision for appropriate variation of the price to reflect consequential increases in the cost of performance. Such a situation is the product of inequality of bargaining power, which contract law generally ignores: courts will not relieve contracting parties of their obligations merely because they are

---

[12] Ibid. 306.   [13] Ibid. 12.

disadvantageous. The other problem arises from the nature of the remedies that contract law provides for defects of quality. In relation to large, complex contracts, non-legal incentives based on long-term 'single supplier' arrangements may provide more effective quality control than price competition backed up by legal sanctions for breach of contract. To the extent that government policy favours promotion of competition over quality assurance, contract law may provide inadequate incentives for the provider to meet contractual quality specifications. Once again, it can be noted that neither problem is peculiar to government contracts. In this light, the point being made seems to be that the problems need to be addressed in this context because government may have a legitimate interest in being free to vary contract terms unilaterally and in favouring promotion of competition over quality assurance.

The first two types of contractual arrangement exemplify contract as a medium of exchange. The third type (adopting Collins's terminology) uses the 'metaphor' of contract as a 'management device'—i.e. as an alternative to 'bureaucratic regulation'.[14] The contract metaphor is ideologically powerful because it bears a connotation of agreement and choice—or, in regulatory jargon, 'responsiveness'—that the idea of bureaucratic regulation lacks (although the reality of both forms of control may be rather different from the rhetoric associated with each). Although many quasi-contracts of this type operate in contexts that are not markets in even a metaphorical sense, the language of contract carries with it the implication that the prime value being promoted by the arrangement is economic efficiency. On the other hand, such contracts are not legally enforceable—in other words, they are not regulated by contract law. This signals the fact that market values that underpin contract law are not considered appropriate to quasi-contracts. In her study of NHS contracts Anne Davies argues (on theoretical and empirical grounds) that lack of enforceability is a serious problem, but also that public law principles would provide a better basis for regulation of NHS contracts than contract law.[15] Davies notes the argument that quasi-contractualization is a fundamentally flawed regulatory technique that should be abandoned,[16] but rejects it on pragmatic grounds. By contrast, Collins is sympathetic to the argument that quasi-contractualization is flawed for the reason that the efficiency-based norms of contract law are in 'considerable tension' with the distributive norms appropriate to the provision of 'public services'.[17] In terms of the regulation of quasi-contracts, the point seems to be that in so far as the market is considered to be an inappropriate mechanism for distributing goods and services that are the subject of quasi-contracts, contract law is an inappropriate tool for their regulation.

Collins's discussion of the use of administrative law, on the one hand, and contract law, on the other, to regulate government contracts well illustrates the

---

[14] Collins, *Regulating Contracts*, 315.

[15] A. C. L. Davies, *Accountability: A Public Law Analysis of Government by Contract* (Oxford: Oxford University Press, 2001), ch. 3.   [16] Ibid., p. xi.

[17] Collins, *Regulating Contracts*, 318–20.

importance of observing the distinction between regulatory tools and regulatory goals. It makes good sense to ask whether a particular regulatory tool is efficient and effective to achieve a given regulatory goal. Answering this (empirical) question in relation to contract law is a major part of Collins's project in *Regulating Contracts*. By contrast, establishing the goals of regulation is, essentially, a prescriptive activity. The prime goal that Collins assigns to contract law is the establishment, maintenance, and support of competitive markets. In Collins's treatment of government contracts the issue being addressed is one about the goals of regulation, not about the effectiveness of regulatory tools given certain regulatory goals.[18] As far as I can judge, the basic proposition that motivates Collins's analysis is that markets do not provide an appropriate mechanism for distributing public services. It follows that the reason why contract law is not an appropriate tool for regulating government contracts is not that contract law is ineffective and inefficient in establishing, maintaining, and supporting a market in public services (although it may be), but rather that establishing, maintaining, and supporting such a market is not an appropriate regulatory goal.[19] In other words, the market values that underpin contract law are inappropriate to regulation of the provision of public services. This is because the patterns of distribution of goods and services that markets tend to generate are not appropriate for public services.

The discussion in this section can, perhaps, be summarized by saying that, from a regulatory point of view, the key to understanding the differences between the various areas into which lawyers divide the law—administrative law, contract law, tort law, and so on—lies in identifying the goals that each body of law promotes. It is to identifying the goals of administrative law that I now turn.

THE REGULATORY GOALS OF ADMINISTRATIVE LAW

The values underlying administrative law can be identified in terms of the 'grounds' on which acts done and decisions made in performance of public functions can be stigmatized as 'illegal'. These grounds can be summarized in three principles: that fair procedures should be followed in the performance of public functions; that public functionaries should observe legal limits on their powers; and that they should respect the rights of individuals. The concept of fair procedure is encapsulated in the two principles of 'natural justice'—the rule against bias and the fair hearing rule. The idea of 'legal limits' addresses substantive

[18] This is reflected in the fact that chapter 13 appears in part IV of *Regulating Contracts*, entitled 'The Distributive Tasks of Regulation'.

[19] Besides contract law, the other major legal foundation of markets is property law. For the development of analogous arguments in that context, see e.g. P. P. Craig, 'Constitutions, Property and Regulation', *Public Law* (1991), 538; M. Taggart, 'Public Utilities and Public Law', in P. A. Joseph (ed.), *Essays on the Constitution* (Wellington: Brookers, 1995); T. Prosser, 'Public Service Law: Privatization's Unexpected Offspring', *Law and Contemporary Problems*, 63 (2000), 63.

concerns: that public functionaries should act consistently with relevant laws, that they should resolve relevant issues of fact within tolerable margins of error, and that they should exercise their powers 'rationally' and for the purposes for which those powers were conferred. Respect for individual rights requires, for instance, that public functionaries should not disappoint legitimate expectations, and that they should respect fundamental human rights.[20]

We might say that the regulatory goal of administrative law is to secure compliance with these principles. On the other hand, defining the regulatory goal of administrative law purely in terms of compliance with these normative principles might be thought not to take seriously the idea of treating administrative law as a regulatory tool. To do that, perhaps we need to identify some goal external, as it were, to the principles of administrative law. Otherwise, we get perilously close to a sort of Weinribian tautology to the effect that the purpose of administrative law is to be administrative law;[21] and we have no basis on which to engage in a regulatory critique of the rules and principles of administrative law, which constitute a given in this analysis.

In the US literature, liberalism and republicanism provide competing interpretations of the point of administrative law.[22] For liberals, the prime goal of administrative law is the protection of individual rights and interests,[23] whereas, for republicans, it is the promotion of rational public deliberation. Richard Stewart famously argued that the function of administrative law is to facilitate the participation of interest groups in administrative decision-making.[24] In the Anglo-Australian literature, a common theme is that judicial review embodies principles of 'good administration'.[25] Typically, such theories are 'normative' in the sense that they recommend or are based on values in terms of which rules and principles of administrative law can be understood and assessed; and in the sense that they are concerned with how public functionaries ought to behave, not how they do behave. Their basic function is to capture 'images of the legitimacy of state action'.[26] But they could also be used 'positively' as hypotheses about why administrative law has the content it does, and as goals by reference to which the effectiveness of administrative law could be judged.

A very different approach seeks to understand administrative law in terms of a hypothesis about how public functionaries actually behave. According to

---

[20] e.g. under s. 6 of the Human Rights Act 1998 (UK).

[21] In his *The Idea of Private Law* (Cambridge, Mass.: Harvard University Press, 1995) Ernest Weinrib argues that 'private law' must be understood 'formally' in terms of its 'structure' and not in terms of its goals or effects. In such formalist terms, he says, the only purpose of private law 'is to be private law' (p. 5).

[22] J. L. Mashaw, *Greed, Chaos and Governance: Using Public Choice to Improve Public Law* (New Haven: Yale University Press, 1997), ch. 5, esp. 111–18.

[23] See n. 7 and the text related to it.

[24] R. B. Stewart, 'The Reformation of American Administrative Law', *Harvard Law Review*, 88 (1975), 1699.

[25] e.g. D. Woodhouse, *In Pursuit of Good Administration: Ministers, Civil Servants and Judges* (Oxford: Oxford University Press, 1997), pt. II.

[26] Mashaw, *Greed, Chaos and Governance*, 108.

public choice theory, public functionaries, like private actors, are motivated by self-interest. This starting point generates a theory of administrative law built on the economics of principal and agent—the 'agency cost' approach.[27] According to this approach, 'judicial review is designed for one purpose: to reduce to an optimal level the agency costs that arise when public officials are appointed as agents to carry out tasks for the benefit of their principals, where the principals are, in various contexts, the people, the legislature, or the ministry'.[28]

Agency costs arise when public functionaries exercise discretion in their own interests, or in the interests of some group, rather than in the interests of their political principals. Under this approach, courts are 'monitors of agency costs in government';[29] and their role is to reduce agency costs to an optimal level—i.e. to the point where any further reduction would produce no benefit to the public. Because it is based on a hypothesis about human behaviour, agency cost theory is typically used positively to explain institutional architecture and the content of legal rules. But there is no theoretical reason why optimum reduction of agency costs should not be adopted as a normative goal for administrative law.

In terms of the principles of judicial review identified above, it is easy to see how the agency cost theory fits the principle that public functionaries should respect legal limits on their powers. So far as procedural requirements are concerned, the rule against bias can obviously be interpreted as designed to reduce agency cost; while the fair hearing rule can be understood as a mechanism for providing necessary information about the likely impact of decisions on affected parties. The agency cost approach does not accommodate the norm of respecting individual rights. Indeed, Bishop sees the agency cost explanation of administrative law as being inconsistent with this norm because success in judicial review does not normally guarantee the complainant a positive outcome, but only provides another opportunity to obtain a favourable decision.[30] In relation to fair procedures, Bishop brands rights-talk as cost–benefit analysis under a different, 'more high sounding name'.[31] Consistently with this approach to the protection of individual rights, Bishop interprets rules of standing as being concerned solely with ensuring that judicial review applications are made by the party best able to 'manage the challenge'[32]—an interpretation rendered plausible by the broadening of standing rules.

A puzzle in the agency cost approach is why courts should be the monitors of agency costs. Because most public functionaries operate under statute, the immediate principal of a public functionary is typically the legislature. Why should the legislature delegate the monitoring task to others who might be tempted to act in their own interest, rather than in that of their principal?[33]

---

[27] W. Bishop, 'A Theory of Administrative Law', *Journal of Legal Studies*, 19 (1990), 489.
[28] Ibid. 490–1.   [29] Ibid. 492.   [30] Ibid. 505–6.   [31] Ibid. 518.
[32] Ibid. 519–21.
[33] The current debate among UK scholars about the constitutional basis of judicial review (see C. Forsyth, *Judicial Review and the Constitution* (Oxford: Hart, 2000)) can be understood as addressing this issue.

The standard public choice answer seems to be that 'judicial independence' minimizes the risk that judges will not act in the public interest.[34] By contrast, Cross argues that courts are more prone to be influenced by special interests than are more democratic branches of government.[35]

It may be argued that however attractive general 'unitary' theories (such as I have surveyed in this section) may be as a normative framework for thinking about what the goals of administrative law should be, they do not provide the most fruitful way of describing or interpreting the actual goals of administrative law. The truth may be (as Jane Stapleton argues in relation to tort law in Chapter 6 of this volume) that administrative law has various 'local' and specific goals that interact in complex ways, and that they compete and conflict with one another.[36] We should be wary of jumping from the proposition that administrative law is goal-oriented to the conclusion that it has one overarching goal as opposed to a multiplicity of goals. Either way, we should be wary also of the idea that the goal(s) of administrative law can easily be read out of (or mapped on to) its rules and principles, whether they be common law or legislative. The task of both judges and legislatures is to make rules. They are under no obligation to specify the purposes and goals of the rules they make, and they typically do not do so, at least not clearly, comprehensively, or with analytical rigour.

JUDICIAL REVIEW AS A REGULATORY TOOL

Assuming that we have identified the regulatory goals of administrative law, the next step in the Project is to give an account of administrative law as a regulatory tool. As noted above, for present purposes a regulatory regime can be taken to have three basic components: the setting of standards, processes for monitoring compliance with the standards, and mechanisms for enforcing the standards. These components provide a helpful framework for this section, in which the focus will be on legal institutions, rather than legal norms.

Standard-Setting

The basic rules and principles of administrative law are products of adjudicatory rule-making by superior courts. In the regulatory literature, two issues about the design of standard-setting institutions loom large. One concerns the relative contribution of technical expertise and political values to the formulation

---

[34] Bishop, 'A Theory of Administrative Law', 491–2; R. D. Cooter, *The Strategic Constitution* (Princeton: Princeton University Press, 2000), 195–8.

[35] F. B. Cross, 'The Judiciary and Public Choice', *Hastings Law Journal*, 50 (1999), 355. See also E. R. Elhauge, 'Does Interest Group Theory Justify More Intrusive Judicial Review?', *Yale Law Journal*, 101 (1991), 31.

[36] P. Cane, 'Theory and Values in Public Law', in P. Craig and R. Rawlings (eds.), *Law and Administration in Europe: Essays in Honour of Carol Harlow* (Oxford: Oxford University Press, 2003), ch. 1.

of standards. The other concerns access to information about the regulated activity. On the first issue, emphasizing the importance of technical expertise tends to favour securing the independence of standard-setters from political influence, whereas emphasizing the role of political values tends to favour subjecting standard-setters to political pressure. The ideal of separation of powers requires that courts have a very high degree of independence from political control. In regulatory terms, the independence of courts exercising judicial review jurisdiction is important not so much because it leaves courts free to exercise technical expertise in setting standards, but in order to minimize the risk that the standard-setter will be unduly influenced by the regulated population— i.e. public functionaries. In fact, the expertise of courts is in adjudication generally, rather than in the subject matter of the disputes that come before them. There is nothing in the training or experience of judges, as such, that is likely to make them technically expert at setting standards for the performance of the wide array of public functions that are the subject of judicial review proceedings. The immunization of courts from control by the political branches of government (to prevent their 'capture' by the regulated population) puts them under constant pressure to deny that the function of setting 'legal' standards of conduct is 'political' in nature.

So far as access to information is concerned, a common criticism of the role of courts in reviewing the exercise of public powers is that the process of bipolar adjudication is not well designed to provide courts with adequate information about the procedures and practices of public functionaries. In regulatory terms, the assumption underlying this criticism is that in order to be effective, regulation must be 'responsive'—i.e. it must take account of the needs, values, expectations, and practices of the regulated population. Otherwise, regulatory standards are likely to be misunderstood or ignored by those to whom they are addressed.[37] This is one limb of Gunther Teubner's famous regulatory trilemma which, on one interpretation, arises out of the fact that different social 'systems' (in this case, administrative law on the one hand, and 'public governance institutions', on the other) may pursue different (and conflicting) goals and promote different (and conflicting) values. However, another limb of the trilemma is that the law may be so responsive to the regulated population that its own goals and values are threatened. In the natural justice literature, it is often argued that in imposing procedural requirements on public functionaries, courts may be insufficiently sensitive to the adverse impact that such requirements may have on the efficient and effective performance of public functions. On the other hand, unless one takes the view that procedures are valuable only to the extent that they contribute to good substantive outcomes, the fact that they may hinder the achievement of such outcomes is no more than a factor to be taken into account in deciding whether, and which, procedural requirements

---

[37] C. Scott, 'The Juridification of Regulatory Relations in the UK Utilities Sector', in J. Black, P. Muchlinski, and P. Walker (eds.), *Commercial Regulation and Judicial Review* (Oxford: Hart, 1998).

should be imposed.[38] Information about regulated activities is needed to assess the potential impact of proposed regulatory standards. But by itself it cannot answer the question whether those standards ought to be imposed. Answering this question requires normative judgments to be made about the desirable balance between regulatory values and the goals and values of the regulated activity.

In some formulations, the 'regulatory approach' seems to assume that the only goal of regulation should be to promote the effective and efficient realization of the (acceptable) goals of the regulated activity. But I would argue that a regulatory understanding of administrative law requires us to allow that a proper goal of regulation may be to impose on the regulated activity values that are, to a greater or lesser extent, in conflict with those of the regulated population but which are, nevertheless, socially desirable. This idea is often expressed in terms of 'checks and balances', contemplating a healthy and creative tension between the goals and values of the various branches of government. In regulatory terms, the idea of checks and balances provides a counterpoint to the value of responsiveness, which may be more appropriate to public regulation of private activity than to public regulation of public activity.[39]

There is another aspect of 'responsiveness' that deserves some discussion. The regulatory literature recognizes various types of standard: 'output', 'input', and 'target' standards.[40] Of these, target standards are most responsive, in the sense that they give the regulated population the largest role in defining the regulatory goal. In these terms, administrative law standards score well. In the first place, they are designed only to impose outer limits on the exercise of public power, and to give public functionaries discretion, within those limits, to choose one outcome over others. Secondly (and as a corollary), administrative law standards are typically open-textured. They require, for instance, that public functionaries pursue 'proper purposes'; not take account of 'irrelevant considerations'; not make decisions that are 'unreasonable' or 'disproportionate'; adopt procedures that are 'fair'. It is only in relation to issues of 'law' that the constraints imposed by administrative law are 'unresponsive'. Ironically, however, it is often argued that the open texture of administrative law standards itself detracts from their potential effectiveness because they give too little

---

[38] Two important theoretical contributions to the debate about the point of procedural fairness are D. J. Galligan, *Due Process and Fair Procedures* (Oxford: Oxford University Press, 1996) and T. R. S. Allan, 'Procedural Fairness and the Duty of Respect', *Oxford Journal of Legal Studies*, 18 (1998), 497. Similar issues underlie debates about the 'proceduralization' of regulation (see J. Black, 'Proceduralising Regulation, Part I', *Oxford Journal of Legal Studies*, 20 (2000), 597, and 'Part II', *Oxford Journal of Legal Studies*, 21 (2001), 33): is responsiveness intrinsically valuable or valuable only on account of whatever contribution it can make to regulatory effectiveness?

[39] This is Collins's view, too: see text surrounding n. 10 above. Another way of framing the dilemma of responsiveness is in terms of a trade-off between knowledge and motivation. The more a regulator knows about the regulated activity, the more the regulator may identify and empathize with the regulated and absorb their values. From this perspective, it may be better that judges do not know too much about those subject to administrative law.

[40] See P. Cane, 'Tort Law as Regulation', *Common Law World Review*, 31 (2002), 305, 314–15.

guidance to the regulated population. Their main function, on this view, is to provide a figleaf of legitimization for ad hoc dispute resolution by the courts.

We may conclude, therefore, that however desirable responsiveness may be in the abstract, regulatory standards may be too responsive either in the sense that they give too much weight to the values and goals of the regulated population at the expense of those of the regulator,[41] or in the sense that they give so much discretion to the regulated population that they provide no effective guidance at all.

Monitoring

Commonly, compliance with regulatory standards is monitored by or on behalf of the standard-setter. This may be called 'public monitoring'. Regulators may, to some extent, rely on third parties to report non-compliance with regulatory standards, but they are generally free to undertake monitoring on their own account. Courts, by contrast, are not monitoring agencies. Compliance with administrative law standards is typically monitored by potential litigants. This may be called 'private monitoring'. The remedies available from courts for such breaches provide the incentive for detecting breaches and bringing them to the attention of the enforcement agency—i.e. the court.

Incentives to monitor compliance with administrative law standards are affected by the rules of standing, which determine who may seek judicial review of the conduct of a public functionary. At their narrowest, standing rules allow an application for judicial review to be made only by a person who has personally been adversely affected by the conduct in question. At their broadest, they allow any citizen to complain about breaches of administrative law standards, regardless of whether the breach has adversely affected the applicant more than it has adversely affected other citizens, or, indeed, of whether it has adversely affected the applicant at all. At one level, there is obviously an important difference in terms of goals between a system that limits access to judicial review to harmed individuals, and one that opens it up to all citizens. Citizen standing puts the focus on controlling illegality in a way that individual standing does not. However, it must be remembered that the grounds on which acts and decisions can be held illegal are the same under both systems; and in this sense, the precise content of the standing rules does not affect the values that administrative law promotes. Citizens as such cannot challenge the conduct of public functionaries on any ground not available (in principle) to an individual adversely affected by the conduct—or vice versa.

In terms of monitoring, courts resemble certain other regulators of the performance of public functions, such as tribunals and ombudsmen. These, too, rely on 'victims' to discover and report breaches of the normative standards they lay down and apply. At the same time, there are various regulatory institutions in

---

[41] At the margin, responsiveness is the antithesis of regulation.

the public sector actively involved in monitoring, such as inspectorates, auditors, and parliamentary committees. An advantage of private monitoring is that beneficiaries of the regulatory regime are more likely to be aware that a breach has occurred than is the regulator. On the other hand, individual beneficiaries are less likely to be able to identify systemic non-compliance with regulatory norms, and they may lack the resources or the incentive to bring the breach to the attention of the enforcing authorities, especially if the harm suffered as a result is small. From this point of view, there may be a case for charging a publicly funded organization with the task of receiving information about breaches of regulatory standards from individuals and taking appropriate action—including judicial review proceedings—in relation to the breaches. Such arrangements have been used in the anti-discrimination area, for instance.

Enforcement

Judicial review standards are enforced by courts, on the application of complainants with standing, by the award of various remedies against respondents. The main remedies are quashing orders, mandatory orders, prohibitory orders, and declaratory orders. Quashing orders are self-executing in the sense that the order of the court, of its own force, deprives some decision of the respondent of legal effect. As a result, any action taken in purported execution of the order would be illegal. Mandatory and prohibitory orders are coercive in the sense that failure to comply with such an order puts the person to whom the order is addressed in contempt of court, and makes them liable to be fined or imprisoned. Securing compliance with coercive orders made against public functionaries is normally not a problem because the cost to a public functionary of failure to comply with a court order would far outweigh any benefit to be gained thereby. Declarations are of two types. Surrogate declarations (as they might be called) provide a non-coercive substitute for a quashing, mandatory, or prohibitory order. Autonomous declarations (as they might be called) merely make a statement of law, and may be awarded even when a quashing, mandatory, or prohibitory order could not be.[42] Quashing orders, mandatory orders, and prohibitory orders (and surrogate declarations that shadow such orders) are all 'corrective' and backward-looking in nature. A quashing order will issue only in relation to an illegal decision that is already in existence. Mandatory orders address refusal or failure to perform duties that ought already to have been performed, and prohibitory orders address anticipated execution of an existing illegal decision. Autonomous declarations are also typically corrective in nature, in the sense that even if the declaration makes only a general statement of law in order to provide guidance for the future, that statement will be made in the context of a live dispute about a particular past decision or action.

---

[42] For more detailed discussion of declarations, see P. Cane, 'The Constitutional Basis of Judicial Remedies in Public Law', in P. Leyland and T. Woods (eds.), *Administrative Law Facing the Future: Old Constraints and New Horizons* (London: Blackstone, 1997), 262–268.

The judicial remedy that gets closest to being 'regulatory' and forward-looking, as opposed to corrective, in nature is the advisory declaration. As a general rule, courts will make pronouncements of law only in the context of, and in order to resolve, a live dispute. In exceptional cases, a court may be prepared to make a declaration of law on a moot issue arising out of a dispute which is no longer alive, for the sole purpose of providing guidance for the future.[43] But courts have been very wary of granting declarations to resolve purely hypothetical questions based on facts that have not yet occurred.[44] Although an important function of judicial review principles is to guide behaviour, judicial review remedies are primarily corrective or reparative in nature. Traditionally, damages have not been available as a remedy for breaches of administrative law standards as such, although such a breach may attract a damages remedy if it is also a breach of contract or a tort. It is not easy to find satisfying reasons for this remedial limitation.[45] Damages are now available against Member States of the European Union for breaches of Community law, and for breaches of human rights—for instance, under the European Convention on Human Rights and the UK Human Rights Act 1998. In the latter context, the operative phrase is 'just satisfaction'. The corrective orientation of the requirement of just satisfaction is made clear by the fact that it may be met merely by a declaration that a breach of the Convention has occurred. Under the Convention, enforcement is primarily directed not at behaviour modification but at vindication of the applicant's rights.

THE IMPACT OF JUDICIAL REVIEW

Although the administrative law enforcement process is corrective in orientation, the main function of rules and principles of administrative law is to guide conduct, not to provide resources for resolving disputes and remedying breaches. There are, therefore, two sorts of empirical questions we might ask about the impact of administrative law: questions about the administrative law enforcement (or 'complaints') process, and questions about the impact of administrative law on the behaviour of the regulated population.[46] In other

---

[43] e.g. *R v Board of Visitors of Dartmoor Prison, ex parte Smith* [1987] QB 106. The procedure for Attorney-General's references under s. 36 of the Criminal Justice Act 1972 (UK) is analogous.

[44] In *Blackburn v Attorney-General* [1971] 1 WLR 1037 the English Court of Appeal refused to make a declaration on the hypothetical question whether, by signing the Treaty of Rome, the British government would partially but irreversibly surrender the sovereignty of Parliament. Perhaps courts come closest to doing this when they set down 'guidelines' for the sentencing of criminals or awards of damages for non-pecuniary loss in personal injury cases (*Heil v Rankin* [2001] QB 272). Both the Government of Wales Act 1998 and the Scotland Act 1998 provide for pre-enactment judicial scrutiny of Acts of the devolved legislature.

[45] P. Cane, 'Damages in Public Law', *Otago Law Review*, 9 (1999), 489.

[46] There is an ongoing debate about the relationship between two different roles of ombudsmen—that of complaints-handling ('fire-fighting') and that of detecting defects in bureaucratic systems ('fire-watching'): Harlow and Rawlings, *Law and Administration*, ch. 13.

words, we might investigate how effective the law is at dealing with *non-compliance* or, alternatively, how effective it is in securing *compliance*. Research into non-compliance and enforcement tends to focus on institutions of enforcement, whereas research into compliance focuses more directly on the substance and intrinsic force of legal norms. The distinction between compliance and non-compliance is also relevant to choice of empirical research techniques. Quantitative ('epidemiological') techniques are more likely to be used (and useful) for the study of non-compliance, whereas qualitative ('ethnographic') methods are more likely to illuminate issues of compliance.

Research into the enforcement of administrative law norms is typically designed to determine the proportion of breaches of administrative law standards that result in successful applications for 'judicial review' (as the process for enforcing administrative law is called) or settlements favourable to the complainant. Because damages are generally not available as a remedy for breach of administrative law standards, the ultimate aim of the typical judicial review application is not merely to reverse an adverse outcome but to obtain a positive result. Often, the awarding of a judicial review remedy will not achieve this effect but will only clear the way for the defendant to make a fresh decision, as a matter of discretion, whether or not to benefit the complainant. This fact has led the Australian researchers Robin Creyke, John McMillan, and Denis Pearce to investigate the frequency with which successful judicial review applications result in the complainant obtaining from the decision-maker the positive outcome they want.[47]

So far as compliance research is concerned, there is a relatively small body of empirical literature about the influence of administrative law on public decision-making in Westminster systems. Some of this literature is concerned with the impact of, and reactions to, decisions in individual enforcement actions.[48] Other contributions deal more generally with the impact of actual enforcement,[49] and the possibility of enforcement, of administrative law norms. Yet others focus more directly on how administrative law norms, as such, figure in and influence public decision-making.[50] Studies have looked at the activities

---

[47] R. Creyke, J. McMillan, and D. Pearce, 'Success at Court: Does the Client Win?', in J. McMillan (ed.), *Administrative Law under the Coalition Government* (Canberra: Australian Institute of Administrative Law, 1997), 239. For some US research on the same issue, see P. H. Schuck and E. D. Elliott, 'To the Chevron Station: An Empirical Study of American Administrative Law', *Duke Law Journal* (1990), 984, 1059–60.

[48] e.g. C. Harlow, 'Administrative Reaction to Judicial Review', *Public Law* (1976), 116; T. Prosser, 'Politics and Judicial Review: The Atkinson Case and its Aftermath', *Public Law* (1979), 59; T. Prosser, *Test Cases for the Poor* (London: Child Poverty Action Group, 1983), ch. 5; L. Bridges, C. Game, O. Lomas, J. McBride, and S. Ranson, *Legality and Local Politics* (Aldershot: Avebury, 1987); M. Loughlin and P. M. Quinn, 'Prisons, Rules and Courts: A Study in Administrative Law', *Modern Law Review*, 56 (1993), 497.

[49] As far as I am aware, all studies so far have dealt with cases in which the applicant for judicial review has succeeded.

[50] For a general consideration of this topic, see G. Richardson and M. Sunkin, 'Judicial Review: Questions of Impact', *Public Law* (1996), 79.

of (for instance) housing authorities,[51] mental health tribunals,[52] and 'internal' social security review bodies.[53] Some studies are concerned with the behaviour of public functionaries, whereas others have focused on their attitudes towards administrative law and judicial review.[54] Most of the available research deals with the behaviour of 'street-level bureaucrats'; but some examines the impact of judicial review on policy- and rule-making.[55]

There is much that could be said about this body of research, and I have discussed it in a little more detail elsewhere.[56] My concern here is with the relationship between the empirical research and the Project. A recurring theme in the empirical literature is that administrative law is only one of a number of influences on the behaviour of public functionaries.[57] Other normative and institutional factors may operate independently of, and in possible conflict with, the rules and principles of administrative law. Researchers often discover that public functionaries routinely disobey the law either as a result of ignorance of the law's requirements or under the pressure of stronger competing influences. This phenomenon is obviously deeply problematic if the goal of administrative law is defined as securing compliance with administrative law norms ('legality'). The fact that this approach is prominent in doctrinal administrative law scholarship[58] no doubt explains the insistence with which empirical researchers point out the competition between legal norms and other influences on decision-making by public functionaries. But the phenomenon is

---

[51] e.g. I. Loveland, 'Housing Benefit: Administrative Law and Administrative Practice', *Public Administration*, 66 (1988), 57; I. Loveland, *Housing Homeless Persons: Administrative Law and the Administrative Process* (Oxford: Oxford University Press, 1995); S. Halliday, 'The Influence of Judicial Review on Bureaucratic Decision-Making', *Public Law* (2000), 110.

[52] G. Richardson and D. Machin, 'Judicial Review and Tribunal Decision-Making: A Study of the Mental Health Review Tribunal', *Public Law* (2000), 494.

[53] M. Sunkin and K. Pick, 'The Changing Impact of Judicial Review: The Independent Review Service of the Social Fund', *Public Law* (2001), 736. See also T. Buck, 'Judicial Review and the Discretionary Social Fund', in Buck (ed.), *Judicial Review and Social Welfare* (London: Pinter, 1998).

[54] e.g. M. Sunkin and A. P. Le Sueur, 'Can Government Control Judicial Review?', *Current Legal Problems*, 44 (1991), 161; Sunkin and Pick, 'The Changing Impact of Judicial Review', 736; R. Creyke and J. McMillan, 'Executive Perceptions of Administrative Law: An Empirical Study', *Australian Journal of Administrative Law*, 9 (2002), 163. There seems little doubt that in the past twenty-five years, both in the UK and in Australia, there has been greatly increasing concern with 'legality' in public administration. See e.g. T. Daintith and A. Page, *The Executive in the Constitution: Structure, Autonomy and Internal Control* (Oxford: Oxford University Press, 1999), ch. 10; E. Willheim, 'Recollections of an Attorney-General's Department Lawyer', *Australian Journal of Administrative Law*, 8 (2001), 151. The precise contribution of administrative law and judicial review to this development is difficult to ascertain. On the whole, researchers have not investigated the impact of judicial review on the behaviour of the beneficiaries of the norms of administrative law as opposed to those subject to them.

[55] e.g. M. Loughlin and P. M. Quinn, 'Prisons, Rules and Courts: A Study in Administrative Law', *Modern Law Review*, 56 (1993), 497.

[56] P. Cane, 'Understanding Judicial Review and its Impact', in M. Hertogh and S. Halliday (eds.), *The Impact of Judicial Review: International and Interdisciplinary Dimensions* (Cambridge: Cambridge University Press, forthcoming).

[57] See esp. Loveland, *Housing Homeless Persons*, ch. 10.

[58] But also in some empirical research: T. Mullen, K. Pick, and T. Prosser, *Judicial Review in Scotland* (Chichester: Wiley, 1996), 113.

less problematic if the goal of administrative law is defined in terms of some broad objective, such as promoting good administration or reducing agency costs. There is no reason to think of law as the only, or even the most import-ant, mechanism for achieving such goals or to define such goals solely in terms of compliance with legal norms.[59]

The goals of administrative law tend to be assumed, rather than explicitly discussed in the empirical literature. This may be a result of the fact that in the non-US theoretical administrative law literature there is little explicit discussion of goals—although the richness of the US theoretical literature has not gener-ated a theoretically robust empirical literature there either. Research seems directed more to discovering what, if any, impact the existence and enforcement of administrative law has than to whether it has any particular impact (beyond securing compliance with administrative law norms). In other words, researchers tend to be looking for regulatory effects, rather than the realization of specific regulatory goals. To the extent that goals are acknowledged, they tend to be framed in terms such as 'good decision-making',[60] 'bureaucratic justice',[61] and 'openness and participation in public decision making'.[62] A common conclusion of such research is that administrative law norms and their enforce-ment have relatively little impact—of any sort—on bureaucratic behaviour. Even when researchers find behaviour that could plausibly be attributed to the enforcement of administrative law norms, the research design is rarely adequate to establish a causal connection.[63]

THE LEGAL AND REGULATORY APPROACHES REVISITED

This discussion allows us, I think, to draw certain conclusions about what the Project of taking a regulatory approach to administrative law, and treating administrative law as one among various mechanisms for achieving certain goals, might involve and how a regulatory approach to administrative law differs from a legal approach.

The Project can be interpreted in at least three different ways. Firstly, it might involve acknowledging that administrative law is goal-oriented. This acknow-ledgement is not without significance, but its significance is severely limited because only extreme formalists (of the ilk of Ernest Weinrib[64]) argue that law can (and must) be understood purely in terms of its own internal normative struc-ture. A second interpretation would involve defining the goal of administrative

---

[59] This conclusion clears the way for consideration of law's strengths and weaknesses in relation to the achievement of specified goals and for an assessment of the distinctive contribution law can make.

[60] e.g. Sunkin and Pick, 'The Changing Impact of Judicial Review', 745; G. Richardson and M. Sunkin, 'Judicial Review: Questions of Impact', *Public Law* (1996), 100.

[61] Halliday, 'The Influence of Judicial Review of Bureaucratic Decision-Making', 111–12; see also pp. 121–2: 'just government'.   [62] Richardson and Sunkin, 'Judicial Review', 101.

[63] See e.g. ibid. 91–4, discussing conclusions of Loughlin and Quinn, 'Prisons, Rules and Courts'.

[64] See n. 21 above.

law as being to secure compliance with the law's norms. This is the goal implicit in much doctrinal legal scholarship; and so this interpretation does not go very far in generating a theoretically fruitful distinction between a legal and a regulatory approach. The third interpretation involves attributing to administrative law some 'external' goal such as promoting good decision-making or rational public deliberation, or achieving optimal reduction of agency costs. It is this interpretation that puts most distance between a legal approach concerned with the substantive doctrines of administrative law and their enforcement by courts, and a regulatory approach concerned with the social effects of administrative law.

Such empirical evidence as we have suggests that administrative law is likely to be able to make only a modest contribution to the promotion of external goals, however they might be conceived and defined. Of course, this conclusion leaves many questions open: for instance, why is administrative law so ineffective as a behaviour modification mechanism? Could its performance in this respect be improved? Does administrative law perform other functions (such as reparation and correction of bad outcomes; or symbolically affording 'constitutional reassurance';[65] or providing a strategic political resource[66]) that make it worthwhile despite its shortcomings as a behaviour modification mechanism? And so on.

---

[65] C. Harlow, 'A Special Relationship? American Influences on Judicial Review in England', in I. Loveland (ed.), *A Special Relationship? American Influences on Public Law in the UK* (Oxford: Oxford University Press, 1995), 96–7.   [66] Prosser, *Test Cases for the Poor*, 69–73.

11

Regulating Constitutions

COLIN SCOTT*

Constitutions are codes of norms which aspire to regulate the allocation of
powers, functions, and duties among the various agencies and officers of
government, and to define the relationship between these and the public.[1]

INTRODUCTION

The project of this book is to apply a regulatory lens to diverse areas of legal
knowledge and practice. The term 'constitutions' encompasses the practice and
knowledge concerned with the allocation and control of state power. Within
this field the legal and political systems meet since constitutional *law* appears
only to be effective and legitimate where it has some resonance and acceptance
within the political world. Equally, governmental practice is reinforced and
legitimized by reference to constitutional norms. There is a sense in which law
and politics are mutually constitutive in their constitutional dimension.[2]

However, the dependence of political and legal systems upon each other
to maintain a 'working constitution' is not unproblematic. The concept of legality within the legal system is premissed upon acting in accordance with a set of
norms which may bear only indirectly on, or which may inhibit compliance
with, the rationales within the political system. Whereas the legal system
is broadly concerned with generating and policing norms of legality, the political system is more focused on exercising power in such a way as to deliver
policy outcomes.[3] Additionally perceptions of fragmentation of power, in the
direction of both supranational governance organizations and civil society
groups, have created doubts concerning traditional assumptions about state
sovereignty.[4]

Constitutional law scholarship has struggled to adapt to the diffusion of public-
like power, causing it to be sidelined in many contemporary discussions of

* I am grateful to Terry Daintith, Michael Dowdle, Sarah Harding, Martin Loughlin, Adam
Tomkins, and Leslie Zines for comments on an earlier draft of this chapter.

[1] S. Finer, V. Bogdanor, and B. Rudden, *Comparing Constitutions* (Oxford: Oxford University
Press, 1995), 1.
[2] N. Walker, 'The Idea of Constitutional Pluralism', *Modern Law Review*, 65 (2002), 317, 343.
[3] J. Elster, Introduction, in Elster (ed.), *Constitutionalism and Democracy* (Cambridge: Cambridge
University Press, 1988), 2–3.
[4] N. McCormick, 'Beyond the Sovereign State', *Modern Law Review*, 56 (1993), 1.

governance.[5] While political science assumes a 'pluralist structure of political power', legal scholarship tends to retain a strong concept of sovereignty vested variously in the legislature or in the legislative, executive, and judicial branches of government.[6] In order to engage similar phenomena to those now taken to be central to understandings of power within political science it appears that constitutional law would need to engage more with ideas of legal pluralism.[7] This would require attention firstly to variety in constitutional norms, perhaps extending beyond traditional constitutional discourse to encompass those structures which effectively steer those exercising public power towards such principles as efficiency and environmental protection. Secondly, it would require an assessment of the diverse mechanisms through which monitoring and enforcement for constitutional norms is carried out, extending beyond judicial review and constitutional litigation to encompass both political and bureaucratic processes. Thirdly, it would require consideration of the constitutional status of non-state organizations exercising public power. Key examples are provided in the various worlds of international rule-making, whether of technical standardization or of the generation of an international *lex mercatoria*.[8] It might be implausible to locate such rule-making as a delegation from one or more parliaments, and thus bring it within conventional constitutional controls. On the other hand, as Teubner suggests, it appears to demand 'an expansion of constitutionalism into private law production which would take into account that "private" governments are "public" governments'.[9]

Such a pluralistic approach is consistent with central themes in contemporary law and society research on regulation.[10] Regulation scholars have been less wedded to hierarchical visions of law and have favoured more broadly based and heterarchical theories of control.[11] We are invited to think about the whole system of control and not just the goals, values, or norms of constitutions. The mutually constitutive character of law and politics in this field creates considerable challenges. It is clearly inappropriate to think of political practice being controlled by constitutional law. Rather we might see two distinct but overlapping sets of discursive practices in relationships which at some times appear to fit

---

[5] J. Morison, 'The Case against Constitutional Reform', *Journal of Law and Society*, 25 (1998), 510; T. Murphy, *The Oldest Social Science? Configurations of Law and Modernity* (Oxford: Oxford University Press, 1997), ch. 6.

[6] S. Gordon, *Controlling the State: Constitutionalism from Ancient Athens to Today* (Cambridge, Mass.: Harvard University Press, 1999).

[7] Cf. Walker, 'The Idea of Constitutional Pluralism', 336–9.

[8] B. de Sousa Santos, *Towards a New Legal Common Sense*, 2nd edn. (London: Butterworth, 2002), 208–14.

[9] G. Teubner, 'Breaking Frames: The Global Interplay of Legal and Social Systems', *American Journal of Comparative Law* (1997), 149.

[10] I use the term 'law and society research' here to encompass research by those who identify themselves as sociological and socio-legal scholars.

[11] J. Black, 'Decentring Regulation: The Role of Regulation and Self-regulation in a "Post-regulatory" World', *Current Legal Problems* (2001), 103; K. Ladeur, *The Theory of Autopoiesis as an Approach to a Better Understanding of Law*, Working Paper of the European University Institute, Florence, 99/3 (1999).

together well while at other times, or in other places, they appear less harmonious. We are as interested in understanding the situations of harmony as we are the constitutional crises.

Within the explanatory regulatory perspective common within law and society scholarship the central question is, what are the mechanisms and processes through which the two distinctive discourses can operate with reasonable harmony? In some cases a certain coherence arises from the simultaneous recognition of constitutional norms in both the political and the legal system. A central example is provided by the class of established practices which are recognized within the legal system as conventions. Conventions have the qualities neither of hard law (in the sense of justiciability and/or enforceability) nor of politics (because they are not simply a matter of expedience and have a degree of fixedness). In other cases such a fit is not immediately to be found, but mechanisms for mediation of tensions can result in outcomes which are recognized as legitimate within both systems. Such mechanisms include both review, for example of legislation by a court, some other constitutional body, or a governmental agency or minister, and the deployment of processes for amending the constitution (whether such amending processes are referred to in a constitutional text or not). A third possibility is constitutional crisis with the possibility that either political practice or constitutional law may have to change profoundly for an accommodation to be reached. Such a revolutionary situation may produce a new accommodation between legal and political systems relatively swiftly. Within some states such accommodations are difficult to find and perceptions of crisis may linger.

In this chapter I look first at the potential of the regulatory lens in the constitutional sphere to illuminate the mechanisms for securing accommodation between political and legal systems. The title to this chapter is a play on words, inspired by Hugh Collins's book *Regulating Contracts*, since it refers both to constitutions as regulatory instruments over government and to the content of constitutions as being subject to regulation. The second main section on constitutions as regulatory regimes takes as its focus the mechanisms by which constitutional norms are made effective within political practice. Thus it considers how the exercise of power is controlled. The analysis sets out the hypothesis that compliance with constitutional norms by political actors represents one workable form of accommodation between law and politics. Modifying political behaviour is only one means to bring constitutional norms and political practice into alignment. The third main section considers the other main set of mechanisms for securing such an alignment, which are concerned with the controls over the contents of constitutions and the mechanisms by which they may be modified. This section addresses the day-to-day practices of constitutional interpretation and change, the more formal processes of amendment, and processes of disruption to constitutional norms in revolutionary situations. A central problem for public law generally is that it is asked to perform certain regulative functions over the polity while at the same time reproducing itself within an external environment which is not well attuned to its requirements.[12] The legal system is constantly subjected to signals from its external environment as to the role the constitution is expected to fulfil. The adaptation of constitutions to those demands is mediated through the normative structure of constitutional law itself.

APPLYING THE REGULATORY LENS TO CONSTITUTIONS

As noted in the Introduction to this volume, a wide range of working definitions are in play in the various disciplines concerned with questions of regulatory governance. Within this project I have found it appropriate to adopt Julia Black's definition of regulation as 'the intentional activity of attempting to control, order, or influence the behaviour of others'.[13] Such a definition clearly implies a concern not just with setting of goals or making of norms, but also with the mechanisms through which behaviour is monitored and sought to be modified so as to realign it with the applicable norms. This moves us well beyond the classic regulatory model of 'sustained and focused control exercised by a public agency over activities which are valued by a community',[14] enabling us to consider a wider range of norms and 'modalities' of control.

Identifying the set of principles which make up the constitution of any particular state is not entirely straightforward. Constitutional norms may be arrayed in a three-way classification which distinguishes higher or fundamental law, ordinary law, and the extra-legal.[15] It is not the form of norms, but rather their subject matter, which distinguishes the constitutional.[16] Constitutional documents, even when constituting higher law, 'are highly incomplete, if not misleading, guides to actual practice, that is to what is sometimes referred to as the "working constitution" or the "governance" of a country'.[17] The diffusion of actors exerting power within the constitutional sphere, considered together with variety in norms and modalities of control, makes it appropriate to think in terms of regulatory regimes[18]—the aggregation of actors, norms, and mechanisms through which constitutions 'live'. Modern government in Britain and many of its former dominions was based on a combination of ordinary legislation, common law, and non-legal convention. While the United Kingdom

---

[12] M. Loughlin, *Public Law and Political Theory* (Oxford: Oxford University Press, 1992), 257.

[13] J. Black, 'Critical Reflections on Regulation', *Australian Journal of Legal Philosophy*, 27 (2002), 1.

[14] P. Selznick, 'Focusing Organisational Research on Regulation', in R. Noll (ed.), *Regulatory Policy and the Social Science* (Berkeley: University of California Press, 1985), 363–8.

[15] T. C. Grey, 'Constitutionalism: An Analytic Framework', in J. R. Pennock and J. W. Chapman (eds.), *Constitutionalism* (New York: New York University Press, 1979), 191; G. Brennan and A. Hamlin, 'Constitutional Choice', in W. F. Shugart and L. Razzaloni (eds.), *The Elgar Companion to Public Choice* (Cheltenham: Edward Elgar, 2001), 117.

[16] Grey, 'Constitutionalism', 194.   [17] Finer *et al.*, *Comparing Constitutions*, 1.

[18] M. A. Eisner, *Regulatory Politics in Transition*, 2nd edn. (Baltimore: Johns Hopkins University Press, 2000), ch. 1.

is among the last to have displaced its 'political constitution' with a more codified superior law of the state,[19] it remains the case that constitutional documents cannot be comprehensive in their regulatory scope and that much within the ambit of constitutional norms everywhere is 'a matter of convention'.[20]

With modalities of control, it is highly relevant to the constitutional sphere to think not only of hierarchical regulation, but also of control exerted through both membership of communities and through competition or rivalry. Thus, within some regimes political behaviour is as likely to be shaped by considerations of what is acceptable to the wider population (perhaps linked to consideration of effects at the ballot box) as it is to the legal enforcement of constitutional norms. This is likely to be particularly true for constitutional norms that lack legal force, notably conventions.

In respect of competition, it is common to build into constitutional systems mechanisms which exploit the potential for rivalry between levels of government and between different branches of government. Thus the practice of federalism includes within it an idea that federal and lower levels of government have incentives both to monitor each other and to seek realignment where behaviour deviates from the applicable norms. Theories of countervailance and the separation of powers are explicitly concerned to exploit the rivalry between different branches of government to promote mutual checks on power. This attempt to control indirectly through the legal structure of a state provides a well-established form of meta-regulation.[21]

The regulatory lens on law, as it has been developed by Hugh Collins, is suggestive also of a set of tensions with the legal system itself. In the Introduction to this volume we suggest that the precise character of this tension is difficult to capture with a single set of terms. It is the contrast between the instrumental norms and purposes associated with regulation, on the one hand, and the universalistic (and implicitly non-instrumental) principles of law, on the other. To render this distinction concretely in the constitutional sphere, the commitment to some version of the rule of law within regimes of constitutional government is an end in itself and provides a central example of the general and universalistic approach to reasoning embodied within the legal mentality. The concept of the

---

[19] M. Loughlin, *Swords and Scales: An Examination of the Relationship between Law and Politics* (Oxford: Hart, 2000), 4. Though recent constitutional reforms have enhanced the justiciability of norms dealing with such matters as human rights and the division of powers between the various levels of government in the UK, the British continue to eschew the creation of any higher constitutional law or a constitutional court. The British government has considered explicitly and rejected the idea of creating a constitutional court in its consultation paper on the abolition of the Judicial Committee of the House of Lords and the creation of a Supreme Court for the United Kingdom: Department of Constitutional Affairs, *Constitutional Reform: A Supreme Court for the United Kingdom*. Consultation Paper 11/03.

[20] R. Hardin, *Liberalism, Constitutionalism, and Democracy* (Oxford: Oxford University Press, 1999), 134; see also J. Elster, 'Forces and Mechanisms in the Constitution-Making Process', *Duke Law Journal*, 45 (1995), 364.

[21] A. Dunsire, 'Tipping the Balance: Autopoiesis and Governance', *Administration and Society*, 28 (1996), 299.

rule of law is widely used to refer to requirements that laws be predictable and stable.[22] There is no immediate, instrumental purpose to the commitment in terms of objectives the states might have in terms of economic or social policy. Indeed, the commitment to the rule of law may positively inhibit states from pursuing their instrumental purposes in what governments deem to be the most appropriate or effective manner.[23]

Thus 'constitutionality' as a property of governance may find itself in tension with efficiency, one of the core values of contemporary politics and public management. One solution to the problem is to suggest that, either as a matter of practice or as a condition to be sought, principles of constitutionality should always trump other more instrumental principles. There does appear to be a bias towards this position within the discourse of constitutional law and politics in the United States. The main international instruments promulgating human rights, the European Convention and the Universal Declaration, each explicitly recognize the tension and seek to balance principles of general application against the more immediate requirements of democratic government. This accommodation between the universal values of law and instrumental principles of regulation (and governance generally) provides a key fault line within constitutional practice. It should not, however, be overstated, since much that is contained within a 'working constitution' will be concerned precisely with generating a workable system of government, both in the sense of maintaining the legitimacy of the political system, and in providing the kind of stability in which society and economy may flourish.[24]

CONSTITUTIONS AS REGULATORY REGIMES

One way in which political and legal systems can be aligned in the constitutional sphere is for political actors to modify their behaviour so as to comply with constitutional norms. This section considers the nature of those norms and the mechanisms for monitoring and enforcing compliance with them so as both to capture the variety of alignment mechanisms of this sort, and to assess the extent to which such practices might provide a workable accommodation.

Constitutional Norms

The normative structure of constitutions is one of the chief concerns of constitutional law scholarship. Such analysis works inductively from the decisions of

---

[22] Elster, Introduction, in *Constitutionalism and Democracy*, 3.

[23] J. Freigang, 'Is Responsive Regulation Compatible with the Rule of Law?', *European Public Law*, 8 (2002), 463.

[24] D. C. North and B. R. Wiengast, 'Constitutions and Commitment: The Evolution of Institutional Governing Public Choice in Seventeenth Century England', *Journal of Economic History*, 49 (1989), 803; B. Levy and P. Spiller (eds.), *Regulation, Institutions and Commitment* (Cambridge: Cambridge University Press, 1996).

authoritative interpreters of the constitution (usually courts) and deductively from ideas about the nature of good governance to reach a view as to what the constitution requires. Contemporary constitutional law scholarship is dominated by normative approaches which emphasize the importance of particular values to modern societies. These values are expressed in terms such as democracy, the rule of law, and freedom of expression. Others proffer functionalist explanations of constitutional norms, emphasizing, for example, their role in coordinating actors with diffuse interests,[25] or in facilitating competition between such actors.[26]

A regulatory lens has more in common with the latter approaches. On the one hand, regulatory scholars will tend to take the normative objectives of a regime to be a given. On the other, the characteristic inductive analysis of a regulatory regime may suggest that, as a matter of practice, the norms which actually operate on public power deviate from constitutional theory. Such an analysis might have a number of aspects. Within those regimes where the focus of constitutional practice is largely on a constitutional text, it might be discovered that some provisions of the constitution are of little or no effect. This is not simply a matter of arguing that certain provisions are never formally enforced. Rather the analysis might be concerned with discovering whether the key actors have sufficient familiarity with the relevant norms to be able to act on them, or whether an inevitable consequence of prioritizing one set of objectives over another is the downplaying of particular principles. A second possibility is the discovery that the authoritative constitutional text does not contain all the norms which are applied and rendered effective in practice. Thus other values may be subject to some form of control. This observation raises some difficulties since it has the potential to challenge a widespread assumption that constitutional norms are indicated definitively only by 'the existence of a self-conscious discourse of constitutionalism'.[27] I think it right to challenge the assumption, not only because it enables us better to see which norms and institutions might be fundamental to the control of public power, but also because without such a move it would be nearly impossible to incorporate the regulation of privately exercised public power into constitutional theory.

It is fair to say that much constitutional analysis focuses on the compliance by legislatures with constitutional norms protective of the rights of citizens. A rather smaller main area of analysis is the application of principles relating to federalism. Clearly the principles that governments should not trample on the rights of citizens or on other levels of government are important. But they hardly exhaust the set of values governing the allocation and control of public power. Thus we might find that there are norms which are routinely applied, for example to the exercise of legislative power, but which are not found either within an authoritative constitutional text nor in the discourse of the

[25] Hardin, *Liberalism, Constitutionalism, and Democracy*.
[26] R. D. Cooter, *The Strategic Constitution* (Princeton: Princeton University Press, 2000).
[27] Walker, 'The Idea of Constitutional Pluralism'.

main organs of constitutional review. For example, there is an international movement directed at requiring government agencies and departments to assess the costs and benefits of new regulatory measures prior to their introduction.[28] These rules require the justification of new regulatory measures contained in primary and secondary legislation and impose a constraint on those agencies and departments which put them forward. Though the institutional details of this kind of regulation over government are extremely varied, their nature is pretty clearly constitutional in character.[29] Similar remarks might be made in respect of the expansion of audit functions over the efficiency of public sector expenditure.

Monitoring

We have in view a range of norms with which bodies exercising public power are expected to comply. Few constitutional regimes have specialized agencies charged with monitoring for compliance with constitutional norms. It is notable that little attention was given to the mechanisms for monitoring and enforcing constitutional norms within the United States Constitution. Madison himself thought of government as self-regulating but added that 'experience has taught mankind the necessity of auxiliary precautions'.[30] The key role of the US Supreme Court in interpreting and applying constitutional norms arises from convention and not from the text of the US Constitution. If we think about constitutional litigation, the monitoring groups which bring actions against governmental bodies are typically aggrieved citizens or, sometimes, other organs of the state. Human rights commissions established in some jurisdictions do have a mission to support such litigants and to carry out more general monitoring. Notwithstanding the absence of specialized monitoring agencies, there are a variety of actors with formal duties or informal capacities to monitor governmental behaviour. Legislative processes provide the strongest examples of mechanisms for what Tushnet calls 'non-judicial review'.[31] In practice the monitoring function is often only visible when linked to enforcement, discussed in the next section.

Capacities and duties to monitor for constitutional behaviour are not restricted to domestic institutions. State power has been diluted through the emergence of international norms and institutions which bear on domestic constitutional regimes. The most extensive such supranational regime (and thus the most intrusive on traditional conceptions of state power) is that of the European Community, which charges the European Commission with enforcing the provisions of the treaties and empowers it to monitor and enforce compliance with

---

[28] OECD, *Regulatory Impact Analysis: Best Practices in OECD Countries* (Paris: OECD, 1997).

[29] J. O. McGinnis, 'Presidential Review as Constitutional Restoration', *Duke Law Journal*, 51 (2001), 901.

[30] G. J. Schochet, 'Introduction: Constitutionalism, Liberalism and the Study of Politics', in Pennock and Chapman (eds.), *Constitutionalism*, 10.

[31] M. Tushnet, 'Non-judicial Review', in T. Campbell, J. Goldsworthy, and A. Stone (eds.), *Protecting Human Rights: Instruments and Institutions* (Oxford: Oxford University Press, 2003).

treaty provisions.[32] A number of treaty provisions affecting member states go to
the heart of constitutional affairs, for example duties to implement EC legislative
instruments, and to act without discrimination on grounds of nationality.[33]
Beyond the EU the European Committee for the Prevention of Torture engages in
regular visits to facilities such as prisons to check on systematic compliance with
international norms states have ratified. The various ways in which states adapt
their constitutions to reflect the impact of these international monitoring mechanisms is less important than the will to power exhibited at international level.

Modifying Behaviour

Where infractions of constitutional norms are detected by monitoring agents,
what is the potential for them or for others to secure the modification of the
behaviour of the agency concerned? The capacity of the United States Supreme
Court to strike legislation down as unconstitutional is not only a key example
of hierarchical enforcement of constitutional norms, but is also often treated as
paradigmatic of constitutional enforcement. While some other jurisdictions,
such as Canada and Germany, give to constitutional courts similar powers, it is
very much the exception.[34]

Within the 'political constitution' of the United Kingdom, the introduction of
justiciable human rights brought with it new powers for the courts. Though the
UK courts may quash administrative behaviour which is in breach of the
convention rights, in respect of legislation their powers are restricted to issuing
a 'declaration of incompatibility'.[35] Such declarations do not affect the continuing validity of the legislation. Consistent with the theory of the supremacy of
Parliament a minister may bring legislation declared incompatible before
Parliament for revision. The decision on whether to align the legislation with
the human rights regime is for Parliament and not the courts. The Canadian
Charter of Rights and Freedoms seeks to balance the protection of rights with
the capacities of democratic legislatures by providing that in respect of some of
the rights protected by the Charter, legislatures may deviate from the requirements by explicit provision that the legislation is to take force, and for a period
of up to five years, 'notwithstanding' its contravention of the protected rights.[36]
This is not untypical of constitutional documents. We could say that the rights-
related constitutional norms are frequently quite significantly qualified by considerations of democratic governance.

Constitutional litigation is one form of 'special' enforcement of constitutional
norms. 'Special' mechanisms involve final arbiters of meaning which lack any
general decision-making capacity in respect of the activities concerned, and are
typically restricted to applying a limited set of tests of validity of the actions scrutinized. *Ex post* judicial review is only one such mechanism.[37] The constitutions

---

[32] Arts. 211, 226, EC.   [33] e.g. Art. 31, EC.   [34] Grey, 'Constitutionalism', 195.
[35] Human Rights Act 1998, s. 4.   [36] Charter of Rights and Freedoms, s. 33.
[37] Tushnet, 'Non-Judicial Review'.

of Ireland and France each permit reference of *proposed* legislation to a special body (the Supreme Court in Ireland[38] and the Conseil Constitutionnel in France[39]). In those spheres or jurisdictions which lack special mechanisms of enforcement such as judicial review, final determination is for ordinary legislative or administrative bodies and the enforcement is said to be political in character.[40] Formal mechanisms for such 'non-judicial review' include the mechanism under which the US Senate may, on a point of order, consider whether a bill violates the Constitution, and the procedure in the UK under which government ministers declare bills to be compatible with the Human Rights Act 1998.[41] In addition to these formal, and relatively transparent mechanisms, we may surmise that officials responsible for advising on the initiation of legislation, and for its drafting, commonly take on an informal but significant role in checking attempts to promulgate legislative rules they deem to breach constitutional norms.[42]

The vindication of constitutional norms achieved by the machinery of constitutional litigation and general mechanisms of review is necessarily partial and sporadic. Less attention has been paid to the machinery of audit and inspection, which are, nevertheless, centrally concerned with monitoring for compliance with values linked to the meta-constitutional principle of the rule of law. Inspection regimes are rather central to governance in jurisdictions as diverse as those of the United States,[43] France, and the United Kingdom.[44] Even within its sphere of citizen rights, constitutional litigation is far from being the only show in town. The international explosion in grievance-handling mechanisms as alternatives to litigation has given ombudspeople and their near kin a central role in enforcing rights, from which position many have taken on a more proactive role in both monitoring and setting standards.[45] Their presence and activities provide a further aspect of the regulatory picture.[46] Thinking about non-judicial enforcement (as opposed to the more limited non-judicial review, discussed above) the formal powers of regulators of the public sector are typically weak.[47] Coercive behavioural modification is frequently the preserve of those who have funding powers, often located within central government departments. Accordingly the activities of finance departments and others wielding funding powers must feature in a regulatory theory of the constitution.[48]

---

[38] Constitution of Ireland, Art. 26(1).
[39] Article 5 of the French Constitution entrusts the president with the duty to see that the Constitution is observed. Article 61(2) provides for reference of bills to the Conseil Constitutionnel by any of the president of the republic, the prime minister, the president of the National Assembly, the president of the Senate, sixty deputies, or sixty senators.
[40] Grey, 'Constitutionalism', 195 ff.
[41] Tushnet, 'Non-judicial Review'; Human Rights Act 1998, s. 19.
[42] I am grateful to Terry Daintith for suggesting this point to me.
[43] P. Light, *Monitoring Government* (Washington: Brookings Institution, 1993).
[44] G. Rhodes, *Inspectorates in British Government* (London: Allen & Unwin, 1981).
[45] C. Hood, C. Scott, O. James, G. Jones, and T. Travers, *Regulation inside Government: Waste-Watchers, Quality Police, and Sleaze-Busters* (Oxford: Oxford University Press, 1999).
[46] Gordon, *Controlling the State*, 342.
[47] J. Q. Wilson and P. Rachal, 'Can Government Regulate Itself?', *Public Interest*, 46 (1997), 3.
[48] T. Daintith and A. Page, *The Executive in the Constitution* (Oxford: Oxford University Press, 1999).

With conventions, the potential for judicial enforcement is limited or non-existent. Constitutional conventions 'grow out of practice and their existence is determined by precedents'.[49] Where conventions are breached, the effects may vary between beginning to effect a change in the convention, causing some form of constitutional crisis, or generating some kind of juridification process as attempts are made to crystallize the convention either through constitutional or legislative amendment or litigation. Arguably the particular virtue of conventions is that they represent an alignment of normative understanding between political and legal systems with consequential benefits in terms of responsiveness and coherence. As one commentator has it, conventions represent 'the marriage of law and politics'.[50] Constitutional conventions provide a key example of norms emerging from and enforced by community mechanisms rather than through formally stipulated mechanisms.

Conventions remain rather central to the operation of the British Constitution. Thus the monarch has the right to dissolve Parliament and, by virtue of the requirement of her assent to bills, the power to veto legislation. By convention the monarch only dissolves Parliament at the request of the incumbent prime minister and does not refuse assent to any bill passed by both houses. Some Commonwealth constitutions retain similar structures of powers for governors-general and thus, necessarily, also require conventions as to their use. Thus the governor-general of Australia's assent is required to bills of the Commonwealth Parliament.[51] Notwithstanding its modern origins, the Australian Constitution does not refer to the office of prime minister. The English convention that the leader of the party holding a majority in the lower house shall be appointed prime minister by the governor-general was followed until the constitutional crisis of 1975, in which the Senate, in breach of convention, refused to pass supply bills which had been passed by the lower house, and the governor-general dismissed the prime minister, notwithstanding the fact of his majority support in the lower house. This breach of convention engendered a constitutional crisis and arguably sowed the seeds of a vigorous republican movement in Australia. It is the threat of such a crisis, or of lower-level pressures on actors, with the potential for public rebuke which provides the main mechanisms for holding the actors to conventional norms.[52] We may surmise that the media is a key part of the machinery, though it is difficult to specify the mechanisms with precision. Constitutional norms protecting freedom of expression are thus intimately linked to the effectiveness of extra-legal constitutional norms.

Federal constitutional structures and the doctrine of the separation of powers each exemplify the combination of competition and institutional design to

[49] I. Jennings, *Cabinet Government*, 3rd edn. (Cambridge: Cambridge University Press, 1959), 5.

[50] A. Heard, *Canadian Constitutional Conventions: The Marriage of Law and Politics* (Toronto: Oxford University Press, 1991).

[51] Australian Constitution, s. 58. Additionally the monarch retains the power to disallow any Act assented to by the governor-general within one year, s. 59. By convention this power is never exercised.

[52] Sir John Kerr, the governor-general who dismissed the Whitlam government in Australia in 1975, left office early in 1977 and voluntarily exiled himself overseas for a period.

create non-hierarchical structures of control (though in each case the invocation of constitutional litigation may, in some systems, add a hierarchical element to the mix).

Federalist 51 asserts explicitly that 'the power surrendered by the people is first divided between two distinct governments, and then the portion allotted to each subdivided among distinct and separate departments. Hence a double security arises to the rights of the people. The different governments will control each other, at the same time that each will be controlled by itself.'[53]

The separation of powers doctrine posits the existence of a dynamic tension between the three arms of government such that we would not expect the courts to have the opportunity to realign the behaviour of legislature and executive in respect of every deviation from constitutional norms, but rather that the system is held in balance by the capacities (as opposed to the actions) of the others in respect of those norms. The theory has considerable attraction to regulation theorists for its deployment of mechanisms of indirect control not premised on hierarchy.[54]

Many constitutions have adopted some form of theory of the separation of powers. It is argued that the doctrine has been widely misunderstood, and that it refers not to a strict functional differentiation of powers as between the executive, the legislature, and judiciary. Rather the separation doctrine requires each branch of government to have sufficient *independence* and, we might add, a distinctive rationality, such that it can constrain the others. 'If each of the separate institutions were endowed with absolute authority in its own specific domain, they could not limit the powers of each other within those jurisdictional boundaries.'[55] Thus independence is partial, rendering the three branches of government interdependent.[56] Each institution of government, it was anticipated by the framers of the US Constitution, 'would *naturally* strive to enlarge its power and dominate the others if it could'.[57]

The application of this theory frequently (though not always) ascribes to courts some constitutional jurisdiction to decide determinatively on the interpretation and application of the constitutional norms. Hence the application of the doctrine is linked to a strong version of the rule of law doctrine, though '. . . the evolutionary British constitution has never accepted the need for institutional differentiation of the State to be regulated by positive law'.[58] This point is further demonstrated by the statutory devolution of powers to a Scottish Parliament and Executive, a Welsh Assembly, and (intermittently) a Northern Ireland Assembly by the first Blair government. There is no question that this major constitutional reform has created new constraints on Westminster government, for example as it is forced to respond to different approaches to

[53] Cited in Gordon, *Controlling the State*, 309.
[54] J. Braithwaite, 'On Speaking Softly and Carrying Big Sticks: Neglected Dimensions of a Republican Separation of Powers', *University of Toronto Law Journal* (1997), 305; Dunsire, 'Tipping the Balance'.   [55] Gordon, *Controlling the State*, 281.
[56] Ibid. 309.   [57] Ibid. 310.   [58] Loughlin, *Swords and Scales*, 193.

policy issues within the devolved governments. The statutory regimes also establish rules for division of competence, and create a new jurisdiction of the Privy Council to adjudicate disputes. But much of the revision to the working constitution has been achieved through the promulgation of 'concordats'— written conventions—recording agreement as to how the division of powers will be handled in practice.[59]

Federalism, while it creates powerful alternative institutional structures for monitoring and enforcing compliance with constitutional norms, also creates the possibility of competition between states as a mechanism for promoting constitutional conduct or delivering innovative or enhanced constitutional standards. The key feature of such arrangements is that they remove the monopoly over the government's provision of legislation and other activities notionally in the public interest.[60] Federalism is said to generate innovation and experimentalism, while being open to a wider range of preferences at the lower level of government. The theory of regulatory competition offers a mechanism through which legislative and other activities are pulled in one direction by voter preferences for governmental activity, and in the opposite direction by the power of capital expressing preferences for less intervention and lower taxes.[61] It is beyond the scope of this chapter to assess the empirical validity of the theory. Suffice it to say there is scepticism about whether the conditions necessary to secure regulatory competition in federal settings (such as mobility of capital) exist widely.

Further dilution, or separation, of powers occurs through the role of non-state actors. There is a widespread phenomenon through which national government is regulated by private actors and, sometimes, non-hierarchical mechanisms. We need only think of the role of credit rating agencies in monitoring sovereign debt and steering governmental behaviour through the publication of its assessments. Such observations require some serious thought as to how private regulators fit into theories of constitutionalism.[62] The very fact of strong institutions of private government may be regarded as a useful check on the power of public government. The emergence of distinct and separate sources of power within contemporary governance inhibits each of the actors who wield power. If we wanted to exploit this observation through deliberate institutional design, we could seek further strategic divisions of power, of the kind that would create mechanisms for holding power in check.[63]

Overall we can see that processes for monitoring and enforcing constitutional norms exhibit considerable variety. We could hypothesize that the mechanisms for the alignment of political practice with constitutional requirements are

---

[59] R. Rawlings, 'Concordats of the Constitution', *Law Quarterly Review*, 116 (2000), 257.

[60] W. Bratton, J. McCahery, S. Picciotto, and C. Scott (eds.), *Regulatory Competition and Coordination* (Oxford: Oxford University Press, 1996), 12.   [61] Ibid. 13.

[62] C. Scott, 'Private Regulation of the Public Sector: A Neglected Facet of Contemporary Governance', *Journal of Law and Society*, 29 (2002), 56.

[63] Braithwaite, 'On Speaking Softly'; C. Scott, 'Accountability in the Regulatory State', *Journal of Law and Society*, 27 (2000), 38.

tailored to the governmental needs of particular societies. An alternative approach is to see the biases of different regimes as linked to accidents of history. Constitutional texts are drafted to address the concerns arising from the immediate preceding history. Such originating texts are hardly neutral in respect of the constitutional practice which then emerges and shapes the working constitution, though texts are not likely to be determinate either.

Thus, the constitutional upheavals in seventeenth-century England were centrally concerned with inhibiting monarchic power partially by transferring it to a sovereign parliament, but also through diffusing it and creating a system of checks and balances.[64] According to Gordon, it was England which first established the 'countervailance system of government', in secure and continuous form only with the Glorious Revolution and the promulgation of the Bill of Rights 1688, and which today represents normative orthodoxy.[65] Taxation was a key area of tension between Parliament and the Crown. The king's attempts to bypass Parliament's power to levy taxes through the exercise of prerogative power stimulated both political tension and litigation.[66] It seems likely that there is a linkage between the king's success in litigation before judges who he personally appointed and dismissed[67] and the development of stronger guarantees of judicial independence in the Act of Settlement 1701.[68] We should note also that the fourth estate, the press, established its power to publish free of censorship in seventeenth-century England.[69] The framers of the United States Constitution (1789) were concerned to limit the capacity of the federal government for arbitrary and capricious rule. Later constitutions, such as that of Switzerland (1874), have been more concerned to address the need for diverse communities to live together amicably. Recent constitutional texts, such as that of South Africa (1996), have sought to address explicitly social inequalities which would be masked by simply incorporating formal commitments to equality.[70]

REGULATING THE CONTENT OF CONSTITUTIONS

The alignment of political practice with constitutional norms, discussed above, provides one mechanism through which political and legal systems may be accommodated within the constitutional sphere. A second possibility is that the content of the constitution may be adapted to the requirements of the political system.

[64] Gordon, *Controlling the State*, 238.   [65] Ibid. 238.

[66] *The Case of Impositions or Bate's Case* (1606) 2 State Tr 371; *Case of Ship Money (R v Hampden)* (1637) 3 State Tr 826; I. Loveland, *Constitutional Law*, 2nd edn. (London: Butterworth, 2000), 77.

[67] Sir Edward Coke, one of the great jurists of the period, was dismissed by James I after only three years as lord chief justice in part because of his attempts to curb prerogative power.

[68] Loveland, *Constitutional Law*, 51.

[69] Gordon, *Controlling the State*, 264. John Milton's *Areopagitica* (1644) provided an influential critique of laws requiring press licensing and permitting censorship, but lasting abolition of such controls was not achieved until 1695. I am grateful to Adam Tomkins for pointing this out to me.

[70] The South African Constitution incorporates social, or third-generation, rights, including rights to housing, health care, food, water, social security, and education (ss. 26, 27, 29).

It is said to be a defining characteristic of constitutions that they are relatively fixed. But, equally, one might say that for all that they are amenable to change.

The role of international organizations in setting, monitoring and enforcing constitutional standards is perhaps most like regulation as it is traditionally conceived. Thus the Council of Europe, the European Union, the OECD, the United Nations, and the World Bank have all used their various levers and monitoring capacities to regulate some aspects of national constitutional regimes. Various mechanisms for enforcing change to constitutional norms may be found in the relationships between international organizations and states. For example, new members of the Council of Europe are required to sign up to the European Convention on Human Rights as a condition for membership of that particular international community. The taking of funds from international organizations such as the World Bank is often tied to conditions relating to institutional (including constitutional) reform. However, it is not unusual to find that such external regulatory oversight restricts its concerns to examining a narrow ambit of constitutional norms encompassed within formal texts. The United Nations Committee on Human Rights is relatively unusual in that its monitoring activities attempt to uncover evidence relating to how constitutional norms concerned with human rights play out in practice, thus bringing it closer to understanding, and thus regulating 'working constitutions'.

Though such international activity may be most 'regulation-like', it is likely to have less prominence than domestic mechanisms for overseeing the content of constitutions. It is common for constitutional texts to provide mechanisms through which constitutional amendment may be made. Just as written constitutional texts are not exhaustive of the norms of the working constitution, so formal processes of amendment are not the only means by which the content of constitutional norms changes. In this sense a constitution is a contingent set of practices with, at least implicitly, monitoring by those with the capacity to initiate, carry out, or influence decisions about amendment. We may think in some sense, then, of mechanisms for regulating the content of constitutions. Some states have specialized institutions of constitutional monitoring (for example, the Conseil Constitutionnel in France).

A substantial economic literature addresses the issues concerning both the choice of constitutional norms and reasons for their relative stability. It is posited that uncertainty as to how choices will affect any individual participant in the process of making constitutional rules means that there is a greater willingness in such processes to privilege the interests of the collectivity over personal self-interest.[71] While the stability of constitutional norms is both a defining feature of constitutions and a virtue for some, this principle is in tension with demands for normative innovation to meet changing social opinion or economic requirements.[72] Once settled on, there is considerable investment

---

[71] Brennan and Hamlin, 'Constitutional Choice', 120–1.
[72] J. Raz, 'On the Authority and Interpretation of Constitutions: Some Preliminaries', in L. Alexander (ed.), *Constitutionalism* (Cambridge: Cambridge University Press, 1998), 186.

made in understanding constitutional norms, and the prospect that decisions affecting matters far in the future will be made on the assumption of the relatively fixed nature of the rules. There are accordingly incentives to maintain the stability of constitutional norms once established.[73]

The most prominent mechanisms for constitutional change are those provided for in foundational constitutional documents themselves. The interest in these mechanisms is understandable given the coherence of finding that the norms governing the adaptation of autonomous law are found within the law itself. Many state constitutions provide for both the supremacy and the entrenchment of constitutional rules.[74] It is common, though not universal, to find that formal acts of amendment require special processes of agreement and consideration (and constitutional norms are thus said to be entrenched). In some jurisdictions amendments to the nominal constitution can only be made following a referendum, in others only with special majorities of applicable legislative bodies. In some federal systems the consent of the constituent states or provinces is required, leading to the calling of conventions of those states to consider constitutional reform. There is consequently a degree of permanence about the standards. The scope for contingency of the norms is clearly greatest, in a formal sense at least, where constitutional norms are neither regarded as supreme and nor are they entrenched, as with the constitutional norms of the United Kingdom. Where constitutional norms are contained in conventions (in the sense of accepted patterned behaviour) then their amendment is achieved through changing the pattern of behaviour.

Consideration of an outlying case like that of the UK makes it clear that there are means by which constitutional norms can be changed other than amendments to constitutional texts by the prescribed means. This may be truer for a jurisdiction like the UK, but is more or less true for all constitutional systems. Administrative, juridical, and political actions may be regulative of constitutional norms, in addition to formal acts of amendment. This is most transparently the case with constitutional litigation which is frequently targeted at recasting the scope or nature of constitutional norms,[75] rather than simply their vindication.

Interpretation of constitutional texts through constitutional litigation has received the most attention as a non-formal mechanism for changing constitutional norms. So, for example, there is a lively debate in the US constitutional literature as to the extent to which the Constitution can be changed by means other than the provisions for amendment provided in Article 5 of the Constitution.[76] Indeed, entrenchment may place pressure on other mechanisms through which the working constitution can be changed. Deductively reasoned positive law analysis suggests that new interpretations are simply disclosing the true and

---

[73] Brennan and Hamlin, 'Constitutional Choice', 123–5.

[74] Finer *et al.*, *Comparing Constitutions*, 13–15.

[75] Raz, 'On the Authority and Interpretation of Constitutions', 191.

[76] B. P. Denning, 'Means to Amend: Theories of Constitutional Change', *Tennessee Law Review* (1997), 155.

original meaning of the constitutional text and hence this is not change at all. An inductively reasoned and empirical approach, associated with regulation scholarship, is more open to recognizing that norms change as they are used. A central example is provided by the Supreme Court's acceptance of the redrawing of boundaries between state and society under the New Deal.[77]

Constitutional courts are just one of a number of loci where new interpretations may be applied. Changing practices or conventions among legislators, administrators, and bureaucrats must be quantitatively much more significant as sources of reinterpretation of constitutional norms. One could add to this the activities of non-state players. Thus we might argue that the practical meaning of rights of free speech, commonly found in modern constitutional texts,[78] is most routinely interpreted (and thus, in most cases, disposed of determinatively) in newsrooms of broadcasters and newspaper journalists.

A wide variety of political and administrative practices can change elements of a constitutional regime.[79] Primary and secondary legislation are the most transparent of these mechanisms (though they may not always be recognized as having constitutional import). So, for example, the scope of public sector audit has been markedly extended in many OECD countries over the past twenty-five years, so as to encompass not only traditional concerns that agencies spend public funds for the purposes for which they were legislated, but also new principles which require such funds to be spent efficiently and effectively.[80] Such changes, which create a performance audit mandate for supreme audit institutions, have typically been effected by ordinary legislation. In the UK and Australia they have been accompanied by measures to enhance the independence of auditors-general.[81]

In addition to amendment to constitutions through legislative acts, legislators may also amend through changing conventions. This form of adaptation occurs where there is a degree of consensus about 'sensible adaptations of existing conventional rules to meet changed or changing political conditions'.[82] Thus it is said the US Senate Judiciary Committee's activities in confirming the nomination of Supreme Court justices have significantly shifted the power of appointment away from the president towards the legislature.[83] This shift is particularly identified with the rejection by the Senate of Robert Bork's nomination by President Reagan in 1987. The requirement of consensus should not, however, be overstated. In some systems governmental activities which are the subject of conventions may not be sufficiently public for it to be apparent that a convention

[77] R. H. Fallon, 'Ruminations on the Work of Frederick Schauer', *Notre Dame Law Review* (1997), 1391, 1407.

[78] e.g. First Amendment, US Constitution; Art. 10, European Convention on Human Rights; Indian Constitution, Art. 19.

[79] My analysis is at variance with that of Grey, 'Constitutionalism', 193, who asserts that 'constitutional norms with the status of ordinary law do not bulk large in practical significance today'.

[80] W. Funnell, 'Enduring Fundamentals: Constitutional Accountability and Auditors General in the Reluctant State', *Critical Perspectives on Accounting*, 14 (2003), 107.

[81] National Audit Act 1983 (UK); Auditor-General Act 1997 (Cwlth).

[82] I. Jennings, *Cabinet Government*, 3rd edn. (Cambridge: Cambridge University Press, 1959), 8.

[83] Denning, 'Means to Amend', 200, 214–15.

exists or that it has been changed. Yet there may be considerable normative pressure within a relatively closed group to hold to particular norms.

A fourth means of accommodation between legal and political systems (in addition to realignment of political actor behaviour, formal constitutional amendment, and informal constitutional change) is found in revolutionary systems where, it is suggested, the basic norm (grundnorm) or underlying suppositions of the constitutional order changes. The legal theory of Hans Kelsen has been extremely influential in framing judicial responses to the constitutional problems of revolutionary change in post-colonial settings, and in particularly in determining when the regime of usurpers should be regarded as not only legitimate but also legal. A recent survey noted eleven such constitutional judgments in countries within the common law jurisdictions.[84] The High Court of Uganda has interpreted Kelsen's theory to entail four cardinal requirements to satisfy a court that a new constitution is effective because of a change in the grundnorm. These are the fact of 'abrupt political change'; that change 'must not have been within the contemplation of an existing Constitution'; 'The change must destroy the entire legal order except what is preserved'; and 'the new Constitution and Government must be effective'.[85]

Kelsenian theory ought also to shed some light on the effectiveness and legitimacy of new constitutional texts. One would anticipate that those constitutional texts which are the outcome of extensive deliberative processes, such as those of the United States, South Africa, and some countries of eastern Europe[86] would be more successful than those which were imposed on states by occupying forces (for example, Japan) or by former colonial powers (as was the case in much of sub-Saharan Africa[87]). So, for example, with the Japanese Constitution it is said that there is a substantial gap between the formal guarantees of rights in the text and the operation of the working constitution, as the transplanted and alien text has been subject to a process of Japonization.[88] Additionally the Japanese Supreme Court has never attained the position of robust independence which might have been anticipated from modelling it on the United States.[89] This is in part a question of cultural sensitivity, or of fit with important preexisting political, social, and legal cultures.[90]

---

[84] T. Mahmud, 'Jurisprudence of Successful Treason: Coup d'État and Common Law', *Cornell International Law Journal* (1994), 49, 53.   [85] Ibid. 60.

[86] M. Krygier, 'Institutional Optimism, Cultural Pessimism and the Rule of Law', in M. Krygier and A. Czarnota (eds.), *The Rule of Law after Communism: Problems and Prospects in East-Central Europe* (Dartmouth: Aldershot, 1999).

[87] 'The Creation of South Africa's Constitution: Interview with Judge Albie Sachs', *New York Law School Review* (1997), 685, 688–9. There is now a substantial literature addressing the issue of 'legal transplants', of which constitutional systems provide key examples: D. Nelken and J. Feest (eds.), *Adapting Legal Cultures* (Oxford: Hart, 2001).

[88] S. B. Hamano, 'Incomplete Revolutions and Not So Alien Transplants: The Japanese Constitution and Human Rights', *University of Pennsylvania Journal of Constitutional Law* (1999), 415, 416.

[89] Ibid. 459 ff.

[90] Krygier, 'Institutional Optimism', 90–1; P. Paczolay, 'Traditional Elements in the Constitutions of Central and East European Democracies', in Krygier and Czarnota (eds.), *The Rule of Law after Communism*.

CONCLUSIONS

Regulatory scholarship has a keen interest in how governance regimes work. Such working arrangements often present in stark terms the problem of control. The actors to be regulated are liable to have different rationalities from the regulators and different ways of thinking about the world. It may be difficult to communicate what the regulatory requirements are, and equally difficult to determine whether they are being met and to realign behaviour where they are not. Just as regulators may be trying to steer the behaviour of regulatees, so the latter may be endeavouring to change the content of the regulatory regime through putting forward alternative interpretations or seeking wider legislative reform. This description of a classic regulatory problem also captures well one perspective on constitutions. In this chapter I have argued that a regulatory approach illuminates the means by which accommodations may be sought between political and legal systems in the constitutional sphere.

The regulatory approach is suggestive of ways of looking beyond the law-centric analysis of constitutional law scholarship. Any assessment of legal constraints on government must be complemented by an understanding of other constraints rooted in community (such as conventions) or in competition (for example, federalism). Key examples are provided by the growing number of mechanisms for scrutinizing compliance with international norms. The reporting organizations are often restricted to naming and shaming states which are not in compliance, but membership of the international community implies some responsibility to take such reports seriously. Public international lawyers describe these community norms in terms of binding obligations of international law.[91]

There is a wide variety of mechanisms and organizations involved in monitoring and enforcement of compliance with constitutional norms (though many of these organizations are not involved in reviewing all the norms). It may be claimed that for those states which have constitutional courts and expansive models of constitutional litigation such processes are special because, in contrast with the other mechanisms I claim belong to the family of constitutional monitors, the courts' jurisdiction extends to the vindication of *all* constitutional norms. But this distinctive quality of constitutional litigation appears questionable. Not all constitutional norms, not even those contained within constitutional texts, are justiciable.[92] This is true a fortiori for conventions. Secondly, constitutional litigation is liable to be sporadic and partial in its scope—driven by the concerns of litigants. The compliance of government with many constitutional norms is, in practice, unlikely to be litigated. Dependence on constitutional litigation as *the* mechanism of monitoring and enforcement leaves government to use power as it wishes unless and until challenged. Though other monitoring mechanisms may be

---

[91] See the discussion by Hilary Charlesworth and Christine Chinkin, Ch. 12 in this volume.
[92] Grey, 'Constitutionalism', mentions the right to pursue and obtain happiness.

more limited in terms of the norms they cover, some of these may be more systematic or proactive in their scrutiny. Furthermore, many states do not have developed systems of constitutional litigation, and are thus more clearly dependent on other mechanisms of monitoring and enforcement, whether through other judicial mechanisms, or through non-judicial institutions.

The juxtaposition of regulation and constitutions set off my initial inquiry in the direction of thinking of constitutions as part of regimes for regulating conduct of governmental actors. Regulatory scholarship is well placed to elaborate and enrich on the working constitutions concept through analysis of the variety of mechanisms through which monitoring and enforcement over constitutional norms is carried out. But such an analysis demotes the constitutional to the level of ordinary legal, social, and market norms. An alternative approach is to think of the constitutive norms of our polities as being concerned not to establish direct regulatory control but rather with acting as meta-legal or meta-regulatory principles which indirectly steer the normative structures of both state and non-state actors towards the direct vindication of those norms.

The hypothesis of this chapter is that the mechanisms by which political and legal systems find some accommodation is central to understanding the workings of the constitutional sphere. The development and operation of constitutional conventions provides one such mechanism. The concept of convention contains within it the idea both of a constraint on political actors by reference to a constitutional norm and the possibility of adaptation of the norms to meet the requirements of the political system. Other means of accommodation are represented by more formal means of both enforcement and adaptation of constitutional norms, whether in processes of constitutional litigation (which may be representative of both enforcement and adaptation), political acts of interpretation, or changes in constitutional norms of a more revolutionary character. Arguably formal mechanisms for amendments of constitutional texts are intended to create a linkage through tying change in constitutional law to more deliberative processes than are required for ordinary legislation (though it is not clear to what extent that is successful). Thus such mechanisms give recognition to the particular difficulties of accommodating law and politics in the constitutional sphere.

12

Regulatory Frameworks in International Law

HILARY CHARLESWORTH and CHRISTINE CHINKIN

INTRODUCTION

The traditional framework for regulation by rules and principles of international law is unsophisticated in comparison with that of national legal systems. Indeed, the threshold question often posed in introducing international law to generations of law students is 'Is international law really law?' A regulatory regime comprises standard-setting, monitoring compliance with the standards, and enforcement of the standards.[1] International law delivers on each of these criteria in a different way from national legal systems. The international legal system has no centralized law-making power for primary legislation, nor any forms of delegated legislation. Standards are typically set directly by the primary objects of international law, sovereign states. This means that international legal norms are highly negotiated, allowing considerable leeway for differences among states. International law offers few schemes of compulsory jurisdiction and no centralized enforcement mechanisms. Monitoring compliance with standards generally allows states broad discretion. Enforcement of international law typically appears as weaker and more porous than domestic law enforcement. The fact that international law does not neatly fit the command and control model of regulation has led some realist scholars of international relations to assert that legal norms are a mere frippery in international politics, used only to decorate a decision reached for overtly political ends, or to be conspicuously discounted.

The realist rejection of the regulatory force of international law has been challenged by 'liberal' international relations scholars who resist the monolithic view of the state and state power that realism adopts. Liberals look instead to the actions of individuals in diverse sectors within the state to determine how their behaviour—and hence that of the state—is influenced by international norms and expectations. On the one hand, technical and sectoral experts work through transnational government networks that are the 'tangible manifestation of a new era of trans-governmental regulatory co-operation'.[2] On the other hand, civil society groups operate across borders both to develop international legal standards

---

[1] Introduction to this volume.

[2] A.-M. Slaughter, 'Governing through Government Networks', in M. Byers (ed.), *The Role of Law in International Politics* (Oxford: Oxford University Press, 2000), 177.

and to monitor compliance with those that exist.[3] Both government networks and non-state actors, notably non-governmental organizations (NGOs), work through the mass of global and regional, general and specialist intergovernmental organizations (INGOs) that have been established, especially since 1945. INGOs provide the space and facilities for intergovernmental negotiation, for the bringing-together of technical experts, and the services of a specialist secretariat for the creation of new rules. For their part, international lawyers comfort themselves that they can validly claim the mantle of law either by showing that many international legal norms are accepted as binding without controversy, or that the language of legal discourse is regularly invoked in international relations.[4] The evolutionary trajectory of international legal reasoning has been from a limited conception of law in the domestic image to the generation of institutions and techniques responsive to the heterogeneity of international society.

Contemporary international law has evolved through an ever-growing array of regulatory instruments and mechanisms for enforcement that make it quite distinct from the traditional inter-state regime. The classic sources of international law—treaties and customary international law[5]—are supplemented by a range of instruments and techniques. Many such instruments are concluded within INGOs, especially where cross-border transactions require detailed regulations or where the effectiveness of the regulatory regime depends upon wide participation and cooperation. This was the case with what might be described as the first international regulatory regime—the Universal Postal Union, created in 1874 by the Treaty of Bern, to organize and enhance global postal services. Today international regulatory regimes for *inter alia* the environment, the control of disease, disarmament and weapons control, human rights, aviation, and maritime pollution all operate within and are developed under the supervisory mechanisms of specialist international institutions. Such institutions have developed their own legal cultures and these come into conflict with each other. For example, there is considerable debate about whether the institutions of international trade regulation (the World Trade Organization) should incorporate the norms of the international human rights bodies. States have to internalize sometimes conflicting principles and account for their implementation to different international institutions. State compliance is no longer seen primarily in terms of sovereignty, but rather in terms of participation, expertise, bureaucracy, and efficiency.[6]

Contemporary regulatory techniques include framework treaties allowing for subsequent detailed protocols to which parties must opt in or out;[7] secondary

---

[3] M. Keck and K. Sikkink, *Activists beyond Borders: Advocacy Networks in International Politics* (Ithaca, NY: Cornell University Press, 1998).

[4] e.g. L. Henkin, *How Nations Behave: Law and Foreign Policy*, 2nd edn. (New York: Columbia University Press, 1979).

[5] Arts. 38(1)(a) and (b) of the Statute of the International Court of Justice, 1945.

[6] A. Chayes and A. Chayes, *The New Sovereignty: Compliance with International Regulatory Agreements* (Cambridge, Mass.: Harvard University Press, 1995).

[7] e.g. United Nations Framework Convention on Climate Change, 9 May 1992; Kyoto Protocol to the United Nations Framework Convention on Climate Change, 11 Dec. 1997; UNIDROIT

mechanisms such as the compliance procedures under environmental treaties;[8] binding agreements in non-treaty form, such as memorandums of understanding adopted between a broader range of actors than states.[9] 'Hard' international law in treaty form is supplemented by 'soft' law—non-binding self-regulatory codes of conduct and commitments,[10] and institutional regulatory codes.[11] Such is the prevalence of non-binding instruments and the degree to which they are formally integrated into the international legal system that actors do not appear to differentiate between them in terms of compliance.[12] These instruments may not be directed solely at states—the traditional actors possessing legal personality in international law—but may include INGOs, NGOs, individuals, and multinational corporations. The number of specialist international tribunals has increased exponentially and their jurisdiction encompasses a broad range of substantive and technical issues that would not previously have been regarded as appropriate for international regulation.[13] Alongside judicial and quasi-judicial systems there are also inspection systems,[14] reporting mechanisms,[15] fact-finding machineries,[16] and expert working groups and commissions. Nevertheless, through both the traditional sources of international law and newer forms of law-making, the international legal system still relies primarily on self-regulation. But this self-regulatory regime operates primarily in a public sphere. International law relationships tend to be subject to public scrutiny that may affect the participants' understanding of their relationship. For example, public debate

Convention on Interests in Mobile Equipment, Cape Town, 16 Nov. 2001; Protocol to the Convention on Interests in Mobile Equipment on Matters Specific to Aircraft Equipment, Cape Town, 16 Nov. 2001.

[8] For example, compliance mechanisms for the Convention for the Protection of the Ozone Layer, Vienna, 1985, were adopted in the Protocol on Substances that Deplete the Ozone Layer, Montreal, 1987 (as amended). Compliance mechanisms provide a combination of 'carrots' and 'sticks' in regulating state behaviour. In problem-solving mode they allow for financial incentives and technical assistance, while allowing for sanction by the Meeting of the Parties.

[9] e.g. Framework for Collaboration among Participating Multilateral Development Banks on Financial Management Diagnostic Work, 18 Feb. 2003.

[10] e.g. the UN Global Compact, launched 26 July 2000, to which corporations may voluntarily adhere.

[11] Institutional regulatory codes, for example, codes of conduct for peacekeepers.

[12] D. Shelton, *Commitment and Compliance: The Role of Non-binding Norms in the International Legal System* (New York: Oxford University Press, 2000).

[13] P. Sands, R. Mackenzie, and Y. Shany (eds.), *Manual on International Courts and Tribunals* (London: Butterworths, 1999).

[14] e.g. Inspection Panels of the World Bank, the Asian Development Bank, and the Inter-American Development Bank; the European Committee for the Prevention of Torture and Inhuman or Degrading Treatment or Punishment, established by the European Convention for the Prevention of Torture and Inhuman or Degrading Treatment or Punishment, Strasbourg, 26 Nov. 1987 (as amended, effective 1 Mar. 2002); Optional Protocol to the Convention against Torture and Other Cruel, Inhuman or Degrading Treatment or Punishment, GA Res. 57/199, 18 Dec. 2002. In all these instances states accept international inspection of some aspect of their internal affairs.

[15] For example, states' obligations for initial and periodic reporting under the UN human rights treaties: P. Alston and J. Crawford (eds.), *The Future of UN Human Rights Treaty Monitoring* (Cambridge: Cambridge University Press, 2000).

[16] e.g. Security Council Resolution 780, 6 Oct. 1992, authorizing the establishment of a Committee of Experts to investigate the commission of crimes in the Former Yugoslavia; Security Council Resolution 935, 1 July 1994, doing the same with respect to Rwanda.

about the meaning of controversial law-making instruments, such as Security Council resolutions, may alter the understanding of their meaning.

International regulation now goes far beyond inter-state behaviour. One of the largely unstudied revolutions in international law has been the shift from macro-level regulation of relations between states to considerable technical micro-management on numerous aspects of the internal affairs of states. An example is in the context of the 'war against terrorism' where international regulation of national affairs has been extended to extraordinary lengths for all states. The UN Counter-Terrorism Committee has taken on the role and function of a national regulator.[17] Its mandate is to 'monitor implementation' of Security Council Resolution 1373, adopted in the wake of the 11 September 2001 attacks on the United States. States must report on the steps they have taken to implement the Resolution, their actions are scrutinized by the Committee, and further measures may be demanded. By December 2002 the Committee had received 175 first-round reports and 101 second-round reports. Under Resolution 1373 states are required to freeze assets of any individual or group suspected of involvement in terrorism, not just those who have been placed on sanctions lists. Thus, international regulations determine state behaviour with respect to the banking activities of private individuals without any systems of scrutiny or due process protection.

Nowhere has this regulatory trend been more marked since the 1990s than in the international reaction to territorial entities that have come to be considered as outsiders in the international system. These entities may be politically designated as 'failed' or 'rogue' entities,[18] while legally they are perceived to constitute a threat to international peace and security. Such entities may be states where civil war has caused the collapse of governmental institutions (e.g. Somalia, Sierra Leone), or new states immersed in or emerging from conflict (Bosnia-Hercegovina, East Timor), or sub-state entities suffering oppressive rule (Kosovo). Designation as a failed or rogue state typically results in punitive measures being imposed on the whole or part of the entity that are supervised by the Security Council Sanctions Committee.[19] Military action to restore order may also be authorized.[20] In the aftermath of the crisis, attention becomes focused on rehabilitating the entity in the eyes of the international community, which may involve its placement under a form of international protection.

[17] Security Council Committee established pursuant to Security Council Resolution 1373, 28 Sept. 2001, concerning counter-terrorism.

[18] Which territories become subject to such treatment is of course a matter of political decision-making primarily within the Security Council. For the depiction of the US as a 'rogue' state, see W. Blum, *The Rogue State: A Guide to the World's Only Superpower* (Claremont, South Africa: Spearhead, 2002).

[19] e.g. Security Council Resolution 864, 15 Sept. 1993, authorizing the imposition of sanctions upon UNITA for its continued actions against the government of Angola. On sanctions generally, see V. Gowlland-Debbas (ed.), *United Nations Sanctions and International Law* (The Hague: Kluwer Law International, 2001).

[20] Under Art. 42, Charter of the United Nations, 1945. Economic sanctions and the use of military force are the two forms of collective coercive regulation provided for within the Charter.

International organizations have been given sweeping control over the internal affairs of such entities in order to rebuild political, social, legal, and economic institutions. For example, in Bosnia-Hercegovina the Office of the High Representative (OHR) has been given wide powers over civilian administration.[21] In Kosovo the Special Representative of the UN Secretary-General has the competence 'to control the implementation of the international civil presence'.[22] In East Timor the UN's Transitional Administration (UNTAET) was endowed with the overall responsibility for the administration of East Timor and empowered to exercise 'all legislative and executive authority, including the administration of justice'.[23]

Two aspects of these territorial regimes should be noted. Firstly, they are established in accordance with a specific ideology, that is, to provide a framework for the establishment of a stable democratic government committed to the rule of law, human rights, and the promotion of trade and free markets. Secondly, scores of NGOs, especially those in the fields of humanitarian assistance and human rights, enter the territory alongside the INGOs. Their close involvement with international governmental and institutional actors on the ground and their reliance upon funding agencies complicates their position.[24] In any event, NGOs must be seen as actors in the international regulation of territory.

Regulatory theory is concerned with how various forms of regulation, including law, govern social interaction. Much of the theoretical work on legal regulation has been developed in the context of domestic law. This chapter examines international law in the particular setting of regulation of outsider entities, such as failed and nascent states, that is where international regulation fills the vacuum caused by the collapse of domestic institutions and the rule of law. Through our brief examination of international regulation in Bosnia-Hercegovina and East Timor, we ask what light a regulatory lens sheds on international law. What are the intended and unintended effects of regulating behaviour through international law? Drawing on Hugh Collins's starting questions in *Regulating Contracts*,[25] we investigate whether the international law in this area conceives of relations in ways that are different from the frameworks in which they operate. We note especially that, although international law pays little attention to sex and gender, such relations are an important aspect of social reconstruction. We hope to identify what can usefully be achieved by legal regulation in a particular international context and how legal regulation may become ineffective and counter-productive.

---

[21] Art. VIII and Annex 10 of the General Framework Agreement for Peace in Bosnia and Hercegovina (GFA). Under Art. 1(2) of Annex 10, the parties requested the designation of the High Representative.

[22] Security Council Resolution 1244, 10 June 1999, para. 6, 10, and 11.

[23] Security Council Resolution 1272, 25 Oct. 1999, para. 1.

[24] D. Rieff, *A Bed for the Night: Humanitarianism in Crisis* (New York: Simon & Schuster, 2002); A. H. Henkin (ed.), *Honoring Human Rights under International Mandates* (Washington: Aspen Institute, 2003).

[25] H. Collins, *Regulating Contracts* (Oxford: Oxford University Press, 1999), preface.

Bosnia-Hercegovina

War in Bosnia-Hercegovina was legally brought to an end by the General Framework Agreement for Peace in Bosnia and Hercegovina (GFA), negotiated in Dayton, Ohio, in 1995.[26] As well as bringing peace, the objectives of the GFA were to create regional stability and to provide a constitutional framework for a democratic state that would be workable within the restraints of its ethnic composition. The GFA centred around three strategies: provision for democratic elections; international controls to ensure compliance with its vision; and international human rights guarantees. The extensive international regulation of all aspects of public life within Bosnia was allocated to a range of European and international institutions. Military responsibility was accorded to the NATO-led Implementation Force (IFOR, subsequently the Stabilization Force, SFOR), while the UN Mission had initial responsibility for the establishment and training of the civilian International Police Task Force (IPTF). The Office of the UN High Commissioner for Refugees was given responsibility over repatriation and relief of refugees and displaced persons,[27] and the Office of the UN High Commissioner for Human Rights (OHCHR) has established a field presence in Sarajevo. The Organization for Security and Cooperation in Europe (OSCE) has responsibility over elections. The European Bank for Reconstruction and Development appoints members of the Commission on Public Corporations.[28]

All these bodies work alongside the OHR. The OHR mandate does not appear particularly broad: to facilitate the parties' own efforts and to mobilize and to coordinate the activities of the organizations and agencies involved in the civilian aspects of the peace settlement.[29] In practice, the OHR has been affirmed as the 'final authority'[30] with a broad executive power in all civilian matters, including the right to overrule the governments of the Bosnian Federation and the Republika Srpska.[31]

It was unclear in 1995 how long the international presence would be required to stay in Bosnia-Hercegovina. Accordingly, the Peace Implementation Council (PIC), comprising the major Western powers and donor countries, was established. The PIC meets twice a year and monitors and updates the regulatory regime as it sees fit. For example, in 1997 the PIC extended the powers of the OHR, allowing him to make 'binding decisions as he judges necessary' on 'other measures to ensure . . . the smooth running of the common institutions'.[32] Yet another international presence since 1999 has been that of the Stability Pact for

---

[26] General Framework Agreement for Peace in Bosnia and Hercegovina with Annexes, 14 Dec. 14, 35 I.L.M. 75(1996). [27] GFA, Art. III of Annex 7.

[28] GFA, Art. 1(2) of Annex 9.   [29] GFA, Annex 10.

[30] Security Council Resolution 1031, 15 Dec. 1995.

[31] M. Chossudovsky, 'Dismantling Former Yugoslavia, Recolonising Bosnia', in D. Eade (ed.), *From Conflict to Peace in a Changing World* (Oxford: Oxfam, 1998), 38, 42. Art. III of the GFA provides for the existence of the two Entities, the Federation of Bosnia and Hercegovina and the Republika Srpska.

[32] Bonn Peace Implementation Conference: Summary of Conclusions, Bonn, 10 Dec. 1997, see esp. XI, (2)(c) http://www.oscebih.org/essentials/pdf/bonn_peace_implementation_council_eng.pdf.

South East Europe, established on the initiative of the European Union on 10 June 1999 in the wake of the NATO bombing of Serbia with respect to Kosovo.

In 2003 the EU enhanced its engagement with Bosnia-Hercegovina as the UN lessened its role. The OHR became also the office of the EU Special Representative, and the IPTF was replaced by the EU Police Mission, whose function is to help the police forces in Bosnia-Hercegovina carry out their duties more professionally and effectively. Bosnia-Hercegovina is moving from post-conflict status to that of a country in transition, looking eventually towards EU accession. Core objectives have been identified in the Mission Implementation Plan as crucial to this transition: entrenching the rule of law; ensuring that extreme nationalists, war criminals, and organized criminal networks cannot reverse peace implementation; reforming the economy; strengthening the capacity of Bosnia-Hercegovina's governing institutions, especially at the state-level; establishing state-level civilian command and control over armed forces, reforming the security sector, and paving the way for integration into the Euro-Atlantic framework; and promoting the sustainable return of refugees and displaced persons.[33]

The GFA confirmed the link between internal state governance and international peace and security by incorporating a state constitution into an international agreement.[34] It therefore sets the legal standards and the competence of the international agencies, which have both law-making and monitoring roles. Enforcement is through a range of bodies, for example, the Constitutional Court and a Commission on Human Rights, comprising an Office of the Ombudsman and a Human Rights Chamber with jurisdiction over alleged or apparent violations of the European Convention for the Protection of Human Rights and Fundamental Freedoms.[35] Internationals play an important role in enforcement: the Constitutional Court has three judges appointed by the president of the European Court of Human Rights, and eight members of the Human Rights Chamber are appointed by the Council of Ministers of the Council of Europe. In addition, those indicted for war crimes, crimes against humanity, or genocide are subject to the jurisdiction of the International Criminal Tribunal for the Former Yugoslavia.[36]

Bosnia-Hercegovina is subject to an extraordinary level of international regulation rendering its sovereignty contingent and flexible. The international community is involved in the running of the internal affairs of a state to a greater extent than had ever previously occurred within a member of the UN. The structure is reminiscent of the UN trusteeship system where non-self-governing

---

[33] Office of the High Representative, 'Mission Implementation Plan', 30 Jan. 2003 http://www.ohr.int/ohr-info/ohr-mip/default.asp?content_id = 29145.

[34] GFA, Art. V and Annex 4.

[35] GFA, Art. 2 of Annex 6. In June 2003 the High Representative for Bosnia-Hercegovina, Paddy Ashdown, announced that the Human Rights Chamber would be disbanded on 31 December 2003 and its caseload transferred to the Constitutional Court.

[36] The International Tribunal for the Prosecution of Persons Responsible for Serious Violations of International Humanitarian Law Committed in the Territory of the Former Yugoslavia since 1991 was established by Security Council Resolution 827, 25 May 1993.

entities were placed under international supervision for the supposed benefit of the territory's inhabitants until such time as they were deemed ready for self-rule.[37] In effect, what has been created is a new form of protectorate or trusteeship-type arrangement. Questions must be asked about how such a degree of international regulation has operated and the extent to which the expectations of those regulated have been met. The international intervention is far-reaching, but in examining the relationship between the international regulators and those subject to regulation, we focus on issues relating to electoral reform, human rights implementation, and an unintended condition within Bosnia, human trafficking.

The OSCE was given extensive control over the electoral process, including supervision of the preparation and conduct of elections.[38] Elections provide a dilemma for international regulators committed to the rule of law and democratization: failure to hold elections undermines the legitimacy of the international presence and causes local resentment, but premature elections may lead to unsatisfactory results by reinforcing the hardline political or nationalist factions that caused institutional collapse and conflict.[39] The GFA provided for elections in September 1996. Although elections were held, when they led to undesired results the OHR intervened, as, for example, in the dismissal in November 1999 of twenty-three elected officials on the grounds that they had pursued anti-Dayton agendas. Yet, it cannot be argued that their policies were unknown to the electorate that had voted them into power.[40] Elections held under a regime of international regulation are problematic in a number of ways. Questions that arise include: when does intervention or regulation in the name of institution consolidation deny the concept of democratization? To what extent can the international community in the name of democracy intervene to ensure election results and national institutions based on the 'morally right'[41] choices approved by the international community, rather than those of internal civil society? Does this mean in practice that no individual may make a 'morally wrong' choice by supporting the nationalist parties and if this is so what becomes of democratic plurality and individual citizenship choice?

The adoption of an Electoral Law in 2001, with input from an international advisory body, was highly controversial.[42] Electoral reform provides an opportunity for social engineering. For example, the Electoral Law has a quota system that provides for greater sex equality within Bosnian political institutions than is the case in the states playing major roles within Bosnia. At least one-third of the lists of all parties and coalitions participating in elections must comprise women candidates and women candidates must be fairly distributed on the lists.[43] The adoption of the Electoral Law was important, as it satisfied one of

---

[37] Art. 75 of the Charter of the United Nations.   [38] GFA, Annex 3.

[39] Sumantra Bose argues that the first post-war elections should be significantly delayed to avoid this outcome: *Bosnia after Dayton, Nationalist Partition and International Intervention* (Oxford: Oxford University Press, 2002), 90. US pressure meant that elections in Bosnia were held only a year after Dayton.   [40] Ibid. 276.

[41] D. Chandler, *Bosnia: Faking Democracy after Dayton*, 2nd edn. (London: Pluto Press, 2000), 28.

[42] Bose, *Bosnia after Dayton*, 215.   [43] Ibid. 219, 225.

the conditions for Bosnia to be admitted to membership of the Council of Europe, ironically entailing still more international regulation by the institutions of the European Convention on Human Rights (ECHR). Since the adoption of the Electoral Law, the OSCE's democratization programme has moved its focus to capacity-building initiatives for newly elected officials and the institutions in which they work.

There is another aspect of democratization especially relevant to international regulation. While democratization is promoted through the holding of elections, the very presence of the international bodies that are responsible for policy-making undermines the concept of democracy. INGOs are neither democratic nor accountable. As the concept of democratic entitlement within national legal structures has gained force, there has been growing concern about the demo-cratic deficit of international institutions themselves, including the EU and UN.[44] The OHR is answerable only to the PIC, not to the local population, and other international agencies operate with little restraint. The lack of accountability has become apparent in the context of human rights.

The GFA provided extensive protection for human rights within Bosnia-Hercegovina, again amounting to detailed domestic regulation based upon international standards and enforced through international mechanisms.[45] Sixteen human rights treaties are included in an Appendix to GFA Annex 6, and the ECHR is made directly applicable in Bosnia-Hercegovina with priority over all other law.[46]

This elaborate regulatory framework for human rights implementation within Bosnia has led to differences between the regulators and those subject to its provisions. The incoherence and inconsistent outcomes have caused cynicism about the international community's double standards and its willingness to go against the regulations it imposed until other imperatives intervened. This is evident in a case that arose before the Human Rights Chamber in early 2003. Post-11 September 2001 the security concerns of the United States caused its military forces based in Bosnia as part of SFOR to demand custody of four people of Algerian origin who had been arrested on the suspicion that they were preparing to commit terrorist activities. Three of them had been accorded Bosnian citizenship and the fourth had permanent residence status in Bosnia. The Bosnian Ministry of the Interior terminated their citizenship or residency status. When the investigative judge of the Bosnian Supreme Court held that there were no grounds to detain them longer, instead of being released they were handed to US military forces and transferred to the US military detention centre in Guantánamo Bay, Cuba.

The four appealed to the Human Rights Chamber on the basis that their rights under the ECHR had been violated. The Chamber, *inter alia*, asserted that the handover to US forces was a breach of the Bosnian government's

---

[44] E. Stein, 'International Integration and Democracy: No Love at First Sight', *American Journal of International Law*, 95 (2001), 489.   [45] GFA, Art. VII.
[46] GFA, Constitution (Annex 4), Art. II (2).

obligation to protect against arbitrary detention by foreign forces.[47] The GFA was intended to protect the Bosnian civilian population against the military forces responsible for the war. The assumption was that the international community through SFOR and the other agencies would act as protectors against further outbreaks of violence. The irony of the position of the Human Rights Chamber is that the acts of those subject to international regulation—the federal government of Bosnia-Hercegovina and the federation government— are subject to scrutiny for acts carried out at the behest of the regulators, SFOR, who are themselves outside such review. The changed role of the protectors– regulators could not be more stark.

International regulation of territory sets up a three-way relationship between the designated leaders, the population, and the international regulators. As war had broken out in Bosnia-Hercegovina immediately on its assertion of independence in 1992, there had been no opportunity for social planning except in the context of war. Peace in Bosnia-Hercegovina provided civil society with its first opportunity for setting local agendas and priorities. However, it also meant the immediate entry into Bosnia-Hercegovina of new military forces (IFOR and subsequently SFOR) and a range of European and international INGOs and NGOs. Such bodies occupied physical, communicative, and social space limiting that available to local bodies and preventing them from independent policy-making. Effective international regulation aimed at long-term stability requires establishing genuine partnerships between regulating agencies and local authorities and between local civil society groups and the regulating agencies. Open channels for communication are needed as well as involvement in local decision-making on the basis of locally set agendas, not those of the international community. Instead of such partnership, international agencies too often treat local people as 'cheap service providers'[48] and undermine their agency for transformation.

International regulators are assumed to be benevolent. This assumption is challenged, for example, when international personnel become involved in sexual abuse and trafficking. Since the adoption of the GFA in 1995, women have been subject to sexual abuse from members of the international agencies.[49] In other contexts sexual exploitation and violence against children by UN peacekeepers, international and local NGOs, and government humanitarian agencies have been exposed.[50] Women have been brought into Bosnia and sold

---

[47] *Boudellaa v Bosnia and Herzegovina and the Federation of Bosnia and Herzegovina*, Butterworths Human Rights Cases, 13 (2003), 297.

[48] J. Mertus, *War's Offensive on Women: The Humanitarian Challenge in Bosnia, Kosovo, and Afghanistan* (West Hartford, Conn.: Kumarian Press, 2000).

[49] S. Payne, 'Teenagers Used for Sex by UN in Bosnia', *Daily Telegraph*, 25 Apr. 2002. Kathryn Bolkovac, a former US policewoman, won an industrial tribunal action in Southampton, UK, for unfair dismissal in which she alleged she was dismissed for exposing the sexual abuse of women by her UN colleagues: S. Payne, 'Investigator Wins UN Sex Abuse Case', *Daily Telegraph*, 7 Aug. 2002.

[50] UNHCR and Save the Children–UK, *Note for Implementing and Operational Partners by UNHCR and Save the Children–UK on Sexual Violence and Exploitation: The Experience of Refugee Children in Guinea, Liberia and Sierra Leone*, 25 Feb. 2002   http://www.reliefweb.int/w/rwb.nsf/ 0/6010F9ED3C651C93C1256B6D00560FCA?OpenDocument.

as commodities. Trafficking is associated with the creation of a potential market for sexual services.[51] The presence of large numbers of international personnel, mostly men, creates just such a market. The obstacles that women face post-conflict in realizing economic security, such as discrimination in employment and in access to credit, enhance their vulnerability to the risk of being trafficked, while privatization as part of post-conflict economic reconstruction reduces the availability of social safety nets.[52]

The spread of trafficking could have been foreseen, especially in a state where women were dehumanized and targeted for sexual abuse throughout the conflict,[53] but the extent of what was happening and the involvement of the international community was not acknowledged until 1998. Since then a coordinated strategy has been developed to tackle trafficking on a long-term basis through the OHCHR, the Gender Task Force of the Stability Pact, and the OHR. The approach has been to bring together the international agencies, civil society (notably women's) groups, and national authorities. The agreement of a national action plan is a significant outcome of this process. An important factor for the development of a regulatory framework against trafficking in Bosnia that is shared by the local community and the international bodies was the appointment of an OHCHR field officer with a commitment to women's empowerment and experience in gender issues. The field officer promoted the collaboration of the various groups to ensure a consolidated and coherent approach to the problem. Her effectiveness was enhanced by a sufficiently long stay to implement proposals and to build up working relationships with both the governmental and non-governmental bodies within Bosnia-Hercegovina.

EAST TIMOR

Timor Lorosa'e, or East Timor, became independent on 20 May 2002. The creation of this new state was a long and painful process after the invasion of the former Portuguese colonial territory by Indonesia in 1975.[54] A UN-sponsored referendum to determine East Timor's future was held on 30 August 1999. The result was a vote of 78.5 per cent against a 'special autonomy' status within

---

[51] Madeleine Rees, OHCHR field officer in Sarajevo, states that an approximate calculation is that the international community constitutes 30 per cent of the customers of foreign women in Bosnia but provides 80 per cent of the revenue of the men who control them: M. Rees, 'International Intervention in Bosnia-Herzegovina: The Cost of Ignoring Gender', in C. Cockburn and D. Zarkov (eds.), *The Postwar Moment: Militaries, Masculinities and International Peacekeeping, Bosnia and the Netherlands* (London: Lawrence & Wishart, 2002), 63.

[52] *Situation of Human Rights in Bosnia and Herzegovina, the Republic of Croatia and the Federal Republic of Yugoslavia*, Report of the Special Rapporteur on Bosnia and Herzegovina, UN Doc. A/54/396, S/1999/1000, 24 Oct. 1999, para. 37.

[53] Rees, 'International Intervention in Bosnia-Herzegovina', 65.

[54] See W. Maley, 'The UN and East Timor', *Pacifica Review*, 12 (2000), 63; C. Chinkin, 'East Timor: A Failure of Decolonisation', *Australian Yearbook of International Law*, 20 (2000), 1.

Indonesia and 21.5 per cent in favour. The announcement of the referendum outcome was met with great violence by opponents of independence. At least 600 people died and many more were attacked in the violence. Local and foreign UN staff were killed. Most of the buildings and much of the infrastructure in Dili, the capital, were destroyed. Prior to the referendum there were 880,000 people living in East Timor. Seven hundred and fifty thousand people were displaced from their homes or became refugees in West Timor during the violence immediately after the independence vote.[55]

A UN force, International Force East Timor (INTERFET), was eventually deployed in September after Indonesia was pressured to agree, to prevent further violence.[56] The UN Security Council decided on 25 October 1999 to extend the peacekeeping role of the international community in East Timor to the formation and operation of a transitional government.[57] The Security Council created the United Nations Transitional Administration in East Timor (UNTAET), granting it 'overall responsibility for the administration of East Timor', which involved 'legislative and executive authority, including the administration of justice'.[58] UNTAET's mandate was, among other things, to 'provide security and maintain law and order' throughout East Timor; to 'support capacity for self-government'; and to 'assist in the establishment of conditions for sustainable development'.[59]

The Special Representative of the UN Secretary-General, also known as the Transitional Administrator, had plenary powers in the UNTAET era.[60] A Brazilian UN official, Sergio Viera de Mello, was appointed to this position. The Transitional Administrator established a fifteen-member National Consultative Council of East Timorese and UN officials to assist him. From August 2000 he delegated part of his executive power to an appointed nine-member Cabinet of East Timorese leaders and international experts.[61] He consulted on legislative matters with a thirty-three-member all-East Timorese legislative body called the National Council.[62] A transitional government was appointed by the Administrator. An eighty-eight-member Constituent Assembly was elected in August 2001 to draft a constitution, which was finally adopted on 22 March 2002 and entered into force on 20 May 2002. Presidential elections were held in April 2002 with Xanana Gusmão, the former leader of the resistance movement Fretilin, elected with a huge popular vote.

The international management of the transition of East Timor from ravaged territory to new state has been hailed as a great success story. The UN's role in East Timor illustrates, however, some of the tensions created by international regulation.

---

[55] J.-C. Cady, 'Building the New State of East Timor', lecture given on 18 May 2000 at the Centre for International and Public Law, Faculty of Law, Australian National University http://www.anu.edu.au/law/cipl.   [56] Security Council Resolution 1264, 15 Sept. 1999.
[57] Security Council Resolution 1272, 25 Oct. 1999.   [58] Ibid.   [59] Ibid., para. 2.
[60] UNTAET/REG/1999/1.   [61] UNTAET/REG/2000/23, 14 July 2000.
[62] UNTAET/REG/2000/22; UNTAET/REG/2000/24.

UNTAET was established under Chapter VII of the UN Charter as a response to threats to international peace and security. Although UNTAET was thus a peacekeeping mission, Resolution 1272 gave UNTAET very broad powers effectively to govern East Timor and to build a capacity for self-governance. Issues such as whether UNTAET personnel should be able to claim immunities from local laws, particularly criminal and taxation laws, caused problems.[63] There was also an inevitable tension in giving UNTAET virtually plenary power over the transition process when the object of that process was to hand governmental control to the East Timorese.[64] The task required a delicate balance between imposing international standards and acknowledging the local historical and political context.

A significant problem faced by the UN's regulatory activity in East Timor was the situation of women.[65] Women had suffered considerable harassment and violence during the Indonesian occupation. Fokupers, an East Timorese women's NGO established in 1998, has documented the sexual violence in September 1999. It found that most of the rapes that occurred in the twelve days between the vote and the arrival of INTERFET were committed by members of the anti-independence militia groups, which were largely composed of East Timorese men. There were also allegations that UN peacekeeping forces were responsible for sexual abuse inflicted on some women who live in isolation on the western borders of East Timor.[66] Responses to violence have dominated the agenda of most East Timorese women activists in the country's UNTAET era. Dealing with the psychological effects of violence remains the focus of most collective women's efforts.

At first sight, UNTAET is an example of women's rights-sensitive nation-building. In establishing UNTAET, the Security Council emphasized the 'importance of including in UNTAET personnel with appropriate training in international humanitarian, human rights and refugee law, including child and gender related provisions'.[67] This was the first such reference in the mandate of a comparable body and was consistent with the UN's commitment to 'mainstreaming' gender perspectives in peace operations.[68] The language of gender-mainstreaming has become prevalent within the UN system.[69] The UN

---

[63] J. Morrow and R. White, 'The United Nations in East Timor: International Standards and the Reality of Governance', *Australian Yearbook of International Law*, 22 (2002), 1.   [64] Ibid.

[65] For a more detailed account of this issue, see H. Charlesworth and M. Wood, 'Women and Human Rights in the Rebuilding of East Timor', *Nordic Journal of International Law*, 71 (2002), 325. Much of the information used in this section is drawn from this paper.

[66] See M. O'Kane, 'Return of the Revolutionaries', *The Guardian*, 15 Jan. 2001.

[67] Security Council Resolution 1272, on the Situation in East Timor, UN Doc. S/RES/1272, 1999, para. 15.

[68] See 'The Namibia Plan of Action on "Mainstreaming a Gender Perspective in Multidimensional Peace Support Operations" ', Windhoek, Namibia, 31 May 2000 http://www.reliefweb.int/library/GHARkit/FilesFeb2001/windhoek_declaration.htm.

[69] e.g. Report of the Secretary-General, *Integration of the Human Rights of Women and the Gender Perspective*, UN Doc. E/CN.4/2000/67, 21 Dec. 1999.

Economic and Social Committee has defined the mainstreaming of a gender perspective as

the process of assessing the implications for women and men of any planned action, including legislation, policies and programmes, in all areas and at all levels. It is a strategy for making women's as well as men's concerns and experiences an integral dimension of the design, implementation, monitoring and evaluation of policies and programmes in all political, economic and societal spheres so that women and men benefit equally and inequality is not perpetuated. The ultimate goal is to achieve gender equality.[70]

Field offices are now encouraged to address particular gender issues or to provide training. However, the United Nations Interim Administration Mission in Kosovo (UNMIK) was the first peacekeeping mission to have an administrative unit dedicated to gender issues.[71]

A proposal for an administrative unit devoted exclusively to gender issues was included in the original structure proposed for the UNTAET in November 1999 but it was not implemented because of budget priorities. The Gender Affairs Unit (GAU) was ultimately reinstated in April 2000 after pressure from senior women within the UN. The quest to establish a gender unit within the corporate structure of UNMIK and UNTAET was a difficult task in both cases. In addition to the absence of institutional precedents, the lack of consistent support for and interest in East Timorese women's concerns by senior UNTAET managers led to the formulation of the GAU's mandate in an ad hoc way and ineffective publicity was given to it.

The initial abandonment of the proposal for a gender unit, however, affected the type of GAU that was ultimately established. Funding that had been allocated for the payment of gender affairs officers was redistributed, and no programme or operational budget was created even when the GAU was reinstated.

The main changes sought by East Timorese women activists in the UNTAET era were relatively modest. They focused on the high rate of female illiteracy (85 per cent), the absence of women in public life, and the issue of violence against women. Advocacy of women's issues was within the context of a deeply Catholic society. Observers of women's participation in political and economic activities in the context of conflict and post-conflict societies suggest that traditional law and indigenous practices that disadvantage women find practical affirmation and reinforcement not only in religious conservatism but also in patriotic expressions of cultural pride by male leaders.[72] This phenomenon is

---

[70] UN Doc. E/1997/L.30, A/52/3/Rev.1, ch. 4.

[71] For an analysis of the successes and failures of UNMIK to enhance the lives and opportunities of Kosovar women up until June 2000, see C. Corrin, 'Gender Audit of Reconstruction Programmes in South Eastern Europe', June 2000 http://www.bndlg.de/~wplarre/GENDER-AUDIT-OF-RECONSTRUCTION-PROGRAMMES-ccGAudit.htm; Kvinna Till Kvinna, *Getting it Right? A Gender Approach to UNMIK Administration in Kosovo* (2002) http://www.iktk.se/english/index.html.

[72] See H. Wallace, 'Gender and the Reform Process in Vanuatu and Solomon Islands', *Development Bulletin*, 51 (2000), 23; S. Mitchell, 'Women in Leadership in Vietnam', *Development Bulletin*, 51 (2000), 30; A. Hellum, 'Human Rights and Gender Relations in Postcolonial Africa: Options and Limits for the Subjects of Legal Pluralism', *Law and Social Inquiry*, 25 (2000), 635.

evident in East Timor, and is mixed with an ambivalent attitude to the UN's presence, combining gratitude and resentment.[73] Thus, in his 2001 New Year's speech to the nation Xanana Gusmão criticized the

> obsessive acculturation to standards that hundreds of international experts try to convey to the East Timorese, who are hungry for values:
>
> - democracy (many of those who teach us never practised it in their own countries because they became UN staff members) . . .
> - gender (many of the women who attend the workshops know that in their countries this issue is no example for others).

He went on:

> It might sound as though I am speaking against these noble values of participation. I do not mind if it happens in the democratic minds of the people. What seems to be absurd is that we absorb standards just to pretend we look like a democratic society and please our masters of independence. What concerns me is the non-critical absorption of (universal) standards . . . [and] that the East Timorese may become detached from their reality and, above all, try to copy something which is not yet clearly understood by them.

Gusmão acknowledged that some of the 'standards' that UNTAET aspired to include in law and administrative practice in East Timor were universal in the sense that they are recognized as such in international law. However, he implied that the standards relating to the rights of women, particularly the right of women to determine their own lives, did not find natural affinity or reflection in East Timorese culture. Gusmão regarded these standards as difficult to absorb locally. He also suggested that the values and the process by which international standards, especially with respect to women's human rights, were being introduced into East Timorese society were beset by strong elements of colonial hypocrisy among the international workers, and unthinking receptiveness by some East Timorese.

There are, however, examples of traditional practices that have been specifically identified and rejected by East Timorese women. For instance, a report publishing the findings of a workshop in Dili organized by Fokupers and the Sahe Institute for Liberation in 2000 describes the institution of *barlaque* (bride price) as oppressive, at least in the current form that it is practised.[74] The report claims that what is now a range of discriminatory practices resulting in married women being

---

[73] One observer noted of East Timor in the UNTAET era: 'The UN presence is huge, like an army of occupation. Watch you don't get squashed by one of the countless UN vehicles while gawking at the massive floating hotel Olympia moored by the deck at the city's [Dili's] heart . . . At the weekend, all the *malai* (foreigners) head for the beach. There you can stand up to your neck in the tepid sea and engage Thai colonels, Swiss economists, globetrotting NGO adventurers, or activists from East Timor's gutsy Yayasan Hak human rights organisation in polite conversation about crocodiles. The locals avert their embarrassed eyes at white flesh in Speedos, and sell beers and Coke from pedicabs': P. Nicholson, 'Goodwill Hunting', *Weekend Australian*, 9–10 Dec. 2000, 28.

[74] Report of 'Women's Liberation in the Process of *Ukun Rasik An* (Self-Government)', workshop held in Dili, 10–11 Feb. 2000.

treated as chattels was once a simpler practice involving a reciprocal exchange of gifts between families.

Gusmão's approach can be contrasted with that of Milena Pires, deputy speaker of the National Council and an active member of the Timorese diaspora in London before she returned to East Timor in 2000. Pires described the common phenomenon whereby men's pride in traditional culture is combined with religiously based social conservatism:

cultural discourse is invoked frequently to quash attempts to introduce discussions on women's rights into the East Timorese political equation. The incompatibility between East Timorese culture and what is popularly cited as a western feminist imposition is used to dismiss even the notion that Timorese women's rights may need to be nurtured and defended so as to become a reality. Undermining the importance of women's human rights because it only considers half of the East Timorese population is another argument put forward to prevent its elaboration.[75]

The arguments Pires describes have been invoked in the context of various proposals to boost the political representation of women in East Timor. For example, a public debate about quotas for women in political positions was ignited by a proposal emanating from a women's NGO, REDE, to entrench a requirement for political parties to field women in at least 30 per cent of their nominated representative positions for election to the Constituent Assembly. Some influential UNTAET officers were very negative about the proposal, arguing that quotas infringed the concept of free and fair elections.[76] The proposal was ultimately defeated in the National Council in March 2001, although in the end 27 per cent of the seats in the Constituent Assembly were held by women.

East Timorese women have expressed frustration at the preoccupation of international organizations and media with the prominence of certain East Timorese women in the various consultative bodies established by UNTAET. They argue that East Timorese women's leadership was conceived by foreigners and by some returned members of the diaspora in excessively narrow terms. The international community regarded leaders as women who were elected to parliament or appointed to decision-making bodies. Some East Timorese women did not see the *number* of women in representative or governmental positions as a significant indicator of women's empowerment, although the National Council rejection of REDE's quota proposal in elections for the Constituent Assembly was regarded with great disappointment.

Women's groups in East Timor were active in the constitution-making process. A Gender and Constitutional Working Group prepared a Charter for Women's Rights based on broad community consultation.[77] The Charter sought

---

[75] Paper presented to the CNRT (National Council of Timorese Resistance) Conference on a Strategic Development Plan for East Timor, Aug. 2000.

[76] Morrow and White, 'The United Nations in East Timor'.

[77] See M. A. Pereira, *Oxfam Community Aid Abroad, Gender and Constitution Working Group* http://www.caa.org.au/world/asia/east_timor/women.html. The Charter appears in *La'O Hamutuk Bulletin*, 2/5 (Aug. 2001) http://www.etan.org/lh/bulletins/bulletinv2n5.html.

the prohibition of all forms of discrimination and the adoption of positive measures to promote equality. It demanded the protection of women's right to live free from any form of violence, both public and private, and regulation of the dowry system to prevent violence against women. The Charter also sought a guarantee of women's participation in traditional decision-making processes.

The Constitution contains some traces of the Charter's provisions. For example, section 37 allows police to enter homes during the night, uninvited, if they believe that there is a serious threat to life or physical integrity. This provision responds to women's concern over the high incidence of domestic violence. The Constitution also refers to non-discrimination on the basis of gender in access to political positions.[78] Many East Timorese women, however, were disappointed with the minimal impact they had on drafting the Constitution and have been critical of UNTAET and the National Council for sidelining their concerns.

The GAU established by UNTAET made some useful initiatives. For example, it organized the collection of gender-sensitive data across East Timor and its collation into statistical form for evaluation; the analysis of regulations proposed by UNTAET for their responsiveness to women's needs and interests; the convening of a group of East Timorese women to discuss proposed UNTAET regulations and the gender issues they raise; the organization of activities in East Timor to commemorate the international observance of sixteen days of activism against gender violence; the publication and distribution of a 'Gender News' bulletin to different sections of UNTAET and to NGOs in Dili; and the establishment of Gender Focal Point officers in some districts of the country.

Overall, however, UNTAET's achievements relating to gender appear to be largely the product of uncoordinated pressures. Although there was implicit recognition in various public statements made by the Transitional Administrator that East Timorese men and women had quite different experiences under the Indonesian regime, and that gender is a significant factor affecting their opportunities in the transitional and independence eras, this was not reflected in resource or management terms.

In the UNTAET era violence against women by male family members was estimated to constitute 40 per cent of all offences committed in East Timor during the year 2000.[79] One explanation for this high rate of domestic violence was the unemployment rate of 80 per cent in urban areas. The long-term economic, social, and physical consequences of severe violence were largely ignored by UNTAET, whose major priority was the construction of public administration and governance units.

The employment of women in UNTAET also suggests a failure in planning and execution. A directive issued from the Transitional Administrator on

---

[78] S. 63.   [79] See M. O'Kane, 'Return of the Revolutionaries', *The Guardian*, 15 Jan. 2001.

7 September 2000, after intense lobbying by REDE, stated that

a minimum of all national and district hiring shall comprise 30% women within every classification/level of employment. Where there are two candidates (male and female) of equal merit, priority will be given to the female candidate; indeed, we shall set as a target gender balance within all hiring. Training shall be given to women on a priority basis.[80]

At 31 January 2001, 33 per cent of the international civilian officials working for UNTAET were women but women comprised only 11 per cent of the UNTAET East Timorese staff. Women were represented in even lower numbers in the civilian police and peacekeeping force in East Timor, composing 4 per cent and 2.4 per cent respectively. The majority of people employed by the GAU (a total of six) were foreigners, newcomers to East Timorese culture and social conditions.

Other criticisms of UNTAET and the GAU by East Timorese women include the failure to produce a clear definition of gender mainstreaming and its subjects. It was unclear whether gender mainstreaming was aimed at UNTAET international workers, or East Timorese women, or East Timorese people in general. This led to misunderstandings about the practical and ethical basis of sex equality rhetoric in the UNTAET mission. There was a gulf between the expectations of the transitional administration and East Timorese people. Many women thought the GAU should offer practical solutions such as counselling to alleviate women's emotional distress, anti-violence education seminars, and money to assist women's NGOs to implement their own agendas.

The UN officially endorses women's ability 'to take their rightful and equal place at the decision-making table in questions of peace and security'.[81] The case of East Timor in the UNTAET era illustrates, however, the complexity of translation of worthy public statements about the equality of women. UNTAET's GAU had an uncertain and little-known mandate. Its funding was constantly being renegotiated. It tended to be marginalized and was without proper institutional support. Language and cultural barriers arose between local women's groups and the GAU. There was little evidence of attention to gender issues outside the small GAU office.

A basic issue arising from the inclusion of gender as the basis for an administrative unit is how it should tackle culturally specific social constructions of gender. In East Timor gender roles assigning men to a public world of politics and employment and women to a private world of home and family pervade social and economic relations. They are supported by religious doctrine, low levels of education, and traditional practices. The most significant counterpressure was the persistence of particular East Timorese women's groups and individuals within UNTAET in using international and local networks to pressure UNTAET to take East Timorese women's concerns seriously.

---

[80] UNTAET internal memo, 7 Sept. 2000, sent to all Cabinet ministers, heads of departments, district administrators, and Chair of the Public Service Commission.
[81] K. Annan, *Secretary-General Calls for Council Action to Ensure Women are Involved in Peace and Security Decisions*, statement at the 4208th meeting of the Security Council, UN Doc. SG/SM/7598, 24 Oct. 2000.

CONCLUDING COMMENTS

International regulation of societies in crisis, while a modest public relations success, has not been well designed from the perspective of regulatory theory. International law imagined its task as the transposition of international standards to transform local chaos, although in neither of the case studies has this been achieved. International regulation in Bosnia-Hercegovina and East Timor suggests a dissonance between the way that international agencies conceive their role as regulators and the experience of those roles by the local participants. Contrary to Hugh Collins's observations with respect to contract law, the apparent objects of the regulatory activity had little impact on the regulatory scheme.

The problems identified by Teubner's 'regulatory trilemma' (effectiveness, responsiveness, coherence[82]) are evident in the case studies, which also show the overlapping of these criteria. Firstly, post-conflict international regulation can be of limited effectiveness. One reason for this is inherent in the project of Western-influenced international institutions intervening in impoverished and chaotic local situations. International regulation is not ideologically neutral but is committed, at least rhetorically, to the supposed universal values of democracy, human rights, and the rule of law. These are considered the bases for a stable economic environment committed to free market principles and foreign investment. The essence of nation-building is the creation of a public and sustainable infrastructure of governance and local capacity-building. This requires micro-management by a range of international actors for an indeterminate period of time. There is likely to be tension between the goals of handing over to a local leadership as speedily as possible, and ensuring that that leadership has sufficient experience to ensure the long-term stability to achieve the prescribed objectives. International regulation in Bosnia-Hercegovina has now lasted for eight years, which has fostered dependency and created further problems for withdrawal. Unemployment is still high and economic and legal stability remain elusive. In East Timor the handover to the local but inexperienced leadership took place after less than three years. Institutional capacity-building—looking long-term— is not necessarily compatible with short-term regulation.

Secondly, international territorial administration of 'failed' territories can appear as a 'civilizing' mission to reconstruct those territories according to the practices and values of the international community, and thus is not always responsive to those of the targets of regulation.[83] This may have resonance in the context of law-making, as international norms have to be incorporated into domestic law and there may be conflict between the two. The Constitution of

---

[82] G. Teubner, 'Juridification: Concepts, Aspects, Limits, Solutions', in Teubner (ed.), *Juridification of Social Spheres: A Comparative Analysis in the Areas of Labor, Corporate, Antitrust, and Social Welfare Law* (New York: Walter de Gruyter, 1987), 3.

[83] C. Parker and J. Braithwaite, 'Regulation', in P. Cane and M. Tushnet (eds.), *Oxford Handbook of Legal Studies* (Oxford: Oxford University Press, 2003), 128.

Bosnia-Hercegovina was negotiated at Dayton and was submitted to the national parliament for adoption. There was no consultation with or participation by local people, nor any examination as to how far the Constitution conformed with their values and expectations. It was not even written in the local language. It is, therefore, difficult to know what expectations local people had either of the international administration or of their new Constitution. The OHR has both made law and applied it, which has caused tension when it conflicts with the wishes of local authorities. Michael Chossudovsky has commented that 'One cannot sidestep the fundamental question: is the Bosnian Constitution formally agreed between heads of State at Dayton really a constitution? . . . There is no constitutional assembly, there are no consultations with citizens' organisations in Bosnia and Hercegovina, and there are to be no "constitutional amendments".'[84] In East Timor international practices ranging from the bureaucratic (such as the tax-free salaries of UN workers) to the normative (such as the commitment to international human rights standards) were at odds with the values of sections of the East Timorese leadership and community.[85] Much of the international regulation was not, in Cotterrell's words, 'deeply rooted in social and cultural life'.[86] This led to disagreement with the international regulators in drafting the Constitution. International regulators have to maintain a balance between becoming too distant from local concerns and becoming embroiled in local politics and disputes. It has been argued that UNTAET was most successful in negotiating the fine line between the imposition of international standards and recognizing the local context when it saw capacity-building as requiring a dialogue between international principles and East Timorese culture, rather than an imposition of international benchmarks.[87] However, this claim raises the question of the content of 'East Timorese culture' being invoked: whose culture was at stake?

Thirdly, the relationship between regulatory standards and local traditions can lead to an incoherent analytic framework. The international agencies' mandate rests upon the negotiated agreement (the GFA) or Security Council resolution (UNTAET). In both cases these top-down mandates cannot detail all aspects of regulation but, rather, set the ground rules for implementation by the relevant international agencies. Indeed, international standards are mediated through the designated international authorities, the international and national agencies responsible for implementation across diverse local communities. Local people—the supposed beneficiaries of all this regulatory activity—tend to be involved in the evolution of rules in only the most minimal way.

While these layers of regulation have the benefit of flexibility and allow for responsiveness to local conditions, in practice the mandates are open to diverse interpretations giving a great deal of discretion to those working on the ground.

---

[84] Chossudovsky, 'Dismantling Former Yugoslavia', 43.
[85] Morrow and White, 'The United Nations in East Timor'.
[86] Quoted in Parker and Braithwaite, 'Regulation', 128.
[87] Morrow and White, 'The United Nations in East Timor'.

For example, the East Timorese Constitution's broad promises of protection of human rights and freedoms were left for enforcement to a readily subverted bureaucratic procedure.[88] The range of international institutions with diverse agendas, working methods, and experience requires effective communication and coordination, which may not be forthcoming. Institutional 'turf protection' may also impede cooperation between agencies. Changed priorities among the regulators may cause shifting objectives. In Bosnia-Hercegovina the government has found itself caught between the internationally created institutions, such as the Human Rights Chamber, and the heightened security concerns of the United States represented through the international regulators. Further, each international agency comprises personnel from different backgrounds and levels of experience that may cause tension between them. For example, peacekeepers and civilian police forces from different countries are likely to have received differing levels of sex and gender awareness training, and may not all share the goals of women's equality and empowerment. This can lead to inconsistent observance of stated norms of behaviour.

There are other observations that can be made when looking at the case studies through the lens of international regulation. There is no template for international regulation of territory. There have been ad hoc responses to events in Cambodia, Bosnia-Hercegovina, Kosovo, and East Timor resulting in the imposition of international agencies in diverse circumstances. Major tensions emerge. On the one hand, there is the need to adjust the mandate to the particular context; on the other, there has been a tendency to replicate the model across all relevant situations. A cadre of international specialists in reconstruction has developed, moving quickly from one trouble spot to another. Short-term appointments are the norm and tasks are not always completed. This prevents the development of institutional memory and best practice. Ad hoc, personal precedents develop in the community of nation-building bureaucrats. The brevity of the contracts also impedes the formation of long-term relationships with the people of the territory and develops the impression of an impersonal international regulatory body only present in a territory until the next emergency requires them to move on. Where there is a longer-term commitment there can be greater coherence between the international agencies and local bodies as has occurred with the development of an integrated anti-trafficking strategy in Bosnia-Hercegovina. Another factor is the willingness of the international community properly to resource international regulation; grand plans agreed in New York acquire political capital but may be frustrated by lack of economic commitment, as illustrated by the delay in the establishment of the GAU in East Timor.

It may be argued that the context of the case studies—local crisis and state-building—is too particularized to draw any general conclusions about international legal regulation in more routine cases. Certainly, other areas of

---

[88] East Timor Constitution.

international regulation do not require the intensive 'hands-on' daily intervention of territorial regulation, but rely on such methods as periodic review and
technical assistance. Nevertheless, a dichotomy between 'crisis' and 'routine'
seems misplaced. International regulation of territory is itself becoming more
regular and routine situations throw up crises and emergencies. For example,
there is a detailed legal regime for the law of the sea.[89] This also requires the
interplay between international regulation and application within domestic law
involving a range of domestic and international agencies. Disputes over fishing,
marine pollution, or overflight[90] belie any assumption of uncontested application of the international regulations, while at the same time much of the daily
international administration of territory is routinely observed.

Typically, international regulatory regimes are created by a multilateral treaty
that sets up an organizing and monitoring INGO. But other existing norms of
international and national law interface with those of the regulatory framework,
for example, the human rights objectives within the regulated territory may conflict with the perceived dictates of international and national security. Another
type of interface is between international and domestic law. International norms
must be incorporated into national law and are applied by a mix of international
and national agencies. Multilateral regimes may also be supplemented by a
network of bilateral agreements determining the operational standards as
between two states.[91] Bilateral agreements may indeed undermine the international regime. For example, the United States has refused to participate in the
International Criminal Court[92] and has entered into bilateral agreements under
Article 98(2) of the Court's Statute to prevent surrender of its citizens to the
Court. This situation highlights the current reality that effective international
regulation is affected by the attitude of the United States.[93] The outcome of negotiations for an international regulatory regime may be largely dictated by US
policy, but frustrated by its eventual unwillingness to participate.[94]

---

[89] UN Convention on the Law of the Sea, 10 Dec. 1982.

[90] e.g. 'The UN says more than a hundred countries are involved in fishing disputes . . .': F. Jonathan,
'Rivalries Grow for Global Fishers as Fleets Expand and Hauls Wane', *Wall Street Journal Interactive*,
25 Feb. 1997 http://zia.hss.cmu.edu/miller/eep/news/fish2.ext.txt; *The Mox Plant Case* (*Ireland v
United Kingdom*, The Hague, 2003) illustrates an inter-state dispute about the national implementation of international environmental standards; available at http://www.pca-cpa.org/ENGLISH/RPC/
#Ireland%20v.%20United%20Kingdom%20("MOX%20Plant%20Case").

[91] For example, the Chicago Convention on Civil Aviation, 7 Dec. 1944, has been supplemented
by numerous bilateral air services agreements.

[92] The International Criminal Court was established under the Rome Statute of the International
Criminal Court, Rome, 17 July 1998.

[93] For example, effective international regulation of climate change is undermined by the refusal
of the United States (and Australia) to become parties to the Kyoto Protocol to the United Nations
Framework Convention on Climate Change, 11 Dec. 1997.

[94] e.g. US participation in the negotiations for the United Nations Convention on the Law of the Sea,
1982. Attempts to facilitate the United States and other industrialized states becoming bound by
the Convention resulted in the Agreement relating to the Implementation of Part XI of the United
Nations Convention on the Law of the Sea of 10 Dec. 1982, which significantly amended the original
Convention. While other states then became parties, the United States has still failed to do so.

International regulation is conceived at the highest level, for example, through treaty-making or Security Council resolution. The legal framework is operationally dependent upon political decision-making. As we have seen, it is implemented by a range of international agencies, both governmental and non-governmental, and local personnel who are far from the original decision-making. Not surprisingly, international regulation can lead to some unintended consequences. For example, the import of large numbers of international personnel distorts the local economy and exacerbates local unemployment at a time when restructuring of the labour market is essential. Resentment can be caused by what appears excessive attention to the accommodation and well-being of the internationals, rather than to reconstruction of local services. The infusion of a large number of mainly unaccompanied men with hard currency has also fuelled sexual abuse and trafficking, as in Cambodia, Bosnia-Hercegovina, and Kosovo.

A final observation is that the public nature of international administrations has also allowed gaps to be identified and pressure for change to be generated at the international level. For example, sex and gender issues did not figure at all in the institutional arrangements in Bosnia-Hercegovina determined at Dayton, leaving particular committed individuals to fill this vacuum. The failure to address sex and gender in the Dayton mandate caused sufficient criticism that an administrative unit dedicated to gender issues was set up first in Kosovo and subsequently in East Timor. But the existence of a gender bureaucracy did not affect the resolution of concerns such as whether there should be quotas for women in political bodies: thus, the Bosnian Electoral Law provides a quota system for women electoral candidates while this could not be achieved in East Timor. At the same time, the larger issue of the sexed and gendered dimensions of structures of regulation remains: who are the regulators; who regulates the regulators? Does regulation affect women and men differently? What gendered patterns of life, work, and politics does regulation support?

Conclusion

JOHN BRAITHWAITE and CHRISTINE PARKER

Introduction

The Introduction to this volume asked if it might be productive to study law as something that both regulates and is regulated. Centuries ago in the common law world, law did not touch as many spheres of life as it does today. There was no corporations law, little financial law, no income tax law, virtually no intellectual property or competition law, little administrative law, tort had yet to be clearly differentiated from criminal law, and an International Criminal Court would have seemed a bizarre notion. While the spread of the institutional reach of law is a centuries-long process, advocates of deregulation accurately point out that most of the exponential growth in the number of pages of law in existence has occurred since 1970, indeed since 1990 in some nations.[1] Even with contemporary developments in labour law, said to be about 'deregulation', Richard Johnstone and Richard Mitchell in Chapter 5 point out that the moves in some countries towards more market-based labour arrangements have required an increase in the quantity of labour law. With labour law, as with competition law in many nations, what we see is legally regulated marketization.[2] Our chapters have touched on many of the different ways that the reach of law has expanded in modern history.

In addition, today we see legal missionaries from the developed economies, supported by institutions like the International Monetary Fund (IMF) and the World Bank, pushing developing countries to acquire a 'rule of law' as one of the 'good governance' essentials for their development. Intellectual property lawyers

---

[1] The Australian case illustrates. In 2002 the Commonwealth Attorney-General's Department estimated there were 1,800 Commonwealth Acts in force; 170 of these were promulgated in 2001, 148 in 2002. But, more tellingly, the number of rules per Act, the complexity and length of Acts, is increasing. For the 1990s the number of pages of law per Act was twice the number for the 1980s and three times the quantity for the 1970s: S. Argy, *Mechanisms for Improving the Quality of Regulations: Australia in an International Context* (Canberra: Productivity Commission, 2003). Tax law is probably the most extreme example, which has grown twenty-seven-fold in its pages of law since 1970 according to Michael Inglis: 'Why we Urgently Need a Proper, Working Systemic Model for the Australian Federal Tax System', Paper presented to Centre for Tax System Integrity, Australian National University, Canberra Sept. 2003. Moreover, it is post-1970s rules in commercial areas such as tax and corporations law that account for the largest part of the growth in litigation. The most dramatic growth in a single locus of litigation has been the use by business litigants of the 1974 Trade Practices Act, Australia's competition and consumer protection law. Globally, growth in the quantity of the latter kind of law has also been from a zero base in most countries, substantial and even more recent than in Australia. Most of the world's nations now have competition laws and competition enforcement agencies. Most have acquired them since 1990: CUTS Centre for Competition, Investment, and Economic Regulation, 'The Role of International Cooperation in Building an Effective Competition Regime', *CUTS Newsletter*, 6/2003, 1.

[2] Maher, Ch. 9 in this volume.

head south and east with Western intellectual property statutes tucked in their suitcases, tax lawyers with Western tax codes in theirs. Some of this missionary work is motivated by a desire to spread justice ideals, but mostly it is explicitly funded to help developing countries regulate their societies in ways that will promote economic growth, either for themselves, or for the developed economies that are 'helping' them. That there has been an empirical proliferation of law across time and space motivated by regulatory objectives and sharp growth in the number of regulatory agencies is beyond question.[3] Whether a regulatory lens for viewing the whole of law is genuinely distinctive and revealing, and whether it is normatively desirable for law, in all its range, to be viewed as primarily a regulatory institution, are both very much in question in this volume. In this concluding chapter we will come to reconsider law, in light of some of the insights in our chapters, as in some ways a 'meta-regulator', a regulator of other (non-legal and quasi-legal) forms of regulation in society. In this conception, law is just one strand, albeit a particularly significant one, in a web of regulatory institutions that regulate one another to greater or lesser degrees. Firstly, we will examine the growth of other mechanisms and institutions of regulation as something that sets up this meta-regulatory web.

LEGAL AND REGULATORY PLURALISM

In Chapter 11, 'Regulating Constitutions', Colin Scott argues that while political science increasingly assumes a pluralist structure of political power, legal research clings more tenaciously to a strong notion of sovereignty 'vested variously in the legislature or in the legislative, executive, and judicial branches of government'.[4] Regulatory scholarship, in the political science governance[5] or Foucauldian governmentality traditions,[6] is less wedded than legal scholarship to hierarchical visions of order as handed down from legislatures and implemented by judiciaries, and favours more heterarchical conceptions of control.[7] For example, Scott illustrates how constitutions work more by conventions

---

[3] J. Jordana and D. Levi-Faur, 'The Rise of the Regulatory State in Latin America: A Study of the Diffusion of Regulatory Reforms across Countries and Sectors', Paper presented to the Annual Meeting of the American Political Science Association, 28 Aug.–2 Sept. 2003.

[4] Ch. 11 in this volume, p. 227.

[5] 'It takes a society to run a society': K. Webb, 'Sustainable Governance in the 21st Century: Moving beyond Instrument Choice', in P. Eliadis, M. Hill, and M. Howlett (eds.), *From Instrument Choice to Governance: Future Directions for the Choice of Governing Instrument* (Montreal: McGill-Queen's University Press, forthcoming). See also M. Bevir and R. Rhodes, *Interpreting British Governance* (London: Routledge, 2003), and R. Rhodes, *Understanding Governance* (Buckingham: Open University Press, 1997).

[6] G. Burchall, C. Gordon, and P. Miller (eds.), *The Foucault Effect: Studies in Governmentality* (London: Harvester Wheatsheaf, 1991); D. Garland, '"Governmentality" and the Problem of Crime: Foucault, Criminology, Sociology', *Theoretical Criminology*, 1 (1997), 173.

[7] J. Black, 'Decentring Regulation: Understanding the Role of Regulation and Self-regulation in a Post-regulating World', *Current Legal Problems*, 54 (2001), 103.

enforced by community opinion from below than by formal law enforced by courts with constitutional jurisdiction. He also points out how international (or supranational) governmental organizations are important enforcers from above of national constitutional norms. To make the picture even more richly plural, Scott shows that horizontal self-regulation of constitutional compliance by the legislature of the legislature (through the variety of mechanisms for review of bills to audit compliance with human rights and other constitutional obligations) is important, and has been for many years. In Chapter 12, Hilary Charlesworth and Christine Chinkin paint a complementary picture of an international law where, in terms of compliance, states do not seem to differentiate between non-binding instruments (enforced at most by naming and shaming) and legally binding instruments.

This basis for legal norms and authority is by no means restricted to constitutional and international law. In the context of 'Regulating Families' (Chapter 4), John Dewar recounts the 'norm-form' project. The norm-form project found that the factors most conducive to settlement of legal cases in a number of core legal fields were 'comprehensibility to the lay person and predictability of result to the lawyer'.[8] But there was no evidence that the form of norms, most notably how precisely they were formulated as rules, explained these factors or indeed anything about lawyers' negotiating behaviour. As in Scott's chapter, it turns out that 'Conventions matter more than formally expressed rules.'[9] Even in criminal law, perhaps the paradigm of centralized top-down legal norm creation, Nicola Lacey (Chapter 7) argues that articulation with community norms is a key to legitimacy, with community norms exerting a pull over the enforcement and even interpretation of formal legal norms. The importance of lay comprehensibility and professional predictability underwrote the take-home message of the norm-form project: 'there is a case for assisting parties to bargain in the *light* of the law rather than its shadow'.[10] The challenge is how to craft the relationship between law and conventions so that both lawyers and ordinary citizens do bargain in that light.

Just as the last two centuries have seen an enormous spread in the regulatory relevance of law, so they have seen a proliferation of non-state forms of regulation. The roots of this pluralization of regulation are themselves plural, yet structurally specific, manifestations of late modernity. In parliamentary systems, backbenchers sidelined by growing centralization of power in the prime minister's office fight back with an opportunity to monitor legislative compliance with human rights obligations through a parliamentary committee system. More subordinated levels of government—local government, provincial governments in federal systems—attempt to reassert some of the regulatory prerogatives they may have exercised in the era before strong nation states entered that regulatory domain. The fourth estate also occasionally seizes

---

[8] Dewar, Ch. 4, in this volume, p. 94. Stephen Bottomley, one of the other authors in this collection, was also a participant in the norm-form project. [9] Ibid. 94.
[10] Quoted ibid. 94.

opportunities to assert their relevance to democratic will formation by stirring up community concern about the flouting of conventions by governments, as in the reporting around the Hutton Inquiry, which threatens the future of the Blair government at the time of writing. Globalization animates a diverse array of supranational regulatory institutions. In part as a reaction against both globalization and its nodes of bureaucratic power (such as the World Trade Organization, IMF, and World Bank) and more centralized and remote national political power, non-governmental organizations (NGOs) and social movements strive, with some success, for more regulatory power.[11]

Yet the most powerful reason for the heterarchic pluralization of regulation is more sociologically fundamental: it is the progressively more pluralized division of labour within societies first theorized a century ago by Émile Durkheim.[12] Once a profession like accounting is differentiated in the division of labour, it is inevitable that part of the professional project will be the creation of accounting standards, the mastery of which becomes a precondition ('barrier') to entering the profession. Julia Black's description, in Chapter 2, of the self-regulatory significance in British financial regulation of the London Stock Exchange, the International Swaps and Dealers Association, the International Accounting Standards Committee, the Basel Committee on Banking Supervision, the International Securities Market Association, and the Bond Market Association, among others, is the most variegated illustration in the volume of how a progressively more complex division of labour institutionalizes a progressively more complex range of self-regulatory orders to which the law has little choice but to respond. As law itself becomes historically more professionalized, self-regulation by the legal profession assumes greater significance.[13] As the Civil Service becomes more professionalized, regulation of government by functionaries of government is given a special new significance.[14] So while there are a lot of drivers of the pluralization of regulatory influences beyond formal law, the three more structurally profound ones are an increasingly elaborated division of labour, globalization (transgovernmental networks that cross national boundaries),[15] and the rise of social movement

---

[11] See Charlesworth and Chinkin, Ch. 12 in this volume, on international NGOs; Johnstone and Mitchell, Ch. 5, on unions; Lacey, Ch. 7, on the social movement for restorative justice.

[12] '... since the division of labor becomes the chief source of social solidarity, it becomes, at the same time, the foundation of the moral order': É. Durkheim, *The Division of Labor in Society* (New York: Free Press, 1960), 401.

[13] While barristers self-regulated for centuries in inns of court, solicitors, the lower branch of the profession, only took on self-regulation as they professionalized in the 19th and early 20th centuries: B. Abel-Smith and R. Stevens, *Lawyers and the Courts: A Sociological Study of the English Legal System 1750–1965* (London: Heinemann, 1967); A. Paterson, 'Legal Ethics: Its Nature and Place in the Curriculum', in R. Cranston (ed.), *Legal Ethics and Professional Responsibility* (Oxford: Clarendon Press, 1995), 175.

[14] C. Hood, O. James, G. Jones, and C. Scott, *Regulation inside Government: Waste-Watchers, Quality Police, and Sleazebusters* (Oxford: Oxford University Press, 1999).

[15] A. M. Slaughter, 'The Real New World Order', *Foreign Affairs*, 76 (1997), 183; G. Teubner, ' "Global Bukowina": Legal Pluralism in the World Society', in Teubner (ed.), *Global Law without a State* (Aldershot: Ashgate, 1997).

politics associated with the exponential growth of NGOs, first in the North but more recently in the South.[16]

Noting this growth in the plurality of regulatory actors is not to deny that non-state regulatory actors of great importance have always been with us. Richard Johnstone and Richard Mitchell give a powerful example in the authority of craft guilds to regulate the terms of labour in medieval Europe. Just as this great medieval regulator no longer regulates, so with one of the most powerful of medieval European regulators, the Catholic Church, we also see a sharp decline in regulatory authority. While the long-run historical trend to regulatory growth seems structurally profound, it is not unidirectional or monotonic, and it is riven with contradictions and puzzles.

At the conference where the draft papers for this volume were presented, one of our commentators, David Soskice, attempted to summarize schematically the array of internal and external regulatory influences on the law that he saw instantiated in our essays. These included private ordering that both lobbies governments and generates cases for judges to digest in their interpretation of the common law and statutes. We think it an instructive exercise for readers to attempt to draw their own diagram of this kind. The sheer diversity of types of regulatory influence on the law rendered the diagrammatic summaries of the multiple directions of influence that we attempted to summarize from our essays troublingly complex, yet incomplete. This could lead to a kind of analytic despair: there are now such a vast plurality of actors and regulatory mechanisms influencing such a plurality of private and public regulatory institutions that we see through the regulatory lens many trees without being able to discern the contours of the forest. Our aim in this conclusion is to suggest that the complexity and plurality required need not lead to analytic despair but to possibilities for a more meta-regulatory analysis.

NETWORKED GOVERNANCE IN THE REGULATORY WEB

If we are right that in the twenty-first century we have both a greater quantity of law than ever, and a greater quantity of private ordering by business associations, professions, standards associations, and NGOs than ever—and proliferating interactions between the two—then standing back to view all this complexity from multiple angles is likely to become more fruitful. When we do, we no longer see a simple hierarchy of legislation handed down to be implemented and interpreted by judges, which results in changes of behaviour. But just as it

---

[16] The Commission on Global Governance found that more than 90 per cent of the growth in NGOs between 1909 and 1995 has occurred since 1970, and it was also after 1970 that the proportion of participation accounted for by Asian and African NGOs grew: Commission on Global Governance, *Our Global Neighbourhood: The Report of the Commission on Global Governance* (Oxford: Oxford University Press, 1995), 32–3. See also J. Braithwaite, and P. Drahos, *Global Business Regulation* (Cambridge: Cambridge University Press, 2000), 497–501.

compels us to reject a simple hierarchical story of how the rule of law is potent to change the world, it also requires us to reject the view that law is unimportant. How could we think that when we observe the metaphor of government by contract gripping the imagination of governments? Peter Cane in Chapter 10 has a different legal interpretation of contracting out from that of Hugh Collins. There is debate over the meaning of what is happening but not over the fact that legal ideas are important to big changes we can see happening in the world. Contracting out of services to the public can be seen as resulting in the erosion of public law values, as traditionally public functions are executed in the private sector.[17] Yet Jody Freeman intriguingly sees contracting out as infiltrating public law values into the private sector.[18] Perhaps there is some truth to both ways of seeing—the privatization of the public and the publicization of the private. With the proliferation of hybrid forms of private–public corporate governance, Angus Corbett and Stephen Bottomley's chapter, 'Regulating Corporate Governance' (Chapter 3), certainly enables us to see both a publicization of the private and privatization of the public.

While we are led to reject both the view that law is the centrally dominant regulatory institution and that law is unimportant to regulation that changes the world, in different ways our authors all see law as somewhere in the loop. As in the rather complex flow diagram that David Soskice put up for our consideration in the conference, there are many non-legal forms of ordering shaping outcomes, but law is also of importance in the complex of forces shaping results. We can understand the regulatory project as delineating a web of regulatory controls where different branches of legal institutions are among the strands in the web. Sometimes when we see law as a weak and unimportant regulatory influence that explains little of the variance in outcomes, we will be failing to grasp the fact that the total fabric of the web of private and public controls has quite profound effects, and that law is important in holding that fabric together. Strategic regulatory action that has big effects, according to this model, involves having the wisdom to know which is the right strand to pull at the right moment to tighten the web. And knowing which strands of control when pulled too forcefully will cause the whole web to unravel. In a majority of cases legal strands will not be the most crucial ones which, when tugged, have the biggest effects in either direction. But it would be wrong to conclude from such an empirical observation that the same result would apply if law were not part of the fabric of the web. Again this leads us to the virtues of seeking a holistic understanding of how whole webs of regulatory controls interact. The web metaphor may also help resolve some of the concerns of our contributors over what regulation is. If regulation is the intentional act of seeking to steer the flow of events by intentionally pulling one of the strands in a web of controls, there

---

[17] A similar analysis of the privatization of the public might also be applied to using contractual practices to control relations between different parts of government: see Collins, Ch. 1 in this volume.

[18] J. Freeman, 'Extending Public Law Norms through Privatization', *Harvard Law Review*, 116 (2003), 1285.

is no implication that any or all of the other strands in that web of control are intentional regulatory creations. They might be a common law that has evolved without any coherence of purpose or mute forms of architectural control.[19]

Jane Stapleton, in Chapter 6, on 'Regulating Torts', warns us against going too far with the implications of this kind of analysis: 'judges seem rightly to appreciate that the system is too complex to allow great accuracy about predictions of how a doctrinal shift will work its way through the complex systems in which it is embedded'.[20] John Dewar also warns that empirical studies of family law in action reveal more about unintended than intended consequences.[21] While this is true, it is also the case that empirical socio-legal research is a comparatively recent branch of the social sciences. So it is too early to say how predictive a more mature body of research will become. Hope can be found in the field where there has been the largest public investment for the longest period in testing the effect of regulatory interventions: criminal law. Right through the 1980s it is probably true that most criminologists subscribed to something close to Robert Martinson's famous review of the evidence on the effectiveness of correctional interventions popularized as 'nothing works'.[22] Most of us who work in this field were therefore more interested in persuading courts to do more justice or less injustice in criminal cases than in having them consider how their actions might regulate crime more or less effectively. By the end of the 1990s, however, few criminologists subscribed to the 'nothing works' philosophy. A lot of different kinds of intervention—mediated through hierarchy, community, competition, and design–architecture[23]—had been shown either to work or to be promising, with growing numbers of randomized controlled trials that provided greater assurance of the robustness of effects than multivariate methods in the traditions of econometrics and epidemiology.[24] Moreover, these demonstrated effects were not just about the narrow regulatory objective of reducing crime, but about a plethora of criminal justice objectives like reducing victim fear and emotional distress, reducing cost, and improving perceived procedural fairness.[25]

---

[19] For examples of mute or self-executing forms of architectural control, see L. Lessig, *Code and Other Laws of Cyberspace* (New York: Basic Books, 1999); and C. Shearing and P. Stenning, 'Say "Cheese!": The Disney Order that is not so Mickey Mouse', in Shearing and Stenning (eds.), *Private Policing* (Newbury Park, Calif.: Sage, 1987).

[20] Ch. 6, p. 139. However, also note Stapleton's argument rehearsed below that in some circumstances courts do and should choose to take other regulatory policies and influences into account.

[21] Ch. 4, p. 91.

[22] R. Martinson, 'What Works? Questions and Answers about Prison Reform', *Public Interest* (Spring 1974), 22; D. Lipton, R. Martinson and J. Wilks, *The Effectiveness of Correctional Treatment: A Survey of Treatment Evaluation Studies* (New York: Praeger, 1975).

[23] See Lacey, Ch. 7 in this volume.

[24] L. Sherman, D. Gottfredson, D. MacKenzie, J. Eck, P. Reuter, and S. Bushway, *Preventing Crime: What Works, What Doesn't, What's Promising: A Report to the United States Congress* (Washington: US Department of Justice, 1997).

[25] On reducing victim fear, see H. Strang, *Repair or Revenge: Victims and Restorative Justice* (Oxford: Oxford University Press, 2003). On emotional distress, see B. Winick and D. Wexler (eds.), *Judging in a Therapeutic Key: Therapeutic Jurisprudence and the Courts* (Durham, NC: Carolina Academic Press, 2003). On reducing cost, see J. Braithwaite, *Restorative Justice and Responsive*

This does not change Jane Stapleton's basic point that most of the time judges will and should make doctrinal judgments on doctrinal grounds. But it does suggest that somewhat more frequently, as socio-legal science improves in the decades ahead, judges, and perhaps more significantly other legal actors, will be able to predict the effects of legal change on regulatory outcomes that are mediated through complex chains of non-legal variables. As the body of higher-quality empirical research on the effects of legal interventions grows, it also becomes less possible for lawyers to say: 'Because judges cannot predict the effects of their cumulated decisions, they should stick to what the law is best at: securing legal certainty and procedural fairness.' This will not wash because socio-legal research reveals that staying on a narrowly legalistic path often empirically reduces certainty and procedural fairness in comparison with law that is purposefully open to influence by private ordering.[26] If we do not allow law to be regulated by changes in custom, it can be the more pervasive rule of custom that will generate most certainty, with occasional guerrilla attacks from the law inflicting uncertainty upon the rule of custom. Legal certainty, like any legal outcome, is mediated through a web of non-legal influences. If there is an uncertainty problem, then the only way legal actors can be effective in seeking to remedy it is by working through the webs of controls that matter for that particular outcome.

Indeed Stapleton argues that even though constantly moving complexes of influence may be hard for all actors, including legal ones, to understand and respond to, they can also deliver productive kinds of dynamism and unpre-dictability that we might relish. Stapleton uses the example of the evolution of a 'plethora of schemes that provide compensation for personal injuries ... each respond[ing] in a subtly specific way to different complex sets of concerns'.[27] Hence, for example, 'we might hold a particular view of the role of tort in this area but still be in favour of there being a separate additional no-fault com-pensation scheme in certain limited contexts because the scheme encourages very specific conduct that we believe benefits society as a whole'.[28] Courts may be the primary location for tensions to emerge between the varying, disparate purposes of law (such as in instrumental law set down by legislatures or bureau-cracies) and older legal norms. In webs of regulatory controls, courtrooms may be distinctive nodes where knots are sometimes tied between different strands of the web. What do courts do in practice when confronted with this complexity?

Regulation (New York: Oxford University Press, 2002), 124–5. Just a few years ago, for example, it was not known that randomly assigning youth violence cases to restorative justice conferences, as opposed to criminal trials, could substantially reduce some types of repeat offending, offender fear and emotional distress, and a variety of different forms of procedural fairness in the eyes of victims, offenders, and their families: Braithwaite, *Restorative Justice*, 45–71. On the procedural justice literature, see T. Tyler, *Why People Obey the Law* (New Haven: Yale University Press, 1990); T. Tyler and Y. Huo, *Trust in the Law* (New York: Russell Sage Foundation, 2002).

[26] J. Braithwaite, 'Rules and Principles: A Theory of Legal Certainty', *Australian Journal of Legal Philosophy*, 27 (2002), 47.   [27] Stapleton, Ch. 6 in this volume, p. 140.
[28] Ibid. 140.

According to Stapleton,

Tort courts have always appreciated that their decisions will have larger social impact than merely on the parties. Indeed, they often speculate as to the ways their decisions might impact on the wider world. Sometimes this speculation influences a decision, sometimes it is given no weight, and sometimes a decision is taken despite the acknowledged inevitability that it will have a profoundly unsettling impact on social or regulatory norms. Sometimes the court declines to address an issue that is critical to the decision of how parties respond to the judgment.[29]

Put another way, sometimes courts cut themselves off from outside regulatory influences upon them, deciding to defend the integrity of a branch of the law's subtly specific way of responding to a particular problem. Sometimes courts succeed in coming to terms with the empirical realities of the complex of social forces surrounding the case and then allow the understanding of that complexity to influence the law. Sometimes they try to understand it and give up in the face of the empirical imponderables of doing so. Stapleton implies that courts should leave all of these options open. We are not inclined to disagree.

Stapleton's observations on what courts do, and should do, are of a piece with Les Metcalfe's observations on how executive agencies should plan.[30] He wonders how state plans can work in a world where state policy prerogatives are increasingly usurped by globally networked governance in which business organizations, voluntary standards bodies, professions, international organizations, and NGOs are all increasingly important players. In the mid-twentieth-century world of top-down state power, it made some sense for state agencies to think in terms of strategic plans, indicative planning, five-year plans, and other such dreams of yesteryear. Metcalfe says that in a world of globally networked governance where there are many and different nodes of local and international regulatory influence in the network, states have stopped doing synoptic top-down planning. Yet he says we cannot and must not give up on steering through planning. In a world of networked governance, Metcalfe suggests that each node in the network, including state nodes, must do their strategic planning taking into account the strategic plans of all the other important nodes of governance in the network.[31] Obviously, these have to be more rolling plans than the old five-year plans because they have to be recursively responsive to changes in the plans of other key nodes in the network. If we want to understand how governance changes the world today, the object of study is not so much government plans as the interplay between the plans of state agencies and those of other nodes of governance with some clout. It is less the ideologies of government regulators and more

---

[29] Ibid. pp. 137–138.
[30] L. Metcalfe, 'The Weakest Links: Building Organisational Networks for Multi-Level Regulation', in Organization for Economic Cooperation and Development, *Regulatory Cooperation for an Interdependent World* (Paris: OECD, 1994), 49.
[31] On the idea of nodal governance, see C. Shearing and J. Wood, 'Nodal Governance, Democracy and the New "Denizens": Challenging the Westphalian Ideal', *Journal of Law and Society*, 30 (2003), 400.

those of epistemic communities or regulatory communities[32] that bring together strategic state, business, legal, and NGO actors to share the sensibilities and the practice recipes that Pierre Bourdieu calls the habitus of a field.[33]

Courts obviously have limited capabilities for data-gathering on the plans of other strategic nodes of governance and the havoc this is likely to create for their decisions. This is why, as Julia Black documents in Chapter 2, courts often simply defer to other strategic nodes of governance, such as the accounting rules of professional or industry associations, and the standards of voluntary standard-setting bodies. The limited data-gathering capabilities of courts is also why Jane Stapleton says it can make more sense for them, in the face of interrelationships they do not have the resources to comprehend, to decide certain matters purely in terms of legal doctrines, oblivious to the imponderables. If, in the event, the decision creates havoc because of the way other nodes of governance respond to it, then executive government has better resources for changing legal plans in ways that are responsive and synoptically prudent.[34]

Yet when courts reasonably believe their decision will have large predictable knock-on effects, they sometimes are and sometimes should be responsive to the plans of other nodes of governance.[35] This is possible more often than one might think in the face of the complexity of regulatory pluralism documented in this collection. This is because regulatory influences that are important in some contexts are almost never important in most contexts. Specific international treaties and their secretariats, for example, are potent regulatory influences in some contexts, but in most contexts are so politically and legally impotent that they are safely ignored by judges. As Julia Black points out, justice might occur in many rooms, but most of the rooms are separated from one another for most specific purposes. So while Hugh Collins may have put a persuasive case that private and public law collide to produce a productive disintegration in the realm

---

[32] P. Haas, 'Do Regimes Matter? Epistemic Communities and Mediterranean Pollution Control', *International Organization*, 43 (1989), 377; E. Meidinger, 'Regulatory Culture: A Theoretical Outline', *Law and Policy*, 9 (1987), 365.

[33] P. Bourdieu, *Distinction: A Social Critique of the Judgment of Taste* (Cambridge, Mass.: Harvard University Press, 1984), 169–244; P. Bourdieu and J. Wacquant, *An Invitation to Reflexive Sociology* (Chicago: University of Chicago Press, 1992). One commentator on this paragraph said that economic forecasting is alive and well and seems to be a form of planning. Yes, and it is a form of planning increasingly dependent for its utility on surveys of the plans of a vast plurality of private actors, central banks from states other than that of the state doing the forecasting, and so on.

[34] By 'synoptically prudent', we mean taking account of a general survey of the risks involved. Executive governments have more resources and time to commission programmes of research and analysis on all the risks and benefits at issue in a legal policy domain. In contrast, as Lon Fuller has argued, the comparative advantage of courts is on 'yes–no questions' (Did she do it?) and 'more or less questions' (How much should be paid?): L. Fuller, *The Morality of Law* (New Haven: Yale University Press, 1964), 33. Polanyi distinguishes 'polycentric' problems from these, as problems not well suited to the judicial model: M. Polanyi, *The Logic of Liberty* (Chicago: University of Chicago Press, 1951), 174–84.

[35] Both Peter Drahos (Ch. 8 in this volume) and Hugh Collins (*Regulating Contracts* (Oxford: Oxford University Press, 1999), 188) cite as a leading example Lord Mansfield's responsiveness to the customs of trade and the nodal governance of merchants' courts in effecting profound improvements in commercial law.

of contract,[36] and Angus Corbett and Stephen Bottomley may see a somewhat similar collision in the domain of corporate governance, this collision may be more absent in tort, family law, labour law, and administrative law. Alternatively, collisions may produce productive integrations rather than productive disintegrations, as Imelda Maher finds in competition law (Chapter 9), or collision may produce what Julia Black prefers to characterize as mutual learning between common law and regulatory law that amounts to 'productive cherry-picking' more than disintegration.

Remember that the Metcalfe thesis of how different state agencies increasingly do strategic planning in an era of networked governance is that they still plan, but in a way that is mindful of the planning at other key nodes in the network— only the key ones. The strategic plans of a national trade union movement may be something the regulatory ambitions of the ministry of labour must be responsive to, but the ministry of justice or the environment ministry can for the most part ignore them. Regulation can occur in many rooms, but for most specific regulatory questions legal decision-makers can assume that the occupants of most of those rooms will be asleep. A law that makes strategic decisions on when to follow its internal logic unencumbered by a consideration of the justice being transacted in different rooms, and when to take a lot of notice of private ordering, should be neither particularly surprising nor offensive. When we drive a car, we can normally do so without paying attention to the mechanics of what is going on in that adjacent room under the bonnet. But occasionally we do and must. A task of regulatory theory might be to develop parsimonious theories of when regulatory actors can and should be selectively responsive to regulation by other nodes in a regulatory network. Metcalfe's method may be one building block towards such theory.

How Many Lenses?

None of this discussion of selective attentiveness to what is seen from a different vantage point is to deny the virtues of having a capability to see through other lenses. In questioning our too simple juxtaposition of the differences between the legal and the regulatory lens in the Introduction, Julia Black admonishes: 'Not all lawyers are concerned with doctrine, and not all regulationists are concerned with effectiveness, coherence, and responsiveness.'[37] Not only is this descriptively correct, but we might obversely hypothesize that, under certain conditions, it is a good prescription for regulationists to be able to see regulation through a legal doctrinal lens, and for lawyers to be able to see law through the lenses of effectiveness, coherence, and responsiveness. Whether their concern is to interpret or to prescribe, it is good for the lawyer to be inquisitive about the regulatory relationships of which law is a part, and good for the

---

[36] Collins, *Regulating Contracts*, and Ch. 1 in this volume.   [37] Chapter 2, p. 40.

regulationist to be inquisitive about doctrine. Yet, while we should not want either to be blind in one eye, we should not want to prescribe endless frenetic alternating of lenses. A strategic approach to seeing and attending is as vital to the legal and regulatory crafts as it is to regulating the movement of a car along the highway. The theory of driving a car is well developed through useful heuristics like 'Try not to be distracted by the scenery, the children in the back seat, or the mobile phone, but do focus on the road signs.' A theory of the heuristics of what to focus on when understanding networks of regulatory governance is still a challenge before us.

Julia Black raises the stakes on this challenge by pointing out that there are not just two lenses we must be concerned about, but multiple lenses.[38] Gareth Morgan has made the same point in his influential contribution to organization theory.[39] Morgan works through a number of different ways of imagining organizations metaphorically, starting with a simple metaphor of a bureaucracy as like a machine. While this machine image is all too simple, the camera in Charlie Chaplin's *Modern Times* captures it as a metaphor far from devoid of insight. What we must do is add perspective to what we see through that lens with the image we imagine through other metaphors of the organization that Morgan proceeds to develop, such as the organization as organism, brain, culture, and psychic prison. Morgan paradoxically argues that seeing a phenomenon, such as an organization or indeed law, through multiple lenses enables us both to see it as many things at once and to see it more holistically. This is the appeal of the lens metaphor. The parable of the blind Hindus and the elephant is about being able to acquire a more holistically veridical understanding by being able to sense the world in more than one way and from more than one angle. While there is no consensus among our contributors on the possibilities for a more holistic vision of the normative purposes of law and regulation, we can agree that we do acquire a more rounded appreciation of law in context by viewing it through a multiplicity of lenses beyond a doctrinal lens.

In different ways our authors have taken up Julia Black's multiple-lens challenge. For example, Hilary Charlesworth and Christine Chinkin productively look at international law through the lens of gender domination.[40] When a case is presented to us of a Bosnian woman raped by a peacekeeper, arguably it is imperative that we view the regulatory encounter through that lens. When the case is a contract dispute between two equally powerful male businessmen, the gender domination lens is one we might ignore. The trick is to have observers and practitioners of the legal process who are sensitized to when they must attend to that recurrently important lens, lawyers who have been made sensible through the stories they heard in law school of how to use that lens.

---

[38] Chapter 2, pp. 34–36.
[39] G. Morgan, *Images of Organization*, 2nd edn. (Thousand Oaks, Calif: Sage, 1997).
[40] Ch. 12.

This collection has demonstrated that regulatory effects are complex, ambiguous, and paradoxical. Our contention is that well-educated judges and other legal actors have access to a rich plurality of lenses for looking at a regulated phenomenon. They read the site of a legal contest diagnostically, applying many metaphors to reveal useful potential interpretations of it. Next they make a critical evaluation of these different interpretations and the possibilities for high-integrity legal interventions that enable change. In the end, legal action is imagined as many things at once, but not everything at once, because there is a critical attitude to the value of all lenses.

COHERENCE AND THE LAW'S RESPONSE TO PLURALISM?

Our conversation about legal and regulatory pluralism certainly raises questions about the coherence of law and regulatory purpose. How can we ever find coherence in doctrine or analysis where such pluralism reigns? In this section we conclude that rather than being cause to jettison coherence as an ideal, pluralism can be a provocation to rethink our notions of what counts as coherence.

A number of the chapters question the coherence of legal doctrine in specific areas of law. One cannot read the essays without concluding that there can be no general answer across the legal domains studied here as to how coherent legal doctrine is or should be. Most legal fields, our authors suggest, tend to normative complexity. Moreover, the political ideology of legal theorists engenders starkly different normative complexes, as Peter Cane illustrates for administrative law: 'For liberals, the prime goal of administrative law is the protection of individual rights and interests, whereas for republicans it is the promotion of rational public deliberation.'[41] Constitutional law doctrines in some significant senses regulate all other areas of national and subnational law towards an element of coherence. In a less profound way, this is also true of international law. While international law doctrines might have limited effects on most private law domains, at least they have an impact when there are international conflicts of laws, which globalization increasingly engenders in private law disputing. In some of our chapters there is a substantial story of mutual influence of private and public law doctrines (such as Chapters 1 and 3 on contract law and corporate governance, respectively). In others there is a story of rather limited influence (such as Chapters 2, 4, 6, and 7 on financial services, family, tort, and criminal law). John Dewar sees a fundamental threat to coherence in family law from the empirical evidence that 'the forum in large part determines the meaning of legal rules'.[42] So the meaning rules have before a judge is very different from the meaning they have in the hands of a solicitor advising a client, a mediator conducting a mediation, or a prosecutor conducting a plea negotiation. On a hierarchical vision of law, we would privilege the interpretations

[41] Cane, Ch. 10, p. 214.   [42] Dewar, Ch. 4, p. 97.

of judges among these multiple sites of legal interpretation. But why, asks Dewar, would we privilege judicial interpretation over mediators' interpretations in a field like family law where 95 per cent of cases do not advance past mediation? It is difficult enough to find coherence within specific fields of law and between different legal areas. But once we begin to consider legal and regulatory fora beyond the courts, doctrinal coherence is all the harder to identify.

It seems plausible to conjecture that as the total number of pages of law in existence doubles or quadruples each decade, the number of purposes being pursued by the law has also grown, though hardly proportionately. Both the quantitative proliferation of law and the proliferation of philosophically incompatible theories of law make coherence at least as elusive today as it has ever been. Jane Stapleton, as we have seen, has an interesting perspective on the reflex response to despair about finding doctrinal coherence, which Peter Cane also endorses in his chapter, 'Administrative Law as Regulation'. Stapleton questions why we should be worried about whether we can find coherence in this complexity. 'We do not regard a complex biodiverse ecosystem in dynamic flux as problematic. Quite the contrary!' As we have seen, there is much to celebrate in constantly moving, plural sources of influence. Indeed it may provide greater scope for dynamism and innovation in proceeding towards normative goals than the alternative.

This does not mean that doctrinal coherence is something we should not care about. But it does mean that coherence is likely to be more complex than simple rule consistency. For example, one view that holds some appeal among the editors of this book is that legal institutions should be organized around the meaning of justice as a social purpose. Yet the meaning and applications of justice will always be contested. Indeed it could be argued that, at the meta-analytical level, justice (and democracy) is all about making sure that people are able to contest exercises of power by reference to their own conceptions of justice.[43] For example, for some political theorists of a deliberative democratic stripe,[44] Hilary Charlesworth and Christine Chinkin's conclusion that international law is mostly devoid of centralized law-making or enforcement mechanisms means that it has the possibility of being constituted and enforced by a more deliberated form of consent. On this account, if there were a world government, international law would be impoverished by becoming less responsive to deliberative norm creation and norm enforcement. Similarly, many legal teachers believe that law schools should not be zones of value-free scholarship, but nor should they indoctrinate students in one unified conception of justice.[45] Rather law schools should be spaces where students (and legal scholars) learn to debate competing visions of what it means to be just. Likewise, a regulatory

---

[43] On the idea of contestatory democracy, see P. Pettit, *Republicanism: A Theory of Freedom and Government* (Oxford: Oxford University Press, 1997), 63, 183–200.

[44] J. Dryzek, *The Politics of the Earth: Environmental Discourses* (Oxford: Oxford University Press, 1997).

[45] C. Menkel-Meadow, 'Can a Law Teacher Avoid Teaching Legal Ethics?', *Journal of Legal Education*, 3 (1991), 3.

space can be conceived as one where plural 'regulators' (legal and non-legal, different areas of law or different legal decision-makers) and citizens can argue over different meanings of justice and how to safeguard justice in the pursuit of regulatory objectives. Justice becomes the subject of ongoing contest and debate. Coherence is contended for at the level of principles and values. But it is rarely found in any simple unity in rules or doctrines. Indeed such unity could be considered insignificant compared to a coherence in principles and values that might never be fully expressed in unified rules.

So our tentative response to the challenge to rethink our notions of what counts as coherence comes at three levels. Firstly, it is to see it as a project that is always necessarily incomplete because, quite properly, it is contested by both democratic actors and environmental change. It is a sandcastle actors keep patting into shape from different sides as waves of change continually erode its form. Secondly, just as there is the possibility of confusion from seeing the castle from different angles, so is there the possibility of a more holistic comprehension of its form(s). The contest of interpretative frames hands us a struggle between chaos and holistic insight. This unresolved struggle is a better dispensation than myopia. Thirdly, it is at the level of rules that chaos is more likely to prevail in that struggle. Sometimes this is a benign, pragmatic chaos that 'works'. Other times it is a chaos that is diabolical, everyone agreeing it to be a mess that works for no one. At the level of values and principles, there is more prospect of holism emergent in the struggle with chaos.[46] Practical reason can settle on a pragmatic chaos of rules as a good outcome that at times passes tests of democratic deliberation.[47] But this does not mean that debates about how to think coherently about our values and principles will not have moments when most citizens in a democracy will feel rewarded by the enhanced clarity that comes from a democratic conversation that, for example, rewrites a values preamble to a post-Apartheid South African Constitution.

A constitution is an institution designed to foster what we call institutional meta-regulation, the regulation of one institution by another. This is no more than a theoretical reframing of the idea that a constitution is about embedding checks and balances in a system of governance of a state, corporation, or other entity. Reciprocal checking of power opens up a path where different institutions

---

[46] There are deeply structured features of human psychology that render high levels of consensus around values, when defined as transituational beliefs, compared to attitudes, defined as beliefs that apply to specific objects, such as rules: M. Rokeach, *The Nature of Human Values* (New York: Free Press, 1968); M. Rokeach, *Beliefs, Attitudes and Values* (San Francisco: Jossey-Bass, 1973). See also J. Braithwaite, 'Community Values and Australian Jurisprudence', *Sydney Law Review*, 17 (1995), 351. Empirically, there tend not to be consensus attitudes around many rules. But in the face of that attitudinal dissensus, there is frequently remarkably high consensus about the values that motivate the rules. So dissensus is rife in attitudes to an abortion law. Yet abortion law debates tend not to be about contesting underlying values—respect for human life, health, freedom of choice. The pro-abortionist does not say, 'Who cares about human life?', but rather argues about the proper context for applying this value and the relative weight to be given to other values.

[47] Cass Sunstein has made a sustained case for this: C. Sunstein, *Legal Reasoning and Political Conflict* (New York: Oxford University Press, 1998).

may learn shared sensibilities about abuse of power each from the other. Meta-regulation is thus one important strategy for the possibility, only the possibility, of coherence to be retrieved at times from contestation in conditions of complexity.

META-REGULATION

Imelda Maher's chapter is distinctive in that the lens she finds to be the most significant juxtaposition to the legal lens in practical regulation is another disciplinary lens—an economic lens. Maher finds competition law to be regulated by the normative ordering of economics, so much so that competition law would make no sense without the discourse of economics. Competition law also, however, regulates economics. The courts and the regulators tell firms with substantial market power what sort of economic analyses they must do, with what level of rigour, before they will be persuaded that, for example, a merger should be permitted. The courts are not resourced and trained to do the econometrics themselves, but they are required to meta-regulate the economic analyses that regulate the private decision-making of firms.

While constitutional and international law meta-regulation of the regulation of other branches of public and private law is decidedly vertical,[48] much meta-regulation is horizontal, as when a branch of private law doctrine regulates a branch of public law or an NGO regulates a business self-regulatory scheme. Indeed perhaps the latter is not even horizontal, but meta-regulation from below. Peter Drahos (Chapter 8, 'Regulating Property') finds in Locke's *Second Treatise of Government* an account of property rights being regulated by government and in turn regulating government. This is a story both of secure property rights for citizens putting a limit on the confiscatory power of government (regulation from below) and of horizontal regulation of the execut-ive by a judiciary that enforces those rights. Yet three centuries on, Locke's beautiful regulatory theory becomes an ugly practice as intellectual property regulation is captured in a way that allows powerful Northern corporations to dictate top-down the terms of intellectual property law on states of the South that are politically weaker than those US corporations.

Whether the regulation of other regulators is top-down, bottom-up, or sideways, it may be that intended regulatory objectives are more likely to be achieved if the regulation is 'responsive' to those being regulated. For example, governments should be responsive to how effectively regulated businesses are regulating themselves through corporate compliance systems and industry-wide self-regulation schemes. But of course regulators must be responsive not only to business interests, but also to public interests represented by governments and NGOs. Tripartite or multi-party mutual responsiveness enables the ideas of

---

[48] However, Hugh Collins seeks to problematize this in the conclusion to Chapter 1 in this volume.

checks and balances and responsiveness to be realized simultaneously, with the concepts applying equally to regulation of the private and public sectors.[49] Thus one theoretical resolution to the limb of the trilemma that institutions may be so responsive to a regulated actor that the integrity of its own values is threatened is: have a multiplicity of separated powers checking and balancing one another in such a responsive manner that none has so much unchecked power that it can dominate, and none is so over-regulated that the integrity of its own regulatory capability is lost.

The theory may be wrong empirically, but it is a theoretical building block that makes some predictions that apply regardless of the direction of regulatory influence. Julia Black is surely right that the rooms where the doctrines of one branch of the law work their effects are often effectively sealed off from other branches of law. Contingency seems to abound in such sealing off. This should mandate an empiricism about a search for doctrinal regulation of one branch by another, as opposed to a theoretical assumption that we will find them. Black's observation should cause a sigh of relief that there are not an infinite number of meta-regulators for the regulating law practitioner to scan.

A responsive regulatory perspective on law certainly overturns the taken-for-granted assumption of some lawyers that access to legal justice in the courts is the normative ideal of justice. Responsiveness means that access to legal justice in the courts is not the normative ideal of the meta-regulatory perspective on law. Rather the ideal is access to justice, where that justice is more likely to be a self-regulatory accomplishment of principles and rules in civil society. The costs of litigation make it economically implausible that access to justice could ever substantially become distributively just, available to the poor, via the courts. The good law is the law that delivers access to justice conceived as a justice that occurs in many rooms beyond the courtroom even when those rooms are rather sealed off one from the other.[50] This normative perspective means the law should often refrain from fixing obligations in detail; often it should even restrict itself to a set of principles and a set of default rules, leaving self-regulation in civil society the flexibility to deliver an access to justice that makes contextual sense. Not only does this leave the justice of the law more democratically open to the contextual justice of the people, it also permits experimentation with novel ways citizens, businesses, and governments might choose to organize their relationships with one another.

This is the ideal of a justice of the law that filters down into the justice of the people and a justice of the people that more effectively bubbles up into the

[49] See J. Braithwaite, 'On Speaking Softly and Carrying Sticks: Neglected Dimensions of a Republican Separation of Powers', *University of Toronto Law Journal*, 47 (1997), 305; I. Ayres and J. Braithwaite, *Responsive Regulation: Transcending the Deregulation Debate* (New York: Oxford University Press), ch. 3; and the discussion of checks and balances in Cane, Ch. 10 and Scott, Ch. 11, in this volume.
[50] M. Galanter, 'Justice in Many Rooms', in M. Cappelletti, (ed.), *Access to Justice and the Welfare State* (Alphen aan den Rijn: Sijthoff, 1981), 147; C. Parker, *Just Lawyers: Regulation and Access to Justice* (Oxford: Oxford University Press, 1999), chs. 3 and 4.

justice of the law.[51] This might involve, for example, a radical rethinking of the relationship between informal justice and courtroom justice to enable the justice of the law and the justice of the people each to be a better check and balance on the other.[52] Even if we get a law that is less holistically coherent as a result of such a productive disintegration, we might get a more holistic infusion of justice into society. This is another version of 'bargaining in the light of the law' where the law filters down to ordinary citizens in a way that makes sense to them (as suggested by John Dewar), and the conventions of private ordering bubble up in a way that clarifies the focus cast by the light of the law, translating it into worlds of naturally occurring custom. On this analysis, observations in some of our chapters that law is not about regulation but about vindicating certain procedural values, or simply about expressing values, can be interpreted as valorizing law's most distinctive regulatory potential for improving justice, even if in limited ways.

Braithwaite has previously argued that there are some tentative empirical grounds for seeing justice as 'immanently holistic'.[53] For example, there is a strong positive correlation between procedural justice and restorative justice.[54] Procedural injustice that allows, say, powerful white people to dominate powerless black people conduces to social injustice. The argument is not that justice is fully holistic—otherwise there would be no point in distinguishing procedural justice and its various facets from restorative justice and social justice[55]—but that it is immanently holistic. Regulatory institutions work most decently when they create spaces where procedural, restorative, and social justice do reinforce one another. Obviously, then, an appeal of Hugh Collins's *Regulating Contracts* for radically rethinking legal institutions in this way is that interpenetration of private law and public regulation might foster the search for more holistic instantiations of justice. For example, if public regulation can transform private conflicts into public issues, the gender dominations that concern feminists, and other forms of social injustice, have better prospects of being flushed into the open and confronted.

Nicola Lacey is dubious about this kind of whole of law, whole of regulation, normative project because what she sees in criminal law is that it tends to be short on real justice and long on the ideology and rhetoric of justice. Critically exposing practical injustice therefore becomes the more pressing immediate

---

[51] Parker, *Just Lawyers*, ch. 3, 4, and 9.

[52] J. Braithwaite and C. Parker, 'Restorative Justice is Republican Justice', in L. Walgrave and G. Bazemore (eds.), *Restoring Juvenile Justice* (Monsey, NY: Criminal Justice Press, 1999), 103; J. Braithwaite, *Restorative Justice and Responsive Regulation* (Oxford: Oxford University Press, 2002), chs. 5 and 8.

[53] J. Braithwaite, 'Holism, Justice and Atonement', *Utah Law Review* (2003), 389. This essay includes a commentary upon Erik Luna's work on holism and justice. See E. Luna, 'Punishment Theory, Holism, and the Procedural Conception of Restorative Justice', *Utah Law Review* (2003), 205.

[54] G. Barnes, 'Procedural Justice in Two Contexts: Testing the Fairness of Diversionary Conferencing for Intoxicated Drivers', Ph.D. diss., Institute of Criminal Justice and Criminology, University of Maryland, 1999.   [55] Tyler, *Why People Obey the Law*.

project than celebrating a justice which is only ideology. It is common ground among our authors that legal institutions can never escape injustice and domination. Even when, as in Peter Drahos's account of property law, the law is established with the purpose of preventing domination (making property secure against the king), Drahos documents empirically that courts are not necessarily less vulnerable than regulatory agencies to capture by powerful business interests. In some ways they may be structurally more vulnerable, because, as Hugh Collins points out in Chapter 1, at least in the common law world, 'litigation about questions of law is a privilege of the rich'.[56] The policy orientation of much empirical regulation research, no less than the doctrinal orientation of much legal research, is wilfully uncritical about analysing and confronting injustice. Principles of law and the practice of democracy in producing justice can interact in a downward spiral of injustice, as Lacey's chapter illustrates, with criminal law infused with both a kind of tyranny of the majority and a tyranny of retributivist doctrine. How to flip this dynamic into an upwards spiral of justice through getting the right checks and balances in the relationship between legal justice and the justice of dispersed deliberative democracy is an unresolved challenge for regulatory theory and praxis.

Meta-regulation is an important topic for regulatory theorists because many of them see it as a way of simultaneously extricating ourselves from the effectiveness and responsiveness horns of Teubner's regulatory trilemma. Peter Grabosky, who first noted the phenomenon of meta-regulation, together with Parker and Braithwaite, find that, in the sociological conditions of a complex division of labour, meta-regulation is likely to be both more responsive and more effective than direct command and control regulation.[57] While some of the early empirical results from this programme of research are encouraging, in areas ranging from environmental enforcement to tax compliance, it is still early days in testing and elaborating meta-regulatory theory.

CONCLUSION

John Dewar's conclusion is that notwithstanding all the incoherence and unpredictability he finds in family law, the language of regulation and meta-regulation can be useful. He also suggests that there are connections between the three horns of the regulatory dilemma, meaning there may be interwoven strategies that enable us to extricate ourselves from all three horns simultaneously. In this

---

[56] Collins, Ch. 1, p. 20.

[57] P. Grabosky, 'Using Non-governmental Resources to Foster Regulatory Compliance', *Governance: An International Journal of Policy and Administration*, 8 (1995), 527; C. Parker, *The Open Corporation* (Cambridge: Cambridge University Press, 2002), ch. 9; J. Braithwaite, 'Meta Risk Management and Responsive Regulation for Tax System Integrity', *Law and Policy*, 25 (2003), 1. See also N. Gunningham and P. Grabosky, *Smart Regulation: Designing Environmental Policy* (Oxford: Clarendon Press, 1998); B. Morgan, *Social Citizenship in the Shadow of Competition: The Bureaucratic Politics of Regulatory Justification* (Aldershot: Ashgate, 2003).

chapter we too have seen responsive meta-regulation as a fruitful topic for future research on just these possibilities.

A reasonable question is whether the lessons from regulatory theory are really likely to be any different from those of the law in action and law in context movements of the 1960s and 1970s. The main difference between them and regulatory theory is simple. Law is their central focus, but law must be understood in terms of how it plays out in action in a particular context. With regulatory theory, regulation—that is, attempts to steer the flow of events—is the focus. With environmental regulation, attempts to preserve and improve the environment are the focus, and environmental law is just one of many institutions implicated in the regulatory space. Angus Corbett and Stephen Bottomley capture the regulatory theoretical perspective when they conceive of corporate governance as 'a body of governance practices, processes, and structures', as well as a body or category of law.[58] There is a law of corporate governance, but corporate governance is not primarily about law. The law of governance matters, yet so does the governance of law. Governance is a more general theoretical domain than regulation in that governance is also about allocating resources in ways that are not intended to steer the flow of events. Even so, it can be argued that in the era of the regulatory state, where rowing (direct provision) is a less important function of states than steering, and where organizations operate so often by contracting out and monitoring the contractors, regulatory theory is becoming an increasingly central part of the theory of governance.[59] So is legal theory in an era where the rule of law is increasingly seen as one of the central planks of 'good governance', as the IMF and World Bank like to put it. One of our claims in this Conclusion is that there is a structural basis for all of this. In a world where there is quantitatively more law and quantitatively more semi-formal self-regulatory ordering, and a proliferation of organizations that do it, in a world where governance is more by regulating than by doing, both legal theory and regulatory theory are bound to assume greater importance, including significance for one another.

Our authors have uncovered rather fewer powerful examples of one sphere of legal doctrine regulating another than Hugh Collins might have liked. While contracting ideas have penetrated public law in an era of government by contract, Peter Cane provides a muted account of the sweep of the doctrinal influences at play. Richard Johnstone and Richard Mitchell provide a more historically cyclical account of the rise and fall and rise of contract in labour law, but at no point are contract law doctrinal influences on the content as opposed to the form of labour law seen as central. Johnstone and Mitchell also detect a sharp *decline* in the influence of criminal law on labour law between the nineteenth and twentieth centuries.[60] While we have considered a large

---

[58] Ch. 3, p. 61.
[59] See M. Dorf and C. Sabel, 'A Constitution of Democratic Experimentalism', *Columbia Law Review*, 98 (1998), 267.   [60] Ch. 5, pp. 106–107.

number of fields of legal doctrine in this volume, each of which has the potential to regulate all of the others, for most doctrines most of the time, there is no influence of great import.

This is not to downplay collisions between different doctrines that we have found do sometimes occur in ways that deliver 'fresh productive capacity for regulation'.[61] The fact that the types of collision that matter are finite rather than infinite makes it feasible to study law as something that is regulated and that regulates. Law is almost never the most important instrument of regulation. Yet important chains of causal influences on regulated phenomena where law is totally absent are hard to think of. When law is one of the links in such loops of causation, it follows that there are a variety of other variables in the loop that are regulating law. The day when we can be evidence-based about most of the regulatory influences of, and on, law is a long way off. Beginning with empirical research on the influences that appear to matter most would be an illuminating start for this inquiry.

---

[61] Collins, *Regulating Contracts*, 361.

Index